JOHN LOCKE

AN ESSAY CONCERNING
HUMAN UNDERSTANDING

IN TWO VOLUMES · VOLUME ONE

EDITED WITH
AN INTRODUCTION BY
JOHN W. YOLTON
*Professor of Philosophy in
the University of Maryland*

LONDON   J. M. DENT & SONS LTD
NEW YORK   E. P. DUTTON & CO INC

CONTENTS

VOLUME ONE

BOOK I

OF INNATE NOTIONS

BOOK II

OF IDEAS

VOLUME TWO

BOOK III

OF WORDS

BOOK IV

OF KNOWLEDGE AND OPINION

INTRODUCTION

LOCKE'S attitude towards his literary productions was that of one who has fathered late in life: over-protective of his progeny and meticulous about their appearance. Both his major works— *Two Treatises of Government* and his *Essay Concerning Human Understanding*—were begun many years before their publication in 1690. Locke kept them by him throughout the years, showing them to a few close friends, re-working sections, allowing his thoughts to mature. Locke was well over fifty before these his first serious works were published; even then, *Two Treatises* appeared anonymously. There may have been special reasons for some of this delay and caution about *Two Treatises*: Laslett has suggested that it was a piece of political writing composed at a time of social unrest, when Locke may have been associated with actions of doubtful legality.[1] But even with *Two Treatises*, Locke was undoubtedly concerned to put his thoughts in proper order before risking publication. It may be too sophisticated to read that work as political theory, a theory whose foundation lies in the epistemology and metaphysics of his *Essay*. Laslett considers it more as a tract for the times, designed as a call to action without a too subtle eye towards its consistency with the *Essay*.[2] But Polin's observations upon the significance of the simultaneous publication of these two works should not be overlooked.[3] Moreover, those lectures which Locke wrote as Censor of Moral Philosophy at Christ Church very likely were never published because of Locke's

---

[1] Laslett, P. Locke's *Two Treatises of Government*, A Critical Edition with Introduction and Notes, Cambridge, 1960, pp. 31-33. While it is certainly true that Locke was a cautious man, even neurotically so, the thesis of Leo Strauss (*Natural Right and History*, Chicago, 1953)—that there is a radical, esoteric doctrine hidden in the printed words of Locke which accounts for his timidity in publishing—is an obvious extravagance and contrivance. *Vide* my 'Locke and the Law of Nature', *The Philosophical Review*, 1958, pp. 477-98.

[2] *Ibid.*, pp. 79-92. Laslett describes *Two Treatises* as a work 'of intuition, insight, and imagination' whose political argument 'is not presented as a part of a general philosophy, and does not seem to be intended to be read as such'. pp. 85, 84.

[3] Polin, R. *La Politique Morale de John Locke*, Paris, 1960, p. 97.

inability to bring their strong claim for laws of nature known by the natural light of reason into harmony with the teachings of his *Essay*.[1] Locke would seem to have been at least doubly motivated. One set of motives belonged to the intellectual, intent upon thinking out his ideas in as harmonious, complete, and inter-locking a fashion as possible. Other motives were associated with his political life. These latter motives may have led Locke into publication even though his thoughts were not all in acceptable order, and despite the loss of a large portion of *Two Treatises*.[2]

THE TEXT OF THIS EVERYMAN EDITION

The *Essay* was begun around 1671. After several redraftings, a long abridgment was published in 1688, in LeClerc's Amsterdam journal, *Bibliothèque Universelle*.[3] Even after its appearance in England in 1690, Locke revised subsequent editions. The last major content additions to his *Essay* were made in the Fourth Edition of 1700; but even after this date, in the last years of his life, Locke continued to re-work and add passages. In the absence of explicit evidence, it is difficult to know whether some of the differences between one edition and another were authorized by the author: many changes were inadvertently introduced by the printers. Especially difficult in this respect is it to determine punctuation and spelling changes, or italicization and paragraphing. Thus, it would be precarious to claim that all of the variants to be found in the Fifth Edition of the *Essay* were changes made by Locke. We do know that Locke was much concerned with the press-work on his *Two Treatises*.[4] Moreover, he himself has told us that he lent his hand to making revisions in the text of his *Essay* after the Fourth Edition.

After 1700, Locke became interested in the posthumous fate

---

[1] Leyden, W. von. *Essays on the Law of Nature*, Oxford, 1954. However, too much should not be made of the inconsistency here; for even in the *Essay*, the law of nature is mentioned. Moreover, although the language of these early *Essays on the Law of Nature* is exactly that of the many proponents of innate moral maxims in the seventeenth century, Locke nowhere says the laws of nature are known before experience. It is the natural light of reason which recognizes the laws as natural and binding. This is very much like the modified or dispositional version of the innate theory. (*Vide* my *John Locke and the Way of Ideas*, chapter II.) Such a version is, of course, not in harmony with the spirit of the *Essay*, but neither does it flatly contradict what the *Essay* says.

[2] Laslett, op. cit., p. ix.

[3] For the full story of the composition of the *Essay*, see Aaron's *John Locke*, pp. 50-74.

[4] Laslett, op. cit., pp. 6-10.

of his books. He took steps to give a number of them to the
Bodleian Library. In a letter of August 1704, Tyrrell lists the
Essay as one such book Locke wanted given to the Bodleian.[1]
This was very probably the Fourth Edition. Locke also had
Peter King send him a form for a codicil to his will. The will
itself was signed in April 1704, the codicil added on 15 Septem-
ber of the same year. One of the items in this codicil was the
following:

Whereas there is intended speedily another edition of my *Essay
Concerning Human Understanding*, wherein there will in the 31
chapter of the second book be some small alterations which I
have made with my own hand, that the university which hath been
pleased to honour it with a place in its library may have that Essay in
that estate that my last thoughts left it in, it is my will that my executor
shall in my name present to the said Bodleian Library one copy of the
next edition of my said Essay, well bound.[2]

No other justification for reprinting the Fifth Edition need be
offered than these words of Locke which place his final approval
upon that edition. Locke died in October 1704, this edition
appeared in 1706.

From the Fifth Edition in 1706 until the beginning of the
nineteenth century, there were at least twenty-five reprintings
of the *Essay*, an indication of the importance and the popularity
accorded it. During the nineteenth century there were a dozen
or more reprintings, sometimes together with his short *Conduct
of the Understanding*. Abstracts of the *Essay* in various lengths
and forms were published, from Wynn's in 1696 (which had
several editions and reprintings) through to the present day.
The only unabridged edition of the *Essay* readily available to
the modern student of Locke has been Fraser's two-volume
edition of 1894. Fraser's edition is neither a straight reprinting
of one of the editions nor a variorum edition, although his
intentions seem to have been closer to the latter than to the
former. He says that his edition was prepared from the first
four editions, with some material incorporated from the French
translation prepared by Pierre Coste under Locke's super-
vision.[3] Fraser also makes some mention of 'the best posthu-

[1]MS Locke C 22, f. 171, in the Lovelace Collection in the Bodleian Library at
Oxford. *Cf.* MS. Locke C 24, f. 57.
[2]MS Locke b. 5 (14). Also reprinted in King's *Life of John Locke*, London, 1829,
p. 267.
[3]*Essai Philosophique concernant l'entendement humain. . . . Traduit de l'anglois
de Mr. Locke, par Pierre Coste, sur la quatrieme edition, revue, corrigee, et augmentee
par l'auteur.* Amsterdam, 1700.

mous edition', apparently the fifth although he does not specifi-
cally say so.[1]   The Epistle to the Reader ends, in Fraser's
reprint, by speaking of the Sixth Edition; Fraser identifies this
as being published in 1706, an identification which suggests he
was not clear about the posthumous editions.   Christophersen,
Locke's bibliographer, was also confused about the Fifth Edition, crediting the fifth as being 'a mere reprint of the fourth' and
saying of the Sixth Edition that it was published 'a short time
afterward, the last in folio, and the last whose manuscript has
been gone through by Locke himself'.[2]

Even allowing for alterations introduced by the printer, the
number of changes between the fourth and fifth editions strongly
suggests Locke's concern with making the text more readable.
From the point of view of printing, there are numerous changes,
e.g., dashes in words like 'wherever' have been eliminated,
italicization changes occur throughout, extensive punctuation
changes appear, larger type and format have been used, a few
paragraphing differences are found.   Stylistic and content
changes also occur. For example, the Epistle to the Reader had
become, by the Fourth Edition, besides an introduction to the
whole work, a repository of reactions to critics, advice to the
reader, and comments upon the various changes in the first four
editions. In the Fifth Edition, the Epistle was made more readable by being carefully edited. In the body of the work, there
are a number of additions of sentences and even paragraphs.
One odd point in this respect is that Locke himself apparently
made a mistake in the codicil of his will in speaking of the 31st
chapter of the Second Book; the main content changes occur,
with few exceptions, in the 21st chapter of that book, the one on
power which gave Locke so much trouble. There are no changes
in the 31st chapter.

The main changes in the text of the Fifth Edition, over the
Fourth, are as follows:

(1) Some half-dozen paragraphs in the Epistle in reply to
Lowde's attack on Locke[3], have been transferred to a long
footnote in Book II, chapter XXVIII, §11.

[1]See vol. I, pp. 17, 20, 325-26; vol. II, p. 396.

[2]Christophersen, H. C.   *A Bibliographical Introduction to the Study of John
Locke*, Oslo, 1930.

[3]Lowde, J. *A Discourse Concerning the Nature of Man*, London, 1694. These
replies of Locke were inserted in the Second Edition and carried on in the Epistles
of the Third and Fourth Editions.

(2) The paragraph which preceded these replies to Lowde in the Epistle has been greatly expanded. It is in that passage that Locke says he has not learnt anything from any of the attacks made upon his book and gives warning that he will not reply to any more.

(3) Book I, chapter III, §9: A new sentence has been added with a reference to Pietro della Valle.

(4) Book I, chapter IV, §8: Two new sentences added with a reference to Churchill's *Collection of Voyages*, recently published in 1704.

(5) Book II, chapter I, §23: The final sentence is new.

(6) Book II, chapter I, §24 has a new beginning, running from 'In time, the mind comes to reflect', to 'Thus the first capacity of human intellect'.

(7) Book II, chapter XV, §9: A long footnote has been added containing Locke's replies to a French critic, M. Barbeyrac, who had worked with Coste when he was revising the French edition.

(8) Book II, chapter XXI, §23: A long section from the Fourth Edition has been omitted after the sentence, 'But the act of volition or preferring'. A number of new phrases are added throughout the paragraph.

(9) Book II, chapter XXI, §24: A new clause was added to the opening sentence, and several new sentences added in the rest of the paragraph.

(10) Book II, chapter XXI, §25 has a new clause in the opening sentence; a parenthetical clause from the Fourth Edition is omitted; and the section ends differently.

(11) Book II, chapter XXI, §48: A long passage is added, beginning 'The very end of our freedom being'.

(12) Book II, chapter XXI, §56: The long first paragraph is new and other changes appear throughout the section. In the Fourth Edition this was a very brief section.

(13) Book II, chapter XXI, §71: A very long paragraph has been added in the Fifth, at the end of the section.

It is of some interest to discover that even when taken as an attempt at a collated edition, Fraser's text is not to be trusted. James Gibson, in his review in *Mind* for 1894, points out a long list of changes introduced in the Fourth Edition which were not so noticed by Fraser. Of the changes listed above, Fraser fails to note that the paragraphs in (1) have merely been transferred, not omitted. He correctly identifies (2) as added in the 'posthumous edition'. All the rest of the above changes are, with a few minor phrases, correctly noted as not occurring in the Fourth Edition, but he says incorrectly that they were added first in the French edition. One would think Fraser meant the first French edition of 1700. But he apparently used only the second French edition of 1729, because all of the above changes, with the exception of (5) and (6), are in the second and subsequent French editions but *not* in the first. All of these changes were new in the Fifth Edition of 1706. Coste says, in the preface to his second, revised edition, that the first is superseded by the second because of the additions and corrections 'faites par Mr. Locke, qu'il me communique lui-meme, et qui n'ont ete imprimees en anglois qu'apres sa mort'. Presumably item (7) was a reply dictated by Locke to Coste, but nonetheless this reply to the French critic, like all the other items above, appears in print first in the 1706 edition.

The concern behind the present Everyman reprinting has been to place before the reader the full text of the Fifth Edition, that edition willed by Locke to the Bodleian with his final approval. No claim is being made for this edition as finally authenticated in every detail; that would be fitting for a scholarly edition seeking to collate all of the first five editions and the French edition, indicating the progressive changes in the text up to the Fifth, and attempting to establish the final text of the *Essay*. Furthermore, some licence has been taken for the sake of the modern reader, e.g., spelling and punctuation have been modernized throughout, although the italicization has been retained, despite the fact that it would be difficult to defend every italicization as employed by Locke. The use of italics was common in the seventeenth century. It was a way, of course, of introducing emphasis upon certain words and phrases; it was also a stylistic habit, not always consistent with stressed words. The retention of the italics will help to give the modern reader something of the flavour of that period. The attention to punctuation was especially necessary, since Locke's own punctuation frequently makes for difficult reading. Obvious printing errors have also been corrected. One of the largest differences between Fourth and Fifth Editions is the insertion of long extracts in the Fifth, in appropriate places throughout the text, of Locke's replies to the Bishop of Worcester. These have not been reprinted in this

Everyman edition. While being interesting commentaries by Locke upon important points in the *Essay*, and evidently approved by him as footnote insertions in the Fifth Edition, they do not constitute the text of that *Essay* itself. Unlike the two long footnotes mentioned in the list of changes in the Fifth Edition—the one of a reply to M. Barbeyrac, the other of his replies to Lowde—Locke's replies to the Bishop of Worcester are available in full as separate books. Another slight change concerns the analytical contents which, in the original appear together with the general contents. For the present edition the analytical contents are placed before their respective books; they constitute a quick, handy guide for each of the books and chapters. The only changes in the index supplied for the original are that the references have been expanded and some entries added.

THE PHILOSOPHY OF THE ESSAY

Locke wrote and thought in an expansive, leisurely fashion. This fact, and not alone the fact that the *Essay* was composed over a number of years and frequently revised, accounts for the prolixity of Locke's style. Locke should be read at one's leisure. I am not suggesting that such a reading of Locke will remove all of the philosophical difficulties, although I do believe that the standard charge about his inconsistencies in this work grossly exaggerates the case. Locke was not a creator of a vast philosophical system, although one of his motives almost certainly was to achieve as much consistency to his many-sided thought as possible. He addressed himself calmly and intensively to a series of questions about human knowledge. These questions had a way of leading to other questions and difficulties. To all and each in turn Locke tried to provide answers in accord with what appeared to him to be the truth. His appeal to truth frequently seems to mask an easy escape from further analysis; and in fact, in the course of his successive analyses of knowledge, language, and reality, he was led to take up positions which went beyond his own account of the origin and extent of human knowledge. His corpuscular, mechanical view of the physical universe, which he took over from his contemporaries; his claim that our knowledge does not extend to the real essences of things; his firm affirmation of the reality of substances as entities causing our ideas but not revealed in those ideas—these are just some of the assertions Locke makes which cannot be derived from those two fountain-heads of experience, sense and reflection, to which he claimed to be able to trace all knowledge. These assertions constitute the conceptual background within which Locke thought and wrote. Given this conceptual orientation, Locke then addressed himself to the questions of the nature, limitation, and scope of knowledge.

If one approaches Locke's *Essay* looking for an analysis of these background attitudes in terms of his programme for tracing all ideas to experience, the *Essay* will split into two parts: the claim for an experiential grounding of all ideas, and those other claims about knowledge and reality which go beyond the experiential grounding. But this split does not occur where it has traditionally been charged as occurring, between the first two and the fourth books. This is a split which runs throughout the *Essay*. These two sides of Locke's thought might be seen as the descriptive and the explanatory sides respectively. His accounts of the origin and extent of knowledge are offered as descriptive accounts within the context of the conceptual orientation in which he operated. The conceptual context forms the explanatory framework of the *Essay*. For instance, the reason we have simple ideas at all is because there are externally existing objects in the world bombarding our senses with tiny particles; the reason our knowledge is limited is that these external objects work in unobservable ways, but in ways which, on the corpuscular hypothesis, account well enough for the ideas and beliefs we do have.

Still a third example can be offered of the difference between descriptive and explanatory concepts in Locke's thought. In Book II, chapter VIII, §9, Locke argues for the inseparability of the primary qualities and matter. He offers three tests for determining primacy. (1) Those qualities are primary which remain the same despite all changes, regardless of how much force is exerted on that bit of matter. (2) Those qualities are primary which are observable to sense in all sizes of matter. (3) Those qualities are primary which the mind always thinks of in conjunction with its thought of body or matter. Only the second of these three tests accords with Locke's claims to ground all knowledge on experience. The first prescribes the physical status of primary qualities but says nothing about how they are discovered. Even if we say that (2) indicates the sensible criteria for (1), the third test clearly indicates that Locke is applying a rational or intelligible criterion along with the sensible one. The same appeal to intelligibility reappears later, when he says that the mind is forced to think of a substance as tying together the perceived qualities of an object. This argument is appealed to in other places in the *Essay*. These appeals to intelligibility—to what the mind thinks—are clearly going beyond the bounds of experience. Or, if it be said that these are nothing but appeals to reflected experience, it needs to be pointed out that in this way a door has been opened which virtually makes it impossible to falsify the thesis that all knowledge is experience-based.

It should not be forgotten that Locke's *Essay* is just as much a contribution to psychology as it is to philosophy. The Second Book is especially concerned with tracing the ways in which we become aware of our world and of our mental operations. Locke tried to show how all the contents of our minds are derived from and rest upon a two-fold experience, external sensation of things and internal inspection of the operations of our minds. He gave ample attention also to the various operations of thought: being aware, discerning, comparing, recollecting, abstracting, willing, etc. Armed with these mental processes, convinced that nothing is in the intellect which is not first in the senses, Locke professes, in Book II, to launch a programme of deriving all ideas from experience. But the exact nature of this programme is not clear. There are places where he seems to interpret it as an attempt to show how every idea, no matter how complex and apparently removed from sensation, is reducible to some set of simple ideas of sense. The faculties of the mind play a role even in the acquisition of simple ideas: the mind must attend to what the senses report. In the case of many other ideas, specific mental operations are necessary before a given idea arises, e.g., we must mentally add quantities before we acquire the idea of finite and infinite; the operations the mind goes through in acquiring the idea of power are complex indeed (II, XXI, §1). In the case of mixed modes, Locke openly recognized these as a species of ideas constructed by the mind. Other ideas, like those of existence and unity, are 'suggested to the mind' by ideas of sense and reflection. Still others, like that of substance, arise because the mind is 'forced to think' of a subject for the individual qualities.

The faculty of reflection is the ambiguous element in this programme. I do not think Locke intended to invoke a concept of experience which was so general and indefinite that the programme of grounding all ideas upon experience was unfalsifiable; but neither does he seem to have been very clear about many of the assumptions behind his arguments, nor clear about the different ways in which ideas can be said to be derived from experience. His attempts to give such a derivation frequently diverge into talk about the meaning of our ideas, e.g., of pleasure, pain, envy, duration, power, infinity, etc. Moreover, the only contrary thesis Locke had in mind concerning the origin of ideas was that of innate inscription. Book I had taken care of that contrary thesis. Book II frequently reminds the reader of that alternative. For these purposes, it was sufficient if Locke could present a case for saying that all ideas are of two sorts: those which we derive from sensory observation and those which we construct from such observation, through reflection and the other faculties of the mind. In its most general form, the empiricist programme of Locke amounts to nothing more than this: an alternative to the innate theory.

The label of 'empiricism' must be used with caution, especially since, of course, Locke knew nothing of such a label. Locke was not out to defend some form of radical reductionism, showing how every idea is either itself a direct result of sensory stimuli or is a complex whose parts are so derived from sense. Some complex ideas were given this sort of analysis by Locke, but by no means all of them. Like those background concepts I have called 'explanatory', many analyses of ideas in Book II interpret the experience-derivation programme in such a liberal way that nothing would count against it save a vindication of innate knowledge.

Thus, on two counts, the reader who approaches Locke with the conviction that the label of 'empiricist' fits him will be disappointed.[1] There are many explanatory concepts functioning

---

[1] The citations of Locke as the father of modern empiricism greatly overstress the experience programme, without taking into account the very wide sense in which 'experience' is used by Locke. Even in the eighteenth century Locke was frequently interpreted as a radical empiricist. There is a similar ignoring of the context of a dictum in the modern appeals to Ockham's razor. Apparently Ockham understood this principle, 'Plurality is not to be posited without necessity', in a much wider sense than those who like to call themselves 'empiricists' mean to allow. Ockham required that 'everyone who makes a statement must have a sufficient reason for its truth'. The scope of sufficient reasons is wide: observation of fact, logical insight, divine revelation, or deduction from any of these. (*Vide* Boehner's introduction to his edition of Ockham's *Philosophical Writings*, Edinburgh, 1957.)

as basic assumptions. There are also many components of knowledge and awareness which owe their origin to a very liberal activity of the mind. These two aspects of Locke's thought often merge together. The idea of substance is a clear instance of such merging, for the idea of substance as a unifying 'something' for sensed particulars was an idea which Locke says the mind is forced to construct. This idea plays, in all men's thinking, just that role which the background assumptions silently play in Locke's: it helps to explain and make sense of the world as experienced.

The explanatory concepts—both as conceptual framework for the *Essay*, and as unifying ideas within all men's knowledge —constitute a rational, intellectualistic facet of Locke's thought. His much vaunted 'plain, historical method' is by no means the dominant motif. A component in Locke's background conceptual attitudes was his view of the 'internal constitution and true nature of things', which thought of the powers and qualities of things as related by necessary connexions. The corpuscular hypothesis is the closest we can come to discovering these necessary connexions in nature. The epistemic analogue to this view of the world is a deductive knowledge of that world: 'our knowledge concerning corporeal substances will be very little advanced . . . till we are made to see what qualities and powers of bodies have a *necessary connexion or repugnancy* one with another' (IV, III, §16). Man's estate is so humble and restricted that this becomes an ideal only. But it was not alone in moral knowledge that this ideal appears: Locke also believed in the possibility of such a deductive knowledge of nature. The only obstruction to such a knowledge is man's limitations as man. An adequate knowledge of nature would be complete and deductive: from a knowledge of the real essence could be read off all the properties of a substance. 'If our knowledge were altogether necessary, all men's knowledge would not only be alike, but every man would know all that is knowable' (IV, XIII, §1). For Locke, this deductive knowledge of nature remains ideal, possible for God but not for man. Nevertheless this idea has affected Locke's account of human knowledge; knowledge is defined in Book IV as being concerned only with ideas and their relations. Were the deductive sort of knowledge actual, we could find out about the world by examining our ideas. Spinoza had proclaimed such an adequation between ideas and things; Locke's scepticism prevented him from saying our ideas reveal the *nature* of things, although he was convinced they do testify to the *existence* of things. But knowledge, whether adequate to things or not, resides in the relations of ideas. Knowledge requires certainty. Certainty is found only in the relations between our ideas, relations of 'connexion or repugnancy'.[1] There can be no certainty where we lack a knowledge of necessary connexions.

This ideal of a deductive knowledge is not characteristic of Book IV alone, nor of our knowledge of external nature. Locke had strongly suggested the possibility of a deductive ethics. There is also a curious section at the end of chapter XXI of Book II where Locke seems to suggest the possibility of a logical derivation of all ideas from only eight original ones. He says that if he were to consider this programme of derivation 'as a philosopher, and examine on what causes they depend and of what they [all our ideas] are made, I believe they all might be reduced to these very few primary and original ones'. He then lists the following eight ideas: extension, solidity, mobility, perceptivity, motivity, existence, duration, and number. The term philosopher' in this statement must mean the 'natural philosopher', but from what Locke says about such a derivation as he here suggests, we cannot be sure just how a natural philosopher would proceed. A psychologist *might* discover that in fact all the ideas of men were causally derived from these eight, although this is a highly dubious possibility. If this were the possibility Locke had envisaged at this point, how are we to understand what he himself has attempted in the preceding twenty chapters? There would seem to be three different sorts of derivation of ideas: (*a*) a physical and physiological one, which Locke suggests in outline only; (*b*) a psychological one, which is what he considers himself to have done in Book II; and (*c*) a logical derivation, which would seek to find some few basic ideas from which all others could be inferred or constructed, regardless of how *in fact* ideas are derived. It may be this third type of analysis which Locke is suggesting at this point. If so, the ideal of a deductive ordering of human knowledge comes forth again, even though it is not fully developed nor adequately stated.

---

[1] The term 'repugnancy' in Locke's definition of knowledge has its strong, late medieval meaning, of contradiction or inconsistency. Knowledge, then, is defined by Locke in terms of these two logical notions, necessary connexion and contradiction.

In stressing the distinction between that which is assumed and that which is accomplished in Locke, I am attempting to overcome some of the prejudices usually brought to the reading of his *Essay*. I have done no more than remind the reader of the structure of any philosophical work. What is assumed cannot, in the system in which it is assumption, be demonstrated or derived, no matter what manner of derivation is being attempted. The assumed is underived, or derived outside the system. Appreciation of this fact about the structure of philosophical systems can help us to read the classics of our tradition with a fresh mind. We too often read the history of philosophy as if each man built upon his predecessors, talking in terms of the problems and the solutions discussed by previous philosophers, the whole forming some kind of progressive development. Even when we do not commit ourselves to such a large-scale philosophy of history, we tend to read past philosophical systems with the present terminology and concepts in mind. Where it is evident from the text of the philosopher that he was talking directly to some of his predecessors—as was the case for many of the eighteenth-century philosophers in relation to Locke—such a reading may not lead to excesses. But it is far from indisputable that Locke wrote with the philosophical tradition in mind. He seems rather to have approached each of his questions and problems on their own terms, trying as best he could to develop a solution which seemed true or reasonable. Pierre Coste's advice for a fruitful reading of Locke could well hold for most philosophers. We must do two things, Coste wrote in the 'Avertissement' to his French translation of the *Essay*: 'La première est de laisser à quartier toutes les opinions dont on est prévenu sur les questions qui sont traitées dans cet ouvrage, et la seconde de juger des raisonnements de l'auteur par rapport à ce qu'on trouve en soi-même, sans se mettre en peine s'ils sont conformés ou non à ce qu'a dit Platon, Aristote, Gassendi, Descartes, ou quelque autre célèbre philosophe.'

Locke did not set out to construct a system of philosophy. The system which is there in his *Essay* grew out of the bits and pieces of his thought and took shape at the same time that he fashioned a product acceptable by him for public examination. Locke's readers in the seventeenth and early eighteenth centuries were, for the most part, unable to examine this work in the unempassioned way in which Locke seems to have

constructed it. The *Essay*, in its own way, was also a tract of the
time, arising out of ethical and theological questioning, analys-
ing—even undermining—many long-held beliefs, calling down
upon itself bitter calumny, arousing extended debates. The
immediate context of the *Essay* has been outgrown by succeeding generations of readers. The significance and relevance of
the problems raised in that work confront us still.

ACKNOWLEDGMENTS

   Mr. Peter Laslett's interest in this work, and his guidance in
the early stages of planning, have been most helpful, as has been
the constant interest of Mr. E. F. Bozman of J. M. Dent and
Sons. Mr. Philip Long's helpful service in the Bodleian Library
at Oxford is also appreciated. A small grant from Kenyon
College has aided my research. The Bodleian Library has
made it possible to use and quote from the Lovelace Collection
and to reproduce the title-page from their copy of the Fifth
Edition. My wife's careful reading of the text, and her assidu-
ous attention to modernizing the spelling and punctuation
have been a major contribution to this edition.

                                            JOHN W. YOLTON.
   Oxford, 1961.

SELECT BIBLIOGRAPHY

Note: For a complete list of Locke's works, as well as the known manuscripts, other contemporary books on Locke, and recent studies in his philosophy, see the bibliographies in Aaron, Long, Polin, and Yolton given below.

1663   *Essays on the Law of Nature*. The Latin text with a translation, edited by W. von Leyden, Oxford, 1954.

1675-9 *Locke's Travels in France, As Related in his Journals, Correspondence, and Other Papers*. Edited by John Lough, Cambridge, 1953.

1686   'Methode Nouvelle de Dresser des Recueils'. In Jean LeClerc's *Bibliothèque Universelle et Historique*, July, p. 315. (Reprinted in English in the *Posthumous Works*, 1706).

1689   *Epistola de Tolerantia ad Clarissimum Verum*, Gouda. (Translated as *A Letter concerning Toleration*, by W. Popple, and published in 1689.)

1690   *A Second Letter concerning Toleration*.

1690   *Two Treatises of Government* (2nd edition, 1694; 3rd edition, 1698). (For a critical edition with introduction and notes, see Laslett's *Locke's Two Treatises of Government*, Cambridge, 1960.)

1690   *An Essay Concerning Human Understanding*. (2nd edition, 1694; 3rd edition, 1695; 4th edition, 1700; 5th edition, 1706.)

1692   *A Third Letter for Toleration*.

1692   *Some Considerations of the Consequences of the Lowering of Interest and the Raising of the Value of Money*.

1693   *Some Thoughts concerning Education*.

1695   *Short Observations on a Printed Paper Intituled For Encouraging the Coinage of Silver Money in England*.

1695   *The Reasonableness of Christianity, As Delivered in the Scriptures*.

1695   *A Vindication of the Reasonableness of Christianity, etc., from Mr. Edwards' Reflections*.

1697   *A Letter to the Right Rev. Edward Lord Bishop of Worcester, concerning Some Passages Relating to Mr. Locke's Essay of Human Understanding*. (Locke's replies to the Bishop's replies appeared in 1697 and 1699.)

1705-7 *Paraphrases of the Epistles of St. Paul*.

1714   *Works of John Locke*, 3 vols. (2nd edition, 1722; 3rd edition, 1727).

BIOGRAPHY AND CRITICISM

Aaron, R. I. *John Locke*, 2nd edition. Oxford, 1955.

Cranston, M. *John Locke: A Biography*. London, 1957.

Gibson, J. *Locke's Theory of Knowledge*. Cambridge, 1917.

James, D. G. *The Life of Reason: Hobbes, Locke and Bolingbroke*. London, 1949.

Klemnt, A. *John Locke: Theoretische Philosophie*. Meisenheim/Glan, 1952.

Lamprecht, S. *The Moral and Political Philosophy of John Locke*. New York, 1918.

Long, P. *A Summary Catalogue of the Lovelace Collection of Papers of John Locke in the Bodleian Library*. Oxford, 1959.

MacLean, K. *John Locke and English Latitudinarians of the Eighteenth Century*. New Haven, Conn., 1936.

MacLachlan, H. *The Religious Opinions of Milton, Locke, and Newton*. London, 1941.

O'Connor, D. J. *John Locke*. London (Pelican), 1952.

Polin, R. *La Politique Morale de John Locke*. Paris, 1960.

Yolton, J. W. *John Locke and the Way of Ideas*. Oxford, 1956.

AN
ESSAY
CONCERNING
Humane Understanding.

In Four BOOKS.

Written by *JOHN LOCKE*, Gent.

The Fifth Edition, with large Additions.

ECCLES. XI. 5.

As thou knowest not what is the Way of the Spirit, nor how the Bones do grow in the Womb of her that is with Child : Even so thou knowest not the Works of God, who maketh all things.

Quam bellum est velle confiteri potius nescire quod nescias, quam ista effutientem nauseare, atque ipsum sibi displicere ! Cic. de Natur. Deor. l. 1.

LONDON:

Printed for *Awnsham* and *John Churchill*, at the *Black Swan* in *Pater-Noster-Row* ; and *Samuel Manship*, at the *Ship* in *Cornhill*, near the *Royal Exchange*, M DCC VI.

To The

Right Honourable

THOMAS

Earl of

Pembroke and Montgomery

Baron Herbert of Cardiff, Lord Ross
of Kendal, Par, Fitzhugh, Marmion,
St. Quintin, and Shurland; Lord
President of his Majesty's most
honourable Privy-Council, and Lord
Lieutenant of the County of Wilts,
and of South Wales.

MY LORD,
This treatise, which is grown up under your lordship's eye, and
has ventured into the world by your order, does now, by a
natural kind of right, come to your lordship for that protection
which you several years since promised it. It is not that I think
any name, how great soever, set at the beginning of a book, will
be able to cover the faults that are to be found in it. Things in
print must stand and fall by their own worth, or the reader's
fancy. But there being nothing more to be desired for truth,
than a fair unprejudiced hearing, nobody is more likely to procure me that than your lordship, who are allowed to have got so
intimate an acquaintance with her, in her more retired recesses.
Your lordship is known to have so far advanced your speculations in the most abstract and general knowledge of things,
beyond the ordinary reach or common methods, that your allowance and approbation of the design of this treatise will at least
preserve it from being condemned without reading, and will
prevail to have those parts a little weighed, which might otherwise perhaps be thought to deserve no consideration, for being
somewhat out of the common road. The imputation of novelty
is a terrible charge amongst those who judge of men's heads, as
they do of their perukes, by the fashion, and can allow none to be
right but the received doctrines. Truth scarce ever yet carried it

by vote anywhere at its first appearance: new opinions are always suspected, and usually opposed, without any other reason but because they are not already common. But truth, like gold, is not the less so for being newly brought out of the mine. It is trial and examination must give it price, and not any antique fashion; and though it be not yet current by the public stamp, yet it may, for all that, be as old as nature, and is certainly not the less genuine. Your lordship can give great and convincing instances of this, whenever you please to oblige the public with some of those large and comprehensive discoveries you have made of truths hitherto unknown, unless to some few, to whom your lordship has been pleased not wholly to conceal them. This alone were a sufficient reason, were there no other, why I should dedicate this *Essay* to your lordship; and its having some little correspondence with some parts of that nobler and vast system of the sciences your lordship has made so new, exact, and instructive a draught of, I think it glory enough, if your lordship permit me to boast, that here and there I have fallen into some thoughts not wholly different from yours. If your lordship think fit that, by your encouragement, this should appear in the world, I hope it may be a reason, some time or other, to lead your lordship further; and you will allow me to say that you here give the world an earnest of something that, if they can bear with this, will be truly worth their expectation. This, my lord, shows what a present I here make to your lordship; just such as the poor man does to his rich and great neighbour, by whom the basket of flowers or fruit is not ill taken, though he has more plenty of his own growth, and in much greater perfection. Worthless things receive a value when they are made the offerings of respect, esteem, and gratitude; these you have given me so mighty and peculiar reasons to have, in the highest degree, for your lordship, that if they can add a price to what they go along with, proportionable to their own greatness, I can present with confidence brag, I here make your lordship the richest present you ever received. This I am sure, I am under the greatest obligation to seek all occasions to acknowledge a long train of favours I have received from your lordship: favours, though great and important in themselves, yet made much more so by the forwardness, concern, and kindness, and other obliging circumstances that never failed to accompany them. To all this, you are pleased to add that which gives yet more weight and relish to all the rest: you vouchsafe to continue me in some degrees of your esteem and allow me a place in your good thoughts, I had almost said friendship. This, my lord, your words and actions so constantly show on all occasions, even to others when I am absent, that it is not vanity in me to mention what everybody knows; but it would be want of good manners not to acknowledge what so many are witnesses of, and every day tell me, I am indebted to your lordship for. I wish they could as easily assist my gratitude, as they convince me of the great growing engagements it has to your lordship. This I am sure, I should write of the *understanding* without having any, if I were not extremely sensible of them, and did not lay hold on this opportunity to testify to the world how much I am obliged to be, and how much I am,

DORSET-COURT,   My Lord,
24th of May, 1689.   Your Lordship's
                        Most Humble, and
                        Most Obedient Servant,

                            JOHN LOCKE

THE EPISTLE TO THE READER

READER,

I here put into thy hands what has been the diversion of some of my idle and heavy hours. If it has the good luck to prove so of any of thine, and thou hast but half so much pleasure in reading as I had in writing it, thou wilt as little think thy money, as I do my pains, ill bestowed. Mistake not this for a commendation of my work; nor conclude, because I was pleased with the doing of it, that therefore I am fondly taken with it now it is done. He that hawks at larks and sparrows has no less sport, though a much less considerable quarry, than he that flies at nobler game; and he is little acquainted with the subject of this treatise, the UNDERSTANDING, who does not know that, as it is the most elevated faculty of the soul, so it is employed with a greater and more constant delight than any of the other. Its searches after truth are a sort of hawking and hunting, wherein the very pursuit makes a great part of the pleasure. Every step the mind takes in its progress towards knowledge makes some discovery, which is not only new, but the best too, for the time at least.

For the understanding, like the eye, judging of objects only by its own sight, cannot but be pleased with what it discovers, having less regret for what has escaped it, because it is unknown. Thus he who has raised himself above the alms-basket, and, not content to live lazily on scraps of begged opinions, sets his own thoughts on work, to find and follow truth, will (whatever he lights on) not miss the hunter's satisfaction; every moment of his pursuit will reward his pains with some delight; and he will have reason to think his time not ill spent, even when he cannot much boast of any great acquisition.

This, Reader, is the entertainment of those who let loose their own thoughts, and follow them in writing; which thou oughtest not to envy them, since they afford thee an opportunity of the like diversion, if thou wilt make use of thy own thoughts in reading. It is to them, if they are thy own, that I refer myself; but if they are taken upon trust from others, it is no great matter what they are, they not following truth, but some meaner consideration; and it is not worth while to be concerned what he says or thinks who says or thinks only as he is directed by another. If thou judgest for thyself I know thou wilt judge candidly, and then I shall not be harmed or offended, whatever be thy censure. For though it be certain that there is nothing in this treatise of the truth whereof I am not fully persuaded, yet I consider myself as liable to mistakes as I can think thee, and know that this book must stand or fall with thee, not by any opinion I have of it, but thy own. If thou findest little in it new or instructive to thee, thou art not to blame me for it. It was not meant for those that had already mastered this subject, and made a thorough acquaintance with their own understandings; but for my own information, and the satisfaction of a few friends, who acknowledged themselves not to have sufficiently considered it. Were it fit to trouble thee with the history of this *Essay*, I should tell thee that five or six friends, meeting at my chamber and discoursing on a subject very remote from this, found themselves quickly at a stand, by the difficulties that rose on every side. After we had awhile puzzled ourselves, without coming any nearer a resolution of those doubts which perplexed us, it came into my thoughts that we took a wrong course; and that before we set ourselves upon inquiries of that nature, it was necessary to examine our own abilities and see what objects our understandings were, or were not, fitted to deal with. This I proposed to the company, who all readily assented; and thereupon it was agreed that this should be our first inquiry. Some hasty and undigested thoughts, on a subject I had never before considered, which I set down against our next meeting, gave the first entrance into this discourse; which having been thus begun by chance, was continued by entreaty; written by incoherent parcels; and after long intervals of neglect, resumed again, as my humour or occasions permitted; and at last, in a retirement where an attendance on my health gave me leisure, it was brought into that order thou now seest it.

This discontinued way of writing may have occasioned, besides others, two contrary faults, viz. that too little and too much may be said in it. If thou findest anything wanting, I shall be glad that what I have writ gives thee any desire that I should have gone further. If it seems too much to thee, thou must blame the subject; for when I first put pen to paper, I thought all I should have to say on this matter would have been contained in one sheet of paper; but the further I went the larger prospect I had;

new discoveries led me still on, and so it grew insensibly to the bulk it now appears in. I will not deny but possibly it might be reduced to a narrower compass than it is, and that some parts of it might be contracted: the way it has been writ in, by catches and many long intervals of interruption, being apt to cause some repetitions. But to confess the truth, I am now too lazy, or too busy, to make it shorter.

I am not ignorant how little I herein consult my own reputation, when I knowingly let it go with a fault, so apt to disgust the most judicious, who are always the nicest readers. But they who know sloth is apt to content itself with any excuse, will pardon me if mine has prevailed on me, where I think I have a very good one. I will not therefore allege in my defence that the same notion, having different respects, may be convenient or necessary to prove or illustrate several parts of the same discourse, and that so it has happened in many parts of this; but waiving that, I shall frankly avow that I have sometimes dwelt long upon the same argument, and expressed it different ways, with a quite different design. I pretend not to publish this *Essay* for the information of men of large thoughts and quick apprehensions; to such masters of knowledge I profess myself a scholar, and therefore warn them beforehand not to expect anything here but what, being spun out of my own coarse thoughts, is fitted to men of my own size, to whom, perhaps, it will not be unacceptable that I have taken some pains to make plain and familiar to their thoughts some truths which established prejudice, or the abstractness of the *ideas* themselves, might render difficult. Some objects had need be turned on every side; and when the notion is new, as I confess some of these are to me, or out of the ordinary road, as I suspect they will appear to others, it is not one simple view of it that will gain it admittance into every understanding or fix it there with a clear and lasting impression. There are few, I believe, who have not observed in themselves or others, that what in one way of proposing was very obscure, another way of expressing it has made very clear and intelligible, though afterward the mind found little difference in the phrases and wondered why one failed to be understood more than the other. But everything does not hit alike upon every man's imagination. We have our understandings no less different than our palates; and he that thinks the same truth shall be equally relished by everyone in the same dress, may as well hope to feast everyone with the same sort of cookery: the meat may be the same, and the nourishment good, yet everyone not be able to receive it with that seasoning; and it must be dressed another way, if you will have it go down with some, even of strong constitutions. The truth is, those who advised me to publish it, advised me, for this reason, to publish it as it is; and since I have been brought to let it go abroad, I desire it should be understood by whoever gives himself the pains to read it. I have so little affection to be in print that, if I were not flattered this *Essay* might be of some use to others, as I think it has been to me, I should have confined it to the view of some friends, who gave the first occasion to it. My appearing therefore in print being on purpose to be as useful as I may, I think it necessary to make what I have to say as easy and intelligible to all sorts of readers as I can. And I had much rather the speculative and quick-sighted should complain of my being in some parts tedious than that anyone, not accustomed to abstract speculations, or prepossessed with different notions, should mistake or not comprehend my meaning.

It will possibly be censured as a great piece of vanity or insolence in me, to pretend to instruct this our knowing age: it amounting to little less, when I own that I publish this *Essay* with hopes it may be useful to others. But, if it may be permitted to speak freely of those who with a feigned modesty condemn as useless what they themselves write, methinks it savours much more of vanity or insolence to publish a book for any other end; and he fails very much of that respect he owes the public, who prints and consequently expects men should read that wherein he intends not they should meet with anything of use to themselves or others; and should nothing else be found allowable in this treatise, yet my design will not cease to be so; and the goodness of my intention ought to be some excuse for the worthlessness of my present. It is that chiefly which secures me from the fear of censure, which I expect not to escape more than better writers. Men's principles, notions, and relishes are so different, that it is hard to find a book which pleases or displeases all men. I acknowledge the age we live in is not the least knowing, and therefore not the most easy to be satisfied. If I have not the good luck to please, yet nobody ought to be offended with me. I plainly tell all my readers, except half a dozen, this treatise was not at first intended for them; and therefore they need not be at the trouble to be of that number.   But yet if anyone thinks fit to be angry and rail at it, he may do it securely, for I shall find some better way of spending my time than in such kind of conversation.   I shall always have the satisfaction to have aimed sincerely at truth and usefulness, though in one of the meanest ways.   The commonwealth of learning is not at this time without master-builders, whose mighty designs, in advancing the sciences, will leave lasting monuments to the admiration of posterity; but everyone must not hope to be a *Boyle* or a *Sydenham*; and in an age that produces such masters as the great *Huygenius* and the incomparable Mr. *Newton,* with some others of that strain, it is ambition enough to be employed as an underlabourer in clearing ground a little, and removing some of the rubbish that lies in the way of knowledge; which certainly had been very much more advanced in the world, if the endeavours of ingenious and industrious men had not been much cumbered with the learned but frivolous use of uncouth, affected, or unintelligible terms, introduced into the sciences, and there made an art of, to that degree that philosophy, which is nothing but the true knowledge of things, was thought unfit or incapable to be brought into well-bred company and polite conversation.   Vague and insignificant forms of speech and abuse of language have so long passed for mysteries of science; and hard or misapplied words, with little or no meaning, have, by prescription, such a right to be mistaken for deep learning and height of speculation, that it will not be easy to persuade either those who speak or those who hear them that they are but the covers of ignorance and hindrance of true knowledge.   To break in upon the sanctuary of vanity and ignorance will be, I suppose, some service to human understanding: though so few are apt to think they deceive or are deceived in the use of words, or that the language of the sect they are of has any faults in it which ought to be examined or corrected, that I hope I shall be pardoned if I have in the Third Book dwelt long on this subject and endeavoured to make it so plain that neither the inveterateness of the mischief nor the prevalency of the fashion shall be any excuse for those who will not take care about the meaning of their own words, and will not suffer the significancy of their expressions to be inquired into.

I have been told that a short epitome of this treatise, which was printed in 1688, was by some condemned without reading, because innate *ideas* were denied in it: they too hastily concluding that, if innate *ideas* were not supposed, there would be little left either of the notion or proof of spirits. If anyone take the like offence at the entrance of this treatise, I shall desire him to read it through; and then I hope he will be convinced that the taking away false foundations is not to the prejudice but advantage of truth, which is never injured or endangered so much as when mixed with, or built on, falsehood. In the Second Edition, I added as followeth:

The bookseller will not forgive me if I say nothing of this Second Edition, which he has promised, by the correctness of it, shall make amends for the many faults committed in the former. He desires, too, that it should be known that it has one whole new chapter concerning *Identity*, and many additions and amendments in other places. These I must inform my reader are not all new matter, but most of them either further confirmation of what I had said, or explications to prevent others being mistaken in the sense of what was formerly printed, and not any variation in me from it. I must only except the alterations I have made in Book 2, Chap. 21.

What I had there writ concerning *Liberty* and the *Will*, I thought deserved as accurate a review as I was capable of: those subjects having in all ages exercised the learned part of the world with questions and difficulties, that have not a little perplexed morality and divinity, those parts of knowledge that men are most concerned to be clear in. Upon a closer inspection into the working of men's minds, and a stricter examination of those motives and views they are turned by, I have found reason somewhat to alter the thoughts I formerly had concerning that which gives the last determination to the *Will* in all voluntary actions. This I cannot forbear to acknowledge to the world with as much freedom and readiness as I at first published what then seemed to me to be right, thinking myself more concerned to quit and renounce any opinion of my own, than oppose that of another, when truth appears against it. For it is truth alone I seek, and that will always be welcome to me, when or from whencesoever it comes.

But what forwardness soever I have to resign any opinion I have, or to recede from anything I have writ, upon the first evidence of any error in it: yet this I must own, that I have not had the good luck to receive any light from those exceptions I have met with in print against any part of my book, nor have, from anything that has been urged against it, found reason to alter my sense in any of the points that have been questioned. Whether the subject I have in hand requires often more thought and attention than cursory readers, at least such as are prepossessed, are willing to allow; or whether any obscurity in my expressions casts a cloud over it, and these notions are made difficult to others' apprehension in my way of treating them: so it is that my meaning, I find, is often mistaken, and I have not the good luck to be everywhere rightly understood. There are so many instances of this, that I think it justice to my reader and myself to conclude that either my book is plainly enough written to be rightly understood by those who peruse it with that attention and indifferency which everyone who will give himself the pains to read ought to employ in reading, or else that I have writ mine so obscurely that it is in vain to go about to mend it. Whichever of these be that truth, it is myself only am affected thereby; and therefore I shall be far from troubling my reader with what I think might be said in answer to those several objections I have met with, to passages here and there of my book: since I persuade myself that he who thinks them of moment enough to be concerned whether they are true or false, will be able to see that what is said is either not well founded, or else not contrary to my doctrine, when I and my opposer come both to be well understood.

If any, careful that none of their good thoughts should be lost, have published their censures of my *Essay*, with this honour done to it, that they will not suffer it to be an *Essay*, I leave it to the public to value the obligation they have to their critical pens, and shall not waste my reader's time in so idle or ill-natured an employment of mine, as to lessen the satisfaction anyone has in himself, or gives to others in so hasty a confutation of what I have written.

The booksellers preparing for the Fourth Edition of my *Essay*, gave me notice of it that I might, if I had leisure, make any additions or alterations I should think fit. Whereupon I thought it convenient to advertise the reader that, besides several corrections I had made here and there, there was one alteration which it was necessary to mention, because it ran through the whole book, and is of consequence to be rightly understood. What I thereupon said was this:

Clear and distinct ideas are terms which, though familiar and frequent in men's mouths, I have reason to think everyone who uses does not perfectly understand. And possibly it is but here and there one who gives himself the trouble to consider them so far as to know what he himself or others precisely mean by them. I have therefore in most places chosen to put *determinate* or *determined*, instead of *clear* and *distinct*, as more likely to direct men's thoughts to my meaning in this matter. By those denominations, I mean some object in the mind, and consequently *determined*, i.e. such as it is there seen and perceived to be. This, I think, may fitly be called a *determinate* or *determined* idea, when, such as it is at any time objectively in the mind and so *determined* there, it is annexed and without variation *determined* to a name or articulate sound, which is to be steadily the sign of that very same object of the mind, or *determinate* idea.

To explain this a little more particularly. By *determinate*, when applied to a simple idea, I mean that simple appearance which the mind has in its view, or perceives in itself, when that idea is said to be in it; by *determined*, when applied to a *complex idea*, I mean such an one as consists of a determinate number of certain simple or less complex ideas, joined in such a proportion and situation as the mind has before its view and sees in itself, when that idea is present in it or should be present in it, when a man gives a name to it. I say *should* be, because it is not everyone, nor perhaps anyone, who is so careful of his language as to use no word till he views in his mind the precise *determined* idea which he resolves to make it the sign of. The want of this is the cause of no small obscurity and confusion in men's thoughts and discourses.

I know there are not words enough in any language to answer all the variety of ideas that enter into men's discourses and reasonings. But this hinders not but that when anyone uses any term, he may have in his mind a *determined* idea, which he makes it the sign of, and to which he should keep it steadily annexed during that present discourse. Where he does not or cannot do this, he in vain pretends to *clear* or *distinct ideas*: it is plain his are not so; and therefore there can be expected nothing but obscurity and confusion, where such terms are made use of which have not such a precise determination.

Upon this ground I have thought *determined* ideas a way of speaking less liable to mistake, than *clear* and *distinct*; and where men have got such *determined* ideas of all that they reason, inquire, or argue about, they will find a great part of their doubts and disputes at an end: the greatest part of the questions and controversies that perplex mankind depending on the doubtful and uncertain use of words or (which is the same) *indetermined ideas*, which they are made to stand for. I have made choice of these terms to signify (1) some immediate object of the mind, which it perceives and has before it, distinct from the sound it uses as a sign of it; (2) that this idea, thus *determined*, i.e. which the mind has in itself and knows and sees there, be *determined* without any change to that name, and that name *determined* to that precise idea. If men had such *determined* ideas in their inquiries and discourses, they would both discern how far their own inquiries and discourses went, and avoid the greatest part of the disputes and wranglings they have with others.

Besides this, the bookseller will think it necessary I should advertise the reader that there is an addition of two chapters wholly new, the one *of the association of ideas*, the other *of enthusiasm*. These, with some other larger additions never before printed, he has engaged to print by themselves after the same manner, and for the same purpose as was done when this *Essay* had the Second Impression.

In this Fifth Edition, there is very little added or altered. The greatest part of what is new is contained in the 21st chapter of the Second Book, which anyone, if he thinks it worth the while, may, with a very little labour, transcribe into the margin of the former edition.

THE ANALYTICAL CONTENTS

BOOK I

CHAPTER I

INTRODUCTION

CHAPTER II

NO INNATE PRINCIPLES IN THE MIND

CHAPTER III

No Innate Practical Principles

CHAPTER IV

OTHER CONSIDERATIONS
CONCERNING INNATE PRINCIPLES,
BOTH SPECULATIVE AND PRACTICAL

SECTION

BOOK I

OF INNATE NOTIONS

CHAPTER I

INTRODUCTION

1. SINCE it is the *understanding* that sets man above the rest of sensible beings, and gives him all the advantage and dominion which he has over them, it is certainly a subject, even for its nobleness, worth our labour to inquire into. The understanding, like the eye, whilst it makes us see and perceive all other things, takes no notice of itself; and it requires art and pains to set it at a distance and make it its own object. But whatever be the difficulties that lie in the way of this inquiry, whatever it be that keeps us so much in the dark to ourselves, sure I am that all the light we can let in upon our own minds, all the acquaintance we can make with our own understandings, will not only be very pleasant, but bring us great advantage, in directing our thoughts in the search of other things.

2. This, therefore, being my *purpose*, to inquire into the original, certainty, and extent of human knowledge, together with the grounds and degrees of belief, opinion, and assent: I shall not at present meddle with the physical consideration of the mind; or trouble myself to examine wherein its essence consists; or by what motions of our spirits or alterations of our bodies we come to have any sensation by our organs, or any *ideas* in our understandings; and whether those *ideas* do in their formation, any or all of them, depend on matter or no. These are speculations which, however curious and entertaining, I shall decline, as lying out of my way in the design I am now upon. It shall suffice to my present purpose to consider the discerning faculties of a man, as they are employed about the objects which they have to do with. And I shall imagine I have not wholly misemployed myself in the thoughts I shall have on this occasion, if, in this historical, plain method, I can give any account of the ways whereby our understandings come to attain those notions of

things we have, and can set down any measures of the certainty
of our knowledge, or the grounds of those persuasions which are
to be found amongst men, so various, different, and wholly con-
tradictory; and yet asserted somewhere or other with such
assurance and confidence that he that shall take a view of the
opinions of mankind, observe their opposition, and at the same
time consider the fondness and devotion wherewith they are
embraced, the resolution and eagerness wherewith they are main-
tained, may perhaps have reason to suspect that either there is
no such thing as truth at all, or that mankind hath no sufficient
means to attain a certain knowledge of it.

3.   It is therefore worth while to search out the *bounds* between
opinion and knowledge, and examine by what measures, in
things whereof we have no certain knowledge, we ought to
regulate our assent and moderate our persuasions. In order
whereunto I shall pursue this following method:

First, I shall inquire into the *original* of those *ideas*, notions, or
whatever else you please to call them, which a man observes
and is conscious to himself he has in his mind; and the ways
whereby the understanding comes to be furnished with them.

Secondly, I shall endeavour to show what *knowledge* the
understanding hath by those *ideas*, and the certainty, evidence,
and extent of it.

Thirdly, I shall make some inquiry into the nature and
grounds of *faith* or *opinion*: whereby I mean that assent which
we give to any proposition as true, of whose truth yet we have no
certain knowledge. And here we shall have occasion to examine
the reasons and degrees of *assent*.

4.   If by this inquiry into the nature of the understanding, I
can discover the powers thereof: *how far* they reach; to what
things they are in any degree proportionate; and where they fail
us, I suppose it may be of use to prevail with the busy mind of
man to be more cautious in meddling with things exceeding its
comprehension; to stop when it is at the utmost extent of its
tether; and to sit down in a quiet ignorance of those things
which upon examination are found to be beyond the reach of
our capacities. We should not then perhaps be so forward, out
of an affectation of an universal knowledge, to raise questions
and perplex ourselves and others with disputes about things to
which our understandings are not suited, and of which we cannot
frame in our minds any clear or distinct perceptions, or whereof

(as it has perhaps too often happened) we have not any notions
at all. If we can find out how far the understanding can extend
its view, how far it has faculties to attain certainty, and in what
cases it can only judge and guess, we may learn to content ourselves with what is attainable by us in this state.

5. For though the *comprehension* of our understandings comes
exceeding short of the vast extent of things, yet we shall have
cause enough to magnify the bountiful Author of our being, for
that portion and degree of knowledge he has bestowed on us,
so far above all the rest of the inhabitants of this our mansion.
Men have reason to be well satisfied with what God hath thought
fit for them, since he has given them (as St. *Peter* says) πάντα
πρὸς ζωὴν καὶ εὐσέβειαν, whatsoever is necessary for the
conveniences of life and information of virtue; and has put
within the reach of their discovery, the comfortable provision
for this life and the way that leads to a better. How short soever
their knowledge may come of an universal or perfect comprehension of whatsoever is, it yet secures their great concernments, that they have light enough to lead them to the knowledge
of their Maker and the sight of their own duties. Men may find
matter sufficient to busy their heads and employ their hands
with variety, delight, and satisfaction, if they will not boldly
quarrel with their own constitution and throw away the bless-
ings their hands are filled with, because they are not big enough
to grasp everything. We shall not have much reason to complain
of the narrowness of our minds, if we will but employ them
about what may be of use to us; for of that they are very capable.
And it will be an unpardonable as well as childish peevishness, if
we undervalue the advantages of our knowledge and neglect to
improve it to the ends for which it was given us, because there
are some things that are set out of the reach of it. It will be no
excuse to an idle and untoward servant, who would not attend
his business by candle light, to plead that he had not broad sunshine. The candle that is set up in us shines bright enough for
all our purposes. The discoveries we can make with this ought
to satisfy us; and we shall then use our understandings right,
when we entertain all objects in that way and proportion that
they are suited to our faculties, and upon those grounds they are
capable of being proposed to us; and not peremptorily or in-
temperately require demonstration and demand certainty, where
probability only is to be had, and which is sufficient to govern all

our concernments. If we will disbelieve everything, because we cannot certainly know all things, we shall do much what as wisely as he who would not use his legs, but sit still and perish because he had no wings to fly.

6. When we know our own *strength*, we shall the better know what to undertake with hopes of success; and when we have well surveyed the *powers* of our own minds, and made some estimate what we may expect from them, we shall not be inclined either to sit still and not set our thoughts on work at all, in despair of knowing anything, nor, on the other side, question everything and disclaim all knowledge, because some things are not to be understood. It is of great use to the sailor to know the length of his line, though he cannot with it fathom all the depths of the ocean. It is well he knows that it is long enough to reach the bottom, at such places as are necessary to direct his voyage, and caution him against running upon shoals that may ruin him. Our business here is not to know all things, but those which concern our conduct. If we can find out those measures whereby a rational creature, put in that state in which man is in this world, may and ought to govern his opinions and actions depending thereon, we need not be troubled that some other things escape our knowledge.

7. This was that which gave the first *rise* to this *Essay* concerning the *understanding*. For I thought that the first step towards satisfying several inquiries the mind of man was very apt to run into was to take a survey of our own understandings, examine our own powers, and see to what things they were adapted. Till that was done I suspected we began at the wrong end and in vain sought for satisfaction in a quiet and sure possession of truths that most concerned us, whilst we let loose our thoughts into the vast ocean of *Being*, as if all that boundless extent were the natural and undoubted possession of our understandings, wherein there was nothing exempt from its decisions or that escaped its comprehension. Thus men, extending their inquiries beyond their capacities, and letting their thoughts wander into those depths where they can find no sure footing, it is no wonder that they raise questions and multiply disputes, which, never coming to any clear resolution, are proper only to continue and increase their doubts and to confirm them at last in perfect scepticism. Whereas, were the capacities of our understandings well considered, the extent of our knowledge once

discovered, and the horizon found which sets the bounds between the enlightened and dark parts of things, between what is and what is not comprehensible by us, men would perhaps with less scruple acquiesce in the avowed ignorance of the one, and employ their thoughts and discourse with more advantage and satisfaction in the other.

8. Thus much I thought necessary to say concerning the occasion of this inquiry into human understanding. But, before I proceed on to what I have thought on this subject, I must here in the entrance beg pardon of my reader for the frequent use of the word *idea*, which he will find in the following treatise. It being that term which, I think, serves best to stand for whatsoever is the object of the understanding when a man thinks, I have used it to express whatever is meant by *phantasm, notion, species*, or whatever it is which the mind can be employed about in thinking; and I could not avoid frequently using it.

I presume it will be easily granted me that there are such *ideas* in men's minds: everyone is conscious of them in himself, and men's words and actions will satisfy him that they are in others.

Our first inquiry then shall be how they come into the mind.

Chapter II

NO INNATE PRINCIPLES IN THE MIND

1. It is an established opinion amongst some men that there are in the *understanding* certain *innate principles*, some primary notions, κοιναὶ ἔννοιαι, characters, as it were, stamped upon the mind of man, which the soul receives in its very first being and brings into the world with it. It would be sufficient to convince unprejudiced readers of the falseness of this supposition, if I should only show (as I hope I shall in the following parts of this discourse) how men, barely by the use of their natural faculties, may attain to all the knowledge they have, without the help of any innate impressions, and may arrive at certainty without any such original notions or principles. For I imagine anyone will easily grant that it would be impertinent to suppose the *ideas* of colours innate in a creature to whom God has given sight, and a power to receive them by the eyes, from external

objects; and no less unreasonable would it be to attribute several
truths to the impressions of nature and innate characters, when
we may observe in ourselves faculties, fit to attain as easy and
certain knowledge of them, as if they were originally imprinted
on the mind.

But because a man is not permitted without censure to follow
his own thoughts in the search of truth, when they lead him ever
so little out of the common road, I shall set down the reasons
that made me doubt of the truth of that opinion, as an excuse
for my mistake, if I be in one; which I leave to be considered by
those who, with me, dispose themselves to embrace truth,
wherever they find it.

2. There is nothing more commonly taken for granted than
that there are certain principles, both *speculative* and *practical*
(for they speak of both), universally agreed upon by all mankind: which therefore, they argue, must needs be constant
impressions which the souls of men receive in their first beings,
and which they bring into the world with them, as necessarily
and really as they do any of their inherent faculties.

3. This argument, drawn from *universal consent*, has this mis-
fortune in it, that if it were true in matter of fact that there were
certain truths wherein all mankind agreed, it would not prove
them innate, if there can be any other way shown how men may
come to that universal agreement, in the things they do consent
in, which I presume may be done.

4. But, which is worse, this argument of universal consent,
which is made use of to prove innate principles, seems to me a
demonstration that there are none such: because there are none
to which all mankind give an universal assent. I shall begin with
the speculative, and instance in those magnified principles of
demonstration, *Whatsoever is, is* and *It is impossible for the same
thing to be and not to be*, which of all others I think have the
most allowed title to innate. These have so settled a reputation
of maxims universally received that it will, no doubt, be thought
strange if anyone should seem to question it. But yet I take
liberty to say that these propositions are so far from having an
universal assent, that there are a great part of mankind to whom
they are not so much as known.

5. For, first, it is evident that all *children* and *idiots* have not
the least apprehension or thought of them. And the want of that
is enough to destroy that universal assent which must needs be

the necessary concomitant of all innate truths: it seeming to me near a contradiction to say that there are truths imprinted on the soul which it perceives or understands not: imprinting, if it signify anything, being nothing else but the making certain truths to be perceived. But to imprint anything on the mind, without the mind's perceiving it, seems to me hardly intelligible. If therefore *children* and *idiots* have souls, have minds, with those impressions upon them, they must unavoidably perceive them, and necessarily know and assent to these truths; which since they do not, it is evident that there are no such impressions. For if they are not notions naturally imprinted, how can they be innate? And if they are notions imprinted, how can they be unknown? To say a notion is imprinted on the mind, and yet at the same time to say that the mind is ignorant of it, and never yet took notice of it, is to make this impression nothing. No proposition can be said to be in the mind, which it never yet knew, which it was never yet conscious of. For if any one may, then by the same reason all propositions that are true and the mind is capable ever of assenting to, may be said to be in the mind and to be imprinted: since, if any one can be said to be in the mind which it never yet knew, it must be only because it is capable of knowing it; and so the mind is of all truths it ever shall know. Nay, thus truths may be imprinted on the mind which it never did nor ever shall know; for a man may live long, and die at last in ignorance of many truths which his mind was capable of knowing, and that with certainty. So that if the capacity of knowing be the natural impression contended for, all the truths a man ever comes to know will, by this account, be every one of them innate; and this great point will amount to no more, but only to a very improper way of speaking; which, whilst it pretends to assert the contrary, says nothing different from those who deny innate principles. For nobody, I think, ever denied that the mind was capable of knowing several truths. The capacity they say is innate, the knowledge acquired. But then to what end such contest for certain innate maxims? If truths can be imprinted on the understanding without being perceived, I can see no difference there can be between any truths the mind is capable of knowing, in respect of their original: they must all be innate, or all adventitious. In vain shall a man go about to distinguish them. He therefore that talks of innate notions in the understanding, cannot (if he intend

thereby any distinct sort of truths) mean such truths to be in the
understanding as it never perceived, and is yet wholly ignorant
of. For if these words (*to be in the understanding*) have any
propriety, they signify to be understood. So that to be in the
understanding and not to be understood, to be in the mind and
never to be perceived, is all one as to say: anything is and is not
in the mind or understanding. If therefore these two propositions, *Whatsoever is, is* and *It is impossible for the same thing to
be and not to be*, are by nature imprinted, children cannot be
ignorant of them; infants, and all that have souls, must necessarily have them in their understandings, know the truth of
them, and assent to it.

6. To avoid this, it is usually answered that all men know and
assent to them, *when they come to the use of reason*; and this is
enough to prove them innate. I answer:

7. Doubtful expressions, that have scarce any signification, go
for clear reasons to those who, being prepossessed, take not the
pains to examine even what they themselves say. For, to apply
this answer with any tolerable sense to our present purpose, it
must signify one of these two things: either, that as soon as men
come to the use of reason these supposed native inscriptions
come to be known and observed by them; or else, that the use
and exercise of men's reason assists them in the discovery of
these principles, and certainly makes them known to them.

8. If they mean that by the *use of reason* men may discover
these principles, and that this is sufficient to prove them innate,
their way of arguing will stand thus: viz. that whatever truths
reason can certainly discover to us and make us firmly assent to,
those are all naturally imprinted on the mind, since that universal
assent, which is made the mark of them, amounts to no more but
this: that by the use of reason we are capable to come to a certain knowledge of and assent to them; and, by this means, there
will be no difference between the maxims of the mathematicians
and theorems they deduce from them: all must be equally
allowed innate, they being all discoveries made by the use of
reason, and truths that a rational creature may certainly come to
know, if he apply his thoughts rightly that way.

9. But how can these men think the *use of reason* necessary
to discover principles that are supposed innate, when reason (if
we may believe them) is nothing else but the faculty of deducing
unknown truths from principles or propositions that are already

known? That certainly can never be thought innate which we have need of reason to discover, unless, as I have said, we will have all the certain truths that reason ever teaches us to be innate. We may as well think the use of reason necessary to make our eyes discover visible objects, as that there should be need of reason, or the exercise thereof, to make the understanding see what is originally engraven in it, and cannot be in the understanding before it be perceived by it. So that to make reason discover those truths thus imprinted is to say that the use of reason discovers to a man what he knew before; and if men have those innate, impressed truths originally, and before the use of reason, and yet are always ignorant of them till they come to the use of reason, it is in effect to say that men know and know them not at the same time.

10. It will perhaps be said that mathematical demonstrations and other truths that are not innate, are not assented to as soon as proposed, wherein they are distinguished from these maxims and other innate truths. I shall have occasion to speak of assent upon the first proposing, more particularly by and by. I shall here only, and that very readily, allow that these maxims and mathematical demonstrations are in this different: that the one have need of reason, using of proofs, to make them out and to gain our assent; but the other, as soon as understood, are, without any the least reasoning, embraced and assented to. But I withal beg leave to observe that it lays open the weakness of this subterfuge which requires the *use of reason* for the discovery of these general truths, since it must be confessed that in their discovery there is no use made of reasoning at all. And I think those who give this answer will not be forward to affirm that the knowledge of this maxim, *That it is impossible for the same thing to be, and not to be,* is a deduction of our reason. For this would be to destroy that bounty of nature they seem so fond of, whilst they make the knowledge of those principles to depend on the labour of our thoughts. For all reasoning is search and casting about and requires pains and application. And how can it with any tolerable sense be supposed that what was imprinted by nature, as the foundation and guide of our reason, should need the use of reason to discover it?

11. Those who will take the pains to reflect with a little attention on the operations of the understanding will find that this ready assent of the mind to some truths depends not either on

native inscription or the *use of reason*, but on a faculty of the
mind quite distinct from both of them, as we shall see hereafter.
Reason, therefore, having nothing to do in procuring our assent
to these maxims, if by saying that *men know and assent to them
when they come to the use of reason* be meant that the use of
reason assists us in the knowledge of these maxims, it is utterly
false; and were it true, would prove them not to be innate.

12.   If by knowing and assenting to them *when we come to the
use of reason* be meant that this is the time when they come to be
taken notice of by the mind; and that as soon as children come
to the use of reason, they come also to know and assent to these
maxims: this also is false and frivolous. *First*, it is false. Because
it is evident these maxims are not in the mind so early as the
use of reason; and therefore the coming to the use of reason is
falsely assigned as the time of their discovery. How many
instances of the use of reason may we observe in children a long
time before they have any knowledge of this maxim, *That it is
impossible for the same thing to be, and not to be*? And a great
part of illiterate people and savages pass many years, even of
their rational age, without ever thinking on this, and the like
general propositions. I grant men come not to the knowledge
of these general and more abstract truths, which are thought
innate, till they come to the use of reason; and I add, nor then
neither. Which is so, because, till after they come to the use of
reason, those general abstract *ideas* are not framed in the mind,
about which those general maxims are which are mistaken for
innate principles, but are indeed discoveries made and verities
introduced and brought into the mind by the same way and
discovered by the same steps as several other propositions,
which nobody was ever so extravagant as to suppose innate.
This I hope to make plain in the sequel of this discourse. I
allow therefore a necessity that men should come to the use of
reason before they get the knowledge of those general truths,
but deny that men's coming to the use of reason is the time of
their discovery.

13.   In the meantime, it is observable that this saying, that
men know and assent to these maxims *when they come to the
use of reason*, amounts in reality of fact to no more but this, that
they are never known nor taken notice of before the use of
reason, but may possibly be assented to sometime after, during
a man's life; but when, is uncertain. And so may all other

knowable truths, as well as these which therefore have no advantage nor distinction from others, by this note of being known when we come to the use of reason; nor are thereby proved to be innate, but quite the contrary.

14. But, *Secondly*, were it true that the precise time of their being known and assented to were when men come to the *use of reason*, neither would that prove them innate. This way of arguing is so frivolous as the supposition of itself is false. For, by what kind of logic will it appear that any notion is originally by nature imprinted in the mind in its first constitution, because it comes first to be observed and assented to when a faculty of the mind, which has quite a distinct province, begins to exert itself? And therefore the coming to the use of speech, if it were supposed the time that these maxims are first assented to (which it may be with as much truth as the time when men come to the use of reason), would be as good a proof that they were innate, as to say they are innate because men assent to them when they come to the use of reason. I agree then with these men of innate principles that there is no knowledge of these general and self-evident maxims in the mind till it comes to the exercise of reason; but I deny that the coming to the use of reason is the precise time when they are first taken notice of; and if that were the precise time, I deny that it would prove them innate. All that can with any truth be meant by this proposition, that men *assent to them when they come to the use of reason*, is no more but this: that the making of general abstract *ideas* and the understanding of general names being a concomitant of the rational faculty and growing up with it, children commonly get not those general *ideas* nor learn the names that stand for them, till having for a good while exercised their reason about familiar and more particular *ideas*, they are by their ordinary discourse and actions with others acknowledged to be capable of rational conversation. If assenting to these maxims, when men come to the use of reason, can be true in any other sense, I desire it may be shown; or at least, how in this or any other sense it proves them innate.

15. The senses at first let in particular *ideas* and furnish the yet empty cabinet; and the mind by degrees growing familiar with some of them, they are lodged in the memory, and names got to them. Afterwards the mind, proceeding further, abstracts them, and by degrees learns the use of general names. In this

manner the mind comes to be furnished with *ideas* and language, the materials about which to exercise its discursive faculty. And the use of reason becomes daily more visible, as these materials that give it employment increase. But though the having of general *ideas* and the use of general words and reason usually grow together, yet I see not how this any way proves them innate. The knowledge of some truths, I confess, is very early in the mind, but in a way that shows them not to be innate. For, if we will observe, we shall find it still to be about *ideas*, not innate, but acquired: it being about those first which are imprinted by external things, with which infants have earliest to do, which make the most frequent impressions on their senses. In *ideas* thus got, the mind discovers that some agree and others differ, probably as soon as it has any use of memory, as soon as it is able to retain and receive distinct *ideas*. But whether it be then or no, this is certain: it does so long before it has the use of words, or comes to that which we commonly call the *use of reason*. For a child knows as certainly, before it can speak, the difference between the *ideas* of sweet and bitter (i.e. that sweet is not bitter) as it knows afterwards (when it comes to speak) that wormwood and sugar-plums are not the same thing.

16. A child knows not that three and four are equal to seven till he comes to be able to count to seven, and has got the name and *idea* of equality; and then upon explaining those words, he presently assents to, or rather perceives the truth of that proposition. But neither does he then readily assent, because it is an innate truth, nor was his assent wanting till then because he wanted the *use of reason*; but the truth of it appears to him as soon as he has settled in his mind the clear and distinct *ideas* that these names stand for. And then he knows the truth of that proposition upon the same grounds and by the same means that he knew before that a rod and cherry are not the same thing, and upon the same grounds also that he may come to know afterwards that *It is impossible for the same thing to be, and not to be*, as shall be more fully shown hereafter. So that the later it is before anyone comes to have those general *ideas* about which those maxims are, or to know the signification of those general terms that stand for them, or to put together in his mind the *ideas* they stand for, the later also will it be before he comes to assent to those maxims; whose terms, with the

ideas they stand for, being no more innate than those of a cat or a weasel, he must stay till time and observation have acquainted him with them; and then he will be in a capacity to know the truth of these maxims, upon the first occasion that shall make him put together those *ideas* in his mind and observe whether they agree or disagree, according as is expressed in those propositions. And therefore it is that a man knows that eighteen and nineteen are equal to thirty-seven, by the same self-evidence that he knows one and two to be equal to three; yet a child knows this not so soon as the other, not for want of the use of reason, but because the *ideas* the words eighteen, nineteen, and thirty-seven stand for are not so soon got as those which are signified by one, two, and three.

17. This evasion therefore of general assent when men come to the use of reason failing as it does, and leaving no difference between those supposed innate and other truths that are afterwards acquired and learnt, men have endeavoured to secure an universal assent to those they call maxims by saying they are generally *assented to, as soon as proposed*, and the terms they are proposed in understood; seeing all men, even children, as soon as they hear and understand the terms, assent to these propositions, they think it is sufficient to prove them innate. For since men never fail, after they have once understood the words, to acknowledge them for undoubted truths, they would infer that certainly these propositions were first lodged in the understanding which, without any teaching, the mind at very first proposal immediately closes with and assents to, and after that never doubts again.

18. In answer to this, I demand whether ready *assent* given to a proposition, *upon first hearing* and understanding the terms, be a certain mark of an innate principle? If it be not, such a general assent is in vain urged as a proof of them; if it be said that it is a mark of innate, they must then allow all such propositions to be innate which are generally assented to as soon as heard, whereby they will find themselves plentifully stored with innate principles. For upon the same ground, viz. of assent at first hearing and understanding the terms, that men would have those maxims pass for innate, they must also admit several propositions about numbers to be innate; and thus, that *One and two are equal to three*, that *Two and two are equal to four*, and a multitude of other the like propositions in numbers that every-

body assents to at first hearing and understanding the terms, must have a place amongst these innate axioms. Nor is this the prerogative of numbers alone, and propositions made about several of them; but even natural philosophy and all the other sciences afford propositions which are sure to meet with assent as soon as they are understood. That *Two bodies cannot be in the same place* is a truth that nobody any more sticks at than at these maxims that *It is impossible for the same thing to be and not to be*, that *White is not black*, that *A square is not a circle*, that *Yellowness is not sweetness*. These and a million of other such propositions, as many at least as we have distinct *ideas*, every man in his wits, at first hearing and knowing what the names stand for, must necessarily assent to. If these men will be true to their own rule and have *assent at first hearing and understanding the terms* to be a mark of innate, they must allow not only as many innate propositions as men have distinct *ideas*, but as many as men can make propositions wherein different *ideas* are denied one of another. Since every proposition wherein one different *idea* is denied of another will as certainly find assent at first hearing and understanding the terms as this general one, *It is impossible for the same to be, and not to be*, or that which is the foundation of it and is the easier understood of the two, *The same is not different*: by which account they will have legions of innate propositions of this one sort, without mentioning any other. But since no proposition can be innate unless the *ideas* about which it is be innate, this will be to suppose all our *ideas* of colours, sounds, tastes, figure, etc., innate, than which there cannot be anything more opposite to reason and experience. Universal and ready assent upon hearing and understanding the terms is (I grant) a mark of self-evidence; but self-evidence, depending not on innate impressions but on something else (as we shall show hereafter), belongs to several propositions, which nobody was yet so extravagant as to pretend to be innate.

19.   Nor let it be said that those more particular self-evident propositions which are assented to at first hearing, as that *One and two are equal to three*, that *Green is not red*, etc., are received as the consequences of those more universal propositions which are looked on as innate principles, since anyone who will but take the pains to observe what passes in the understanding will certainly find that these and the like less general propositions are certainly known and firmly assented to by those who are

utterly ignorant of those more general maxims, and so, being earlier in the mind than those (as they are called) first principles, cannot owe to them the assent wherewith they are received at first hearing.

20. If it be said that these propositions, viz., *Two and two equal to four*, *Red is not blue*, etc., are not general maxims nor of any great use, I answer that makes nothing to the argument of universal assent upon hearing and understanding. For, if that be the certain mark of innate, whatever proposition can be found that receives general assent as soon as heard and understood, that must be admitted for an innate proposition, as well as this maxim, that *It is impossible for the same thing to be, and not to be*, they being upon this ground equal. And as to the difference of being more general, that makes this maxim more remote from being innate, those general and abstract *ideas* being more strangers to our first apprehensions than those of more particular self-evident propositions, and therefore it is longer before they are admitted and assented to by the growing understanding. And as to the usefulness of these magnified maxims, that perhaps will not be found so great as is generally conceived when it comes to its due place to be more fully considered.

21. But we have not yet done with *assenting to propositions at first hearing and understanding their terms.* It is fit we first take notice that this, instead of being a mark that they are innate, is a proof of the contrary, since it supposes that several, who understand and know other things, are ignorant of these principles till they are proposed to them, and that one may be unacquainted with these truths till he hears them from others. For if they were innate, what need they be proposed in order to gaining assent, when, by being in the understanding, by a natural and original impression (if there were any such) they could not but be known before? Or doth the proposing them print them clearer in the mind than nature did? If so, then the consequence will be that a man knows them better after he has been thus taught them than he did before. Whence it will follow that these principles may be made more evident to us by others' teaching than nature has made them by impression: which will ill agree with the opinion of innate principles, and give but little authority to them, but on the contrary makes them unfit to be the foundations of all our other knowledge, as

they are pretended to be. This cannot be denied: that men grow first acquainted with many of these self-evident truths upon their being proposed; but it is clear that whosoever does so finds in himself that he then begins to know a proposition which he knew not before, and which from thenceforth he never questions, not because it was innate, but because the consideration of the nature of the things contained in those words would not suffer him to think otherwise, how or whensoever he is brought to reflect on them. And if whatever is assented to at first hearing and understanding the terms must pass for an innate principle, every well-grounded observation drawn from particulars into a general rule must be innate. When yet it is certain that not all but only sagacious heads light at first on these observations and reduce them into general propositions, not innate but collected from a preceding acquaintance and reflection on particular instances. These, when observing men have made them, unobserving men, when they are proposed to them, cannot refuse their assent to.

22. If it be said the understanding hath an *implicit knowledge* of these principles, but not an explicit, before this first hearing (as they must who will say that they are in the understanding before they are known), it will be hard to conceive what is meant by a principle imprinted on the understanding implicitly, unless it be this, that the mind is capable of understanding and assenting firmly to such propositions. And thus all mathematical demonstrations, as well as first principles, must be received as native impressions on the mind; which I fear they will scarce allow them to be, who find it harder to demonstrate a proposition than assent to it when demonstrated. And few mathematicians will be forward to believe that all the diagrams they have drawn were but copies of those innate characters which nature had engraven upon their minds.

23. There is, I fear, this further weakness in the foregoing argument, which would persuade us that therefore those maxims are to be thought innate which men *admit at first hearing*, because they assent to propositions which they are not taught nor do receive from the force of any argument or demonstration, but a bare explication or understanding of the terms. Under which there seems to me to lie this fallacy, that men are supposed not to be *taught* nor to *learn* anything *de novo*, when, in truth, they are taught and do learn something they were ignorant of

before. For, first, it is evident they have learned the terms and their signification, neither of which was born with them. But this is not all the acquired knowledge in the case: the *ideas* themselves, about which the proposition is, are not born with them, no more than their names, but got afterwards. So that in all propositions that are assented to at first hearing: the terms of the proposition, their standing for such *ideas*, and the *ideas* themselves that they stand for being neither of them innate, I would fain know what there is remaining in such propositions that is innate. For I would gladly have anyone name that proposition whose terms or *ideas* were either of them innate. We by degrees get *ideas* and names, and learn their appropriated connection one with another; and then to propositions made in such terms, whose signification we have learnt, and wherein the agreement or disagreement we can perceive in our *ideas* when put together is expressed, we at first hearing assent; though to other propositions, in themselves as certain and evident, but which are concerning *ideas* not so soon or so easily got, we are at the same time no way capable of assenting. For though a child quickly assent to this proposition, that *An apple is not fire*, when by familiar acquaintance he has got the *ideas* of those two different things distinctly imprinted on his mind, and has learnt that the names *apple* and *fire* stand for them: yet it will be some years after, perhaps, before the same child will assent to this proposition, that *It is impossible for the same thing to be, and not to be*. Because, though perhaps the words are as easy to be learnt, yet the signification of them, being more large, comprehensive, and abstract than of the names annexed to those sensible things the child hath to do with, it is longer before he learns their precise meaning, and it requires more time plainly to form in his mind those general *ideas* they stand for. Till that be done, you will in vain endeavour to make any child assent to a proposition made up of such general terms; but as soon as ever he has got those *ideas* and learned their names, he forwardly closes with the one as well as the other of the fore-mentioned propositions, and with both for the same reason, viz. because he finds the *ideas* he has in his mind to agree or disagree, according as the words standing for them are affirmed or denied one of another in the proposition. But if propositions be brought to him in words which stand for *ideas* he has not yet in his mind, to such propositions, however evidently true or false in themselves, he affords neither assent nor dissent but is ignorant. For words being but empty sounds, any further than they are signs of our *ideas* we cannot but assent to them as they correspond to those *ideas* we have, but no further than that. But the showing by what steps and ways knowledge comes into our minds, and the grounds of several degrees of assent, being the business of the following discourse, it may suffice to have only touched on it here, as one reason that made me doubt of those innate principles.

24. To conclude this argument of *universal consent*, I agree with these defenders of innate principles that if they are *innate* they must needs *have universal assent*. For that a truth should be innate and yet not assented to is to me as unintelligible as for a man to know a truth and be ignorant of it at the same time. But then, by these men's own confession, they cannot be innate, since they are not assented to by those who understand not the terms; nor by a great part of those who do understand them, but have yet never heard nor thought of those propositions; which I think, is at least one-half of mankind. But were the number far less, it would be enough to destroy *universal assent*, and thereby show these propositions not to be innate, if children alone were ignorant of them.

25. But that I may not be accused to argue from the thoughts of infants, which are unknown to us, and to conclude from what passes in their understandings before they express it, I say next that these two general propositions are not the truths that *first possess the minds* of children, nor are antecedent to all acquired and adventitious notions: which if they were innate, they must needs be. Whether we can determine it or no, it matters not: there is certainly a time when children begin to think, and their words and actions do assure us that they do so. When therefore they are capable of thought, of knowledge, of assent, can it rationally be supposed they can be ignorant of those notions that nature has imprinted, were there any such? Can it be imagined, with any appearance of reason, that they perceive the impressions from things without, and be at the same time ignorant of those characters which nature itself has taken care to stamp within? Can they receive and assent to adventitious notions and be ignorant of those which are supposed woven into the very principles of their being and imprinted there in indelible characters, to be the foundation and guide of all their acquired knowledge and future reasonings? This would be to

make nature take pains to no purpose, or, at least, to write very ill, since its characters could not be read by those eyes which saw other things very well; and those are very ill-supposed the clearest parts of truth, and the foundations of all our knowledge, which are not first known and without which the undoubted knowledge of several other things may be had. The child certainly knows that the *nurse* that feeds it is neither the *cat* it plays with nor the *blackamoor* it is afraid of, that the *wormseed* or *mustard* it refuses is not the *apple* or *sugar* it cries for: this it is certainly and undoubtedly assured of; but will anyone say it is by virtue of this principle, that *It is impossible for the same thing to be and not to be*, that it so firmly assents to these and other parts of its knowledge? Or that the child has any notion or apprehension of that proposition at an age wherein yet, it is plain, it knows a great many other truths? He that will say children join in these general abstract speculations with their sucking-bottles and their rattles, may perhaps, with justice, be thought to have more passion and zeal for his opinion, but less sincerity and truth, than one of that age.

26. Though therefore there be several general propositions that meet with constant and ready assent, as soon as proposed to men grown up, who have attained the use of more general and abstract *ideas*, and names standing for them: yet they not being to be found in those of tender years, who nevertheless know other things, they cannot pretend to universal assent of intelligent persons, and so by no means can be supposed innate, it being impossible that any truth which is innate (if there were any such) should be unknown, at least to anyone who knows anything else. Since, if they are innate truths, they must be innate thoughts, there being nothing a truth in the mind that it has never thought on. Whereby it is evident, if there be any *innate truths*, they *must necessarily be the first of any thought on*, the first that appear there.

27. That the general maxims we are discoursing of are not known to *children*, *idiots*, and a great part of *mankind*, we have already sufficiently proved; whereby it is evident they have not an universal assent nor are general impressions. But there is this further argument in it against their being innate: that these characters, if they were native and original impressions, *should appear fairest and clearest in* those persons in whom yet we find no footsteps of them; and it is, in my opinion, a strong presumption

that they are not innate, since they are least known to those
in whom, if they were innate, they must needs exert themselves
with most force and vigour. For *children, idiots, savages,* and
illiterate people, being of all others the least corrupted by custom
or borrowed opinions; learning and education having not cast
their native thoughts into new moulds, nor by super-inducing
foreign and studied doctrines confounded those fair characters
nature had written there: one might reasonably imagine that in
their minds these innate notions should lie open fairly to everyone's view, as it is certain the thoughts of children do. It might
very well be expected that these principles should be perfectly
known to naturals, which being stamped immediately on the
soul (as these men suppose) can have no dependence on the
constitutions or organs of the body, the only confessed difference between them and others. One would think, according to
these men's principles, that all these native beams of light
(were there any such) should in those who have no reserves, no
arts of concealment, shine out in their full lustre and leave us in
no more doubt of their being there than we are of their love of
pleasure and abhorrence of pain. But alas, amongst *children,
idiots, savages* and the grossly *illiterate,* what general maxims
are to be found? what universal principles of knowledge? Their
notions are few and narrow, borrowed only from those objects
they have had most to do with, and which have made upon their
senses the frequentest and strongest impressions. A child knows
his nurse and his cradle, and by degrees the play-things of a little
more advanced age; and a young savage has, perhaps, his head
filled with love and hunting, according to the fashion of his
tribe. But he that, from a child untaught, or a wild inhabitant
of the woods, will expect these abstract maxims and reputed
principles of science will, I fear, find himself mistaken. Such
kind of general propositions are seldom mentioned in the huts
of *Indians,* much less are they to be found in the thoughts of
children, or any impressions of them on the minds of *naturals.*
They are the language and business of the schools and academies
of learned nations, accustomed to that sort of conversation or
learning, where disputes are frequent, these maxims being suited
to artificial argumentation and useful for conviction, but not much
conducing to the discovery of truth or advancement of knowledge. But of their small use for the improvement of knowledge,
I shall have occasion to speak more at large, IV, ch. vii.

28. I know not how absurd this may seem to the masters of demonstration. And probably it will hardly down with anybody at first hearing. I must therefore beg a little truce with prejudice and the forbearance of censure, till I have been heard out in the sequel of this discourse, being very willing to submit to better judgments. And since I impartially search after truth, I shall not be sorry to be convinced that I have been too fond of my own notions; which I confess we are all apt to be, when application and study have warmed our heads with them.

Upon the whole matter, I cannot see any ground to think these two famed speculative maxims innate, since they are not universally assented to; and the assent they so generally find is no other than what several propositions, not allowed to be innate, equally partake in with them; and since the assent that is given them is produced another way, and comes not from natural inscription, as I doubt not but to make appear in the following discourse. And if *these first principles* of knowledge and science *are* found *not* to be *innate, no other speculative maxims can* (I suppose) *with better right pretend to be so.*

CHAPTER III

NO INNATE PRACTICAL PRINCIPLES

1. IF those speculative maxims, whereof we discoursed in the foregoing chapter, have not an actual universal assent from all mankind, as we there proved, it is much more visible concerning *practical principles* that they *come short of an universal reception*; and I think it will be hard to instance any one moral rule which can pretend to so general and ready an assent as *What is, is,* or to be so manifest a truth as this, that *It is impossible for the same thing to be and not to be.* Whereby it is evident that they are further removed from a title to be innate, and the doubt of their being native impressions on the mind is stronger against these moral principles than the others. Not that it brings their truth at all in question. They are equally true, though not equally evident. Those speculative maxims carry their own evidence with them; but moral principles require reasoning and discourse, and some exercise of the mind, to discover the

C 332

certainty of their truth. They lie not open as natural characters engraven on the mind; which if any such were, they must needs be visible by themselves, and by their own light be certain and known to everybody. But this is no derogation to their truth and certainty, no more than it is to the truth or certainty of the three angles of a triangle being equal to two right ones: because it is not so evident as *The whole is bigger than a part,* nor so apt to be assented to at first hearing. It may suffice that these moral rules are capable of demonstration, and therefore it is our own faults if we come not to a certain knowledge of them. But the ignorance wherein many men are of them, and the slowness of assent wherewith others receive them, are manifest proofs that they are not innate and such as offer themselves to their view without searching.

2.   Whether there be any such moral principles wherein all men do agree, I appeal to any who have been but moderately conversant in the history of mankind, and looked abroad beyond the smoke of their own chimneys. Where is that practical truth that is universally received, without doubt or question, as it must be if innate? *Justice,* and keeping of contracts, is that which *most men seem to agree in.* This is a principle which is thought to extend itself to the dens of thieves, and the confederacies of the greatest villains; and they who have gone furthest towards the putting off of humanity itself, keep faith and rules of justice one with another. I grant that outlaws themselves do this one amongst another, but it is without receiving these as the innate laws of nature. They practise them as rules of convenience within their own communities; but it is impossible to conceive that he embraces justice as a practical principle, who acts fairly with his fellow highwayman and at the same time plunders or kills the next honest man he meets with. Justice and truth are the common ties of society; and therefore even outlaws and robbers, who break with all the world besides, must keep faith and rules of equity amongst themselves, or else they cannot hold together. But will anyone say that those that live by fraud and rapine have innate principles of truth and justice which they allow and assent to?

3.   Perhaps it will be urged that the *tacit assent of their minds agrees to what their practice contradicts.* I answer, *first,* I have always thought the actions of men the best interpreters of their thoughts. But, since it is certain that most men's practice, and

some men's open professions have either questioned or denied these principles, it is impossible to establish an universal consent (though we should look for it only amongst grown men), without which it is impossible to conclude them innate. *Secondly,* it is very strange and unreasonable to suppose innate practical principles that terminate only in contemplation. Practical principles, derived from nature, are there for operation, and must produce conformity of action, not barely speculative assent to their truth, or else they are in vain distinguished from speculative maxims. Nature, I confess, has put into man a desire of happiness and an aversion to misery: these indeed are innate practical principles which (as practical principles ought) do continue constantly to operate and influence all our actions without ceasing; these may be observed in all persons and all ages, steady and universal; but these are inclinations of the appetite to good, not impressions of truth on the understanding. I deny not that there are natural tendencies imprinted on the minds of men, and that from the very first instances of sense and perception, there are some things that are grateful and others unwelcome to them, some things that they incline to, and others that they fly: but this makes nothing for innate characters on the mind, which are to be the principles of knowledge, regulating our practice. Such natural impressions on the understanding are so far from being confirmed hereby, that this is an argument against them, since, if there were certain characters imprinted by nature on the understanding, as the principles of knowledge, we could not but perceive them constantly operate in us and influence our knowledge, as we do those others on the will and appetite; which never cease to be the constant springs and motives of all our actions to which we perpetually feel them strongly impelling us.

4.   Another reason that makes me doubt of any innate practical principles is that I think *there cannot any one moral rule be proposed whereof a man may not justly demand a reason*: which would be perfectly ridiculous and absurd if they were innate, or so much as self-evident, which every innate principle must needs be, and not need any proof to ascertain its truth, nor want any reason to gain it approbation. He would be thought void of common sense who asked on the one side, or on the other side went to give a reason *why it is impossible for the same thing to be and not to be*. It carries its own light and evidence with it, and

needs no other proof: he that understands the terms assents to it
for its own sake, or else nothing will ever be able to prevail with
him to do it. But should that most unshaken rule of morality and
foundation of all social virtue, that *One should do as he would be
done unto*, be proposed to one who never heard of it before,
but yet is of capacity to understand its meaning, might he not
without any absurdity ask a reason why? And were not he that
proposed it bound to make out the truth and reasonableness of it
to him? Which plainly shows it not to be innate; for if it were it
could neither want nor receive any proof, but must needs (at
least as soon as heard and understood) be received and assented
to as an unquestionable truth, which a man can by no means
doubt of. So that the truth of all these moral rules plainly
depends upon some other, antecedent to them and from which
they must be deduced: which could not be if either they were
innate or so much as self-evident.

5.   That men should keep their compacts is certainly a great
and undeniable rule in morality. But yet, if a Christian, who
has the view of happiness and misery in another life, be asked
why a man must keep his word, he will *give* this as a *reason*:
because God, who has the power of eternal life and death,
requires it of us. But if a *Hobbist* be asked why, he will answer:
because the public requires it, and the *Leviathan* will punish
you if you do not. And if one of the old *heathen* philosophers
had been asked, he would have answered: because it was dis-
honest, below the dignity of a man, and opposite to virtue, the
highest perfection of human nature, to do otherwise.

6.   Hence naturally flows the great variety of opinions concerning moral rules which are to be found amongst men, according
to the different sorts of happiness they have a prospect of, or
propose to themselves; which could not be if practical principles
were innate and imprinted in our minds immediately by the
hand of God. I grant the existence of God is so many ways
manifest, and the obedience we owe him so congruous to the
light of reason, that a great part of mankind give testimony to
the law of nature: but yet I think it must be allowed that
several moral rules may receive from mankind a very general
approbation, without either knowing or admitting the true
ground of morality; which can only be the will and law of a
god, who sees men in the dark, has in his hand rewards and
punishments, and power enough to call to account the proudest

offender. For, God having, by an inseparable connexion, joined *virtue* and *public happiness* together, and made the practice thereof necessary to the preservation of society, and visibly *beneficial* to all with whom the virtuous man has to do, it is no wonder that everyone should not only allow, but recommend and magnify those rules to others, from whose observance of them he is sure to reap advantage to himself. He may, out of interest as well as conviction, cry up that for sacred, which if once trampled on and profaned, he himself cannot be safe nor secure. This, though it takes nothing from the moral and eternal obligation which these rules evidently have, yet it shows that the outward acknowledgment men pay to them in their words proves not that they are innate principles. Nay, it proves not so much as that men assent to them inwardly in their own minds as the inviolable rules of their own practice, since we find that self-interest and the conveniences of this life make many men own an outward profession and approbation of them, whose actions sufficiently prove that they very little consider the Law-giver that prescribed these rules, nor the hell he has ordained for the punishment of those that transgress them.

7.   For, if we will not in civility allow too much sincerity to the professions of most *men*, but think their actions to be the interpreters of their thoughts, we shall find that they have *no* such internal veneration for these rules, nor so *full a persuasion of their certainty* and obligation. The great principle of morality, *To do as one would be done to*, is more commended than practised. But the breach of this rule cannot be a greater vice than to teach others that it is no moral rule, nor obligatory, would be thought madness and contrary to that interest men sacrifice to when they break it themselves. Perhaps *conscience* will be urged as checking us for such breaches, and so the internal obligation and establishment of the rule be preserved.

8.   To which I answer that I doubt not but without being written on their hearts, many men may, by the same way that they come to the knowledge of other things, come to assent to several moral rules and be convinced of their obligation. Others also may come to be of the same mind, from their education, company, and customs of their country; which *persuasion, however got, will serve to set conscience on work*, which is nothing else but our own opinion or judgment of the moral rectitude or pravity of our own actions. And if conscience be a proof of

innate principles, contraries may be innate principles: since some men, with the same bent of conscience, prosecute what others avoid.

9.   But I cannot see how any *men* should ever *transgress* those *moral rules with confidence* and *serenity*, were they innate and stamped upon their minds.   View but an army at the sacking of a town, and see what observation or sense of moral principles or what touch of conscience for all the outrages they do.   *Robberies, murders, rapes* are the sports of men set at liberty from punishment and censure.   Have there not been whole nations, and those of the most civilized people, amongst whom the exposing their children, and leaving them in the fields to perish by want or wild beasts has been the practice, as little condemned or scrupled as the begetting them?   Do they not still, in some countries, put them into the same graves with their mothers, if they die in childbirth; or dispatch them, if a pretended astrologer declares them to have unhappy stars?   And are there not places where, at a certain age, they kill or expose their parents without any remorse at all?   In a part of *Asia*, the sick, when their case comes to be thought desperate, are carried out and laid on the earth before they are dead, and left there, exposed to wind and weather, to perish without assistance or pity.[1]   It is familiar amongst the *Mingrelians*, a people professing Christianity, to bury their children alive without scruple.[2]   There are places where they eat their own children.[3]   The *Caribbees* were wont to geld their children, on purpose to fat and eat them.[4]   And *Garcilasso de la Vega* tells us of a people in *Peru* which were wont to fat and eat the children they got on their female captives, whom they kept as concubines for that purpose, and when they were past breeding, the mothers themselves were killed too and eaten.[5]   The virtues whereby the *Tououpinambos* believed they merited paradise were revenge and eating abundance of their enemies. They have not so much as the name for God[6], no acknowledgment of any god, no religion, no worship (p. 223).   The saints

---

[1]Grueber, G. *in* Thévenot, Melchisedec, ed. *Relations de divers voyages curieux.* Nouv. éd., 1696. t. ii, pt. iv, p. 23.

[2]Lambert *in* Thévenot, t. i, pt. i, p. 38.

[3]Voss, Isaac. *De Nili . . . origine.* 1666. ch. 18, 19.

[4]Martyrus, Peter (i.e., Anglerius) *De orbe novo . . . & . . . Decades octo.* 1587 Dec. 1, p. 5.

[5]*Histoire des Incas.* 1704. lib. i, ch. xii.

[6]Léry, Jean de. *Historia navigationis in Brasiliam.* 1594. p. 220.

who are canonized amongst the *Turks,* lead lives which one
cannot with modesty relate. A remarkable passage to this
purpose, out of the voyage of *Baumgarten,* which is a book not
every day to be met with, I shall set down at large, in the
language it is published in. *Ibi (sc. prope* Belbes *in* Aegypto)
*vidimus sanctum unum Saracenicum inter arenarum cumulos, ita
ut ex utero matris prodiit nudum sedentem. Mos est, ut didicimus
eo tempore* Mahometistis, *ut eos qui amentes et sine ratione sunt,
pro* sanctis *colant et venerentur. Insuper et eos qui cum diu vitam
egerint inquinatissimam, voluntariam demum poenitentiam et
paupertatem, sanctitate venerandos deputant. Ejusmodi vero genus
hominum libertatem quandam effraenem habent: domos quas
volunt intrandi, edendi, bibendi, et quod majus est, concumbendi;
ex quo concubitu, si proles secuta fuerit, sancta similiter habetur.
His ergo hominibus, dum vivunt, magnos exhibent honores;
mortuis verò vel templa vel monumenta extruunt amplissima,
eosque contingere ac sepelire maximae fortunae ducunt loco.
Audivimus haec dicta et dicenda per interpretem à Mucrelo nostro.
Insuper* sanctum *illum, quem eo loci vidimus, publicitus apprimé
commendari, eum esse hominem sanctum, divinum ac integritate
praecipuum; eo quod nec foeminarum umquam esset nec puerorum,
sed tantum modo asellarum concubitor atque mularum.*[1] More
of the same kind, concerning these precious saints amongst the
Turks, may be seen in *Pietro della Valle,* in his letter of the 25*th*
of *January,* 1616.[2] Where then are those innate principles
of justice, piety, gratitude, equity, chastity? Or where is that
universal consent that assures us there are such inbred rules?
Murders in duels, when fashion has made them honourable, are
committed without remorse of conscience: nay, in many places
innocence in this case is the greatest ignominy. And if we look
abroad, to take a view of men as they are, we shall find that they
have remorse in one place for doing or omitting that which
others, in another place, think they merit by.

10. He that will carefully peruse the history of mankind, and
look abroad into the several tribes of men, and with indifferency
survey their actions, will be able to satisfy himself that there is
scarce that principle of morality to be named, or *rule* of *virtue*
to be thought on (those only excepted, that are absolutely
necessary to hold society together, which commonly too are

[1]Baumgarten, M. *Peregrinatio in Aegytum, Arabiam* . . . 1594. lib. ii, ch. i, p. 73.
[2]Valle, P. della. *Viaggio* . . . 1667. (pt. 4.)

neglected betwixt distinct societies) which is not, somewhere or
other, *slighted* and condemned by the general fashion of *whole
societies* of men, governed by practical opinions and rules of
living quite opposite to others.

11.   Here perhaps it will be objected that it is no argument that
the *rule* is *not known*, *because* it is *broken*. I grant the objection
good where men, though they transgress, yet disown not the
law; where fear of shame, censure, or punishment carries the
mark of some awe it has upon them. But it is impossible to
conceive that *a whole nation* of men should all *publicly reject* and
renounce what everyone of them certainly and infallibly knew
to be a law; for so they must, who have it naturally imprinted on
their minds. It is possible men may sometimes own *rules of
morality* which in their private thoughts they do not believe to
be true, only to keep themselves in reputation and esteem
amongst those who are persuaded of their obligation. But it is
not to be imagined that a whole society of men should publicly
and professedly disown and cast off a rule which they could not
in their own minds but be infallibly certain was a law, nor be
ignorant that all men they should have to do with knew it to be
such; and therefore must everyone of them apprehend from
others all the contempt and abhorrence due to one who professes himself void of humanity, and one who confounding the
known and natural measures of right and wrong cannot but be
looked on as the professed enemy of their peace and happiness.
Whatever practical principle is innate cannot but be known to
everyone to be just and good. It is therefore little less than a
contradiction to suppose that whole nations of men should both
in their professions and practice unanimously and universally
give the lie to what, by the most invincible evidence, everyone
of them knew to be true, right and good. This is enough to
satisfy us that no practical rule, which is anywhere universally
and with public approbation or allowance transgressed, can be
supposed innate. But I have something further to add in answer
to this objection.

12.   The breaking of a rule, say you, is no argument that it is
unknown. I grant it: but the *generally allowed breach of it anywhere*, I say, *is a proof that it is not innate*. For example, let us
take any of these rules, which, being the most obvious deductions of human reason and conformable to the natural inclination of the greatest part of men, fewest people have had the

impudence to deny or inconsideration to doubt of. If any can be thought to be naturally imprinted, none, I think, can have a fairer pretence to be innate than this: *Parents, preserve and cherish your children.* When therefore you say that this is an innate rule, what do you mean? Either that it is an innate principle which upon all occasions excites and directs the actions of all men, or else that it is a truth which all men have imprinted on their minds and which therefore they know and assent to. But in neither of these senses is it innate. *First,* that it is not a principle which influences all men's actions is what I have proved by the examples before cited; nor need we seek so far as *Mingrelia* or *Peru* to find instances of such as neglect, abuse, nay and destroy their children, or look on it only as the more than brutality of some savage and barbarous nations, when we remember that it was a familiar and uncondemned practice amongst the *Greeks* and *Romans* to expose without pity or remorse their innocent infants. *Secondly,* that it is an innate truth, known to all men, is also false. For *Parents, preserve your children* is so far from an innate truth that it is no truth at all, it being a command and not a proposition, and so not capable of truth or falsehood. To make it capable of being assented to as true, it must be reduced to some such proposition as this: *It is the duty of parents to preserve their children.* But what duty is cannot be understood without a law, nor a law be known or supposed without a law-maker, or without reward and punishment; so that it is impossible that this or any other practical principle should be innate, i.e. be imprinted on the mind as a duty, without supposing the *ideas* of God, of law, of obligation, of punishment, of a life after this innate. For, that punishment follows not in this life the breach of this rule, and consequently that it has not the force of a law in countries where the generally allowed practice runs counter to it, is in itself evident. But these *ideas* (which must be all of them innate, if anything as a duty be so) are so far from being innate that it is not every studious or thinking man, much less everyone that is born, in whom they are to be found clear and distinct; and that one of them, which of all others seems most likely to be innate, is not so (I mean the *idea* of God), I think, in the next chapter will appear very evident to any considering man.

13.   From what has been said, I think we may safely conclude that *whatever practical rule is in any place generally and with*

* C 332

allowance broken, cannot be supposed innate, it being impossible
that men should, without shame or fear, confidently and serenely,
break a rule which they could not but evidently know that God
had set up, and would certainly punish the breach of (which
they must, if it were innate), to a degree to make it a very ill
bargain to the transgressor. Without such a knowledge as this,
a man can never be certain that anything is his duty. Ignorance
or doubt of the law, hopes to escape the knowledge or power of
the law-maker, or the like may make men give way to a present
appetite; but let anyone see the fault, and the rod by it, and
with the transgression, a fire ready to punish it: a pleasure
tempting, and the hand of the Almighty visibly held up and
prepared to take vengeance (for this must be the case where any
duty is imprinted on the mind), and then tell me whether it be
possible for people with such a prospect, such a certain knowledge as this, wantonly and without scruple, to offend against a
law which they carry about them in indelible characters, and
that stares them in the face whilst they are breaking it? Whether
men at the same time that they feel in themselves the imprinted
edicts of an omnipotent law-maker can, with assurance and
gaiety, slight and trample under foot his most sacred injunctions?
And lastly, whether it be possible that, whilst a man thus openly
bids defiance to this innate law and supreme law-giver, all the
bystanders, yea, even the governors and rulers of the people,
full of the same sense both of the law and law-maker, should
silently connive without testifying their dislike or laying the
least blame on it? Principles of actions indeed there are lodged
in men's appetites, but these are so far from being innate moral
principles that, if they were left to their full swing, they would
carry men to the over-turning of all morality. Moral laws are
set as a curb and restraint to these exorbitant desires, which
they cannot be but by rewards and punishments that will over-
balance the satisfaction anyone shall propose to himself in the
breach of the law. If therefore anything be imprinted on the
mind of all men as a law, all men must have a certain and
unavoidable knowledge that certain and unavoidable punishment will attend the breach of it. For if men can be ignorant or
doubtful of what is innate, innate principles are insisted on and
urged to no purpose: truth and certainty (the things pretended)
are not at all secured by them; but men are in the same
uncertain, floating estate with as without them. An evident

indubitable knowledge of unavoidable punishment, great enough to make the transgression very ineligible, must accompany an innate law, unless with an innate law they can suppose an innate gospel too. I would not be here mistaken as if, because I deny an innate law, I thought there were none but positive laws. There is a great deal of difference between an innate law and a law of nature, between something imprinted on our minds in their very original, and something that we, being ignorant of, may attain to the knowledge of, by the use and due application of our natural faculties. And I think they equally forsake the truth who, running into the contrary extremes, either affirm an innate law, or deny that there is a law knowable by the light of nature, i.e. without the help of positive revelation.

14. The difference there is amongst men in their practical principles is so evident that I think I need say no more to evince that it will be impossible to find any innate moral rules by this mark of general assent; and it is enough to make one suspect that the supposition of such innate principles is but an opinion taken up at pleasure, since those who talk so confidently of them are so sparing to *tell* us *which they are.* This might with justice be expected from those men who lay stress upon this opinion; and it gives occasion to distrust either their knowledge or charity who, declaring that God has imprinted on the minds of men the foundations of knowledge and the rules of living, are yet so little favourable to the information of their neighbours or the quiet of mankind as not to point out to them which they are in the variety men are distracted with. But in truth, were there any such innate principles, there would be no need to teach them. Did men find such innate propositions stamped on their minds, they would easily be able to distinguish them from other truths that they afterwards learned and deduced from them; and there would be nothing more easy than to know what and how many they were. There could be no more doubt about their number than there is about the number of our fingers; and it is like, then, every system would be ready to give them us by tale. But since nobody that I know has ventured yet to give a catalogue of them, they cannot blame those who doubt of these innate principles, since even they who require men to believe that there are such innate propositions do not tell us what they are. It is easy to foresee that, if different men of different sects should go about to give us a list of those innate practical principles,

they would set down only such as suited their distinct hypotheses and were fit to support the doctrines of their particular schools or churches: a plain evidence that there are no such innate truths. Nay, a great part of men are so far from finding any such innate moral principles in themselves that by denying freedom to mankind and thereby making men no other than bare machines, they take away not only innate but all moral rules whatsoever, and leave not a possibility to believe any such to those who cannot conceive how anything can be capable of a law that is not a free agent; and upon that ground, they must necessarily reject all principles of virtue who cannot *put morality and mechanism together*, which are not very easy to be reconciled or made consistent.

15. When I had writ this, being informed that my Lord *Herbert* had in his books *De Veritate* assigned these innate principles, I presently consulted him, hoping to find, in a man of so great parts, something that might satisfy me in this point and put an end to my inquiry. In his chapter *De Instinctu Naturali* (1656, pp. 76-78), I met with these six marks of his *notitiae communes*. 1. *Prioritas*. 2. *Independentia*. 3. *Universalitas*. 4. *Certitudo*. 5. *Necessitas*, i.e., as he explains it, *faciunt ad hominis conservationem*. 6. *Modus conformationis*, i.e., *assensus nullà interpositâ morà*.   And at the latter end of his little treatise, *De Religione Laici*, he says this of these innate principles: *Adeo ut non uniuscujusvis* religionis *confinio arctentur quae ubique vigent semperque vigebunt veritates. Sunt enim in ipsa mente coelitùs descriptae nullisque traditionibus, sive scriptis, sive non scriptis, obnoxiae*, p. 3. And *Veritates nostrae catholicae, quae tanquam indubia Dei effata in foro interiori descripta*. Thus having given the marks of the innate principles or common notions, and asserted their being imprinted on the minds of men by the hand of God, he proceeds to set them down, and they are these: 1. *Esse aliquod supremum numen*. 2. *Numen illud coli debere*. 3. *Virtutem cum pietate conjunctam optimam esse rationem cultus divini*. 4. *Resipiscendum esse à peccatis*. 5. *Dari praemium vel poenam post hanc vitam transactam*. Though I allow these to be clear truths and such as, if rightly explained, a rational creature can hardly avoid giving his assent to, yet I think he is far from proving them innate impressions *in foro interiori descriptae*. For I must take leave to observe:

16. First, that these five propositions are either not all, or

more than all, those common notions writ on our minds by the finger of God, if it were reasonable to believe any at all to be so written. Since there are other propositions, which even by his own rules have as just a pretence to such an original and may be as well admitted for innate principles as, at least, some of these five he enumerates, viz. *Do as thou wouldst be done unto*, and perhaps some hundreds of others, when well considered.

17. *Secondly*, that all his marks are not to be found in each of his five propositions, viz. his first, second, and third marks agree perfectly to neither of them; and the first, second, third, fourth, and sixth marks agree but ill to his third, fourth, and fifth propositions. For besides that we are assured from history of many men, nay, whole nations, who doubt or disbelieve some or all of them, I cannot see how the third, viz. *that virtue joined with piety is the best worship of God*, can be an innate principle when the name or sound, *virtue*, is so hard to be understood, liable to so much uncertainty in its signification, and the thing it stands for so much contended about and difficult to be known. And therefore this can be but a very uncertain rule of human practice, and serve but very little to the conduct of our lives, and is therefore very unfit to be assigned as an innate practical principle.

18. For let us consider this proposition as to its meaning (for it is the sense, and not sound, that is and must be the principle or common notion), viz. *virtue is the best worship of God*, i.e. is most acceptable to him: which, if *virtue* be taken, as most commonly it is, for those actions which according to the different opinions of several countries are accustomed laudable, will be a proposition so far from being certain that it will not be true. If *virtue* be taken for actions conformable to God's will, or to the rule prescribed by God, which is the true and only measure of virtue when virtue is used to signify what is in its own nature right and good, then this proposition, *that virtue is the best worship of God*, will be most true and certain, but of very little use in human life, since it will amount to no more but this, viz. *that God is pleased with the doing of what he commands*, which a man may certainly know to be true without knowing what it is that God doth command, and so be as far from any rule or principles of his actions as he was before. And I think very few will take a proposition which amounts to no more than this, viz. that God is pleased with the doing of what

he himself commands, for an innate moral principle writ on the minds of all men (however true and certain it may be) since it teaches so little. Whosoever does so will have reason to think hundreds of propositions innate principles, since there are many which have as good a title as this to be received for such, which nobody yet ever put into that rank of innate principles.

19.   Nor is the fourth proposition, viz. *Men must repent of their sins*, much more instructive till what those actions are that are meant by sins be set down. For the word *peccata* or *sins* being put, as it usually is, to signify in general ill actions that will draw on punishment upon the doers, what great principle of morality can that be to tell us we should be sorry and cease to do that which will bring mischief upon us without knowing what those particular actions are that will do so? Indeed, this is a very true proposition and fit to be inculcated on and received by those who are supposed to have been taught what actions in all kinds are *sins*; but neither this, nor the former, can be imagined to be innate principles, nor to be of any use if they were innate, unless the particular measures and bounds of all virtues and vices were engraven in men's minds and were innate principles also, which I think is very much to be doubted. And therefore, I imagine it will scarce seem possible that God should engrave principles in men's minds in words of uncertain signification, such as *virtues* and *sins*, which amongst different men stand for different things: nay, it cannot be supposed to be in words at all which, being in most of these principles very general names, cannot be understood but by knowing the particulars comprehended under them. And in the practical instances, the measures must be taken from the knowledge of the actions themselves, and the rules of them abstracted from words and antecedent to the knowledge of names; which rules a man must know, what language soever he chance to learn, whether *English* or *Japan*, or if he should learn no language at all, or never should understand the use of words, as happens in the case of dumb and deaf men. When it shall be made out that men ignorant of words, or untaught by the laws and customs of their country, know that it is part of the worship of God not to kill another man; not to know more women than one; not to procure abortion; not to expose their children; not to take from another what is his though we want it ourselves, but on the contrary, relieve and supply his wants; and whenever we have

done the contrary, we ought to repent, be sorry, and resolve to do so no more: when, I say, all men shall be proved actually to know and allow all these and a thousand other such rules, all which come under these two general words made use of above, viz. *virtutes* and *peccata, virtues* and *sins*, there will be more reason for admitting these and the like for common notions and practical principles. Yet after all, universal consent (were there any in moral principles) to truths, the knowledge whereof may be attained otherwise, would scarce prove them to be innate; which is all I contend for.

20. Nor will it be of much moment here to offer that very ready, but not very material answer, viz. that the *innate principles* of morality *may, by education and custom* and the general opinion of those amongst whom we converse, *be darkened* and at last *quite worn out* of the minds of men. Which assertion of theirs, if true, quite takes away the argument of universal consent by which this opinion of innate principles is endeavoured to be proved, unless those men will think it reasonable that their private persuasions, or that of their party, should pass for universal consent: a thing not infrequently done when men, presuming themselves to be the only masters of right reason, cast by the votes and opinions of the rest of mankind as not worthy the reckoning. And then their argument stands thus: the principles which all mankind allow for true are innate; those that men of right reason admit are the principles allowed by all mankind; we and those of our mind are men of reason; therefore we agreeing, our principles are innate: which is a very pretty way of arguing and a short cut to infallibility. For otherwise it will be very hard to understand how there be some principles which all men do acknowledge and agree in; and yet there are none of those *principles* which are *not by depraved custom and ill education blotted out* of the minds of many men: which is to say that all men admit but yet many men do deny, and dissent from them. And indeed, the supposition of such first principles will serve us to very little purpose; and we shall be as much at a loss with as without them, if they may, by any human power such as is the will of our teachers or opinions of our companions, be altered or lost in us; and notwithstanding all this boast of first principles and innate light, we shall be as much in the dark and uncertainty as if there were no such thing at all, it being all one to have no rule and one that will warp any way, or amongst

various and contrary rules not to know which is the right. But concerning innate principles, I desire these men to say whether they can or cannot by education and custom be blurred and blotted out; if they cannot, we must find them in all mankind alike and they must be clear in everybody; and if they may suffer variation from adventitious notions, we must then find them clearest and most perspicuous, nearest the fountain, in children and illiterate people who have received least impression from foreign opinions. Let them take which side they please, they will certainly find it inconsistent with visible matter of fact and daily observation.

21. I easily grant that there are great numbers of *opinions* which, by men of different countries, educations, and tempers are received and *embraced as first and unquestionable principles*; *many whereof*, both for their absurdity as well as oppositions one to another, *it is impossible should be true*. But yet all those propositions, how remote soever from reason, are so sacred somewhere or other, that men even of good understanding in other matters will sooner part with their lives, and whatever is dearest to them, than suffer themselves to doubt, or others to question, the truth of them.

22. This, however strange it may seem, is that which every day's experience confirms; and will not, perhaps, appear so wonderful, if we consider the *ways* and *steps by which* it is brought about, and how really it may come to pass that *doctrines* that have been derived from no better original than the superstition of a nurse or the authority of an old woman, may, by length of time and consent of neighbours, *grow up to the dignity of principles* in religion or morality. For such who are careful (as they call it) to principle children well (and few there be who have not a set of those principles for them which they believe in) instil into the unwary and, as yet, unprejudiced understanding (for white paper receives any characters) those doctrines they would have them retain and profess. These, being taught them as soon as they have any apprehension and still as they grow up confirmed to them, either by the open profession or tacit consent of all they have to do with, or at least by those of whose wisdom, knowledge, and piety they have an opinion, who never suffer those propositions to be otherwise mentioned but as the basis and foundation on which they build their religion or manners, come by these means to have the

reputation of unquestionable, self-evident, and innate truths.
23.   To which we may add that, when *men* so instructed are
grown up and reflect on their own minds, they cannot find anything more ancient there than those opinions which were taught
them before their memory began to keep a register of their
actions or date the time when any new thing appeared to them;
and therefore make no scruple to *conclude that those propositions, of whose knowledge they can find in themselves no original,
were certainly the impress of God and nature* upon their minds,
and not taught them by anyone else.   These they entertain and
submit to, as many do to their parents, with veneration, not
because it is natural; nor do children do it where they are not so
taught; but because, having been always so educated, and having
no remembrance of the beginning of this respect, they think it
is natural.
24.   This will appear very likely and almost unavoidable to
come to pass, if we consider the nature of mankind and the constitution of human affairs, wherein *most men cannot live without
employing their time in the daily labours of their callings, nor be
at quiet in their minds without some foundation or principle to
rest their thoughts on.*   There is scarce anyone so floating and
superficial in his understanding who hath not some reverenced
propositions, which are to him the principles on which he
bottoms his reasonings, and by which he judgeth of truth and
falsehood, right and wrong; which some, wanting skill and
leisure, and others the inclination, and some being taught that
they ought not to examine, there are few to be found who are not
exposed by their ignorance, laziness, education, or precipitancy,
to *take them upon trust.*
25.   This is evidently the case of all children and young folk;
and custom, a greater power than nature, seldom failing to make
them worship for divine what she hath inured them to bow their
minds and submit their understandings to, it is no wonder that
grown *men*, either perplexed in the necessary affairs of life or
hot in the pursuit of pleasures, should *not* seriously sit down to
examine their own tenets, especially when one of their principles
is that principles ought not to be questioned.   And had men
leisure, parts, and will, who is there almost that dare shake the
foundations of all his past thoughts and actions and endure to
bring upon himself the shame of having been a long time
wholly in mistake and error?   Who is there hardy enough to

contend with the reproach which is everywhere prepared for
those who dare venture to dissent from the received opinions of
their country or party? And where is the man to be found that
can patiently prepare himself to bear the name of whimsical,
sceptical, or atheist; which he is sure to meet with who does in
the least scruple any of the common opinions? And he will be
much more *afraid to question those principles* when he shall
think them, as most men do, the standards set up by God in his
mind, to be the rule and touchstone of all other opinions. And
what can hinder him from thinking them sacred when he finds
them the earliest of all his own thoughts and the most reverenced by others?

26. It is easy to imagine *how*, by these means, it comes to pass
that *men* worship the idols that have been set up in their minds,
grow fond of the notions they have been long acquainted with
there, and *stamp the characters of divinity upon absurdities and
errors*, become zealous votaries to bulls and monkeys, and contend too, fight and die in defence of their opinions. *Dum solos
credit habendos esse Deos, quos ipse colit.* For since the reasoning
faculties of the soul, which are almost constantly though not
always warily nor wisely employed, would not know how to
move for want of a foundation and footing, in most men who
through laziness or avocation do not, or for want of time or true
helps or for other causes, cannot penetrate into the principles
of knowledge and trace truth to its fountain and original, it is
natural for them, and almost unavoidable, to take up with some
borrowed principles, which being reputed and presumed to be
the evident proofs of other things are thought not to need any
other proof themselves. Whoever shall receive any of these into
his mind and entertain them there with the reverence usually
paid to principles, never venturing to examine them, but accus-
toming himself to believe them because they are to be believed,
may take up from his education and the fashions of his country
any absurdity for innate principles; and by long poring on the
same objects, so dim his sight as to take monsters lodged in his
own brain for the images of the Deity and the workmanship of
His hands.

27. By this progress, how many there are, who arrive at principles which they believe innate, may be easily observed in the
variety of opposite principles held and contended for by all sorts
and degrees of men. And he that shall deny this to be the

method wherein most men proceed to the assurance they have of the truth and evidence of their principles, will perhaps find it a hard matter any other way to account for the contrary tenets, which are firmly believed, confidently asserted, and which great numbers are ready at any time to seal with their blood. And indeed, if it be the privilege of innate principles to be received upon their own authority, without examination, I know not what may not be believed, or how anyone's *principles* can be questioned. If they may and *ought to be examined* and tried, I desire to know how first and innate principles can be tried; or at least it is reasonable to demand the marks and characters whereby the genuine innate principles may be distinguished from others, that so, amidst the great variety of pretenders, I may be kept from mistakes in so material a point as this. When this is done, I shall be ready to embrace such welcome and useful propositions; and till then I may with modesty doubt, since I fear universal consent, which is the only one produced, will scarce prove a sufficient mark to direct my choice and assure me of any innate principles. From what has been said, I think it past doubt that there are no practical principles wherein all men agree, and therefore none innate.

CHAPTER IV

OTHER CONSIDERATIONS CONCERNING INNATE PRINCIPLES, BOTH SPECULATIVE AND PRACTICAL

1. HAD those who would persuade us that there are innate principles not taken them together in gross, but considered separately the parts out of which those propositions are made, they would not, perhaps, have been so forward to believe they were innate: since, if the *ideas* which made up those truths were not, it was impossible that the propositions made up of them should be innate or our knowledge of them be born with us. For if the *ideas* be not *innate*, there was a time when the mind was without those principles; and then they will not be innate, but be derived from some other original. For, where the *ideas* themselves are not, there can be no knowledge, no assent, no mental or verbal propositions about them.

2.   If we will attentively consider new-born *children*, we shall
have little reason to think that they bring many *ideas* into the
world with them.   For, bating perhaps some faint *ideas* of
hunger, and thirst, and warmth, and some pains which they
may *have* felt in the womb, there is *not* the least appearance of
any settled *ideas* at all in them, especially of *ideas answering the
terms which make up those universal propositions* that are
esteemed innate principles.   One may perceive how, by degrees,
afterwards, *ideas* come into their minds, and that they get no
more nor no other than what experience and the observation of
things that come in their way furnish them with: which might be
enough to satisfy us that they are not original characters stamped
on the mind.

3.   *It is impossible for the same thing to be and not to be* is
certainly (if there be any such) an innate principle.   But can
anyone think, or will anyone say that *impossibility* and *identity*
are two innate *ideas*?   Are they such as all mankind have and
bring into the world with them?   And are they those that are the
first in children and antecedent to all acquired ones?   If they
are innate, they must needs be so.   Hath a child an *idea* of
impossibility and *identity* before it has of *white* or *black*, *sweet* or
bitter?   And is it from the knowledge of this principle that it
concludes that wormwood rubbed on the nipple hath not the
same taste that it used to receive from thence?   Is it the actual
knowledge of *impossibile est idem esse et non esse* that makes a
child distinguish between its mother and a stranger, or that
makes it fond of the one and fly the other?   Or does the mind
regulate itself and its assent by *ideas* that it never yet had?   Or
the understanding draw conclusions from principles which it
never yet knew or understood?   The names *impossibility* and
identity stand for two *ideas* so *far from being innate* or born with
us that I think it requires great care and attention to form them
right in our understandings.   They are so far from being brought
into the world with us, so remote from the thoughts of infancy
and childhood that, I believe, upon examination it will be found
that many grown men want them.

4.   If *identity* (to instance in that alone) be a native impression,
and consequently so clear and obvious to us that we must needs
know it even from our cradles, I would gladly be resolved by
one of seven or seventy years old, whether a man, being a
creature consisting of soul and body, be the same man when his

body is changed? Whether *Euphorbus* and *Pythagoras*, having had the same soul, were the same man though they lived several ages asunder? Nay, whether the cock too, which had the same soul, were not the same with both of them? Whereby, perhaps, it will appear that our *idea of sameness* is *not* so settled and clear as to deserve to be thought *innate* in us. For if those innate *ideas* are not clear and distinct so as to be universally known and naturally agreed on, they cannot be subjects of universal and undoubted truths, but will be the unavoidable occasion of perpetual uncertainty. For, I suppose, everyone's *idea* of *identity* will not be the same, that *Pythagoras* and thousands others of his followers have. And which then shall be the true? Which innate? Or are there two different *ideas* of *identity*, both innate?

5. Nor let anyone think that the questions I have here proposed about the *identity* of man are bare, empty speculations; which, if they were, would be enough to show that there was in the understandings of men *no innate* idea *of* identity. He that shall, with a little attention, reflect on the Resurrection and consider that divine justice shall bring to judgment, at the last day, the very same persons to be happy or miserable in the other who did well or ill in this life, will find it perhaps not easy to resolve with himself what makes the same man or wherein *identity* consists, and will not be forward to think he and everyone, even children themselves, have naturally a clear *idea* of it.

6. Let us examine that principle of mathematics, viz. that *The whole is bigger than a part*. This, I take it, is reckoned amongst innate principles. I am sure it has as good a title as any to be thought so; which yet nobody can think it to be, when he considers the *ideas* it comprehends in it, *whole* and *part*, are perfectly relative; but the positive *ideas* to which they properly and immediately belong are extension and number, of which alone *whole* and *part* are relations. So that if *whole* and *part* are innate *ideas*, extension and number must be so too: it being impossible to have an *idea* of a relation, without having any at all of the thing to which it belongs, and in which it is founded. Now, whether the minds of men have naturally imprinted on them the *ideas* of extension and number, I leave to be considered by those who are the patrons of innate principles.

7. That *God is to be worshipped* is, without doubt, as great a truth as any can enter into the mind of man and deserves the

first place amongst all practical principles. But yet, it can by no
means be thought innate, unless the *ideas* of *God* and *worship*
are innate. That the *idea* the term *worship* stands for is not in
the understanding of children and a character stamped on the
mind in its first original, I think will be easily granted by anyone that considers how few there be amongst grown men who
have a clear and distinct notion of it. And, I suppose, there
cannot be anything more ridiculous than to say that children
have this practical principle innate, *that God is to be worshipped*,
and yet that they know not what that worship of God is which is
their duty. But to pass by this.

8. If any *idea* can be imagined *innate*, the *idea of God* may, of
all others, for many reasons be thought so, since it is hard to
conceive how there should be innate moral principles without
an innate *idea* of a *deity*. Without a notion of a law-maker, it is
impossible to have a notion of a law and an obligation to observe
it. Besides the atheists taken notice of amongst the ancients and
left branded upon the records of history, hath not navigation
discovered, in these latter ages, whole nations, at the bay of
Saldanha[1], in *Brazil*[2], in *Boranday*[3], and the *Caribbee* islands
amongst whom there was to be found no notion of a god, no
religion. Nicholaus de Techo, *In literis, ex Paraquaria de
Caiguarum conversione* has these words[4]: *Reperi eam gentem
nullum nomen habere, quod Deum, et Hominis animam significet,
nulla sacra habet, nulla idola.* These are instances of nations
where uncultivated nature has been left to itself, without the
help of letters and discipline and the improvements of arts and
sciences. But there are others to be found who have enjoyed
these in a very great measure who yet, for want of a due application of their thoughts this way, want the *idea* and knowledge of
God. It will I doubt not be a surprise to others, as it was to me,
to find the *Siamites* of this number. But for this, let them consult the King of *France's* late envoy thither[5] who gives no better
account of the *Chinese* themselves[6]. And if we will not believe

[1]Roe *in* Thévenot, t. i, pt. i, p. 2.
[2]Léry, ch. 16.
[3]La Martiniére, P. M. de. *Voyages des pays septentrionaux.* 1676. p. 201. Terry,
E. *A Voyage to East-India.* 1655. p. 17. Ovington, J. *A Voyage to the Suratt.*
1696. p. 489.
[4]In *Relatio triplex de rebus Indicis Caaiguarum,* 1654. p. 43.
[5]La Loubère, S. de. *Du royaume de Siam.* 1691. t. i, ch. 9, §15 et seq.; ch. 20,
§22; ch. 22, §6.
[6]*Ibid.,* t. i, ch. 20, §4; ch. 23.

La Loubère, the missionaries of *China*, even the Jesuits themselves, the great encomiasts of the *Chinese*, do all to a man agree and will convince us that the sect of the *litterati* or *learned*, keeping to the old religion of *China* and the ruling party there, are all of them *atheists*. *Vide* D. Fernandez Navarrete's 'An Account of the Empire of China' in vol. I of A. & J. Churchill's *A Collection of voyages and travels* (1704) and *Historia Cultus Sinensium* (1700). And, perhaps, if we should with attention mind the lives and discourses of people not so far off, we should have too much reason to fear that many in more civilized countries have no very strong and clear impressions of a deity upon their minds, and that the complaints of atheism made from the pulpit are not without reason. And though only some profligate wretches own it too bare-facedly now, yet perhaps we should hear, more than we do, of it from others, did not the fear of the magistrate's sword or their neighbour's censure tie up people's tongues; which, were the apprehensions of punishment or shame taken away, would as openly proclaim their *atheism* as their lives do.

9. But had all mankind everywhere a *notion of a God* (whereof yet history tells us the contrary) it would *not* from thence follow that the *idea* of him was *innate*. For, though no nation were to be found without a name and some few dark notions of him, yet that would not prove them to be natural impressions on the mind, no more than the names of fire or the sun, heat, or number do prove the *ideas* they stand for to be innate; because the names of those things and the *ideas* of them, are so universally received and known amongst mankind. Nor on the contrary is the want of such a name, or the absence of such a notion out of men's minds, any argument against the being of a god; any more than it would be a proof that there was no load-stone in the world, because a great part of mankind had neither a notion of any such thing nor a name for it; or be any show of argument to prove that there are no distinct and various species of angels or intelligent beings above us, because we have no *ideas* of such distinct species or names for them; for, men being furnished with words by the common language of their own countries, can scarce avoid having some kind of *ideas* of those things whose names those they converse with have occasion frequently to mention to them. And if it carry with it the notion of excellency, greatness, or something extraordinary; if apprehension and

concernment accompany it; if the fear of absolute and irresistible power set it on upon the mind, the *idea* is likely to sink the deeper and spread the further, especially if it be such an *idea* as is agreeable to the common light of reason and naturally deducible from every part of our knowledge, as that of a god is. For the visible marks of extraordinary wisdom and power appear so plainly in all the works of the creation that a rational creature who will but seriously reflect on them cannot miss the discovery of a *deity*; and the influence that the discovery of such a being must necessarily have on the minds of all that have but once heard of it is so great and carries such a weight of thought and communication with it, that it seems stranger to me that a whole nation of men should be anywhere found so brutish as to want the notion of a god, than that they should be without any notion of numbers or fire.

10.   The name of God being once mentioned in any part of the world, to express a superior, powerful, wise, invisible being: the suitableness of such a notion to the principles of common reason and the interest men will always have to mention it often must necessarily spread it far and wide, and continue it down to all generations: though yet the general *reception of this name, and some imperfect and unsteady notions conveyed thereby* to the unthinking part of mankind *prove not the* idea *to be innate*, but only that they who made the discovery had made a right use of their reason, thought maturely of the causes of things, and traced them to their original; from whom other less considering people, having once received so important a notion, it could not easily be lost again.

11.   This is all could be inferred from the notion of a *god*, were it to be found universally in all the tribes of mankind and generally acknowledged by men grown to maturity in all countries. For the generality of the acknowledging of a god, as I imagine, is extended no further than that; which, if it be sufficient to prove the *idea of God innate*, will as well prove the *idea* of fire innate, since I think it may truly be said that there is not a person in the world who has a notion of a *god* who has not also the *idea* of fire. I doubt not but if a colony of young children should be placed in an island where no fire was, they would certainly neither have any notion of such a thing nor name for it, how generally soever it were received and known in all the world besides; and perhaps too their apprehensions

would be as far removed from any name or notion of a god, until someone amongst them had employed his thoughts to inquire into the constitution and causes of things, which would easily lead him to the notion of a *god*; which having once taught to others, reason and the natural propensity of their own thoughts would afterwards propagate and continue amongst them.

12. Indeed it is urged that it is *suitable to the goodness of God to imprint upon the minds of men characters and notions of Himself*, and not to leave them in the dark and doubt in so grand a concernment; and also, by that means, to secure to himself the homage and veneration due from so intelligent a creature as man; and therefore he has done it.

This argument, if it be of any force will prove much more than those who use it in this case expect from it. For, if we may conclude that *God* hath done for men all that men shall judge is best for them, because it is suitable to his goodness so to do, it will prove not only that God has imprinted on the minds of men an *idea* of himself, but that he hath plainly stamped there, in fair characters, all that men ought to know or believe of him, all that they ought to do in obedience to his will, and that he hath given them a will and affections conformable to it. This, no doubt, everyone will think it better for men than that they should, in the dark, grope after knowledge, as St. *Paul* tells us all nations did after God (*Acts* xvii, 27) than that their wills should clash with their understandings, and their appetites cross their duty. The *Romanists* say it is best for men, and so suitable to the goodness of God, that there should be an infallible judge of controversies on earth; and therefore there is one. And I, by the same reason, say it is better for men that every man himself should be infallible. I leave them to consider whether by the force of this argument they shall think that every man is so. I think it a very good argument to say: the infinitely wise God hath made it so, and therefore it is best. But it *seems to me a little too much confidence of our own wisdom to say, I think it best and therefore God hath made it so.* And in the matter in hand, it will be in vain to argue from such a topic that God hath done so, when certain experience shows us that he hath not. But the goodness of God hath not been wanting to men without such original impressions of knowledge or *ideas* stamped on the mind, since he hath furnished man with those faculties which

will serve for the sufficient discovery of all things requisite to
the end of such a being; and I doubt not but to show that a man
by the right use of his natural abilities may, without any innate
principles, attain the knowledge of a god and other things that
concern him. God, having endued man with those faculties of
knowing which he hath, was no more obliged by his goodness
to implant those innate notions in his mind than that having
given him reason, hands, and materials he should build him
bridges or houses, which some people in the world, however of
good parts, do either totally want or are but ill provided of, as
well as others are wholly without *ideas of God* and principles of
morality, or at least have but very ill ones. The reason in both
cases being that they never employed their parts, faculties, and
powers industriously that way, but contented themselves with
the opinions, fashions, and things of their country as they found
them, without looking any further. Had you or I been born at
the Bay of *Saldanha*, possibly our thoughts and notions had not
exceeded those brutish ones of the *Hottentots* that inhabit there.
And had the *Virginia* king *Apochancana* been educated in
England, he had perhaps been as knowing a divine and as good
a mathematician as any in it: the difference between him and
a more improved *Englishman* lying barely in this, that exercise
of his faculties was bounded within the ways, modes and
notions of his own country and never directed to any other or
further inquiries. And if he had not any *idea* of a god, it was
only because he pursued not those thoughts that would have
led him to it.

13. I grant that *if* there were *any ideas* to be found *imprinted*
on the minds of men, we have reason to expect *it should be the
notion of his maker*, as a mark GOD set on his own workmanship,
to mind man of his dependence and duty; and that herein
should appear the first instances of human knowledge. But how
late is it before any such notion is discoverable in children? And
when we find it there, how much more does it resemble the
opinion and notion of the teacher than represent the true God?
He that shall observe in children the progress, whereby their
minds attain the knowledge they have, will think that the objects
they do first and most familiarly converse with are those that
make the first impressions on their understandings; nor will he
find the least footsteps of any other. It is easy to take notice
how their thoughts enlarge themselves, only as they come to be

acquainted with a greater variety of sensible objects, to retain the *ideas* of them in their memories, and to get the skill to compound and enlarge them, and several ways put them together. How by these means they come to frame in their minds an *idea* men have of a deity, I shall hereafter show.

14. Can it be thought that the *ideas* men have of God are the characters and marks of himself, engraven in their minds by his own finger, when we see that, in the same country, under one and the same name, *men have far different*, nay often *contrary and inconsistent ideas* and conceptions *of him*? Their agreeing in a name, or sound, will scarce prove an innate notion of him.

15. What true or tolerable notion of a *deity* could they have, who acknowledged and worshipped hundreds? Every deity that they owned above one was an infallible evidence of their ignorance of Him, and a proof that they had no true notion of God, where unity, infinity, and eternity were excluded. To which, if we add their gross conceptions of corporeity, expressed in their images and representations of their deities; the amours, marriages, copulations, lusts, quarrels, and other mean qualities attributed by them to their gods, we shall have little reason to think that the heathen world, i.e. the greatest part of mankind, had such *ideas* of God in their minds as he himself, out of care that they should not be mistaken about him, was author of. And this universality of consent, so much argued, if it prove any native impressions, it will be only this: that God imprinted on the minds of all men speaking the same language a name for himself, but not any *idea*, since those people who agreed in the name had, at the same time, far different apprehensions about the thing signified. If they say that the variety of deities worshipped by the heathen world were but figurative ways of expressing the several attributes of that incomprehensible being or several parts of his providence, I answer: what they might be in their original I will not here inquire; but that they were so in the thoughts of the vulgar I think nobody will affirm. And he that will consult the voyage of the Bishop of *Beryte*[1] (not to mention other testimonies) will find that the theology of the *Siamites* professedly owns a plurality of gods: or, as the *Abbé de Choisy* more judiciously remarks in his *Journal du Voyage de Siam*[2], it consists properly in acknowledging no god at all.

[1]Bourges, J. de. *Relation du voyage de Monseigneur* (P. de la Motte-Lambert) *'Evèque de Beryte* (i.e., Beirut). 1668. ch. 13.
[2]Choisy, F. T. de. *Journal, ou Suite du voyage de Siam.* 1687. p. 301.

16.   If it be said that *wise men* of all nations came to *have true conceptions* of the unity and infinity *of the Deity*, I grant it. But then this,

First, excludes universality of consent in anything but the name, for those wise men being very few, perhaps one of a thousand, this universality is very narrow.

Secondly, it seems to me plainly to prove that the truest and best notions men had of God were not imprinted but acquired by thought and meditation and a right use of their faculties: since the wise and considerate men of the world, by a right and careful employment of their thoughts and reason, attained true notions in this as well as other things; whilst the lazy and inconsiderate part of men, making the far greater number, took up their notions by chance from common tradition and vulgar conceptions, without much beating their heads about them. And if it be a reason to think *the notion of God innate*, because all wise men had it, virtue too must be thought innate, for that also wise men have always had.

17.   This was evidently the case of all *Gentilism*; nor hath even amongst *Jews*, *Christians*, and *Mahometans*, who acknowledge but one God, this doctrine (and the care is taken in those nations to teach men to have true notions of a GOD) prevailed so far as to make men to have the same and true *ideas* of him. How many, even amongst us, will be found upon inquiry to fancy him in the shape of a man, sitting in heaven, and to have many other absurd and unfit conceptions of him? Christians, as well as Turks, have had whole sects owning and contending earnestly for it that the Deity was corporeal and of human shape; and though we find few amongst us who profess themselves *anthropomorphites* (though some I have met with that own it) yet, I believe, he that will make it his business may find amongst the ignorant and uninstructed Christians many of that opinion. Talk but with country people, almost of any age, or young people almost of any condition, and you shall find that, though the name of GOD be frequently in their mouths, yet the notions they apply this name to are so odd, low, and pitiful that nobody can imagine they were taught by a rational man, much less that they were characters writ by the finger of God himself. Nor do I see how it derogates more from the goodness of God that he has given us minds unfurnished with these *ideas* of himself, than that he hath sent us into the world with bodies unclothed,

and that there is no art or skill born with us. For being fitted
with faculties to attain these, it is want of industry and consideration in us and not of bounty in him if we have them not. It is
as certain that there is a god, as that the opposite angles made
by the intersection of two straight lines are equal. There
was never any rational creature that set himself sincerely to
examine the truth of these propositions that could fail to assent
to them, though yet it be past doubt that there are many men
who, having not applied their thoughts that way, are ignorant
both of the one and the other. If any one think fit to call this
(which is the utmost of its extent) universal consent, such an one
I easily allow; but such an universal consent as this proves not
the *idea* of *God*, no more than it does the *idea* of such angles,
innate.

18.   Since then, though the knowledge of a GOD be the most
natural discovery of human reason, yet *the idea of him* is *not
innate*, as I think is evident from what has been said; I imagine
there will be scarce any other *idea* found that can pretend to it;
since, if God had set any impression, any character on the
understanding of men, it is most reasonable to expect it should
have been some clear and uniform *idea* of himself, as far as our
weak capacities were capable to receive so incomprehensible and
infinite an object. But our minds being at first void of that *idea*
which we are most concerned to have, it *is a strong presumption
against all other innate characters*. I must own, as far as I can
observe, I can find none and would be glad to be informed by
any other.

19.   I confess there is another *idea* which would be of general
use for mankind to have, as it is of general talk as if they had it;
and that is the *idea of substance*, which we neither have nor can
have by *sensation* or *reflection*. If nature took care to provide us
any *ideas*, we might well expect they should be such as by our
own faculties we cannot procure to ourselves; but we see on the
contrary that, since, by those ways whereby other *ideas* are
brought into our minds, this is not, we have no such *clear idea*
at all; and therefore signify nothing by the word *substance* but
only an uncertain supposition of we know not what (i.e. of something whereof we have no particular distinct positive) *idea*,
which we take to be the *substratum*, or support, of those *ideas*
we do know.

20.   Whatever then we talk of innate, either *speculative* or

practical, principles, it may with as much probability be said that a man hath £100 sterling in his pocket, and yet denied that he hath either penny, shilling, crown, or any other coin out of which the sum is to be made up, as to think that certain propositions are innate when the *ideas* about which they are can by no means be supposed to be so. The general reception and assent that is given doth *not* at all prove that the *ideas* expressed in them are *innate*; for in many cases, however the *ideas* came there, the assent to words expressing the agreement or disagreement of such *ideas* will necessarily follow. Everyone that hath a true *idea* of *God* and *worship* will assent to this proposition, that God is to be worshipped, when expressed in a language he understands; and every rational man that hath not thought on it today, may be ready to assent to this proposition tomorrow; and yet millions of men may be well supposed to want one or both those *ideas* today. For if we will allow savages and most country-people to have *ideas* of *God* and *worship* (which conversation with them will not make one forward to believe), yet I think few children can be supposed to have those *ideas* which therefore they must begin to have sometime or other, and then they will also begin to assent to that proposition and make very little question of it ever after. But such an assent upon hearing no more proves the *ideas* to be innate than it does that one born blind (with cataracts, which will be couched tomorrow) had the innate *ideas* of the sun or light or saffron or yellow; because, when his sight is cleared, he will certainly assent to this proposition: that the sun is lucid, or that saffron is yellow. And therefore if such an assent upon hearing cannot prove the *ideas* innate, it can much less the propositions made up of those *ideas*. If they have any innate *ideas*, I would be glad to be told what and how many they are.

21. To which let me add: if there be any innate *ideas*, any *ideas* in the mind which the mind does not actually think on, they must be lodged in the memory and from thence must be brought into view by remembrance, i.e. must be known when they are remembered to have been perceptions in the mind before, unless remembrance can be without remembrance. For to remember is to perceive anything with memory, or with a consciousness, that it was known or perceived before; without this, whatever *idea* comes into the mind is new and not remembered: this consciousness of its having been in the mind before

being that which distinguishes remembering from all other ways of thinking. Whatever *idea* was never perceived by the mind was never in the mind. Whatever *idea* is in the mind is either an actual perception or else, having been an actual perception, is so in the mind that by the memory it can be made an actual perception again. Whenever there is the actual perception of an *idea* without memory, the *idea* appears perfectly new and unknown before to the understanding. Whenever the memory brings any *idea* into actual view, it is with a consciousness that it had been there before and was not wholly a stranger to the mind. Whether this be not so, I appeal to everyone's observation. And then I desire an instance of an *idea* pretended to be innate which (before any impression of it by ways hereafter to be mentioned) anyone could revive and remember as an *idea* he had formerly known: without which consciousness of a former perception there is no remembrance; and whatever *idea* comes into the mind without that consciousness is not remembered, or comes not out of the memory, nor can be said to be in the mind before that appearance. For what is not either actually in view, or in the memory, is in the mind no way at all, and is all one as if it never had been there. Suppose a child had the use of his eyes till he knows and distinguishes colours; but then cataracts shut the windows and he is forty or fifty years perfectly in the dark; and in that time perfectly loses all memory of the *ideas* of colours he once had. This was the case of a blind man I once talked with, who lost his sight by the smallpox when he was a child and had no more notion of colours than one born blind. I ask whether anyone can say this man had then any *ideas* of colours in his mind, any more than one born blind? And I think nobody will say that either of them had in his mind any *idea* of colours at all. His cataracts are couched and then he has the *ideas* (which he remembers not) of colours, *de novo*, by his restored sight conveyed to his mind, and that without any consciousness of a former acquaintance. And these now he can revive and call to mind in the dark. In this case all these *ideas* of colours, which when out of view can be revived with a consciousness of a former acquaintance, being thus in the memory, are said to be in the mind. The use I make of this is that whatever *idea*, being not actually in view, is in the mind is there only by being in the memory; and if it be not in the memory, it is not in the mind; and if it be in the memory, it cannot by the memory be brought into actual view without a perception that it comes out of the memory: which is this, that it had been known before and is now remembered. If therefore there be any innate *ideas*, they must be in the memory or else nowhere in the mind; and if they be in the memory, they can be revived without any impression from without; and whenever they are brought into the mind, they are remembered, i.e. they bring with them a perception of their not being wholly new to it. This being a constant and distinguishing difference between what is and what is not in the memory, or in the mind: that what is not in the memory, whenever it appears there, appears perfectly new and unknown before; and what is in the memory or in the mind, whenever it is suggested by the memory, appears not to be new, but the mind finds it in itself and knows it was there before. By this it may be tried whether there be any innate *ideas* in the mind before impression from *sensation* or *reflection*. I would fain meet with the man who, when he came to the use of reason or at any other time, remembered any of them, and to whom, after he was born, they were never new. If anyone will say there are *ideas* in the mind that are not in the memory, I desire him to explain himself and make what he says intelligible.

22. Besides what I have already said, there is another reason why I doubt that neither these nor any other principles are innate. I, that am fully persuaded that the infinitely wise GOD made all things in perfect wisdom, cannot satisfy myself why he should be supposed to print upon the minds of men some universal *principles*, whereof those *that* are pretended innate, and *concern speculation, are of no great use; and those that concern practice, not self-evident; and neither of them distinguishable from some other truths not allowed to be innate.* For to what purpose should characters be graven on the mind by the finger of God, which are not clearer there than those which are afterwards introduced, or cannot be distinguished from them? If anyone thinks there are such innate *ideas* and propositions, which by their clearness and usefulness are distinguishable from all that is adventitious in the mind and acquired, it will not be a hard matter for him to tell us which they are; and then everyone will be a fit judge whether they be so or no. Since if there be such innate *ideas* and impressions, plainly different from all other perceptions and knowledge, everyone will find it true in himself. Of the evidence of these supposed innate

maxims, I have spoken already; of their usefulness, I shall have occasion to speak more hereafter.

23. To conclude: some *ideas* forwardly offer themselves to all men's understanding; some sorts of truths result from any *ideas*, as soon as the mind puts them into propositions; other truths require a train of *ideas* placed in order, a due comparing of them, and deductions made with attention, before they can be discovered and assented to. Some of the first sort, because of their general and easy reception, have been mistaken for innate; but the truth is, *ideas* and notions are no more born with us than arts and sciences, though some of them indeed offer themselves to our faculties more readily than others and therefore are more generally received, though that too be according as the organs of our bodies and powers of our minds happen to be employed: *God having fitted men with faculties and means to discover, receive, and retain truths, accordingly as they are employed.* The great difference that is to be found in the notions of mankind is from the different use they put their faculties to; whilst some (and those the most), taking things upon trust, misemploy their power of assent, by lazily enslaving their minds to the dictates and dominion of others, in doctrines which it is their duty carefully to examine and not blindly, with an implicit faith, to swallow; others, employing their thoughts only about some few things, grow acquainted sufficiently with them, attain great degrees of knowledge in them, and are ignorant of all other, having never let their thoughts loose in the search of other inquiries. Thus, that the three angles of a triangle are equal to two right ones is a truth as certain as anything can be, and I think more evident than many of those propositions that go for principles; and yet there are millions, however expert in other things, who know not this at all because they never set their thoughts on work about such angles; and he that certainly knows this proposition may yet be utterly ignorant of the truth of other propositions in mathematics itself, which are as clear and evident as this, because, in his search of those mathematical truths, he stopped his thoughts short and went not so far. The same may happen concerning the notions we have of the being of a deity. For, though there be no truth which a man may more evidently make out to himself than the existence of a god, yet he that shall content himself with things as he finds them in this world, as they minister to his pleasures and passions, and not

make inquiry a little further into their causes, ends, and admirable contrivances, and pursue the thoughts thereof with diligence and attention, may live long without any notion of such a being. And if any person hath, by talk, put such a notion into his head, he may, perhaps, believe it; but if he hath never *examined* it, his knowledge of it will be no perfecter than his who, having been told that the three angles of a triangle are equal to two right ones, takes it upon trust without examining the demonstration, and may yield his assent as a probable opinion but hath no knowledge of the truth of it; which yet his faculties, if carefully employed, were able to make clear and evident to him. But this only by the by, to show how much our *knowledge depends upon the right use of those powers nature hath bestowed upon us*, and how little upon such innate principles as are in vain supposed to be in all mankind for their direction; which all men could not but know if they were there, or else they would be there to no purpose; and which, since all men do not know, nor can distinguish from other adventitious truths, we may well conclude there are no such.

24. What censure doubting thus of innate principles may deserve from men, who will be apt to call it pulling up the old foundations of knowledge and certainty, I cannot tell; I persuade myself at least that the way I have pursued, being conformable to truth, lays those foundations surer. This I am certain, I have not made it my business either to quit or follow any authority in the ensuing discourse. Truth has been my only aim; and wherever that has appeared to lead, my thoughts have impartially followed, without minding whether the footsteps of any other lay that way or no. Not that I want a due respect to other men's opinions; but after all, the *greatest reverence is due to truth*: and I hope it will not be thought arrogance to say that perhaps we should make greater progress in the discovery of rational and contemplative *knowledge*, if we *sought* it in the fountain, *in the consideration of things themselves*, and made use rather of our own thoughts than other men's to find it. For I think we may as rationally hope to see with other men's eyes as to know by other men's understandings. So much as we ourselves consider and comprehend of truth and reason, so much we possess of real and true knowledge. The floating of other men's opinions in our brains makes us not one jot the more knowing, though they happen to be true. What in them was science is in

us but opiniatrety, whilst we give up our assent only to reverend names and do not, as they did, employ our own reason to *understand* those *truths* which gave them reputation. *Aristotle* was certainly a knowing man, but nobody ever thought him so because he blindly embraced and confidently vented the opinions of another. And if the taking up of another's principles, without examining them, made not him a philosopher, I suppose it will hardly make anybody else so. In the sciences, everyone has so much as he really knows and comprehends: what he believes only and takes upon trust are but shreds; which, however well in the whole piece, make no considerable addition to his stock who gathers them. Such borrowed wealth, like fairy-money, though it were gold in the hand from which he received it, will be but leaves and dust when it comes to use.

25. When men have found some general propositions that could not be doubted of, as soon as understood, it was, I know, *a short and easy way to conclude them innate*. This being once received, it eased the lazy from the pains of search and stopped the inquiry of the doubtful concerning all that was once styled innate; and it was of no small advantage, to those who affected to be masters and teachers, to make this the principle of *principles*: that principles must not be questioned. For having once established this tenet, that there are innate principles, it put their followers upon a necessity of receiving some doctrines as such; which was to take them off from the use of their own reason and judgment and put them upon believing and taking them upon trust, without further examination: in which posture of blind credulity, they might be more easily governed by and made useful to some sort of men, who had the skill and office to principle and guide them. Nor is it a small power it gives one man over another to have the authority to be the dictator of principles and teacher of unquestionable truths, and to make a man swallow that for an innate principle which may serve to his purpose who teacheth them. Whereas had they examined the ways whereby men came to the knowledge of many universal *truths*, they would have found them to result in the minds of men from the being of things themselves, when duly considered, and that they were discovered by the application of those faculties that were fitted by nature to receive and judge of them, when duly employed about them.

26. *To show how the understanding proceeds herein is the design
of the following discourse*; which I shall proceed to, when I have
first premised that hitherto, to clear my way to those foundations which I conceive are the only true ones whereon to establish those notions we can have of our own knowledge, it hath
been necessary for me to give an account of the reasons I had to
doubt of innate principles. And since the arguments which are
against them do some of them rise from common received
opinions, I have been forced to take several things for granted,
which is hardly avoidable to anyone whose task it is to show
the falsehood or improbability of any tenet: it happening in
controversial discourses, as it does in assaulting of towns, where,
if the ground be but firm whereon the batteries are erected,
there is no further inquiry of whom it is borrowed nor whom it
belongs to, so it affords but a fit rise for the present purpose.
But in the future part of this discourse, designing to raise an
edifice uniform and consistent with itself, as far as my own
experience and observation will assist me, I hope to erect it on
such a basis that I shall not need to shore it up with props and
buttresses, leaning on borrowed or begged foundations; or at
least if mine prove a castle in the air, I will endeavour it shall be
all of a piece and hang together. Wherein I warn the reader not
to expect undeniable cogent demonstrations, unless I may be
allowed the privilege, not seldom assumed by others, to take my
principles for granted; and then, I doubt not but I can demonstrate too. All that I shall say for the principles I proceed on is
that I can only *appeal* to men's own unprejudiced *experience* and
observation whether they be true or no; and this is enough for a
man who professes no more than to lay down candidly and freely
his own conjectures concerning a subject lying somewhat in the
dark, without any other design than an unbiased inquiry after
truth.

THE ANALYTICAL CONTENTS

BOOK II

CHAPTER I

OF IDEAS IN GENERAL, AND THEIR ORIGINAL

CHAPTER II

OF SIMPLE IDEAS

CHAPTER III

OF IDEAS OF ONE SENSE

CHAPTER IV

OF SOLIDITY

CHAPTER V

OF SIMPLE IDEAS OF DIVERS SENSES

CHAPTER VI

OF SIMPLE IDEAS OF REFLECTION

CHAPTER VII

OF SIMPLE IDEAS
OF BOTH SENSATION AND REFLECTION

CHAPTER VIII

SOME FURTHER CONSIDERATIONS CONCERNING
OUR SIMPLE IDEAS

CHAPTER IX

OF PERCEPTION

CHAPTER X

OF RETENTION

CHAPTER XI

OF DISCERNING, AND OTHER OPERATIONS OF THE MIND

CHAPTER XII

OF COMPLEX IDEAS

CHAPTER XIII

OF SIMPLE MODES; AND FIRST, OF THE SIMPLE MODES OF SPACE

*D 832

CHAPTER XIV

OF DURATION AND ITS SIMPLE MODES

CHAPTER XV

OF DURATION AND
EXPANSION, CONSIDERED TOGETHER

CHAPTER XVI

Of Number

CHAPTER XVII

Of Infinity

CHAPTER XVIII

OF OTHER SIMPLE MODES

SECTION

CHAPTER XIX

OF THE MODES OF THINKING

SECTION

CHAPTER XX

OF MODES OF PLEASURE AND PAIN

SECTION

CHAPTER XXI

OF POWER

CHAPTER XXII

OF MIXED MODES

CHAPTER XXIII

OF OUR COMPLEX IDEAS OF SUBSTANCES

CHAPTER XXIV

OF COLLECTIVE IDEAS OF SUBSTANCES

SECTION

CHAPTER XXV

OF RELATION

SECTION

CHAPTER XXVI

Of Cause and Effect, and Other Relations

CHAPTER XXVII

Of Identity and Diversity

CHAPTER XXVIII

Of Other Relations

CHAPTER XXIX

Of Clear and Obscure, Distinct and Confused Ideas

CHAPTER XXX

OF REAL AND FANTASTICAL IDEAS

CHAPTER XXXI

OF ADEQUATE AND INADEQUATE IDEAS

CHAPTER XXXII

OF TRUE AND FALSE IDEAS

CHAPTER XXXIII

OF THE ASSOCIATION OF IDEAS

BOOK II

OF IDEAS

CHAPTER I

OF IDEAS IN GENERAL, AND THEIR ORIGINAL

1. Every man being conscious to himself that he thinks, and
that which his mind is applied about whilst thinking being the
ideas that are there, it is past doubt that men have in their minds
several *ideas* such as are those expressed by the words *whiteness,
hardness, sweetness, thinking, motion, man, elephant, army,
drunkenness* and others: it is in the first place then to be inquired, how he comes by them? I know it is a received doctrine
that men have native *ideas* and original characters stamped
upon their minds in their very first being. This opinion I have
at large examined already; and, I suppose, what I have said in
the foregoing book will be much more easily admitted when I
have shown whence the understanding may get all the *ideas* it
has, and by what ways and degrees they may come into the
mind; for which I shall appeal to everyone's own observation
and experience.

2. Let us then suppose the mind to be, as we say, white paper
void of all characters, without any *ideas*. How comes it to be
furnished? Whence comes it by that vast store which the busy
and boundless fancy of man has painted on it with an almost
endless variety? Whence has it all the materials of reason and
knowledge? To this I answer, in one word, from *experience*;
in that all our knowledge is founded, and from that it ultimately
derives itself. Our observation, employed either about *external
sensible objects, or about the internal operations of our minds perceived and reflected on by ourselves, is that which supplies our
understandings with all the materials of thinking*. These two are
the fountains of knowledge, from whence all the *ideas* we have,
or can naturally have, do spring.

3. First, *our senses*, conversant about particular sensible
objects, do *convey into the mind* several distinct *perceptions* of

things, according to those various ways wherein those objects do affect them. And thus we come by those *ideas* we have of *yellow, white, heat, cold, soft, hard, bitter, sweet,* and all those which we call sensible qualities; which when I say the senses convey into the mind, I mean, they from external objects convey into the mind what produces there those *perceptions*. This great source of most of the *ideas* we have, depending wholly upon our senses, and derived by them to the understanding, I call SENSATION.

4. Secondly, the other fountain from which experience furnisheth the understanding with *ideas* is the *perception of the operations of our own minds* within us, as it is employed about the *ideas* it has got; which operations, when the soul comes to reflect on and consider, do furnish the understanding with another set of *ideas*, which could not be had from things without. And such are *perception, thinking, doubting, believing, reasoning, knowing, willing,* and all the different actings of our own minds; which we, being conscious of and observing in ourselves, do from these receive into our understandings as distinct *ideas* as we do from bodies affecting our senses. This source of *ideas* every man has wholly in himself; and though it be not sense, as having nothing to do with external objects, yet it is very like it, and might properly enough be called internal sense. But as I call the other *sensation*, so I call this REFLECTION, the *ideas* it affords being such only as the mind gets by reflecting on its own operations within itself. By REFLECTION then, in the following part of this discourse, I would be understood to mean that notice which the mind takes of its own operations, and the manner of them, by reason whereof there come to be *ideas* of these operations in the understanding. These two, I say, viz. external material things as the objects of SENSATION, and the operations of our own minds within as the objects of REFLECTION, are to me the only originals from whence all our *ideas* take their beginnings. The term *operations* here I use in a large sense, as comprehending not barely the actions of the mind about its *ideas*, but some sort of passions arising sometimes from them, such as is the satisfaction or uneasiness arising from any thought.

5. The understanding seems to me not to have the least glimmering of any *ideas* which it doth not receive from one of these two. *External objects furnish the mind with the* ideas *of sensible qualities,* which are all those different perceptions they

produce in us; and the *mind furnishes the understanding with*
ideas *of its own operations.*

These, when we have taken a full survey of them and their
several modes, combinations, and relations, we shall find to
contain all our whole stock of *ideas*, and that we have nothing in
our minds which did not come in one of these two ways. Let
anyone examine his own thoughts and thoroughly search into
his understanding and then let him tell me whether all the
original *ideas* he has there are any other than of the objects of
his *senses*, or of the operations of his mind, considered as
objects of his *reflection.* And how great a mass of knowledge
soever he imagines to be lodged there, he will, upon taking a
strict view, see that he has *not any* idea *in his mind but what one
of these two have imprinted*, though perhaps, with infinite
variety compounded and enlarged by the understanding, as we
shall see hereafter.

6. He that attentively considers the state of a *child*, at his first
coming into the world, will have little reason to think him stored
with plenty of *ideas*, that are to be the matter of his future
knowledge. It is by degrees he comes to be furnished with them.
And though the *ideas* of obvious and familiar qualities imprint
themselves before the memory begins to keep a register of time
and order, yet it is often so late before some unusual qualities
come in the way, that there are few men that cannot recollect the
beginning of their acquaintance with them. And if it were
worthwhile, no doubt a child might be so ordered as to have but
a very few, even of the ordinary *ideas*, till he were grown up to
a man. But all that are born into the world being surrounded
with bodies that perpetually and diversely affect them, variety
of *ideas*, whether care be taken about it or no, are imprinted on
the minds of children. *Light* and *colours* are busy at hand everywhere when the eye is but open; *sounds* and some *tangible
qualities* fail not to solicit their proper senses and force an
entrance to the mind; but yet, I think it will be granted easily
that, if a child were kept in a place where he never saw any
other but black and white till he were a man, he would have no
more *ideas* of scarlet or green than he that from his childhood
never tasted an oyster or a pineapple has of those particular
relishes.

7. Men then come to be furnished with fewer or more simple
ideas from without, according as the *objects* they converse with

afford greater or less variety; and from the operation of their minds within, according as they more or less *reflect* on them. For, though he that contemplates the operations of his mind cannot but have plain and clear *ideas* of them: yet, unless he turn his thoughts that way and consider them *attentively*, he will no more have clear and distinct *ideas* of all the *operations of his mind*, and all that may be observed therein, than he will have all the particular *ideas* of any landscape, or of the parts and motions of a clock, who will not turn his eyes to it and with attention heed all the parts of it. The picture or clock may be so placed that they may come in his way every day, but yet he will have but a confused *idea* of all the parts they are made up of, till he *applies himself with attention* to consider them each in particular.

8. And hence we see the reason why it is pretty late before most children get *ideas* of the operations of their own minds; and some have not any very clear or perfect *ideas* of the greatest part of them all their lives. Because, though they pass there continually, yet, like floating visions, they make not deep impressions enough to leave in the mind clear, distinct, lasting *ideas*, till the understanding turns inwards upon itself, *reflects* on its own *operations*, and makes them the object of its own contemplation. Children, when they come first into it, are surrounded with a world of new things which, by a constant solicitation of their senses, draw the mind constantly to them, forward to take notice of new and apt to be delighted with the variety of changing objects. Thus the first years are usually employed and diverted in looking abroad. Men's business in them is to acquaint themselves with what is to be found without; and so growing up in a constant attention to outward sensations, seldom make any considerable reflection on what passes within them, till they come to be of riper years; and some scarce ever at all.

9. To ask *at what time a man has first any* ideas is to ask when he begins to perceive: having *ideas* and perception being the same thing. I know it is an opinion that the soul always thinks, and that it has the actual perception of *ideas* in itself constantly, as long as it exists; and that actual thinking is as inseparable from the soul as actual extension is from the body; which if true, to inquire after the beginning of a man's *ideas* is the same as to inquire after the beginning of his soul. For, by this

account, soul and its *ideas*, as body and its extension, will begin
to exist both at the same time.

10.   But whether the soul be supposed to exist antecedent to,
or coeval with, or some time after, the first rudiments of organization, or the beginnings of life in the body, I leave to be disputed by those who have better thought of that matter.   I
confess myself to have one of those dull souls, that doth not
perceive itself always to contemplate *ideas*; nor can conceive it
any more necessary for the *soul always to think*, than for the body
always to move: the perception of *ideas* being (as I conceive) to
the soul what motion is to the body: not its essence, but one of
its operations.   And therefore, though thinking be supposed
never so much the proper action of the soul, yet it is not necessary to suppose that it should be always thinking, always in
action.   That, perhaps, is the privilege of the infinite Author and
Preserver of things, *who never slumbers nor sleeps*; but is not
competent to any finite being, at least not to the soul of man.
We know certainly, by experience, that we sometimes think;
and thence draw this infallible consequence, that there is something in us that has a power to think.   But whether that substance perpetually thinks or no, we can be no further assured
than experience informs us.   For to say that actual thinking is
essential to the soul and inseparable from it is to beg what is in
question and not to prove it by reason; which is necessary to be
done, if it be not a self-evident proposition.   But whether this,
that the soul always thinks, be a self-evident proposition that
everybody assents to at first hearing, I appeal to mankind.   It is
doubted whether I thought all last night or no; the question
being about a matter of fact, it is begging it to bring as a proof
for it an hypothesis which is the very thing in dispute: by which
way one may prove anything, and it is but supposing that all
watches, whilst the balance beats, think, and it is sufficiently
proved and past doubt that my watch thought all last night.
But he that would not deceive himself ought to build his hypothesis on matter of fact and make it out by sensible experience
and not presume on matter of fact because of his hypothesis,
that is, because he supposes it to be so; which way of proving
amounts to this, that I must necessarily think all last night
because another supposes I always think, though I myself cannot perceive that I always do so.

But men in love with their opinions may not only suppose

what is in question, but allege wrong matter of fact. How else could anyone make it an *inference* of mine *that a thing is not because we are not sensible of it in our sleep*? I do not say there is no soul in a man, because he is not sensible of it in his sleep; but I do say he cannot think at any time waking or sleeping without being sensible of it. Our being sensible of it is not necessary to anything but to our thoughts; and to them it is and to them it will always be necessary, until we can think without being conscious of it.

11. I grant that the soul, in a waking man, is never without thought, because it is the condition of being awake. But whether sleeping without dreaming be not an affection of the whole man, mind as well as body, may be worth a waking man's consideration: it being hard to conceive that anything should think and not be conscious of it. If the *soul* doth *think in a sleeping man* without being conscious of it, I ask whether, during such thinking, it has any pleasure or pain, or be capable of happiness or misery? I am sure the man is not, no more than the bed or earth he lies on. For to be happy or miserable without being conscious of it seems to me utterly inconsistent and impossible. Or if it be possible that the soul can, whilst the body is sleeping, have its thinking, enjoyments, and concerns, its pleasure or pain, apart, which the man is not conscious of nor partakes in, it is certain that *Socrates* asleep and *Socrates* awake is not the same person; but his soul, when he sleeps, and *Socrates* the man consisting of body and soul, when he is waking, are two persons, since waking *Socrates* has no knowledge of or concernment for that happiness or misery of his soul which it enjoys alone by itself whilst he sleeps, without perceiving anything of it, no more than he has for the happiness or misery of a man in the *Indies*, whom he knows not. For, if we take wholly away all consciousness of our actions and sensations, especially of pleasure and pain, and the concernment that accompanies it, it will be hard to know wherein to place personal identity.

12. The soul, during sound sleep, thinks, say these men. *Whilst it thinks* and perceives, it is capable certainly of those of delight or trouble, as well as any other perceptions; and *it must necessarily be conscious of its own perceptions*. But it has all this apart: the sleeping man, it is plain, is conscious of nothing of all this. Let us suppose, then, the soul of *Castor*, whilst he is sleeping, retired from his body; which is no impossible supposition

for the men I have here to do with, who so liberally allow life
without a thinking soul to all other animals. These men cannot
then judge it impossible or a contradiction that the body should
live without the soul; nor that the soul should subsist and think,
or have perception, even perception of happiness or misery,
without the body. Let us then, as I say, suppose the soul of
Castor separated during his sleep from his body, to think apart.
Let us suppose, too, that it chooses for its scene of thinking the
body of another man, e.g. *Pollux*, who is sleeping without a
soul. For, if *Castor's* soul can think whilst *Castor* is asleep,
what *Castor* is never conscious of, it is no matter what place it
chooses to think in. We have here, then, the bodies of two men
with only one soul between them, which we will suppose to
sleep and wake by turns; and the soul still thinking in the
waking man, whereof the sleeping man is never conscious, has
never the least perception. I ask, then, whether *Castor* and
Pollux, thus with only one soul between them which thinks and
perceives in one what the other is never conscious of nor is concerned for, are not two as distinct persons as *Castor* and *Her-
cules*, or as *Socrates* and *Plato* were? And whether one of them
might not be very happy, and the other very miserable? Just by
the same reason, they make the soul and the man two persons,
who make the soul think apart what the man is not conscious of.
For, I suppose, nobody will make identity of persons to consist
in the soul's being united to the very same numerical particles of
matter. For if that be necessary to identity, it will be impossible, in that constant flux of the particles of our bodies, that any
man should be the same person two days, or two moments,
together.

13.　Thus, methinks, every drowsy nod shakes their doctrine,
who teach that the soul is always thinking. Those, at least, who
do at any time *sleep without dreaming* can never be convinced
that their thoughts are sometimes for four hours busy without
their knowing of it; and if they are taken in the very act, waked
in the middle of that sleeping contemplation, can give no manner
of account of it.

14.　It will perhaps be said that the *soul thinks* even *in* the
soundest *sleep, but the memory retains it not*. That the soul in a
sleeping man should be this moment busy a-thinking, and the
next moment in a waking man not remember nor be able to
recollect one jot of all those thoughts, is very hard to be

conceived and would need some better proof than bare assertion
to make it be believed. For who can, without any more ado, but
being barely told so, imagine that the greatest part of men do,
during all their lives, for several hours every day, think of something, which if they were asked, even in the middle of these
thoughts, they could remember nothing at all of?

Most men, I think, pass a great part of their sleep without
dreaming. I once knew a man that was bred a scholar and had
no bad memory who told me he had never dreamed in his life
till he had that fever he was then newly recovered of, which was
about the five or six and twentieth year of his age. I suppose the
world affords more such instances: at least everyone's acquaintance will furnish him with examples enough of such as pass
most of their nights without dreaming.

15.   *To think often and never to retain it so much as one moment
is a very useless sort of thinking*; and the soul in such a state of
thinking does very little if at all excel that of a looking-glass,
which constantly receives variety of images or *ideas* but retains
none: they disappear and vanish and there remain no footsteps
of them; the looking-glass is never the better for such *ideas*, nor
the soul for such thoughts. Perhaps it will be said that in a
waking man the materials of the body are employed and made
use of in thinking, and that the memory of thoughts is retained
by the impressions that are made on the brain, and the traces
there left after such thinking; but that in the *thinking of the soul*,
which is not perceived *in a sleeping man*, there the soul thinks
apart, and *making no use* of the organs of *the body, leaves no
impressions on it, and consequently no memory* of such thoughts.
Not to mention again the absurdity of two distinct persons
which follows from this supposition, I answer further that
whatever *ideas* the mind can receive and contemplate without
the help of the body, it is reasonable to conclude it can retain
without the help of the body too, or else the soul or any separate
spirit will have but little advantage by thinking. If it has no
memory of its own thoughts; if it cannot lay up them for its
own use and be able to recall them upon occasion; if it cannot
reflect upon what is past and make use of its former experiences,
reasonings, and contemplations, to what purpose does it think?
They, who make the soul a thinking thing, at this rate will not
make it a much more noble being than those do whom they condemn for allowing it to be nothing but the subtlest parts of

matter. Characters drawn on dust that the first breath of wind effaces, or impressions made on a heap of atoms or animal spirits are altogether as useful and render the subject as noble as the thoughts of a soul that perish in thinking, that once out of sight are gone for ever and leave no memory of themselves behind them. Nature never makes excellent things for mean or no uses; and it is hardly to be conceived that our infinitely wise Creator should make so admirable a faculty as the power of thinking, that faculty which comes nearest the excellency of his own incomprehensible being, to be so idly and uselessly employed, at least one-fourth part of its time here, as to think constantly without remembering any of those thoughts, without doing any good to itself or others or being any way useful to any other part of the creation. If we will examine it, we shall not find, I suppose, the motion of dull and senseless matter anywhere in the universe made so little use of and so wholly thrown away.
16. It is true, we have sometimes instances of perception whilst we are *asleep*, and retain the memory of those *thoughts*: but how *extravagant* and incoherent for the most part they are, how little conformable to the perfection and order of a rational being, those who are acquainted with dreams need not be told. This I would willingly be satisfied in: whether the soul, when it thinks thus apart and as it were separate from the body, acts less rationally than when conjointly with it, or no. If its separate thoughts be less rational, then these men must say that the soul owes the perfection of rational thinking to the body; if it does not, it is a wonder that our dreams should be, for the most part, so frivolous and irrational, and that the soul should retain none of its more rational soliloquies and meditations.
17. Those who so confidently tell us that the soul always actually thinks, I would they would also tell us what those *ideas* are that are in the soul of a child before or just at the union with the body, before it hath received any by *sensation*. The *dreams* of sleeping men *are*, as I take it, all *made up of the waking man's* ideas, though for the most part oddly put together. It is strange, if the soul has *ideas* of its own that it derived not from *sensation* or *reflection* (as it must have, if it thought before it received any impressions from the body), that it should never in its private thinking (so private that the man himself perceives it not) retain any of them the very moment it wakes out of them and then make the man glad with new discoveries. Who can find it

reasonable that the soul should, in its retirement during sleep, have so many hours' thoughts and yet never light on any of those *ideas* it borrowed not from *sensation* or *reflection*; or at least preserve the memory of none but such, which being occasioned from the body, must needs be less natural to a spirit? It is strange the soul should never once in a man's whole life recall over any of its pure, native thoughts and those *ideas* it had before it borrowed anything from the body, never bring into the waking man's view any other *ideas* but what have a tang of the cask and manifestly derive their original from that union. If it always thinks and so had *ideas* before it was united or before it received any from the body, it is not to be supposed but that during sleep it recollects its native *ideas*; and during that retirement from communicating with the body, whilst it thinks by itself, the *ideas* it is busied about should be, sometimes at least, those more natural and congenial ones which it had in itself, underived from the body or its own operations about them: which since the waking man never remembers, we must from this hypothesis conclude either that the soul remembers something that the man does not, or else that memory belongs only to such *ideas* as are derived from the body or the mind's operations about them.

18.   I would be glad also to learn from these men who so confidently pronounce that the human soul or, which is all one, that a man always thinks, how they come to know it; nay, *how they come to know that they themselves think, when they themselves do not perceive it*. This, I am afraid, is to be sure without proofs, and to know without perceiving; it is, I suspect, a confused notion, taken up to serve an hypothesis, and none of those clear truths that either their own evidence forces us to admit or common experience makes it impudence to deny. For the most that can be said of it is that it is possible the soul may always think, but not always retain it in memory. And I say, it is as possible that the soul may not always think, and much more probable that it should sometimes not think, than that it should often think, and that a long while together, and not be conscious to itself, the next moment after, that it had thought.

19.   To suppose the soul to think, and the man not to perceive it is, as has been said, to make two persons in one man. And if one considers well these men's way of speaking, one should be led into a suspicion that they do so. For they who tell us that the soul always thinks do never, that I remember, say that a

man always thinks. Can the soul think and not the man? Or a
man think and not be conscious of it? This perhaps would be
suspected of *jargon* in others. If they say the man thinks always
but is not always conscious of it, they may as well say his body is
extended without having parts. For it is altogether as intelligible
to say that a body is extended without parts, as that anything
thinks without being conscious of it or perceiving that it does so.
They who talk thus may, with as much reason, if it be necessary
to their hypothesis, say that a man is always hungry but that he
does not always feel it; whereas hunger consists in that very
sensation, as thinking consists in being conscious that one thinks.
If they say that a man is always conscious to himself of thinking,
I ask how they know it? Consciousness is the perception of
what passes in a man's own mind. Can another man perceive
that I am conscious of anything when I perceive it not myself?
No man's knowledge here can go beyond his experience. Wake
a man out of a sound sleep, and ask him what he was that
moment thinking on. If he himself be conscious of nothing he
then thought on, he must be a notable diviner of thoughts that
can assure him that he was thinking. May he not, with more
reason, assure him he was not asleep? This is something beyond
philosophy, and it cannot be less than revelation that discovers to
another thoughts in my mind, when I can find none there
myself. And they must needs have a penetrating sight who can
certainly see that I think when I cannot perceive it myself and
when I declare that I do not, and yet can see that dogs or
elephants do not think, when they give all the demonstration of
it imaginable, except only telling us that they do so. This some
may suspect to be a step beyond the *Rosicrucians*: it seeming
easier to make one's self invisible to others than to make
another's thoughts visible to me, which are not visible to himself. But it is but defining the soul to be a substance that always
thinks, and the business is done. If such definition be of any
authority, I know not what it can serve for but to make many
men suspect that they have no souls at all, since they find a good
part of their lives pass away without thinking. For no definitions that I know, no suppositions of any sect, are of force
enough to destroy constant experience; and perhaps, it is the
affectation of knowing beyond what we perceive that makes so
much useless dispute and noise in the world.

20.   I see no reason therefore to believe that the *soul thinks*

before the senses have furnished it with ideas to think on; and as those are increased and retained, so it comes by exercise to improve its faculty of thinking in the several parts of it; as well as, afterwards, by compounding those *ideas* and reflecting on its own operations, it increases its stock as well as facility in remembering, imagining, reasoning, and other modes of thinking.

21. He that will suffer himself to be informed by observation and experience, and not make his own hypothesis the rule of nature, will find few signs of a soul accustomed to much thinking in a new-born child and much fewer of any reasoning at all. And yet it is hard to imagine that the rational soul should think so much and not reason at all. And he that will consider that infants newly come into the world spend the greatest part of their time in sleep and are seldom awake but when either hunger calls for the teat or some pain (the most importunate of all sensations) or some other violent impression on the body forces the mind to perceive and attend to it. He, I say, who considers this will perhaps find reason to imagine that a *foetus in the mother's womb differs not much from the state of a vegetable*, but passes the greatest part of its time without perception or thought, doing very little but sleep in a place where it needs not seek for food, and is surrounded with liquor, always equally soft, and near of the same temper, where the eyes have no light and the ears, so shut up, are not very susceptible of sounds, and where there is little or no variety or change of objects to move the senses.

22. Follow a *child* from its birth and observe the alterations that time makes, and you shall find, as the mind by the senses comes more and more to be furnished with *ideas*, it comes to be more and more awake; thinks more, the more it has matter to think on. After some time it begins to know the objects which, being most familiar with it, have made lasting impressions. Thus it comes by degrees to know the persons it daily converses with, and distinguish them from strangers; which are instances and effects of its coming to retain and distinguish the *ideas* the senses convey to it. And so we may observe how the mind, *by degrees*, improves in these, and *advances* to the exercise of those other faculties of *enlarging*, *compounding*, and *abstracting* its *ideas*, and of reasoning about them, and reflecting upon all these, of which I shall have occasion to speak more hereafter.

23. If it shall be demanded then *when a man begins to have any*

ideas, I think the true answer is, when he first has any *sensation.* For, since there appear not to be any *ideas* in the mind before the senses have conveyed any in, I conceive that *ideas* in the understanding are coeval with *sensation;* which is such an impression or motion made in some part of the body, as produces some perception in the understanding. It is about these impressions made on our senses by outward objects that the mind seems first to employ itself in such operations as we call *perception, remembering, consideration, reasoning,* etc.

24. In time, the mind comes to reflect on its own *operations* about the *ideas* got by *sensation* and thereby stores itself with a new set of *ideas,* which I call *ideas* of *reflection.* These are the *impressions* that are made on our *senses* by outward objects that are extrinsical to the mind; and *its own operations,* proceeding from powers intrinsical and proper to itself, which when reflected on by itself become also objects of its contemplation, are, as I have said, *the original of all knowledge.* Thus the first capacity of human intellect is that the mind is fitted to receive the impressions made on it either through the *senses* by outward objects, or by its own operations when it *reflects* on them. This is the first step a man makes towards the discovery of anything and the ground-work whereon to build all those notions which ever he shall have naturally in this world. All those sublime thoughts, which tower above the clouds and reach as high as heaven itself, take their rise and footing here: in all that great extent wherein the mind wanders, in those remote speculations it may seem to be elevated with, it stirs not one jot beyond those *ideas* which *sense* or *reflection* have offered for its contemplation.

25. In this part the *understanding* is merely *passive*; and whether or no it will have these beginnings and, as it were, materials of knowledge, is not in its own power. For the objects of our senses do, many of them, obtrude their particular *ideas* upon our minds whether we will or no; and the operations of our minds will not let us be without, at least, some obscure notions of them. No man can be wholly ignorant of what he does when he thinks. These *simple ideas,* when offered to the mind, *the understanding can* no more refuse to have, nor alter when they are imprinted, nor blot them out and make new ones itself, than a mirror can refuse, alter, or obliterate the images or *ideas* which the objects set before it do therein produce. As the bodies that surround us do diversely affect our

organs, the mind is forced to receive the impressions; and cannot avoid the perception of those *ideas* that are annexed to them.

CHAPTER II

OF SIMPLE IDEAS

1.   THE better to understand the nature, manner, and extent of our knowledge, one thing is carefully to be observed concerning the *ideas* we have, and that is that *some* of them are *simple* and *some complex*.

Though the qualities that affect our senses are, in the things themselves, so united and blended that there is no separation, no distance between them, yet it is plain the *ideas* they produce in the mind enter by the senses simple and unmixed.   For, though the sight and touch often take in from the same object, at the same time, different *ideas*, as a man sees at once motion and colour, the hand feels softness and warmth in the same piece of wax: yet the simple *ideas* thus united in the same subject are as perfectly distinct as those that come in by different senses. The coldness and hardness which a man feels in a piece of *ice* being as distinct *ideas* in the mind as the smell and whiteness of a lily, or as the taste of sugar, and smell of a rose; and there is nothing can be plainer to a man than the clear and distinct perception he has of those simple *ideas*; which, being each in itself uncompounded, contains in it nothing but *one uniform appearance* or conception in the mind, and is not distinguishable into different *ideas*.

2.   These simple *ideas*, the materials of all our knowledge, are suggested and furnished to the mind only by those two ways above mentioned, viz. *sensation* and *reflection*. When the understanding is once stored with these simple *ideas*, it has the power to repeat, compare, and unite them, even to an almost infinite variety, and so can make at pleasure new complex *ideas*.   But it is not in the power of the most exalted wit or enlarged understanding, by any quickness or variety of thought, to *invent or frame one new simple* idea in the mind, not taken in by the ways before mentioned; nor can any force of the understanding

destroy those that are there, the dominion of man in this little world of his own understanding being much what the same as it is in the great world of visible things; wherein his power, however managed by art and skill, reaches no further than to compound and divide the materials that are made to his hand, but can do nothing towards the making the least particle of new matter, or destroying one atom of what is already in being. The same inability will everyone find in himself, who shall go about to fashion in his understanding any simple *idea*, not received in by his senses from external objects, or by reflection from the operations of his own mind about them. I would have anyone try to fancy any taste which had never affected his palate, or frame the *idea* of a scent he had never smelt; and when he can do this, I will also conclude that a blind man hath *ideas* of colours and a deaf man true distinct notions of sounds.

3. This is the reason why, though we cannot believe it impossible to God to make a creature with other organs and more ways to convey into the understanding the notice of corporeal things than those five, as they are usually counted, which he has given to man: yet I think it is *not possible* for anyone *to imagine* any other *qualities* in bodies, howsoever constituted, whereby they can be taken notice of besides sounds, tastes, smells, visible and tangible qualities. And had mankind been made with but four senses, the qualities then which are the object of the fifth sense had been as far from our notice, imagination, and conception as now any *belonging to a sixth, seventh, or eighth sense* can possibly be; which, whether yet some other creatures in some other parts of this vast and stupendous universe may not have, will be a great presumption to deny. He that will not set himself proudly at the top of all things, but will consider the immensity of this fabric and the great variety that is to be found in this little and inconsiderable part of it which he has to do with, may be apt to think that in other mansions of it there may be other and different intelligent beings of whose faculties he has as little knowledge or apprehension as a worm shut up in one drawer of a cabinet hath of the senses or understanding of a man, such variety and excellency being suitable to the wisdom and power of the Maker. I have here followed the common opinion of man's having but five senses, though perhaps there may be justly counted more; but either supposition serves equally to my present purpose.

Chapter III

OF IDEAS OF ONE SENSE

1.   The better to conceive the *ideas* we receive from sensation, it may not be amiss for us to consider them in reference to the different ways whereby they make their approaches to our minds and make themselves perceivable by us.

First, then, There are some which come into our minds *by one sense* only.

Secondly, There are others that convey themselves into the mind *by more senses than one*.

Thirdly, Others that are had from *reflection* only.

Fourthly, There are some that make themselves way and are suggested to the mind *by all the ways of sensation and reflection*.

We shall consider them apart under these several heads.

First, There are *some* ideas *which have admittance only through one sense*, which is peculiarly adapted to receive them. Thus light and colours, as white, red, yellow, blue, with their several degrees or shades and mixtures, as green, scarlet, purple, sea-green, and the rest, come in only by the eyes. All kinds of noises, sounds, and tones, only by the ears. The several tastes and smells, by the nose and palate. And if these organs or the nerves which are the conduits to convey them from without to their audience in the brain, the mind's presence-room (as I may so call it), are any of them so disordered as not to perform their functions, they have no postern to be admitted by, no other way to bring themselves into view and be perceived by the understanding.

The most considerable of those belonging to the touch are heat and cold, and solidity; all the rest—consisting almost wholly in the sensible configuration, as smooth and rough; or else, more or less firm adhesion of the parts, as hard and soft, tough and brittle—are obvious enough.

2.   I think it will be needless to enumerate all the particular *simple ideas* belonging to each sense. Nor indeed is it possible if we would, there being a great many *more* of them belonging to

most of the senses *than we have names for*. The variety of smells, which are as many almost, if not more, than species of bodies in the world, do most of them want names. *Sweet* and *stinking* commonly serve our turn for these *ideas*, which in effect is little more than to call them pleasing or displeasing; though the smell of a rose and violet, both sweet, are certainly very distinct *ideas*. Nor are the different tastes, that by our palates we receive *ideas* of, much better provided with names. Sweet, bitter, sour, harsh, and salt are almost all the epithets we have to denominate that numberless variety of relishes which are to be found distinct, not only in almost every sort of creatures, but in the different parts of the same plant, fruit, or animal. The same may be said of colours and sounds. I shall, therefore, in the account of simple *ideas* I am here giving, content myself to set down only such as are most material to our present purpose, or are in themselves less apt to be taken notice of, though they are very frequently the ingredients of our complex *ideas*; amongst which, I think, I may well account solidity, which therefore I shall treat of in the next chapter.

CHAPTER IV

OF SOLIDITY

1. THE *idea* of *solidity* we receive by our touch; and it arises from the resistance which we find in body to the entrance of any other body into the place it possesses, till it has left it. There is no *idea* which we receive more constantly from sensation than *solidity*. Whether we move or rest, in what posture soever we are, we always feel something under us that supports us and hinders our further sinking downwards; and the bodies which we daily handle make us perceive that, whilst they remain between them, they do, by an insurmountable force, hinder the approach of the parts of our hands that press them. That which thus hinders the approach of two bodies, when they are moving one towards another, I call *solidity*. I will not dispute whether this acceptation of the word *solid* be nearer to its original signification than that which mathematicians use it in: it

suffices that I think the common notion of solidity will allow, if not justify this use of it; but if anyone think it better to call it *impenetrability*, he has my consent. Only I have thought the term *solidity* the more proper to express this *idea*, not only because of its vulgar use in that sense, but also because it carries something more of positive in it than *impenetrability*; which is negative, and is perhaps more a consequence of *solidity*, than *solidity* itself. This, of all others, seems the *idea* most intimately connected with and essential to body, so as nowhere else to be found or imagined, but only in matter. And though our senses take no notice of it, but in masses of matter, of a bulk sufficient to cause a sensation in us: yet the mind, having once got this *idea* from such grosser sensible bodies, traces it further and considers it, as well as figure, in the minutest particle of matter that can exist, and finds it inseparably inherent in body, wherever or however modified.

2. This is the *idea* which belongs to body, whereby we conceive it *to fill space*. The *idea* of which filling of space is that, where we imagine any space taken up by a solid substance, we conceive it so to possess it that it excludes all other solid substances, and will for ever hinder any two other bodies, that move towards one another in a straight line, from coming to touch one another, unless it removes from between them in a line not parallel to that which they move in. This *idea* of it, the bodies which we ordinarily handle sufficiently furnish us with.

3. This resistance, whereby it keeps other bodies out of the space which it possesses, is so great that no force, how great soever, can surmount it. All the bodies in the world, pressing a drop of water on all sides, will never be able to overcome the resistance which it will make, as soft as it is, to their approaching one another, till it be removed out of their way: whereby our *idea* of *solidity* is *distinguished* both *from pure space*, which is capable neither of resistance nor motion, and from the ordinary *idea* of *hardness*. For a man may conceive two bodies at a distance so as they may approach one another without touching or displacing any solid thing till their superficies come to meet; whereby, I think, we have the clear *idea* of space without *solidity*. For (not to go so far as annihilation of any particular body) I ask whether a man cannot have the *idea* of the motion of one single body alone, without any other succeeding immediately into its place? I think it is evident he can: the *idea* of motion in

one body no more including the *idea* of motion in another, than the *idea* of a square figure in one body includes the *idea* of a square figure in another. I do not ask whether bodies do so exist that the motion of one body cannot really be without the motion of another. To determine this either way is to beg the question for or against a *vacuum*. But my question is whether one cannot have the *idea* of one body moved, whilst others are at rest. And I think this no one will deny. If so, then the place it deserted gives us the *idea* of pure space without solidity, whereinto another body may enter without either resistance or protrusion of anything. When the sucker in a pump is drawn, the space it filled in the tube is certainly the same, whether another body follows the motion of the sucker or no; nor does it imply a contradiction that, upon the motion of one body, another that is only contiguous to it should not follow it. The necessity of such a motion is built only on the supposition that the world is full; but not on the distinct *ideas* of space and solidity, which are as different as resistance and not resistance, protrusion and not protrusion. And that men have *ideas* of space without body, their very disputes about a *vacuum* plainly demonstrate, as is shown in another place.

4. *Solidity* is hereby also *differenced from hardness*, in that solidity consists in repletion, and so an utter exclusion of other bodies out of the space it possesses: but hardness, in a firm cohesion of the parts of matter making up masses of a sensible bulk, so that the whole does not easily change its figure. And indeed, hard and soft are names that we give to things only in relation to the constitutions of our own bodies: that being generally called hard by us which will put us to pain sooner than change figure by the pressure of any part of our bodies; and that, on the contrary, soft, which changes the situation of its parts upon an easy and unpainful touch.

But this difficulty of changing the situation of the sensible parts amongst themselves, or of the figure of the whole, gives no more solidity to the hardest body in the world than to the softest; nor is an adamant one jot more solid than water. For, though the two flat sides of two pieces of marble will more easily approach each other, between which there is nothing but water or air, than if there be a diamond between them: yet it is not that the parts of the diamond are more solid than those of water or resist more, but because, the parts of water being more easily separable from each other, they will, by a side motion, be more easily removed and give way to the approach of the two pieces of marble. But if they could be kept from making place by that side motion, they would eternally hinder the approach of these two pieces of marble, as much as the diamond; and it would be as impossible by any force to surmount their resistance, as to surmount the resistance of the parts of a diamond. The softest body in the world will as invincibly resist the coming together of any two other bodies, if it be not put out of the way but remain between them, as the hardest that can be found or imagined. He that shall fill a yielding soft body well with air or water will quickly find its resistance. And he that thinks that nothing but bodies that are hard can keep his hands from approaching one another, may be pleased to make a trial with the air enclosed in a football. The experiment I have been told was made at *Florence* with a hollow globe of gold, filled with water and exactly closed, further shows the solidity of so soft a body as water. For the golden globe thus filled being put into a press, which was driven by the extreme force of screws, the water made itself way through the pores of that very close metal and, finding no room for a nearer approach of its particles within, got to the outside where it rose like a dew and so fell in drops before the sides of the globe could be made to yield to the violent compression of the engine that squeezed it.

5. By this *idea* of solidity is the extension of body distinguished from the extension of space: the extension of body being nothing but the cohesion or continuity of solid, separable, moveable parts; and the extension of space, the continuity of unsolid, inseparable, and immoveable parts. *Upon the solidity of bodies* also *depend their mutual impulse, resistance, and protrusion.* Of pure space then and solidity, there are several (amongst which I confess myself one) who persuade themselves they have clear and distinct *ideas*, and that they can think on space without anything in it that resists or is protruded by body. This is the *idea* of pure space which they think they have as clear as any *idea* they can have of the extension of body: the *idea* of the distance between the opposite parts of a concave superficies being equally as clear without, as with the *idea* of any solid parts between; and on the other side they persuade themselves that they have, distinct from that of pure space, the *idea* of

something that fills space, that can be protruded by the impulse of other bodies or resist their motion. If there be others that have not these two *ideas* distinct, but confound them and make but one of them, I know not how men who have the same *idea* under different names, or different *ideas* under the same name, can in that case talk with one another: any more than a man who, not being blind or deaf, has distinct *ideas* of the colour of scarlet and the sound of a trumpet, could discourse concerning scarlet-colour with the blind man I mention in another place, who fancied that the *idea* of scarlet was like the sound of a trumpet.

6. If anyone asks me *what this solidity is*, I send him to his senses to inform him. Let him put a flint or a football between his hands and then endeavour to join them, and he will know. If he thinks this not a sufficient explication of solidity, what it is and wherein it consists, I promise to tell him what it is and wherein it consists when he tells me what thinking is or wherein it consists, or explains to me what extension or motion is, which perhaps seems much easier. The simple *ideas* we have are such as experience teaches them us; but if, beyond that, we endeavour by words to make them clearer in the mind, we shall succeed no better than if we went about to clear up the darkness of a blind man's mind by talking, and to discourse into him the *ideas* of light and colours. The reason of this I shall show in another place.

Chapter V

OF SIMPLE IDEAS OF DIVERS SENSES

THE *ideas* we get by more than one sense are of *space* or *extension, figure, rest*, and *motion*. For these make perceivable impressions, both on the eyes and touch; and we can receive and convey into our minds the *ideas* of the extension, figure, motion, and rest of bodies, both by seeing and feeling. But having occasion to speak more at large of these in another place, I here only enumerate them.

CHAPTER VI

OF SIMPLE IDEAS OF REFLECTION

1.   THE mind, receiving the *ideas* mentioned in the foregoing chapters from without, when it turns its view inward upon itself and observes its own actions about those *ideas* it has, takes from thence other *ideas*, which are as capable to be the objects of its contemplation as any of those it received from foreign things.

2.   The two great and principal actions of the mind, which are most frequently considered, and which are so frequent that everyone that pleases may take notice of them in himself, are these two:

Perception, or *Thinking*; and
Volition, or *Willing*.

The power of thinking is called the *understanding* and the power of volition is called the *will*, and these two powers or abilities in the mind are denominated *faculties*.   Of some of the modes of these simple *ideas* of reflection, such as are *remembrance, discerning, reasoning, judging, knowledge, faith*, etc., I shall have occasion to speak hereafter.

CHAPTER VII

OF SIMPLE IDEAS OF BOTH SENSATION AND REFLECTION

1.   THERE be other simple *ideas* which convey themselves into the mind by all the ways of sensation and reflection, viz:

Pleasure or *Delight*, and its opposite.
Pain, or *Uneasiness*.
Power.
Existence.
Unity.

2.   *Delight* or *uneasiness*, one or other of them, join themselves to almost all our *ideas* both of sensation and reflection: and there is scarce any affection of our senses from without, any retired thought of our mind within, which is not able to produce in us *pleasure* or *pain*. By *pleasure* and *pain* I would be understood to signify whatsoever delights or molests us, whether it arises from the thoughts of our minds, or anything operating on our bodies. For, whether we call it satisfaction, delight, pleasure, happiness, etc., on the one side, or uneasiness, trouble, pain, torment, anguish, misery, etc., on the other, they are still but different degrees of the same thing, and belong to the *ideas* of *pleasure* and *pain*, delight or uneasiness; which are the names I shall most commonly use for those two sorts of *ideas*.

3.   The infinite wise Author of our being, having given us the power over several parts of our bodies to move or keep them at rest as we think fit; and also, by the motion of them, to move ourselves and other contiguous bodies, in which consists all the actions of our body; having also given a power to our minds, in several instances, to choose, amongst its *ideas*, which it will think on, and to pursue the inquiry of this or that subject with consideration and attention: to excite us to these actions of thinking and motion that we are capable of, has been pleased to join to several thoughts and several sensations a *perception* of *delight*. If this were wholly separated from all our outward sensations and inward thoughts, we should have no reason to prefer one thought or action to another, negligence to attention, or motion to rest. And so we should neither stir our bodies, nor employ our minds, but let our thoughts (if I may so call it) run adrift, without any direction or design, and suffer the *ideas* of our minds, like unregarded shadows, to make their appearances there, as it happened, without attending to them. In which state man, however furnished with the faculties of understanding and will, would be a very idle, inactive creature, and pass his time only in a lazy, lethargic dream. It has therefore pleased our wise Creator to annex to several objects and to the *ideas* which we receive from them, as also to several of our thoughts, a concomitant pleasure, and that in several objects, to several degrees: that those faculties which he had endowed us with might not remain wholly idle and unemployed by us.

4.   *Pain* has the same efficacy and use to set us on work that pleasure has, we being as ready to employ our faculties to avoid

that as to pursue this; only this is worth our consideration: that *pain is often produced by the same objects and* ideas *that produce pleasure* in us. This their near conjunction, which makes us often feel pain in the sensations where we expected pleasure, gives us new occasion of admiring the wisdom and goodness of our Maker, who, designing the preservation of our being, has annexed pain to the application of many things to our bodies, to warn us of the harm that they will do, and as advices to withdraw from them. But he, not designing our preservation barely, but the preservation of every part and organ in its perfection, hath in many cases annexed pain to those very *ideas* which delight us. Thus heat, that is very agreeable to us in one degree, by a little greater increase of it proves no ordinary torment; and the most pleasant of all sensible objects, light itself, if there be too much of it, if increased beyond a due proportion to our eyes, causes a very painful sensation. Which is wisely and favourably so ordered by nature that, when any object does by the vehemency of its operation disorder the instruments of sensation, whose structures cannot but be very nice and delicate, we might, by the pain, be warned to withdraw, before the organ be quite put out of order, and so be unfitted for its proper functions for the future. The consideration of those objects that produce it may well persuade us that this is the end or use of pain. For though great light be insufferable to our eyes, yet the highest degree of darkness does not at all disease them; because that, causing no disorderly motion in it, leaves that curious organ unharmed in its natural state. But yet excess of cold as well as heat pains us: because it is equally destructive to that temper which is necessary to the preservation of life and the exercise of the several functions of the body, and which consists in a moderate degree of warmth or, if you please, a motion of the insensible parts of our bodies confined within certain bounds.

5.   Beyond all this, we may find another reason *why* God hath scattered up and down *several degrees of pleasure and pain in all the things that environ and affect us* and blended them together in almost all that our thoughts and senses have to do with, that we, finding imperfection, dissatisfaction, and want of complete happiness in all the enjoyments which the creatures can afford us, might be led to seek it in the enjoyment of Him, *with whom there is fullness of joy and at whose right hand are pleasures for evermore.*

6. Though what I have here said may not, perhaps, make the *ideas of pleasure and pain* clearer to us than our own experience does, which is the only way that we are capable of having them: yet the consideration of the reason why they are annexed to so many other *ideas*, serving to give us due sentiments of the wisdom and goodness of the Sovereign Disposer of all things, may not be unsuitable to the main end of these inquiries: the knowledge and veneration of Him being the chief end of all our thoughts, and the proper business of all understandings.

7. *Existence* and *unity* are two other *ideas* that are suggested to the understanding by every object without, and every *idea* within. When *ideas* are in our minds, we consider them as being actually there, as well as we consider things to be actually without us; which is, that they exist or have *existence*. And whatever we can consider as one thing, whether a real being or *idea*, suggests to the understanding the *idea* of *unity*.

8. *Power* also is another of those simple *ideas* which we receive from *sensation and reflection*. For, observing in ourselves that we can at pleasure move several parts of our bodies which were at rest; the effects, also, that natural bodies are able to produce in one another occurring every moment to our senses, we both these ways get the *idea* of *power*.

9. Besides these there is another *idea*, which, though suggested by our senses, yet is more constantly offered us by what passes in our own minds, and that is the *idea* of *succession*. For if we look immediately into ourselves, and reflect on what is observable there, we shall find our *ideas* always, whilst we are awake or have any thought, passing in train, one going and another coming, without intermission.

10. These, if they are not all, are at least (as I think) the most considerable of those *simple ideas* which the mind has, and out of which is made all its other knowledge, all which it receives only by the two forementioned ways of *sensation* and *reflection*.

Nor let anyone think these too narrow bounds for the capacious mind of man to expatiate in, which takes its flight further than the stars and cannot be confined by the limits of the world, that extends its thoughts often even beyond the utmost expansion of matter, and makes excursions into that incomprehensible *inane*. I grant all this, but desire anyone to assign any *simple idea* which is not *received from* one of *those inlets* before mentioned, or any *complex idea* not *made out of those simple ones.* Nor will it be so strange to think these few simple *ideas* sufficient to employ the quickest thought or largest capacity, and to furnish the materials of all that various knowledge and more various fancies and opinions of all mankind, if we consider how many words may be made out of the various composition of twenty-four letters; or if, going one step further, we will but reflect on the variety of combinations that may be made with barely one of the above-mentioned *ideas*, viz. number, whose stock is inexhaustible and truly infinite; and what a large and immense field doth extension alone afford the mathematicians!

CHAPTER VIII

SOME FURTHER CONSIDERATIONS CONCERNING OUR SIMPLE IDEAS

1. CONCERNING the simple *ideas* of sensation, it is to be considered that whatsoever is so constituted in nature as to be able, by affecting our senses, to cause any perception in the mind, doth thereby produce in the understanding a simple *idea*; which, whatever be the external cause of it, when it comes to be taken notice of by our discerning faculty, it is by the mind looked on and considered there to be a real *positive idea* in the understanding, as much as any other whatsoever, though perhaps the cause of it be but a privation of the subject.

2. Thus the *ideas* of heat and cold, light and darkness, white and black, motion and rest, are equally clear and *positive ideas* in the mind, though perhaps some of *the causes* which produce them are barely *privations* in those subjects from whence our senses derive those *ideas*. These the understanding, in its view of them, considers all as distinct positive *ideas*, without taking notice of the causes that produce them: which is an inquiry not belonging to the *idea*, as it is in the understanding, but to the nature of the things existing without us. These are two very different things, and carefully to be distinguished: it being one thing to perceive and know the *idea* of white or black, and quite another to examine what kind of particles they must be and how ranged in the superficies, to make any object appear white or black.

3. A painter or dyer who never inquired into their causes hath the *ideas* of white and black, and other colours, as clearly, perfectly, and distinctly in his understanding, and perhaps more distinctly, than the philosopher who hath busied himself in considering their natures and thinks he knows how far either of them is, in its cause, positive or privative; and the *idea of black* is no less *positive* in his mind than that of white, *however the cause* of that colour in the external object may *be only a privation*.

4. If it were the design of my present undertaking to inquire into the natural causes and manner of perception, I should offer this as a reason *why a privative cause might*, in some cases at least, *produce a positive idea*, viz. that all sensation being produced in us only by different degrees and modes of motion in our animal spirits, variously agitated by external objects, the abatement of any former motion must as necessarily produce a new sensation as the variation or increase of it, and so introduce a new *idea*, which depends only on a different motion of the animal spirits in that organ.

5. But whether this be so or no, I will not here determine but appeal to everyone's own experience whether the shadow of a man, though it consists of nothing but the absence of light (and the more the absence of light is, the more discernible is the shadow) does not, when a man looks on it, cause as clear and positive an *idea* in his mind as a man himself, though covered over with clear sunshine? And the picture of a shadow is a positive thing. Indeed, we have *negative names* which stand not directly for positive *ideas* but for their absence, such as *insipid, silence, nihil*, etc., which words denote positive *ideas*, v.g., *taste, sound, being* with a signification of their absence.

6. And thus one may truly be said to see darkness. For supposing a hole perfectly dark, from whence no light is reflected, it is certain one may see the figure of it, or it may be painted; or, whether the ink I write with makes any other *idea* is a question. The privative causes I have here assigned of positive *ideas* are according to the common opinion; but in truth it will be hard to determine whether there be really any *ideas* from a privative cause, till it be determined *whether rest be any more a privation than motion*.

7. To discover the nature of our *ideas* the better, and to discourse of them intelligibly, it will be convenient to distinguish them as they are *ideas* or perceptions in our minds, and as they

are modifications of matter in the bodies that cause such perceptions in us: that so we *may not* think (as perhaps usually is done) that they are exactly the images and *resemblances* of something inherent in the subject: most of those of sensation being in the mind no more the likeness of something existing without us, than the names that stand for them are the likeness of our *ideas*, which yet upon hearing they are apt to excite in us.

8. Whatsoever the mind perceives in itself, or is the immediate object of perception, thought, or understanding, that I call *idea*; and the power to produce any *idea* in our mind, I call *quality* of the subject wherein that power is. Thus a snowball having the power to produce in us the *ideas* of *white, cold,* and *round,* the power to produce those *ideas* in us as they are in the snowball I call *qualities*; and as they are sensations or perceptions in our understandings, I call them *ideas*; which *ideas,* if I speak of sometimes as in the things themselves, I would be understood to mean those qualities in the objects which produce them in us.

9. Qualities thus considered in bodies are:

First, such as are utterly inseparable from the body, in what state soever it be; such as in all the alterations and changes it suffers, all the force can be used upon it, it constantly keeps; and such as sense constantly finds in every particle of matter which has bulk enough to be perceived; and the mind finds inseparable from every particle of matter, though less than to make itself singly be perceived by our senses. V.g., take a grain of wheat, divide it into two parts, each part has still *solidity, extension, figure,* and *mobility*; divide it again, and it retains still the same qualities; and so divide it on, till the parts become insensible: they must retain still each of them all those qualities. For division (which is all that a mill or pestle or any other body does upon another in reducing it to insensible parts) can never take away either solidity, extension, figure, or mobility from any body, but only makes two or more distinct separate masses of matter, of that which was but one before; all which distinct masses, reckoned as so many distinct bodies, after division make a certain number. These I call *original* or *primary qualities* of body; which I think we may observe to produce simple *ideas* in us, viz. solidity, extension, figure, motion or rest, and number.

10. Secondly, such *qualities* which in truth are nothing in the objects themselves but powers to produce various sensations in us by their *primary qualities,* i.e. by the bulk, figure, texture,

and motion of their insensible parts, as colours, sounds, tastes, etc. These I call *secondary qualities*. To these might be added a third sort, which are allowed to be barely powers, though they are as much real qualities in the subject as those which I, to comply with the common way of speaking, call *qualities*, but for distinction, *secondary qualities*. For the power in fire to produce a new colour, or consistency in wax or clay, by its primary qualities, is as much a quality in fire as the power it has to produce in me a new *idea* or sensation of warmth or burning, which I felt not before, by the same primary qualities, viz. the bulk, texture, and motion of its insensible parts.

11. The next thing to be considered is how *bodies* produce *ideas* in us; and that is manifestly *by impulse*, the only way which we can conceive bodies operate in.

12. If then external objects be not united to our minds when they produce *ideas* in it and yet we perceive *these original qualities* in such of them as singly fall under our senses, it is evident that some motion must be thence continued by our nerves or animal spirits, by some parts of our bodies, to the brains or the seat of sensation, there to *produce in our minds the particular* ideas *we have of them*. And since the extension, figure, number, and motion of bodies of an observable bigness may be perceived at a distance *by* the sight, it is evident some singly imperceptible bodies must come from them to the eyes, and thereby convey to the brain some *motion*, which produces these *ideas* which we have of them in us.

13. After the same manner that the *ideas* of these original qualities are produced in us, we may conceive that the *ideas of secondary qualities* are also *produced*, viz. *by the operation of insensible particles on our senses*. For it being manifest that there are bodies and good store of bodies, each whereof are so small that we cannot by any of our senses discover either their bulk, figure, or motion, as is evident in the particles of the air and water and others extremely smaller than those, perhaps as much smaller than the particles of air or water as the particles of air or water are smaller than peas or hail-stones: let us suppose at present that the different motions and figures, bulk and number, of such particles, affecting the several organs of our senses, produce in us those different sensations which we have from the colours and smells of bodies: v.g. that a violet, by the impulse of such insensible particles of matter, of peculiar

figures and bulks, and in different degrees and modifications of
their motions, causes the *ideas* of the blue colour and sweet
scent of that flower to be produced in our minds. It being no
more impossible to conceive that God should annex such *ideas*
to such motions, with which they have no similitude, than that
he should annex the *idea* of pain to the motion of a piece of steel
dividing our flesh, with which that *idea* hath no resemblance.

14. What I have said concerning *colours* and *smells* may be
understood also of *tastes* and *sounds, and other the like sensible
qualities*; which, whatever reality we by mistake attribute to
them, are in truth nothing in the objects themselves but powers
to produce various sensations in us, and depend *on those primary
qualities*, viz. bulk, figure, texture, and motion of parts, as I
have said.

15. From whence I think it easy to draw this observation: that
the *ideas of primary qualities* of bodies *are resemblances* of them,
and their patterns do really exist in the bodies themselves; but
the *ideas produced* in us *by* these *secondary qualities have no resemblance* of them at all. There is nothing like our *ideas* existing
in the bodies themselves. They are, in the bodies we denominate
from them, only a power to produce those sensations in us; and
what is sweet, blue, or warm in *idea* is but the certain bulk,
figure, and motion of the insensible parts in the bodies themselves, which we call so.

16. *Flame* is denominated *hot* and *light*; *snow, white* and *cold*;
and *manna, white* and *sweet*, from the *ideas* they produce in us.
Which qualities are commonly thought to be the same in those
bodies that those *ideas* are in us, the one the perfect resemblance
of the other, as they are in a mirror, and it would by most men
be judged very extravagant if one should say otherwise. And
yet he that will consider that *the same fire* that at one distance
produces in us the sensation of *warmth* does, at a nearer approach,
produce in us the far different sensation of *pain*, ought to bethink
himself what reason he has to say that his *idea* of *warmth*,
which was produced in him by the fire, is actually *in the fire*; and
his *idea* of *pain*, which the same fire produced in him the same
way, is *not* in the *fire*. Why are whiteness and coldness in snow,
and pain not, when it produces the one and the other *idea* in us;
and can do neither, but by the bulk, figure, number, and motion
of its solid parts?

17. The particular *bulk, number, figure, and motion of the parts*

of fire or snow are really in them, whether anyone's senses perceive them or no; and therefore they may be called *real qualities,*
because they really exist in those bodies. But *light, heat, whiteness,* or *coldness are no more really in them than sickness or pain
is in* manna. Take away the sensation of them; let not the eyes
see light or colours, nor the ears hear sounds; let the palate not
taste, nor the nose smell; and all colours, tastes, odours, and
sounds, as they are such particular *ideas,* vanish and cease, and
are reduced to their causes, i.e. bulk, figure, and motion of parts.
18. A piece of *manna* of a sensible bulk is able to produce in us
the *idea* of a round or square figure; and by being removed from
one place to another, the *idea* of motion. This *idea* of motion
represents it as it really is in the *manna* moving; a circle or square
are the same, whether in *idea* or existence, in the mind or in the
manna; and this, both *motion and figure, are really in the
manna,* whether we take notice of them or no: this everybody is
ready to agree to. Besides, *manna,* by the bulk, figure, texture,
and motion of its parts, has a power to produce the sensations of
sickness, and sometimes of acute pains or gripings in us. That
these *ideas* of *sickness and pain are not in the* manna, but effects
of its operations on us, and are nowhere when we feel them not:
this also everyone readily agrees to. And yet men are hardly to
be brought to think that *sweetness and whiteness are not really in
manna,* which are but the effects of the operations of *manna,* by
the motion, size, and figure of its particles, on the eyes and
palate, as the pain and sickness caused by *manna* are confessedly
nothing but the effects of its operations on the stomach and guts,
by the size, motion, and figure of its insensible parts (for by
nothing else can a body operate, as has been proved): as if it could
not operate on the eyes and palate and thereby produce in the
mind particular distinct *ideas* which in itself it has not, as well as
we allow it can operate on the guts and stomach and thereby
produce distinct *ideas* which in itself it has not. These *ideas*
being all effects of the operations of *manna* on several parts of
our bodies by the size, figure, number, and motion of its parts,
why those produced by the eyes and palate should rather be
thought to be really in the *manna* than those produced by the
stomach and guts; or why the pain and sickness, *ideas* that are
the effects of *manna,* should be thought to be nowhere, when
they are not felt: and yet the sweetness and whiteness, effects of
the same *manna* on other parts of the body by ways equally as

unknown, should be thought to exist in the *manna*, when they
are not seen nor tasted, would need some reason to explain.

19. Let us consider the red and white colours in *porphyry*.
Hinder light but from striking on it, and its colours vanish: it no
longer produces any such *ideas* in us; upon the return of light
it produces these appearances on us again. Can anyone think
any real alterations are made in the *porphyry* by the presence
or absence of light; and that those *ideas* of whiteness and redness are really in *porphyry* in the light, when it is plain *it has no
colour in the dark*? It has, indeed, such a configuration of particles, both night and day, as are apt, by the rays of light re-
bounding from some parts of that hard stone, to produce in us
the *idea* of redness, and from others the *idea* of whiteness; but
whiteness or redness are not in it at any time, but such a texture
that hath the power to produce such a sensation in us.

20. Pound an almond, and the clear white *colour* will be altered
into a dirty one, and the sweet *taste* into an oily one. What
real alteration can the beating of the pestle make in any body,
but an alteration of the *texture* of it?

21. *Ideas* being thus distinguished and understood, we may be
able to give an account how the same water, at the same time,
may produce the *idea* of cold by one hand and of heat by the
other, whereas it is impossible that the same water, if those
ideas were really in it, should at the same time be both hot and
cold. For if we imagine *warmth* as it is *in our hands* to be
*nothing but a certain sort and degree of motion in the minute
particles of our nerves, or animal spirits*, we may understand how
it is possible that the same water may at the same time produce
the sensation of heat in one hand and cold in the other; which
yet figure never does, that never producing the *idea* of a square
by one hand which has produced the *idea* of a globe by another.
But if the sensation of heat and cold be nothing but the increase
or diminution of the motion of the minute parts of our bodies,
caused by the corpuscles of any other body, it is easy to be
understood that, if that motion be greater in one hand than in
the other, if a body be applied to the two hands, which has in its
minute particles a greater motion than in those of one of the
hands, and a less than in those of the other, it will increase the
motion of the one hand and lessen it in the other, and so cause
the different sensations of heat and cold that depend
thereon.

22. I have in what just goes before been engaged in physical inquiries a little further than perhaps I intended. But, it being necessary to make the nature of sensation a little understood; and to make the *difference between the qualities in bodies, and the* ideas *produced by them in the mind*, to be distinctly conceived, without which it were impossible to discourse intelligibly of them: I hope I shall be pardoned this little excursion into natural philosophy, it being necessary in our present inquiry to distinguish the *primary* and *real qualities* of bodies, which are always in them (viz. solidity, extension, figure, number, and motion or rest; and are sometimes perceived by us, viz. when the bodies they are in are big enough singly to be discerned), from those *secondary* and *imputed qualities*, which are but the powers of several combinations of those primary ones, when they operate without being distinctly discerned; whereby we also may come to know what *ideas* are, and what are not, resemblances of something really existing in the bodies we denominate from them.

23. The *qualities*, then, that are in *bodies*, rightly considered, are of *three sorts*:

First, The *bulk, figure, number, situation*, and *motion or rest* of their solid parts. Those are in them, whether we perceive them or no; and when they are of that size that we can discover them, we have by these an *idea* of the thing as it is in itself, as is plain in artificial things. These I call *primary qualities*.

Secondly, The *power* that is in any body, by reason of *its* insensible *primary qualities*, to operate after a peculiar manner on any of our senses, and thereby *produce in us* the *different ideas* of several colours, sounds, smells, tastes, etc. These are usually called sensible qualities.

Thirdly, The *power* that is in any body, *by* reason of the particular constitution of *its primary qualities, to* make such a *change* in the *bulk, figure, texture, and motion of another body*, as to make it operate on our senses differently from what it did before. Thus the sun has a power to make wax white, and fire to make lead fluid. These *are* usually called powers.

The first of these, as has been said, I think may be properly called *real, original*, or *primary qualities*, because they are in the things themselves, whether they are perceived or no; and upon their different modifications it is that the secondary qualities depend.

The other two are only powers to act differently upon other

things, which powers result from the different modifications of
those primary qualities.

24. But though *these two latter sorts of qualities are powers
barely*, and nothing but powers relating to several other bodies
and resulting from the different modifications of the original
qualities, yet they are generally otherwise thought of. For *the
second sort*, viz. the powers to produce several *ideas* in us by
our senses, *are looked upon as real qualities in the things* thus
affecting us; but *the third sort are called and esteemed barely
powers*, v.g. the *idea* of heat or light which we receive by our
eyes or touch from the sun are commonly thought *real qualities*
existing in the sun and something more than mere powers in it.
But when we consider the sun in reference to wax, which it
melts or blanches, we look upon the whiteness and softness produced in the wax not as qualities in the sun but effects produced
by *powers* in it: whereas, if rightly considered, these qualities of
light and warmth, which are perceptions in me when I am
warmed or enlightened by the sun, are no otherwise in the sun
than the changes, made in the wax when it is blanched or melted,
are in the sun. They are all of them equally powers in the sun,
depending on its primary qualities; whereby it is able in the one
case so to alter the bulk, figure, texture, or motion of some of the
insensible parts of my eyes or hands as thereby to produce in
me the *idea* of light or heat; and in the other, it is able so to
alter the bulk, figure, texture, or motion of the insensible parts
of the wax, as to make them fit to produce in me the distinct
ideas of white and fluid.

25. The reason *why the one are ordinarily taken for real
qualities and the other only for bare powers* seems to be because
the *ideas* we have of distinct colours, sounds, etc., containing
nothing at all in them of bulk, figure, or motion, we are apt to
think them the effects of these primary qualities which appear
not to our senses to operate in their production, and with which
they have not any apparent congruity or conceivable connexion.
Hence it is that we are so forward to imagine that those *ideas* are
the resemblances of something really existing in the objects
themselves, since sensation discovers nothing of bulk, figure, or
motion of parts in their production, nor can reason show how
bodies by their bulk, figure, and motion should produce in the
mind the *ideas* of blue or yellow, etc. But in the other case, in
the operations of bodies changing the qualities one of another,

we plainly discover that the quality produced hath commonly no resemblance with anything in the thing producing it; wherefore we look on it as a bare effect of power. For, though receiving the *idea* of heat or light from the sun, we are apt to think it is a perception and resemblance of such a quality in the sun: yet when we see wax or a fair face receive change of colour from the sun, we cannot imagine that to be the reception or resemblance of anything in the sun, because we find not those different colours in the sun itself. For, our senses being able to observe a likeness or unlikeness of sensible qualities in two different external objects, we forwardly enough conclude the production of any sensible quality in any subject to be an effect of bare power, and not the communication of any quality which was really in the efficient, when we find no such sensible quality in the thing that produced it. But our senses not being able to discover any unlikeness between the *idea* produced in us and the quality of the object producing it, we are apt to imagine that our *ideas* are resemblances of something in the objects, and not the effects of certain powers placed in the modification of their primary qualities, with which primary qualities the *ideas* produced in us have no resemblance.

26. To conclude, beside those before-mentioned *primary qualities* in bodies, viz. bulk, figure, extension, number, and motion of their solid parts: all the rest, whereby we take notice of bodies and distinguish them one from another, are nothing else but several powers in them, depending on those primary qualities; whereby they are fitted, either by immediately operating on our bodies to produce several different *ideas* in us, or else, by operating on other bodies, so to change their primary qualities as to render them capable of producing *ideas* in us different from what before they did. The former of these, I think, may be called *secondary qualities immediately perceivable*, the latter *secondary qualities, mediately perceivable*.

CHAPTER IX

OF PERCEPTION

1. PERCEPTION, as it is the first faculty of the mind exercised about our *ideas*, so it is the first and simplest *idea* we have from

reflection, and is by some called thinking in general. Though thinking, in the propriety of the *English* tongue, signifies that sort of operation in the mind about its *ideas*, wherein the mind is active, where it, with some degree of voluntary attention, considers anything. For in bare naked *perception*, the mind is, for the most part, only passive; and what it perceives, it cannot avoid perceiving.

2. *What perception is*, everyone will know better by reflecting on what he does himself, when he sees, hears, feels, etc., or thinks, than by any discourse of mine. Whoever reflects on what passes in his own mind cannot miss it. And if he does not reflect, all the words in the world cannot make him have any notion of it.

3. This is certain: that whatever alterations are made in the body, if they reach not the mind; whatever impressions are made on the outward parts, if they are not taken notice of within, there is no perception. Fire may burn our bodies with no other effect than it does a billet, unless the motion be continued to the brain, and there the sense of heat, or *idea* of pain, be produced in the mind; wherein consists *actual perception*.

4. How often may a man observe in himself that, whilst his mind is intently employed in the contemplation of some objects, and curiously surveying some *ideas* that are there, it takes no notice of impressions of sounding bodies made upon the organ of hearing, with the same alteration that used to be for the producing the idea of sound. A sufficient impulse there may be on the organ, but it not reaching the observation of the mind, there follows no perception; and though the motion that used to produce the *idea* of sound be made in the ear, yet no sound is heard. Want of sensation, in this case, is not through any defect in the organ, or that the man's ears are less affected than at other times when he does hear: but that which used to produce the *idea*, though conveyed in by the usual organ, not being taken notice of in the understanding, and so imprinting no *idea* in the mind, there follows no sensation. *So that wherever there is sense or perception, there some* idea *is actually produced, and present in the understanding.*

5. Therefore I doubt not but *children*, by the exercise of their senses about objects that affect them *in the womb, receive some few* ideas, before they are born, as the unavoidable effects either of the bodies that environ them or else of those wants or diseases

they suffer; amongst which (if one may conjecture concerning things not very capable of examination) I think the *ideas* of hunger and warmth are two: which probably are some of the first that children have and which they scarce ever part with again.

6. But though it be reasonable to imagine that *children* receive some *ideas* before they come into the world, yet these simple *ideas* are *far from* those *innate principles* which some contend for and we above have rejected. These here mentioned, being the effects of sensation, are only from some affections of the body which happen to them there, and so depend on something exterior to the mind, no otherwise differing in their manner of production from other *ideas* derived from sense but only in the precedency of time; whereas those innate principles are supposed to be quite of another nature, not coming into the mind by any accidental alterations in or operations on the body, but, as it were, original characters impressed upon it in the very first moment of its being and constitution.

7. As there are some *ideas* which we may reasonably suppose may be introduced into the minds of children in the womb, subservient to the necessities of their life and being there, so after they are born *those* ideas are the *earliest imprinted which happen to be the sensible qualities which first occur* to them; amongst which light is not the least considerable nor of the weakest efficacy. And how covetous the mind is to be furnished with all such *ideas* as have no pain accompanying them may be a little guessed by what is observable in children new-born, who always turn their eyes to that part from whence the light comes, lay them how you please. But the *ideas* that are most familiar at first, being various according to the divers circumstances of children's first entertainment in the world, the order wherein the several *ideas* come at first into the mind is very various and uncertain also; neither is it much material to know it.

8. We are further to consider concerning perception that the *ideas we receive by sensation are often* in grown people *altered by the judgment,* without our taking notice of it. When we set before our eyes a round globe of any uniform colour, v.g. gold, alabaster, or jet, it is certain that the *idea* thereby imprinted in our mind is of a flat circle, variously shadowed, with several degrees of light and brightness coming to our eyes. But we having, by use, been accustomed to perceive what kind of

appearance convex bodies are wont to make in us, what alterations are made in the reflections of light by the difference of the
sensible figures of bodies: the judgment presently, by an
habitual custom, alters the appearances into their causes. So
that from that which is truly variety of shadow or colour,
collecting the figure, it makes it pass for a mark of figure and
frames to itself the perception of a convex figure and an uniform
colour, when the *idea* we receive from thence is only a plane
variously coloured, as is evident in painting. To which purpose
I shall here insert a problem of that very ingenious and studious
promoter of real knowledge, the learned and worthy Mr.
Molyneux, which he was pleased to send me in a letter some
months since; and it is this: *Suppose a man born blind, and now
adult, and taught by his touch to distinguish between a cube and
a sphere of the same metal, and nighly of the same bigness, so as to
tell, when he felt one and the other, which is the cube, which the
sphere. Suppose then the cube and sphere placed on a table, and
the blind man to be made to see:* quaere, *whether by his sight, before
he touched them, he could now distinguish and tell which is the
globe, which the cube?* To which the acute and judicious pro-
poser answers: *Not. For, though he has obtained the experience
of how a globe, how a cube affects his touch, yet he has not yet
obtained the experience that what affects his touch so or so must
affect his sight so or so; or that a protuberant angle in the cube,
that pressed his hand unequally, shall appear to his eye as it does
in the cube.* I agree with this thinking gentleman, whom I am
proud to call my friend, in his answer to this problem; and am
of opinion that the blind man, at first sight, would not be able
with certainty to say which was the globe, which the cube,
whilst he only saw them, though he could unerringly name
them by his touch, and certainly distinguish them by the
difference of their figures felt. This I have set down and leave
with my reader as an occasion for him to consider how much
he may be beholding to experience, improvement, and acquired
notions, where he thinks he has not the least use of or help
from them; and the rather, because this observing *gentleman*
further adds that, *having upon the occasion of my book proposed
this to divers very ingenious men, he hardly ever met with one that
at first gave the answer to it which he thinks true, till by hearing
his reasons they were convinced.*

9.   But this is not, I think, usual in any of our *ideas,* but those

received by *sight*. Because sight, the most comprehensive of all our senses, conveying to our minds the *ideas* of light and colours, which are peculiar only to that sense; and also the far different *ideas* of space, figure, and motion, the several varieties whereof change the appearances of its proper object, viz. light and colours: we bring ourselves by use to judge of the one by the other. This, in many cases by a settled habit, in things whereof we have frequent experience, is performed so constantly and so quick, that we take that for the perception of our sensation which is an *idea* formed by our judgment; so that one, viz. that of sensation, serves only to excite the other, and is scarce taken notice of itself; as a man who reads or hears with attention and understanding, takes little notice of the characters or sounds, but of the *ideas* that are excited in him by them.

10. Nor need we wonder that this is done with so little notice, if we consider how very *quick* the *actions of the mind* are performed; for, as itself is thought to take up no space, to have no extension, so its actions seem to require no time, but many of them seem to be crowded into an instant. I speak this in comparison to the actions of the body. Anyone may easily observe this in his own thoughts, who will take the pains to reflect on them. How, as it were in an instant, do our minds, with one glance, see all the parts of a demonstration, which may very well be called a long one, if we consider the time it will require to put it into words, and step by step show it another? *Secondly*, we shall not be so much surprised that this is done in us with so little notice, if we consider how the facility which we get of doing things by a custom of doing makes them often pass in us without our notice. *Habits*, especially such as are begun very early, come at last to *produce actions in us which often escape our observation*. How frequently do we, in a day, cover our eyes with our eye-lids, without perceiving that we are at all in the dark? Men that by custom have got the use of a by-word do almost in every sentence pronounce sounds which though taken notice of by others they themselves neither hear nor observe. And therefore it is not so strange that our mind should often change the *idea* of its sensation into that of its judgment, and make one serve only to excite the other, without our taking notice of it.

11. This faculty of *perception* seems to me to be that which *puts the distinction betwixt the animal kingdom and the inferior parts of nature*. For, however vegetables have, many of them,

some degrees of motion, and upon the different application of other bodies to them, do very briskly alter their figures and motions, and so have obtained the name of sensitive plants, from a motion which has some resemblance to that which in animals follows upon sensation: yet I suppose it is all bare mechanism, and no otherwise produced than the turning of a wild oat-beard by the insinuation of the particles of moisture, or the shortening of a rope by the affusion of water. All which is done without any sensation in the subject, or the having or receiving any *ideas*.

12. *Perception*, I believe, is, in some degree, *in all sorts of animals*; though in some possibly the avenues provided by nature for the reception of sensations are so few, and the perception they are received with so obscure and dull, that it comes extremely short of the quickness and variety of sensation which is in other animals; but yet it is sufficient for, and wisely adapted to, the state and condition of that sort of animals who are thus made, so that the wisdom and goodness of the Maker plainly appear in all the parts of this stupendous fabric and all the several degrees and ranks of creatures in it.

13. We may, I think, from the make of an *oyster* or *cockle* reasonably conclude that it has not so many, nor so quick senses as a man or several other animals; nor if it had would it, in that state and incapacity of transferring itself from one place to another, be bettered by them. What good would sight and hearing do to a creature that cannot move itself to or from the objects wherein at a distance it perceives good or evil? And would not quickness of sensation be an inconvenience to an animal that must lie still where chance has once placed it, and there receive the afflux of colder or warmer, clean or foul water, as it happens to come to it?

14. But yet I cannot but think there is some small dull perception whereby they are distinguished from perfect insensibility. And that this may be so, we have plain instances, even in mankind itself. Take one in whom decrepit old age has blotted out the memory of his past knowledge and clearly wiped out the *ideas* his mind was formerly stored with, and has, by destroying his sight, hearing, and smell quite, and his taste to a great degree, stopped up almost all the passages for new ones to enter; or, if there be some of the inlets yet half open, the impressions made are scarce perceived or not at all retained. How far such an one (notwithstanding all that is boasted of innate principles) is in his

knowledge and intellectual faculties above the condition of a *cockle* or an *oyster*, I leave to be considered. And if a man had passed sixty years in such a state, as it is possible he might, as well as three days, I wonder what difference there would have been, in any intellectual perfections, between him and the lowest degree of animals.

15. *Perception* there being the *first step and degree towards knowledge and the inlet of all the materials of it:* the fewer senses any man, as well as any other creature, hath; and the fewer and duller the impressions are that are made by them; and the duller the faculties are that are employed about them: the more remote are they from that knowledge which is to be found in some men. But this, being in great variety of degrees (as may be perceived amongst men), cannot certainly be discovered in the several species of animals, much less in their particular individuals. It suffices me only to have remarked here that perception is the first operation of all our intellectual faculties, and the inlet of all knowledge in our minds. And I am apt, too, to imagine that it is perception in the lowest degree of it which puts the boundaries between animals and the inferior ranks of creatures. But this I mention only as my conjecture by the by, it being indifferent to the matter in hand which way the learned shall determine of it.

CHAPTER X

OF RETENTION

1. THE next faculty of the mind, whereby it makes a further progress towards knowledge, is that which I call *retention*, or the keeping of those simple *ideas* which from sensation or reflection it hath received. This is done two ways. First, by keeping the *idea* which is brought into it, for some time actually in view, which is called *contemplation*.

2. The other way of retention is the power to revive again in our minds those *ideas* which, after imprinting, have disappeared, or have been as it were laid aside out of sight; and thus we do, when we conceive heat or light, yellow or sweet, the object being removed. This is *memory*, which is as it were the storehouse of our *ideas*. For, the narrow mind of man not being

capable of having many *ideas* under view and consideration at once, it was necessary to have a repository, to lay up those *ideas* which, at another time, it might have use of. But, our *ideas* being nothing but actual perceptions in the mind, which cease to be anything when there is no perception of them, this *laying up* of our *ideas* in the repository of the memory signifies no more but this: that the mind has a power in many cases to revive perceptions which it has once had, with this additional perception annexed to them, that it has had them before. And in this sense it is that our *ideas* are said to be in our memories, when indeed they are actually nowhere; but only there is an ability in the mind when it will to revive them again, and as it were paint them anew on itself, though some with more, some with less difficulty, some more lively, and others more obscurely. And thus it is by the assistance of this faculty that we are said to have all those *ideas* in our understandings which, though we do not actually contemplate, yet we can bring in sight and make appear again and be the objects of our thoughts, without the help of those sensible qualities which first imprinted them there.

3. *Attention* and *repetition help* much to the fixing any *ideas* in *the memory*; but those which naturally at first make the deepest and most lasting impression are those which are accompanied with *pleasure* or *pain*. The great business of the senses being to make us take notice of what hurts or advantages the body, it is wisely ordered by nature (as has been shown) that pain should accompany the reception of several *ideas*; which, supplying the place of consideration and reasoning in children, and acting quicker than consideration in grown men, makes both the young and old avoid painful objects with that haste which is necessary for their preservation, and in both settles in the memory a caution for the future.

4. Concerning the several *degrees of* lasting, wherewith *ideas* are imprinted on the *memory*, we may observe that some of them have been produced in the understanding by an object affecting the senses once only and no more than once; others that have more than once offered themselves to the senses have yet been little taken notice of: the mind either heedless, as in children, or otherwise employed, as in men, intent only on one thing, not setting the stamp deep into itself. And in some, where they are set on with care and repeated impressions, either through the temper of the body or some other default, the memory is very

weak. In all these cases, *ideas* in the mind quickly fade and often vanish quite out of the understanding, leaving no more footsteps or remaining characters of themselves than shadows do flying over fields of corn; and the mind is as void of them as if they never had been there.

5. Thus many of those *ideas* which were produced in the minds of children in the beginning of their sensation (some of which, perhaps, as of some pleasures and pains, were before they were born and others in their infancy) if in the future course of their lives they are not repeated again, are quite lost without the least glimpse remaining of them. This may be observed in those who by some mischance have lost their sight when they were very young, in whom the *ideas* of colours, having been but slightly taken notice of and ceasing to be repeated, do quite wear out; so that some years after there is no more notion nor memory of colours left in their minds than in those of people born blind. The memory in some men, it is true, is very tenacious, even to a miracle; but yet there seems to be a constant decay of all our *ideas*, even of those which are struck deepest and in minds the most retentive: so that, if they be not sometimes renewed by repeated exercise of the senses of reflection on those kind of objects which at first occasioned them, the print wears out and at last there remains nothing to be seen. Thus the *ideas* as well as children of our youth often die before us; and our minds represent to us those tombs to which we are approaching: where, though the brass and marble remain, yet the inscriptions are effaced by time and the imagery moulders away. *The pictures drawn in our minds are laid in fading colours*, and if not sometimes refreshed, vanish and disappear. How much the constitution of our bodies and the make of our animal spirits are concerned in this, and whether the temper of the brain make this difference that in some it retains the characters drawn on it like marble, in others like freestone, and in others little better than sand, I shall not here inquire, though it may seem probable that the constitution of the body does sometimes influence the memory, since we oftentimes find a disease quite strip the mind of all its *ideas*, and the flames of a fever, in a few days, calcine all those images to dust and confusion which seemed to be as lasting as if graved in marble.

6. But concerning the *ideas* themselves, it is easy to remark that those that are *oftenest refreshed* (amongst which are those

that are conveyed into the mind by more ways than one) by a frequent return of the objects or actions that produce them, *fix themselves best in the memory*, and remain clearest and longest there; and therefore those which are of the original qualities of bodies, viz. *solidity, extension, figure, motion* and *rest*; and those that almost constantly affect our bodies, as *heat* and *cold*; and those which are the affections of all kinds of beings, as *existence, duration*, and *number*, which almost every object that affects our senses, every thought which employs our minds, bring along with them: these, I say, and the like *ideas* are seldom quite lost, whilst the mind retains any *ideas* at all.

7.   In this secondary perception, as I may so call it, or viewing again the *ideas* that are lodged *in* the *memory, the mind is oftentimes more than barely passive*: the appearance of those dormant pictures depending sometimes on the will. The mind very often sets itself on work in search of some hidden *idea*, and turns as it were the eye of the soul upon it: though sometimes too they start up in our minds of their own accord, and offer themselves to the understanding, and very often are roused and tumbled out of their dark cells into open daylight, by turbulent and tempestuous passion: our affections bringing *ideas* to our memory, which had otherwise lain quiet and unregarded. This further is to be observed concerning *ideas* lodged in the memory and upon occasion revived by the mind, that they are not only (as the word *revive* imports) none of them new ones, but also that the mind takes notice of them, as of a former impression, and renews its acquaintance with them, as with *ideas* it had known before. So that though *ideas* formerly imprinted are not all constantly in view, yet in remembrance they are constantly known to be such as have been formerly imprinted, i.e. in view and taken notice of before by the understanding.

8.   *Memory*, in an intellectual creature, is necessary in the next degree to perception. It is of so great moment that, where it is wanting, all the rest of our faculties are in a great measure useless; and we in our thoughts, reasonings, and knowledge, could not proceed beyond present objects, were it not for the assistance of our memories, wherein there may be *two defects*:

First, That it *loses the idea* quite, and so far it produces perfect ignorance. For, since we can know nothing further than we have the idea of it, when that is gone, we are in perfect *ignorance*.

Secondly, That it moves slowly and *retrieves not the ideas* that it has and are laid up in store *quick enough* to serve the mind upon occasion. This, if it be to a great degree, is *stupidity*; and he who, through this default in his memory, has not the *ideas* that are really preserved there ready at hand when need and occasion call for them, were almost as good be without them quite, since they serve him to little purpose. The dull man, who loses the opportunity, whilst he is seeking in his mind for those *ideas* that should serve his turn, is not much more happy in his knowledge than one that is perfectly ignorant. It is the business therefore of the memory to furnish to the mind those dormant *ideas* which it has present occasion for; in the having them ready at hand on all occasions consists that which we call *invention*, *fancy*, and quickness of parts.

9. These are defects we may observe in the memory of one man compared with another. There is another defect which we may conceive to be in the memory of man in general, compared with some superior created intellectual beings, which in this faculty may so far excel man, that they may have constantly in view the whole scene of all their former actions, wherein no one of the thoughts they have ever had may slip out of their sight. The omniscience of God, who knows all things, past, present, and to come, and to whom the thoughts of men's hearts always lie open, may satisfy us of the possibility of this. For who can doubt but God may communicate to those glorious spirits, his immediate attendants, any of his perfections, in what proportions he pleases, as far as created finite beings can be capable? It is reported of that prodigy of parts, Monsieur *Pascal*, that till the decay of his health had impaired his memory, he forgot nothing of what he had done, read, or thought, in any part of his rational age. This is a privilege so little known to most men that it seems almost incredible to those who, after the ordinary way, measure all others by themselves; but yet, when considered, may help us to enlarge our thoughts towards greater perfections of it, in superior ranks of spirits. For this of Monsieur *Pascal* was still with the narrowness that human minds are confined to here, of having greater variety of *ideas* only by succession, not all at once; whereas the several degrees of angels may probably have larger views, and some of them be endowed with capacities able to retain together and constantly set before them, as in one picture, all their past knowledge at once. This, we may conceive, would be no small advantage to the knowledge of a thinking man,

if all his past thoughts and reasonings could be always present to him. And therefore we may suppose it one of those ways wherein the knowledge of separate spirits may exceedingly surpass ours.
10. This faculty of laying up and retaining the *ideas* that are brought into the mind, several *other animals* seem to have to a great degree, as well as man. For, to pass by other instances, birds learning of tunes, and the endeavours one may observe in them to hit the notes right, put it past doubt with me that they have perception and retain *ideas* in their memories and use them for patterns. For it seems to me impossible that they should endeavour to conform their voices to notes (as it is plain they do) of which they had no *ideas*. For though I should grant sound may mechanically cause a certain motion of the animal spirits in the brains of those birds whilst the tune is actually playing; and that motion may be continued on to the muscles of the wings and so the bird mechanically be driven away by certain noises, because this may tend to the bird's preservation: yet that can never be supposed a reason why it should cause mechanically, either whilst the tune was playing, much less after it has ceased, such a motion in the organs of the bird's voice as should conform it to the notes of a foreign sound, which imitation can be of no use to the bird's preservation. But which is more, it cannot with any appearance of reason be supposed (much less proved) that birds, without sense and memory, can approach their notes nearer and nearer by degrees to a tune played yesterday; which, if they have no *idea* of in their memory, is now nowhere, nor can be a pattern for them to imitate, or which any repeated essays can bring them nearer to: since there is no reason why the sound of a pipe should leave traces in their brains which not at first but by their after endeavours should produce the like sounds; and why the sounds they make themselves should not make traces which they should follow, as well as those of the pipe, is impossible to conceive.

CHAPTER XI

OF DISCERNING, AND OTHER OPERATIONS OF THE MIND

1. ANOTHER faculty we may take notice of in our minds is that of *discerning* and distinguishing between the several *ideas* it has.

It is not enough to have a confused perception of something in general; unless the mind had a distinct perception of different objects and their qualities, it would be capable of very little knowledge, though the bodies that affect us were as busy about us as they are now, and the mind were continually employed in thinking. On this faculty of distinguishing one thing from another depends the *evidence and certainty* of several, even very general, propositions, which have passed for innate truths: because men, overlooking the true cause why those propositions find universal assent, impute it wholly to native uniform impressions; whereas it in truth *depends upon this clear discerning faculty* of the mind whereby it perceives two *ideas* to be the same, or different. But of this more hereafter.

2. How much the imperfection of accurately discriminating *ideas* one from another lies either in the dullness or faults of the organs of sense, or want of acuteness, exercise, or attention in the understanding, or hastiness and precipitancy natural to some tempers, I will not here examine; it suffices to take notice that this is one of the operations that the mind may reflect on and observe in itself. It is of that consequence to its other knowledge that, so far as this faculty is in itself dull or not rightly made use of, for the distinguishing one thing from another, so far our notions are confused, and our reason and judgment disturbed or misled. If in having our *ideas* in the memory ready at hand consists quickness of parts: in this, of having them unconfused and being able nicely to distinguish one thing from another, where there is but the least difference, consists, in a great measure, the exactness of judgment and clearness of reason which is to be observed in one man above another. And hence perhaps may be given some reason of that common observation, that men who have a great deal of wit, and prompt memories, have not always the clearest judgment or deepest reason. For *wit* lying most in the assemblage of *ideas*, and putting those together with quickness and variety, wherein can be found any resemblance or congruity, thereby to make up pleasant pictures and agreeable visions in the fancy: *judgment*, on the contrary, lies quite on the other side, in separating carefully, one from another, *ideas* wherein can be found the least difference, thereby to avoid being misled by similitude, and by affinity to take one thing for another. This is a way of proceeding quite contrary to metaphor and allusion, wherein for the most part

lies that entertainment and pleasantry of wit, which strikes so
lively on the fancy, and therefore is so acceptable to all people:
because its beauty appears at first sight, and there is required no
labour of thought to examine what truth or reason there is in it.
The mind, without looking any further, rests satisfied with the
agreeableness of the picture and the gaiety of the fancy; and it
is a kind of affront to go about to examine it by the severe
rules of truth and good reason; whereby it appears that it consists in something that is not perfectly conformable to them.

3.   To the well distinguishing our *ideas*, it chiefly contributes
that they be *clear and determinate*; and when they are so, *it
will not breed any confusion* or mistake about them, though the
senses should (as sometimes they do) convey them from the
same object differently on different occasions, and so seem to
err.   For, though a man in a fever should from a sugar have a
bitter taste, which at another time would produce a sweet one,
yet the *idea* of bitter in that man's mind would be as clear and
distinct from the *idea* of sweet as if he had tasted only gall.   Nor
does it make any more confusion between the two *ideas* of
sweet and bitter that the same sort of body produces at one
time, one and at another time another *idea* by the taste, than it
makes a confusion in two *ideas* of white and sweet or white and
round that the same piece of sugar produces them both in the
mind at the same time.   And the *ideas* of orange colour and azure
that are produced in the mind by the same parcel of the infusion
of *lignum nephriticum* are no less distinct *ideas* than those of the
same colours, taken from two very different bodies.

4.   The COMPARING them one with another, in respect of extent,
degrees, time, place, or any other circumstances, is another
operation of the mind about its *ideas*, and is that upon which
depends all that large tribe of *ideas* comprehended under
relation; which, of how vast an extent it is, I shall have occasion
to consider hereafter.

5.   How far brutes partake in this faculty is not easy to determine.   I imagine they have it not in any great degree: for though
they probably have several *ideas* distinct enough, yet it seems to
me to be the prerogative of human understanding, when it has
sufficiently distinguished any *ideas*, so as to perceive them to be
perfectly different and so consequently two, to cast about and
consider in what circumstances they are capable to be compared.   And therefore, I think, *beasts compare* not their *ideas*

further than some sensible circumstances annexed to the objects themselves. The other power of comparing, which may be observed in men, belonging to general *ideas*, and useful only to abstract reasonings, we may probably conjecture beasts have not.

6. The next operation we may observe in the mind about its *ideas* is COMPOSITION, whereby it puts together several of those simple ones it has received from sensation and reflection, and combines them into complex ones. Under this of composition may be reckoned also that of ENLARGING, wherein, though the composition does not so much appear as in more complex ones, yet it is nevertheless a putting several *ideas* together, though of the same kind. Thus, by adding several units together, we make the *idea* of a dozen; and putting together the repeated *ideas* of several perches, we frame that of furlong.

7. In this also, I suppose, *brutes* come far short of men. For, though they take in and retain together several combinations of simple *ideas*, as possibly the shape, smell, and voice of his master make up the complex *idea* a dog has of him, or rather are so many distinct marks whereby he knows him: yet I *do not* think they do of themselves ever compound them and *make complex* ideas. And perhaps even where we think they have complex *ideas*, it is only one simple one that directs them in the knowledge of several things, which possibly they distinguish less by their sight than we imagine. For I have been credibly informed that a bitch will nurse, play with, and be fond of young foxes, as much as and in place of her puppies, if you can but get them once to suck her so long that her milk may go through them. And those animals, which have a numerous brood of young ones at once, appear not to have any knowledge of their number; for though they are mightily concerned for any of their young that are taken from them whilst they are in sight or hearing, yet if one or two of them be stolen from them in their absence or without noise, they appear not to miss them or to have any sense that their number is lessened.

8. When children have, by repeated sensations, got *ideas* fixed in their memories, they begin by degrees to learn the use of signs. And when they have got the skill to apply the organs of speech to the framing of articulate sounds, they begin to make *use of words* to signify their *ideas* to others. These verbal signs they sometimes borrow from others and sometimes make

themselves, as one may observe among the new and unusual
names children often give to things in their first use of language.
9. The use of words then being to stand as outward marks of
our internal *ideas*, and those *ideas* being taken from particular
things, if every particular *idea* that we take in should have a
dictinct name, names must be endless. To prevent this, the
mind makes the particular *ideas* received from particular objects
to become general; which is done by considering them as they
are in the mind such appearances, separate from all other
existences and the circumstances of real existence, as time,
place, or any other concomitant *ideas*. This is called ABSTRAC-
TION, whereby *ideas* taken from particular beings become
general representatives of all of the same kind; and their names,
general names, applicable to whatever exists conformable to
such abstract *ideas*. Such precise, naked appearances in the
mind, without considering how, whence, or with what others
they came there, the understanding lays up (with names commonly annexed to them) as the standards to rank real existences
into sorts, as they agree with these patterns, and to *denominate*
them accordingly. Thus the same colour being observed to-day
in chalk or snow, which the mind yesterday received from milk,
it considers that appearance alone, makes it a representative of
all of that kind; and having given it the name *whiteness*, it by
that sound signifies the same quality wheresoever to be imagined
or met with; and thus universals, whether *ideas* or terms, are made.
10. If it may be doubted whether *beasts* compound and enlarge
their *ideas* that way to any degree: this, I think, I may be positive in, that the power of *abstracting* is not at all in them; and
that the having of general *ideas* is that which puts a perfect distinction betwixt man and brutes, and is an excellency which the
faculties of brutes do by no means attain to. For it is evident
we observe no footsteps in them of making use of general signs
for universal *ideas*; from which we have reason to imagine that
they have not the faculty of abstracting, or making general *ideas*,
since they have no use of words or any other general signs.
11. Nor can it be imputed to their want of fit organs to frame
articulate sounds that they have no use or knowledge of general
words, since many of them, we find, can fashion such sounds
and pronounce words distinctly enough, but never with any such
application. And on the other side, men who through some
defect in the organs want words, yet fail not to express their

universal *ideas* by signs which serve them instead of general words, a faculty which we see beasts come short in. And therefore I think we may suppose that it is in this that the species of *brutes* are discriminated from man, and it is that proper difference wherein they are wholly separated and which at last widens to so vast a distance. For if they have any *ideas* at all and are not bare machines (as some would have them) we cannot deny them to have some reason. It seems as evident to me that they do some of them in certain instances reason, as that they have sense; but it is only in particular *ideas*, just as they received them from their senses. They are the best of them tied up within those narrow bounds and *have not* (as I think) the faculty to enlarge them by any kind of *abstraction*.

12. How far *idiots* are concerned in the want or weakness of any or all of the foregoing faculties, an exact observation of their several ways of faltering would no doubt discover. For those who either perceive but dully or retain the *ideas* that come into their minds but ill, who cannot readily excite or compound them, will have little matter to think on. Those who cannot distinguish, compare, and abstract would hardly be able to understand and make use of language, or judge or reason to any tolerable degree, but only a little and imperfectly about things present and very familiar to their senses. And indeed, any of the forementioned faculties, if wanting or out of order, produce suitable defects in men's understandings and knowledge.

13. In fine the defect in *naturals* seems to proceed from want of quickness, activity, and motion in the intellectual faculties, whereby they are deprived of reason; whereas *madmen*, on the other side, seem to suffer by the other extreme. For they do not appear to me to have lost the faculty of reasoning, but having joined together some *ideas* very wrongly, they mistake them for truths, and they err as men do that argue right from wrong principles. For, by the violence of their imaginations, having taken their fancies for realities, they make right deductions from them. Thus you shall find a distracted man, fancying himself a king, with a right inference require suitable attendance, respect, and obedience; others, who have thought themselves made of glass, have used the caution necessary to preserve such brittle bodies. Hence it comes to pass that a man who is very sober, and of a right understanding in all other things, may in one particular be as frantic as any in *Bedlam*, if either by any sudden

very strong impression, or long fixing his fancy upon one sort of thoughts, incoherent *ideas* have been cemented together so powerfully as to remain united. But there are degrees of madness, as of folly: the disorderly jumbling *ideas* together is in some more and some less. In short, herein seems to lie the difference between idiots and madmen: that madmen put wrong ideas together, and so make wrong propositions, but argue and reason right from them; but idiots make very few or no propositions, and reason scarce at all.

14. These I think are the first faculties and operations of the mind which it makes use of in understanding; and though they are exercised about all its *ideas* in general, yet the instances I have hitherto given have been chiefly in simple *ideas*. And I have subjoined the explication of these faculties of the mind to that of simple *ideas* before I come to what I have to say concerning complex ones, for these following reasons:

First, Because several of these faculties being exercised at first principally about simple *ideas*, we might, by following nature in its ordinary method, trace and discover them in their rise, progress, and gradual improvements.

Secondly, Because, observing the faculties of the mind, how they operate about simple *ideas*, which are usually, in most men's minds, much more clear, precise, and distinct than complex ones, we may the better examine and learn how the mind abstracts, denominates, compares, and exercises its other operations about those which are complex, wherein we are much more liable to mistake.

Thirdly, Because these very operations of the mind about *ideas* received from *sensation* are themselves, when reflected on, another set of *ideas*, derived from that other source of our knowledge, which I call *reflection*, and therefore fit to be considered in this place after the simple *ideas* of *sensation*. Of compounding, comparing, abstracting, etc., I have but just spoken, having occasion to treat of them more at large in other places.

15. And thus I have given a short and, I think, true *history of the first beginnings of human knowledge*: whence the mind has its first objects, and by what steps it makes its progress to the laying in and storing up those *ideas* out of which is to be framed all the knowledge it is capable of; wherein I must appeal to experience and observation whether I am in the right, the best way to come

to truth being to examine things as really they are, and not to conclude they are as we fancy of ourselves or have been taught by others to imagine.

16. To deal truly, *this is the only way* that I can discover *whereby* the *ideas* of things *are brought into the understanding.* If other men have either innate *ideas* or infused principles, they have reason to enjoy them; and if they are sure of it, it is impossible for others to deny them the privilege that they have above their neighbours. I can speak but of what I find in myself and is agreeable to those notions, which, if we will examine the whole course of men in their several ages, countries, and educations, seem to depend on those foundations which I have laid and to correspond with this method, in all the parts and degrees thereof.

17. I pretend not to teach, but to inquire; and therefore cannot but confess here again that external and internal sensation are the only passages that I can find of knowledge to the understanding. These alone, as far as I can discover, are the windows by which light is let into this *dark room.* For, methinks, the *understanding* is not much unlike a closet wholly shut from light, with only some little opening left, to let in external visible resemblances, or *ideas* of things without; would the pictures coming into such a dark room but stay there, and lie so orderly as to be found upon occasion, it would very much resemble the understanding of a man in reference to all objects of sight and the *ideas* of them.

These are my guesses concerning the means whereby the understanding comes to have and retain simple *ideas* and the modes of them, with some other operations about them. I proceed now to examine some of these simple *ideas* and their modes a little more particularly.

CHAPTER XII

OF COMPLEX IDEAS

1. WE have hitherto considered those *ideas* in the reception whereof the mind is only passive, which are those simple ones received from *sensation* and *reflection* before mentioned, whereof

the mind cannot make one to itself, nor have any *idea* which does not wholly consist of them. But as the mind is wholly passive in the reception of all its simple *ideas*, so it exerts several acts of its own whereby out of its simple *ideas*, as the materials and foundations of the rest, the others are framed. The acts of the mind, wherein it exerts its power over its simple *ideas*, are chiefly these three: (1) Combining several simple *ideas* into one compound one; and thus all complex *ideas* are made. (2) The second is bringing two *ideas*, whether simple or complex, together, and setting them by one another, so as to take a view of them at once, without uniting them into one; by which way it gets all its *ideas* of relations. (3) The third is separating them from all other *ideas* that accompany them in their real existence: this is called *abstraction*; and thus all its general *ideas* are made. This shows man's power, and its way of operation, to be much the same in the material and intellectual world. For the materials in both being such as he has no power over either to make or destroy, all that man can do is either to unite them together, or to set them by one another, or wholly separate them. I shall here begin with the first of these in the consideration of complex *ideas*, and come to the other two in their due places. As simple *ideas* are observed to exist in several combinations united together, so the mind has a power to consider several of them united together as one *idea*, and that not only as they are united in external objects, but as itself has joined them. *Ideas* thus made up of several simple ones put together, I call *complex*, such as are *beauty, gratitude, a man, an army, the universe*; which, though complicated of various simple *ideas*, or *complex ideas* made up of simple ones, yet are, when the mind pleases, considered each by itself as one entire thing, and signified by one name.

2. In this faculty of repeating and joining together its *ideas*, the mind has great power in varying and multiplying the objects of its thoughts, infinitely beyond what *sensation* or *reflection* furnished it with, but all this still confined to those simple *ideas* which it received from those two sources, and which are the ultimate materials of all its compositions. For simple *ideas* are all from things themselves, and of these *the mind can* have no more, nor other than what are suggested to it. It can have no other *ideas* of sensible qualities than what come from without by the senses; nor any *ideas* of other kind of operations of a thinking

substance, than what it finds in itself. But when it has once got these simple *ideas* it is not confined barely to observation and what offers itself from without: it can, by its own power, put together those *ideas* it has and *make new complex ones*, which it never received so united.

3. *Complex ideas*, however compounded and decompounded, though their number be infinite and the variety endless wherewith they fill and entertain the thoughts of men, yet I think they may be all reduced under these three heads:

1. *Modes.*
2. *Substances.*
3. *Relations.*

4. First, *Modes* I call such complex *ideas* which, however compounded, contain not in them the supposition of subsisting by themselves, but are considered as dependences on, or affections of substances; such are the *ideas* signified by the words *triangle, gratitude, murder*, etc. And if in this I use the word *mode* in somewhat a different sense from its ordinary signification, I beg pardon: it being unavoidable in discourses differing from the ordinary received notions either to make new words or to use old words in somewhat a new signification, the latter whereof in our present case is perhaps the more tolerable of the two.

5. Of these *modes*, there are two sorts which deserve distinct consideration: First, there are some which are only variations, or different combinations of the same simple *idea*, without the mixture of any other, as a dozen, or score; which are nothing but the *ideas* of so many distinct units added together; and these I call *simple modes* as being contained within the bounds of one simple *idea*. Secondly, there are others compounded of simple *ideas* of several kinds, put together to make one complex one: v.g. *beauty*, consisting of a certain composition of colour and figure, causing delight in the beholder; *theft*, which being the concealed change of the possession of anything, without the consent of the proprietor, contains, as is visible, a combination of several *ideas* of several kinds: and these I call *mixed modes*.

6. Secondly, the *ideas* of *substances* are such combinations of simple *ideas* as are taken to represent distinct particular things subsisting by themselves, in which the supposed or confused *idea* of substance, such as it is, is always the first and chief. Thus

if to substance be joined the simple *idea* of a certain dull whitish colour, with certain degrees of weight, hardness, ductility, and fusibility, we have the *idea* of *lead*; and a combination of the *ideas* of a certain sort of figure, with the powers of motion, thought, and reasoning, joined to substance, make the ordinary *idea* of *a man*. Now of substances also, there are two sorts of *ideas:* one of single substances, as they exist separately, as of *a man* or *a sheep;* the other of several of those put together, as an *army* of men, or *flock* of sheep; which *collective* ideas *of* several *substances* thus put together are as much each of them one single *idea* as that of a man or an unit.

7.   Thirdly, the last sort of complex *ideas* is that we call *relation*, which consists in the consideration and comparing one *idea* with another.

Of these several kinds we shall treat in their order.

8.   If we will trace the progress of our minds, and with attention observe how it repeats, adds together, and unites its simple *ideas* received from sensation or reflection, it will lead us further than at first perhaps we should have imagined. And I believe we shall find, if we warily observe the originals of our notions, that even *the most abstruse ideas*, how remote soever they may seem from sense, or from any operation of our own minds, are yet only such as the understanding frames to itself, by repeating and joining together *ideas* that it had either from objects of sense, or from its own operations about them: so that those even large *and abstract* ideas *are derived from sensation or reflection*, being no other than what the mind, by the ordinary use of its own faculties, employed about *ideas* received from objects of sense or from the operations it observes in itself about them, may and does attain unto. This I shall endeavour to show in the *ideas* we have of *space, time*, and *infinity*, and some few other that seem the most remote from those originals.

CHAPTER XIII

OF SIMPLE MODES; AND FIRST, OF THE SIMPLE MODES OF SPACE

1.   THOUGH in the foregoing part I have often mentioned simple *ideas*, which are truly the materials of all our knowledge,

yet having treated of them there rather in the way that they come into the mind than as distinguished from others more compounded, it will not be perhaps amiss to take a view of some of them again under this consideration, and examine those different *modifications of the same* idea, which the mind either finds in things existing, or is able to make within itself without the help of any extrinsical object, or any foreign suggestion.

Those *modifications of any one simple* idea (which, as has been said, I call *simple modes*) are as perfectly different and distinct *ideas* in the mind as those of the greatest distance or contrariety. For the *idea* of *two* is as distinct from that of *one*, as *blueness* from *heat*, or either of them from any number: and yet it is made up only of that simple *idea* of an unit repeated; and repetitions of this kind joined together make those distinct *simple modes*, of a *dozen*, a *gross*, a *million*.

2. I shall begin with the *simple idea* of *space*. I have shown above, ch. iv, that we get the *idea* of space, both by our sight and touch; which, I think, is so evident that it would be as needless to go to prove that men perceive, by their sight, a distance between bodies of different colours, or between the parts of the same body, as that they see colours themselves; nor is it less obvious that they can do so in the dark by feeling and touch.

3. This space, considered barely in length between any two beings, without considering anything else between them, is called *distance*; if considered in length, breadth, and thickness, I think it may be called *capacity*. The term extension is usually applied to it in what manner soever considered.

4. Each different distance is a different modification of space; and *each* idea *of any different distance, or space, is a simple mode of this* idea. Men, for the use and by the custom of measuring, settle in their minds the *ideas* of certain stated lengths, such as are an *inch*, *foot*, *yard*, *fathom*, *mile*, *diameter of the earth*, etc., which are so many distinct *ideas* made up only of space. When any such stated lengths or measures of space are made familiar to men's thoughts, they can in their minds repeat them as often as they will without mixing or joining to them the *idea* of body or anything else; and frame to themselves the *ideas* of long, square, or cubic, *feet*, *yards*, or *fathoms*, here amongst the bodies of the universe, or else beyond the utmost bounds of all bodies; and by adding these still one to another, enlarge their *idea* of space as much as they please. This power of repeating or

doubling any *idea* we have of any distance and adding it to the former as often as we will without being ever able to come to any stop or stint, let us enlarge it as much as we will, is that which gives us the *idea* of immensity.

5.   There is another modification of this *idea* which is nothing but the relation which the parts of the termination of extension or circumscribed space have amongst themselves.   This the touch discovers in sensible bodies whose extremities come within our reach, and the eye takes both from bodies and colours whose boundaries are within its view; where observing how the extremities terminate either in straight lines, which meet at discernible angles, or in crooked lines, wherein no angles can be perceived: by considering these as they relate to one another in all parts of the extremities of any body or space, it has that *idea* we call *figure*, which affords to the mind infinite variety.   For, besides the vast number of different figures that do really exist in the coherent masses of matter, the stock that the mind has in its power, by varying the *idea* of space and thereby making still new compositions by repeating its own *ideas* and joining them as it pleases, is perfectly inexhaustible.   And so it can multiply figures *in infinitum*.

6.   For the mind having a power to repeat the *idea* of any length directly stretched out, and join it to another in the same direction, which is to double the length of that straight line or else join it to another with what inclination it thinks fit and so make what sort of angle it pleases: and being able also to shorten any line it imagines by taking from it one-half or one-fourth or what part it pleases, without being able to come to an end of any such divisions, it can make an angle of any bigness.   So also the lines that are its sides, of what length it pleases, which joining again to other lines of different lengths and at different angles till it has wholly enclosed any space, it is evident that it can multiply *figures* both in their shape and capacity *in infinitum*; all which are but so many different *simple modes of space*.

The same that it can do with straight lines, it can do also with crooked, or crooked and straight together; and the same it can do in lines, it can also in superficies, by which we may be led into further thoughts of the endless variety of *figures* that the mind has a power to make and thereby to multiply the *simple modes* of space.

7.   Another *idea* coming under this head and belonging to this

tribe is that we call *place*. As in simple space, we consider the relation of distance between any two bodies or points; so in our *idea* of *place*, we consider the relation of distance betwixt anything, and any two or more points, which are considered as keeping the same distance one with another, and so considered as at rest. For when we find anything at the same distance now which it was yesterday, from any two or more points which have not since changed their distance one with another, and with which we then compared it, we say it hath kept the same *place*; but if it hath sensibly altered its distance with either of those points, we say it hath changed its place, though, vulgarly speaking, in the common notion of *place*, we do not always exactly observe the distance from precise points, but from larger portions of sensible objects, to which we consider the thing placed to bear relation, and its distance from which we have some reason to observe.

8. Thus, a company of chess-men standing on the same squares of the chess-board where we left them, we say they are all in the *same place*, or unmoved, though perhaps the chess-board hath been in the meantime carried out of one room into another; because we compared them only to the parts of the chess-board, which keep the same distance one with another. The chess-board, we also say, is in the *same place* it was, if it remain in the same part of the cabin, though perhaps the ship which it is in sails all the while. And the ship is said to be in the *same place*, supposing it kept the same distance with the parts of the neighbouring land, though perhaps the earth hath turned round; and so both chess-men, and board, and ship, have every one *changed place*, in respect of remoter bodies, which have kept the same distance one with another. But yet the distance from certain parts of the board being that which determines the place of the chess-men; and the distance from the fixed parts of the cabin (with which we made the comparison) being that which determined the place of the chess-board; and the fixed parts of the earth that by which we determined the place of the ship: these things may be said to be in the *same place* in those respects; though their distance from some other things, which in this matter we did not consider, being varied, they have undoubtedly *changed place* in that respect; and we ourselves shall think so, when we have occasion to compare them with those other.

9. But this modification of distance we call *place*, being made by men for their common use, that by it they might be able to design the particular position of things where they had occasion for such designation: men consider and determine of this *place* by reference to those adjacent things which best served to their present purpose, without considering other things which to another purpose would better *determine the place* of the same thing. Thus in the chess-board, the use of the *designation of* the *place* of each chess-man being determined only within that chequered piece of wood, it would cross that purpose to measure it by anything else; but when these very chess-men are put up in a bag, if anyone should ask where the black king is, it would be proper to *determine the place* by the parts of the room it was in and not by the chess-board: there being another use of *designing the place* it is now in than when in play it was on the chess-board, and so must be determined by other bodies. So if anyone should ask in what place are the verses which report the story of *Nisus* and *Eurialus*, it would be very improper to determine this place by saying they were in such a part of the earth, or in *Bodley's* library; but the right designation of the place would be by the parts of *Virgil's* works; and the proper answer would be that these verses were about the middle of the ninth book of his *Aeneids*, and that they have been always constantly in the same place ever since *Virgil* was printed; which is true, though the book itself hath moved a thousand times, the use of the *idea* of place here being to know only in what part of the book that story is, that so, upon occasion, we may know where to find it and have recourse to it for our use.

10. That our *idea* of place is nothing else but such a relative position of anything as I have before mentioned, I think is plain and will be easily admitted, when we consider that we can have no *idea* of the place of the universe, though we can of all the parts of it; because beyond that, we have not the *idea* of any fixed, distinct, particular beings, in reference to which we can imagine it to have any relation of distance, but all beyond it is one uniform space or expansion, wherein the mind finds no variety, no marks. For to say that the world is somewhere means no more than that it does exist; this, though a phrase borrowed from place, signifying only its existence, not location; and when one can find out and frame in his mind clearly and distinctly the place of the universe, he will be able to tell us

whether it moves or stands still in the undistinguishable *inane* of infinite space: though it be true that the word place has sometimes a more confused sense and stands for that space which any body takes up; and so the universe is in a place. The *idea* therefore of *place* we have by the same means that we get the *idea* of space (whereof this is but a particular limited consideration), viz. by our sight and touch, by either of which we receive into our minds the *ideas* of extension or distance.

11.   There are some that would persuade us that *body and extension are the same thing*, who either change the signification of words, which I would not suspect them of, they having so severely condemned the philosophy of others because it hath been too much placed in the uncertain meaning or deceitful obscurity of doubtful or insignificant terms. If therefore they mean by *body and extension the same* that other people do, viz. by *body*, something that is solid and extended, whose parts are separable and movable different ways; and by extension, only the space that lies between the extremities of those solid coherent parts, and which is possessed by them, they confound very different *ideas* one with another. For I appeal to every man's own thoughts whether the *idea* of space be not as distinct from that of solidity as it is from the *idea* of scarlet colour? It is true, solidity cannot exist without extension, neither can scarlet colour exist without extension; but this hinders not but that they are distinct *ideas*. Many *ideas* require others as necessary to their existence or conception which yet are very distinct *ideas*. Motion can neither be nor be conceived without space, and yet motion is not space nor space motion; space can exist without it and they are very distinct *ideas*; and so, I think, are those of space and solidity. Solidity is so inseparable an *idea* from body that upon that depends its filling of space, its contact, impulse, and communication of motion upon impulse. And if it be a reason to prove that spirit is different from body because thinking includes not the *idea* of extension in it, the same reason will be as valid, I suppose, to prove that *space is not body*, because it includes not the *idea* of solidity in it: *space* and *solidity* being *as distinct ideas* as thinking and extension, and as wholly separable in the mind one from another. *Body* then and *extension*, it is evident, are two distinct *ideas*. For,

12.   *First, Extension* includes no solidity, nor resistance to the motion of *body*, as body does.

13.   *Secondly,* The parts of pure space are inseparable one from
the other; so that the continuity cannot be separated, neither
really nor mentally.   For I demand of anyone to remove any
part of it from another, with which it is continued, even so much
as in thought.   To divide and separate actually is, as I think, by
removing the parts one from another, to make two superficies,
where before there was a continuity; and to divide mentally is
to make in the mind two superficies, where before there was a
continuity, and consider them as removed one from the other;
which can only be done in things considered by the mind as
capable of being separated and, by separation, of acquiring new
distinct superficies, which they then have not, but are capable of.
But neither of these ways of separation, whether real or mental,
is, as I think, compatible to pure *space*.

It is true, a man may consider so much of such a *space* as is
answerable or commensurate to a foot, without considering the
rest; which is indeed a partial consideration, but not so much a
mental separation or division, since a man can no more mentally
divide without considering two superficies separate one from
the other, than he can actually divide without making two superficies disjoined one from the other; but a partial consideration is
not separating.   A man may consider light in the sun without its
heat, or mobility in body without its extension, without thinking
of their separation.   One is only a partial consideration, terminating in one alone; and the other is a consideration of both as
existing separately.

14.   *Thirdly,* The parts of pure *space* are immovable, which
follows from their inseparability, *motion* being nothing but
change of distance between any two things; but this cannot be
between parts that are inseparable, which, therefore, must needs
be at perpetual rest one amongst another.

Thus the determined *idea* of simple *space* distinguishes it
plainly and sufficiently from *body*, since its parts are inseparable,
immovable, and without resistance to the motion of body.

15.   If anyone ask me *what* this *space* I speak of *is*, I will tell
him when he tells me what his *extension* is.   For to say, as is
usually done, that extension is to have *partes extra partes* is to
say only that *extension* is *extension*.   For what am I the better
informed in the nature of *extension* when I am told that *extension is to have parts that are extended, exterior to parts that are
extended,* i.e. *extension* consists of extended parts?   As if one

asking what a fibre was, I should answer him that it was a thing made up of several fibres. Would he hereby be enabled to understand what a fibre was better than he did before? Or rather, would he not have reason to think that my design was to make sport with him, rather than seriously to instruct him?

16. Those who contend that *space and body are the same* bring this *dilemma*: either this *space* is something or nothing; if nothing be between two bodies, they must necessarily touch; if it be allowed to be something, they ask: Whether it be body or spirit? To which I answer by another question: Who told them that there was, or could be, nothing but solid beings which could not think, and thinking beings that were not extended? Which is all they mean by the terms *body* and *spirit*.

17. If it be demanded (as usually it is) whether this *space*, void of *body*, be *substance* or *accident*, I shall readily answer I know not, nor shall be ashamed to own my ignorance, till they that ask show me a clear distinct *idea* of *substance*.

18. I endeavour as much as I can to deliver myself from those fallacies which we are apt to put upon ourselves, by taking words for things. It helps not our ignorance to feign a knowledge where we have none by making a noise with sounds, without clear and distinct significations. Names made at pleasure neither alter the nature of things, nor make us understand them, but as they are signs of and stand for determined *ideas*. And I desire those who lay so much stress on the sound of these two syllables, *substance*, to consider whether applying it as they do to the infinite incomprehensible GOD, to finite spirit, and to body, it be in the same sense; and whether it stands for the same *idea*, when each of those three so different beings are called *substances*? If so, whether it will not thence follow that God, spirits, and body, agreeing in the same common nature of *substance*, differ not any otherwise than in a bare different modification of that *substance*: as a tree and a pebble, being in the same sense body and agreeing in the common nature of body, differ only in a bare modification of that common matter; which will be a very harsh doctrine. If they say that they apply it to God, finite spirits, and matter in three different significations, and that it stands for one *idea* when GOD is said to be a *substance*, for another when the soul is called *substance*, and for a third when a body is called so: if the name *substance* stands for

three several distinct *ideas*, they would do well to make known those distinct *ideas*, or at least to give three distinct names to them, to present in so important a notion the confusion and errors that will naturally follow from the promiscuous use of so doubtful a term; which is so far from being suspected to have three distinct, that in ordinary use it has scarce one clear distinct signification. And if they can thus make three distinct *ideas* of *substance*, what hinders why another may not make a fourth?

19. They who first ran into the notion of *accidents*, as a sort of real beings that needed something to inhere in, were forced to find out the word *substance* to support them. Had the poor *Indian* philosopher (who imagined that the earth also wanted something to bear it up) but thought of this word *substance*, he needed not to have been at the trouble to find an elephant to support it, and a tortoise to support his elephant: the word *substance* would have done it effectually. And he that inquired might have taken it for as good an answer from an *Indian* philosopher that *substance*, without knowing what it is, is that which supports the earth, as we take it for a sufficient answer and good doctrine from our *European* philosophers that *substance*, without knowing what it is, is that which supports *accidents*. So that of *substance*, we have no *idea* of what it is, but only a confused, obscure one of what it does.

20. Whatever a learned man may do here, an intelligent *American*, who inquired into the nature of things, would scarce take it for a satisfactory account if, desiring to learn our architecture, he should be told that a pillar was a thing supported by a *basis* and a *basis* something that supported a pillar. Would he not think himself mocked instead of taught with such an account as this? And a stranger to them would be very liberally instructed in the nature of books and the things they contained if he should be told that all learned books consisted of paper and letters, and that letters were things inhering in paper and paper a thing that held forth letters: a notable way of having clear *ideas* of letters and paper! But were the *Latin* words *inhaerentia* and *substantia* put into the plain *English* ones that answer them, and were called *sticking on* and *under-propping*, they would better discover to us the very great clearness there is in the doctrine of *substance* and *accidents*, and show of what use they are in deciding of questions in philosophy.

21. But to return to our *idea* of *space*. If *body* be not supposed infinite (which I think no one will affirm), I would ask whether, if GOD placed a man at the extremity of corporeal beings, he could not stretch his hand beyond his body? If he could, then he would put his arm where there was before *space* without *body*; and if there he spread his fingers, there would still be *space* between them without *body*. If he could not stretch out his hand, it must be because of some external hindrance (for we suppose him alive, with such a power of moving the parts of his body that he hath now, which is not in itself impossible if GOD so pleased to have it; or at least it is not impossible for God so to move him); and then I ask whether that which hinders his hand from moving outwards be substance or accident, something or nothing? And when they have resolved that, they will be able to resolve themselves what that is which is, or may be between two bodies at a distance, that is not body, has no solidity. In the meantime, the argument is at least as good that where nothing hinders (as beyond the utmost bounds of all bodies), a *body* put into motion may move on, as where there is nothing between, there two bodies must necessarily touch; for pure *space* between is sufficient to take away the necessity of mutual contact, but bare *space* in the way is not sufficient to stop motion. The truth is, these men must either own that they think body infinite, though they are loath to speak it out, or else affirm that *space* is not *body*. For I would fain meet with that thinking man that can in his thoughts set any bounds to space, more than he can to duration, or by thinking hope to arrive at the end of either. And therefore, if his *idea* of eternity be infinite, so is his *idea* of immensity: they are both finite or infinite alike.

22. Further, those who assert the impossibility of *space* existing without *matter*, must not only make body infinite, but must also deny a power in God to annihilate any part of matter. No one, I suppose, will deny that God can put an end to all motion that is in matter, and fix all the bodies of the universe in a perfect quiet and rest and continue them so long as he pleases. Whoever then will allow that God can, during such a general rest, annihilate either this book or the body of him that reads it, must necessarily admit the possibility of a *vacuum*; for it is evident that the space that was filled by the parts of the annihilated body will still remain and be a space without body. For the circum-

ambient bodies being in perfect rest are a wall of adamant and in
that state make it a perfect impossibility for any other body to
get into that space. And indeed the necessary motion of one
particle of matter into the place from whence another particle
of matter is removed is but a consequence from the supposition
of plenitude; which will therefore need some better proof than
a supposed matter of fact, which experiment can never make
out: our own clear and distinct *idea* plainly satisfying us that
there is no necessary connexion between *space* and *solidity*,
since we can conceive the one without the other. And those who
dispute for or against a *vacuum* do thereby confess they have
distinct *ideas* of *vacuum* and *plenum*, i.e. that they have an *idea*
of extension void of solidity, though they deny its existence; or
else they dispute about nothing at all. For they who so much
alter the signification of words as to call *extension, body,* and
consequently make the whole essence of body to be nothing but
pure extension without solidity, must talk absurdly whenever
they speak of *vacuum*, since it is impossible for extension to be
without extension. For *vacuum*, whether we affirm or deny its
existence, signifies space without body, whose very existence no
one can deny to be possible who will not make matter
infinite and take from God a power to annihilate any particle
of it.

23. But not to go so far as beyond the utmost bounds of body
in the universe, nor appeal to God's omnipotency to find a
vacuum, the *motion* of bodies that are in our view and neighbourhood seem to me plainly to evince it. For I desire anyone
so to divide a solid body, of any dimension he pleases, as to
make it possible for the solid parts to move up and down freely
every way within the bounds of that superficies, if there be not
left in it a void space as big as the least part into which he has
divided the said solid body. And if, where the least particle of
the body divided is as big as a mustard-seed, a void space
equal to the bulk of a mustard-seed be requisite to make room
for the free motion of the parts of the divided body within the
bounds of its superficies, where the particles of matter are
100,000,000 less than a mustard-seed, there must also be a
space void of solid matter as big as 100,000,000th part of a
mustard-seed; for if it hold in one it will hold in the other,
and so on *in infinitum*. And let this void space be as little as it
will, it destroys the hypothesis of *plenitude*. For if there can be

a space void of body equal to the smallest separate particle of matter now existing in nature, it is still space without body and makes as great a difference between space and body as if it were μέγα χάσμα, a distance as wide as any in nature. And therefore, if we suppose not the void space necessary to motion equal to the least parcel of the divided solid matter, but to one-tenth or one-thousandth of it, the same consequence will always follow of space without matter.

24. But the question being here, whether the *idea of space* or *extension* be *the same with the idea of body*, it is not necessary to prove the real existence of a *vacuum*, but the *idea* of it; which it is plain men have when they inquire and dispute whether there be a *vacuum* or no. For if they had not the *idea* of space without body, they could not make a question about its existence; and if their *idea* of body did not include in it something more than the bare *idea* of space, they could have no doubt about the plenitude of the world; and it would be as absurd to demand whether there were space without body, as whether there were space without space, or body without body, since these were but different names of the same *idea*.

25. It is true, the *idea* of *extension* joins itself so inseparably with all visible and most tangible qualities that it suffers us to see no one, or feel very few external objects, without taking in impressions of extension too. This readiness of extension to make itself be taken notice of so constantly with other *ideas* has been the occasion, I guess, that some have made the whole essence of *body* to consist in extension; which is not much to be wondered at, since some have had their minds, by their eyes and touch (the busiest of all our senses), so filled with the *idea* of extension and, as it were, wholly possessed with it, that they allowed no existence to anything that had not extension. I shall not now argue with those men who take the measure and possibility of all being only from their narrow and gross imaginations; but having here to do only with those who conclude the essence of body to be *extension*, because they say they cannot imagine any sensible quality of any body without extension, I shall desire them to consider that, had they reflected on their *ideas* of tastes and smells as much as on those of sight and touch, nay, had they examined their *ideas* of hunger and thirst and several other pains, they would have found that they included in them no *idea* of extension at all, which is but an

affection of body, as well as the rest discoverable by our senses, which are scarce acute enough to look into the pure essences of things.

26.   If those *ideas* which are constantly joined to all others must therefore be concluded to be the essence of those things which have constantly those *ideas* joined to them and are inseparable from them, then unity is without doubt the essence of everything.   For there is not any object of sensation or reflection which does not carry with it the *idea* of one; but the weakness of this kind of argument we have already shown sufficiently.

27.   To conclude: Whatever men shall think concerning the existence of a *vacuum*, this is plain to me: that we have as clear an *idea of space distinct from solidity*, as we have of solidity distinct from motion, or motion from space.   We have not any two more distinct *ideas*; and we can as easily conceive space without solidity, as we can conceive body or space without motion, though it be never so certain that neither body nor motion can exist without space.   But whether anyone will take space to be only a relation resulting from the existence of other beings at a distance; or whether they will think the words of the most knowing King *Solomon, The heaven, and the heaven of heavens, cannot contain thee,* or those more emphatical ones of the inspired philosopher St. *Paul, In him we live, move, and have our being,* are to be understood in a literal sense, I leave everyone to consider: only our *idea* of *space* is, I think, such as I have mentioned, and distinct from that of *body.*   For, whether we consider, in matter itself, the distance of its coherent solid parts, and call it, in respect of those solid parts, *extension;* or whether, considering it as lying between the extremities of any body in its several dimensions, we call it *length, breadth,* and *thickness;* or else, considering it as lying between any two bodies or positive beings, without any consideration whether there be any matter or no between, we call it *distance:* however named or considered, it is always the same uniform simple *idea* of *space,* taken from objects about which our senses have been conversant; whereof, having settled *ideas* in our minds, we can revive, repeat, and add them one to another as often as we will, and consider the space or distance so imagined either as filled with solid parts, so that another body cannot come there without displacing and thrusting out the body that was there before, or else as void of solidity, so

that a body of equal dimensions to that empty or pure space may be placed in it, without the removing or expulsion of anything that was there. But, to avoid confusion in discourses concerning this matter, it were possibly to be wished that the name *extension* were applied only to matter, or the distance of the extremities of particular bodies; and the term *expansion* to space in general, with or without solid matter possessing it, so as to say *space* is *expanded*, and *body extended*. But in this everyone has his liberty; I propose it only for the more clear and distinct way of speaking.

28. The knowing precisely what our words stand for would, I imagine, in this as well as a great many other cases, quickly end the dispute. For I am apt to think that men, when they come to examine them, find their simple *ideas* all generally to agree, though in discourse with one another they perhaps confound one another with different names. I imagine that *men* who abstract their thoughts, and do well examine the *ideas* of their own minds, *cannot much differ in thinking*, however they may perplex themselves with words, according to the way of speaking of the several schools or sects they have been bred up in: though amongst unthinking men, who examine not scrupulously and carefully their own *ideas*, and strip them not from the marks men use for them, but confound them with words, there must be endless dispute, wrangling, and jargon, especially if they be learned, bookish men, devoted to some sect and accustomed to the language of it, and have learned to talk after others. But if it should happen that any two thinking men should really have different *ideas*, I do not see how they could discourse or argue one with another. Here I must not be mistaken to think that every floating imagination in men's brains is presently of that sort of *ideas* I speak of. It is not easy for the mind to put off those confused notions and prejudices it has imbibed from custom, inadvertency, and common conversation. It requires pains and assiduity to examine its *ideas*, till it resolves them into those clear and distinct simple ones, out of which they are compounded; and to see which, amongst its simple ones, have or have not a necessary connexion and dependence one upon another. Till a man doth this in the primary and original notions of things, he builds upon floating and uncertain principles, and will often find himself at a loss.

CHAPTER XIV

OF DURATION AND ITS SIMPLE MODES

1. THERE is another sort of distance, or length, the *idea* whereof we get not from the permanent parts of space, but from the fleeting and perpetually perishing parts of succession. This we call *duration*: the simple modes whereof are any different lengths of it whereof we have distinct *ideas*, as *hours*, *days*, *years*, etc., *time* and *eternity*.

2. The answer of a great man, to one who asked what time was, *Si non rogas intelligo* (which amounts to this: The more I set myself to think of it, the less I understand it), might perhaps persuade one that *time*, which reveals all other things, is itself not to be discovered. *Duration*, *time*, and *eternity* are, not without reason, thought to have something very abstruse in their nature. But however remote these may seem from our comprehension, yet if we trace them right to their originals, I doubt not but one of those sources of all our knowledge, viz. *sensation* and *reflection*, will be able to furnish us with these *ideas*, as clear and distinct as many others which are thought much less obscure; and we shall find that the *idea* of eternity itself is derived from the same common original with the rest of our *ideas*.

3. To understand *time* and *eternity* aright, we ought with attention to consider what *idea* it is we have of *duration*, and how we came by it. It is evident, to anyone who will but observe what passes in his own mind, that there is a train of *ideas* which constantly succeed one another in his understanding, as long as he is awake. *Reflection* on these appearances of several *ideas* one after another in our minds is that which furnishes us with the *idea* of *succession*; and the distance between any parts of that succession, or between the appearance of any two *ideas* in our minds, is that we call *duration*. For whilst we are thinking or whilst we receive successively several *ideas* in our minds, we know that we do exist; and so we call the existence or the continuation of the existence of ourselves, or anything else commensurate to the succession of any *ideas* in our minds, the *duration*

of ourselves or any such other thing co-existing with our thinking.

4.   That we have our notion of *succession* and *duration* from this original, viz. from reflection on the train of *ideas* which we find to appear one after another in our own minds, seems plain to me in that we have no perception of *duration* but by considering the train of *ideas* that take their turns in our understandings. When that succession of *ideas* ceases, our perception of duration ceases with it; which everyone clearly experiments in himself, whilst he sleeps soundly, whether an hour or a day, a month or a year; of which duration of things, while he sleeps or thinks not, he has no perception at all, but it is quite lost to him; and the moment wherein he leaves off to think, till the moment he begins to think again, seems to him to have no distance. And so I doubt not but it would be to a waking man, if it were possible for him to keep only one *idea* in his mind, without variation and the succession of others; and we see that one who fixes his thoughts very intently on one thing so as to take but little notice of the succession of *ideas* that pass in his mind whilst he is taken up with that earnest contemplation, lets slip out of his account a good part of that duration and thinks that time shorter than it is. But if sleep commonly unites the distant parts of duration, it is because during that time we have no succession of *ideas* in our minds. For if a man during his sleep dreams, and variety of *ideas* make themselves perceptible to his mind one after another, he hath then, during such a dreaming, a sense of *duration* and of the length of it. By which it is to me very clear that men derive their *ideas* of duration from their *reflection on the train of the* ideas they observe to succeed one another in their own understandings, without which observation they can have no notion of *duration*, whatever may happen in the world.

5.   Indeed a man having, from reflecting on the succession and number of his own thoughts, got the notion or *idea* of *duration*, he can apply that notion to things which exist while he does not think: as he that has got the *idea* of extension from bodies by his sight or touch can apply it to distances, where no body is seen or felt. And therefore, though a man has no perception of the length of duration which passed whilst he slept or thought not: yet, having observed the revolution of days and nights and found the length of their duration to be in appearance regular and constant, he can, upon the supposition that that revolution

has proceeded after the same manner whilst he was asleep or thought not, as it used to do at other times, he can, I say, imagine and make allowance for the length of *duration* whilst he slept. But if *Adam* and *Eve* (when they were alone in the world) instead of their ordinary night's sleep, had passed the whole twenty-four hours in one continued sleep, the duration of that twenty-four hours had been irrecoverably lost to them, and been forever left out of their account of time.

6.   Thus *by reflecting on the appearing of various* ideas *one after another in our understandings, we get the notion of succession*; which if anyone should think we did rather get from our observation of motion by our senses, he will perhaps be of my mind when he considers that even motion produces in his mind an *idea* of succession no otherwise than as it produces there a continued train of distinguishable *ideas*. For a man looking upon a body really moving perceives yet no motion at all unless that motion produces a constant train *of successive* ideas: v.g. a man becalmed at sea, out of sight of land, in a fair day, may look on the sun, or sea, or ship a whole hour together and perceive no motion at all in either, though it be certain that two, and perhaps all of them, have moved during that time a great way; but as soon as he perceives either of them to have changed distance with some other body, as soon as this motion produces any new *idea* in him, then he perceives that there has been motion. But wherever a man is with all things at rest about him, without perceiving any motion at all, if during this hour of quiet he has been thinking, he will perceive the various *ideas* of his own thoughts in his own mind appearing one after another, and thereby observe and find succession where he could observe no motion.

7.   And this, I think, is the reason *why motions very slow, though they are constant, are not perceived* by us: because in their remove from one sensible part towards another, their change of distance is so slow that it causes no new *ideas* in us, but a good while one after another. And so not causing a constant train of new *ideas* to follow one another immediately in our minds, we have no perception of motion; which consisting in a constant succession, we cannot perceive that succession without a constant succession of varying *ideas* arising from it.

8.   On the contrary, *things that move* so swift as not to affect the senses distinctly with several distinguishable distances of

their motion, and so cause not any train of *ideas* in the mind, *are not* also *perceived* to move. For anything that moves round about in a circle, in less time than our *ideas* are wont to succeed one another in our minds, is not perceived to move, but seems to be a perfect entire circle of that matter or colour, and not a part of a circle in motion.

9. Hence I leave it to others to judge whether it be not probable that our *ideas* do, whilst we are awake, succeed one another in our minds at certain distances, not much unlike the images in the inside of a lantern, turned round by the heat of a candle. This appearance of theirs in train, though perhaps it may be sometimes faster and sometimes slower, yet, I guess, varies not very much in a waking man: there seem to be *certain bounds to the quickness and slowness of the succession of* those *ideas* one to another in our minds beyond which they can neither delay nor hasten.

10. The reason I have for this odd conjecture is from observing that, in the impressions made upon any of our senses, we can but to a certain degree perceive any succession; which if exceeding quick, the sense of succession is lost, even in cases where it is evident that there is a real succession. Let a cannon-bullet pass through a room, and in its way take with it any limb or fleshy parts of a man, it is as clear as any demonstration can be that it must strike successively the two sides of the room; it is also evident that it must touch one part of the flesh first, and another after, and so in succession; and yet, I believe, nobody who ever felt the pain of such a shot, or heard the blow against the two distant walls, could perceive any succession either in the pain or sound of so swift a stroke. Such a part of duration as this, wherein we perceive no succession, is that which we may call an *instant*, and is *that which takes up the time of only one idea* in our minds, without the succession of another, wherein therefore we perceive no succession at all.

11. This also happens *where the motion is* so *slow* as not to supply a constant train of fresh *ideas* to the senses, as fast as the mind is capable of receiving new ones into it; and so other *ideas* of our own thoughts having room to come into our minds between those offered to our senses by the moving body, *there the sense of motion is lost*; and the body, though it really moves, yet not changing perceivable distance with some other bodies as fast as the *ideas* of our own minds do naturally follow one another

in train, the thing seems to stand still; as is evident in the hands
of clocks, and shadows of sun-dials, and other constant but slow
motions where, though after certain intervals we perceive. by
the change of distance that it hath moved, yet the motion itself
we perceive not.

12.   So that to me it seems that *the constant and regular succession of ideas* in a waking man *is*, as it were, *the measure* and standard *of all other successions*: whereof, if anyone either exceeds
the pace of our *ideas*, as where two sounds or pains, etc., take up
in their succession the duration of but one *idea*, or else where any
motion or succession is so slow as that it keeps not pace with the
ideas in our minds or the quickness in which they take their
turns, as when any one or more *ideas* in their ordinary course
come into our mind between those which are offered to the
sight by the different perceptible distances of a body in motion,
or between sounds or smells following one another, there also
the sense of a constant continued succession is lost, and we
perceive it not but with certain gaps of rest between.

13.   If it be so, that the *ideas* of our minds, whilst we have any
there, do constantly change and shift in a continual succession,
it would be impossible, may anyone say, for a man to think
long of any one thing; by which, if it be meant that a man may
have one self-same single idea *a long time alone in his mind, without any variation at all*, I think, in matter of fact, it is *not
possible*: for which (not knowing how the *ideas* of our minds are
framed, of what materials they are made, whence they have their
light, and how they come to make their appearances), I can give
no other reason but experience; and I would have anyone try
whether he can keep one unvaried single *idea* in his mind, without any other, for any considerable time together.

14.   For trial, let him take any figure, any degree of light or
whiteness, or what other he pleases, and he will, I suppose, find
it difficult to keep all other *ideas* out of his mind; but that some,
either of another kind, or various considerations of that *idea*
(each of which considerations is a new *idea*) will constantly
succeed one another in his thoughts, let him be as wary as he can.

15.   All that is in a man's power in this case, I think, is only to
mind and observe what the *ideas* are that take their turns *in* his
understanding, or else to direct the sort and call in such as he
hath a desire or use of; but hinder the *constant succession* of
fresh ones I think he cannot, though he may commonly choose

whether he will heedfully observe and consider them.
16. Whether these several *ideas* in a man's mind be made by
certain motions, I will not here dispute; but this I am sure, that
they include no *idea* of motion in their appearance; and if a man
had not the *idea* of motion otherwise, I think he would have
none at all; which is enough to my present purpose and sufficiently shows that the notice we take of the *ideas* of our own
minds, appearing there one after another, is that which gives us
the *idea* of succession and duration, without which we should
have no such *ideas* at all. It is *not*, then, *motion*, but the constant
train of *ideas* in our minds, whilst we are waking, *that furnishes
us with the* idea *of duration*, whereof motion no otherwise gives
us any perception than as it causes in our minds a constant
succession of *ideas*, as I have before shown; and we have as
clear an *idea* of succession and duration by the train of other
ideas succeeding one another in our minds, without the *idea* of
any motion, as by the train of *ideas* caused by the uninterrupted
sensible change of distance between two bodies, which we have
from motion; and therefore we should as well have the *idea* of
duration, were there no sense of motion at all.
17. Having thus got the *idea* of duration, the next thing
natural for the mind to do is to get some *measure of* this common
duration whereby it might judge of its different lengths, and
consider the distinct order wherein several things exist, without
which a great part of our knowledge would be confused and a
great part of history be rendered very useless. This consideration as set out by certain periods and marked by certain
measures or *epochs* is that, I think, which most properly we
call *time*.
18. In the measuring of extension, there is nothing more
required but the application of the standard or measure we make
use of to the thing of whose extension we would be informed.
But in the measuring of duration this cannot be done, because
no two different parts of succession can be put together to
measure one another; and nothing being a *measure of duration*
but duration, as nothing is of extension but extension, we cannot keep by us any standing, unvarying measure of duration,
which consists in a constant fleeting succession, as we can of
certain lengths of extension, as inches, feet, yards, etc., marked
out in permanent parcels of matter. Nothing then could serve
well for a convenient measure of time but what has divided the

whole length of its duration into apparently equal portions, by constantly repeated periods. What portions of duration are not distinguished, or considered as distinguished and measured by such periods, come not so properly under the notion of time, as appears by such phrases as these, viz., *before all time, and when time shall be no more*.

19. The diurnal and annual *revolutions of the sun*, as having been from the beginning of nature constant, regular, and universally observable by all mankind, and supposed equal to one another, have been with reason *made use of for the measure of duration*. But the distinction of days and years having depended on the motion of the sun, it has brought this mistake with it, that it has been thought that motion and duration were the measure one of another. For men in the *measuring of the length of time*, having been accustomed to the *ideas* of minutes, hours, days, months, years, etc., which they found themselves upon any mention of time or duration presently to think on, all which portions of time were measured out by the motion of those heavenly bodies, they were apt to confound time and motion, or at least to think that they had a necessary connexion one with another: whereas any constant periodical appearance or alteration of *ideas*, in seemingly equidistant spaces of duration, if constant and universally observable, would have as well distinguished the intervals of time as those that have been made use of. For, supposing the sun, which some have taken to be a fire, had been lighted up at the same distance of time that it now every day comes about to the same meridian, and then gone out again about twelve hours after, and that in the space of an annual revolution it had sensibly increased in brightness and heat, and so decreased again: would not such regular appearances serve to measure out the distances of duration to all that could observe it, as well without as with motion? For if the appearances were constant, universally observable, and in equidistant periods, they would serve mankind for measure of time as well were the motion away.

20. For the freezing of water or the blowing of a plant, returning at equidistant periods in all parts of the earth, would as well serve men to reckon their years by as the motions of the sun; and in effect we see that some people in *America* counted their years by the coming of certain birds amongst them at their certain seasons and leaving them at others. For a fit of an ague, the

sense of hunger or thirst, a smell or a taste, or any other *idea* returning constantly at equidistant periods and making itself universally be taken notice of, *would* not fail to *measure* out the course of succession and distinguish the distances of *time*. Thus we see that men born blind count time well enough by years, whose revolutions yet they cannot distinguish by motions that they perceive not; and I ask whether a blind man who distinguished his years either by heat of summer or cold of winter, by the smell of any flower of the spring or taste of any fruit of the autumn, would not have a better measure of time than the *Romans* had, before the reformation of their *calendar* by *Julius Caesar*, or many other people whose years, notwithstanding the motion of the sun, which they pretend to make use of, are very irregular? And it adds no small difficulty to chronology that the exact lengths of the years that several nations counted by are hard to be known, they differing very much one from another, and I think I may say all of them from the precise motion of the sun. And if the sun moved from the creation to the flood constantly in the equator, and so equally dispersed its light and heat to all the habitable parts of the earth, in days all of the same length, without its annual variations to the tropics, as a late ingenious author supposes, I do not think it very easy to imagine that (notwithstanding the motion of the sun) men should in the *antediluvian* world, from the beginning count by years, or measure their time by periods that had no sensible marks very obvious to distinguish them by.

21. But perhaps it will be said, without a regular motion, such as of the sun or some other, how could it ever be known that such periods were equal? To which I answer: The equality of any other returning appearances might be known by the same way that that of days was known, or presumed to be so at first, which was only by judging of them by the train of *ideas* which had passed in men's minds in the intervals; by which train of *ideas* discovering inequality in the natural days, but none in the artificial days, the artificial days or νυχθήμερα were guessed to be equal, which was sufficient to make them serve for a measure: though exacter search has since discovered inequality in the diurnal revolutions of the sun, and we know not whether the annual also be not unequal; these yet, by their presumed and apparent equality, serve as well to reckon time by (though not to measure the parts of duration exactly) as if they could be

proved to be exactly equal. We must, therefore, carefully distinguish betwixt duration itself, and the measures we make use of to judge of its length. Duration, in itself, is to be considered as going on in one constant, equal, uniform course; but none of the measures of it which we make use of can be known to do so, nor can we be assured that their assigned parts or periods are equal in duration one to another: for two successive lengths of duration, however measured, can never be demonstrated to be equal. The motion of the sun, which the world used so long and so confidently for an exact measure of duration, has, as I said, been found in its several parts unequal; and though men have, of late, made use of a pendulum as a more steady and regular motion than that of the sun or (to speak more truly) of the earth: yet if anyone should be asked how he certainly knows that the two successive swings of a pendulum are equal, it would be very hard to satisfy him that they are infallibly so, since we cannot be sure that the cause of that motion, which is unknown to us, shall always operate equally; and we are sure that the medium in which the pendulum moves is not constantly the same: either of which, varying, may alter the equality of such periods and thereby destroy the certainty and exactness of the measure by motion, as well as any other periods of other appearances, the notion of duration still remaining clear though our measures of it cannot any of them be demonstrated to be exact. Since then no two portions of succession can be brought together, it is impossible ever certainly to know their equality. All that we can do for a measure of time is to take such as have continual successive appearances at seemingly equidistant periods; *of* which *seeming equality we have no other measure but* such as *the train of our own ideas* have lodged in our memories, with the concurrence of other probable reasons, to persuade us of their equality.

22.   One thing seems strange to me: that whilst all men manifestly measured time by the motion of the great and visible bodies of the world, *time* yet should be *defined* to be the *measure of motion*: whereas it is obvious to everyone who reflects ever so little on it, that to measure motion, space is as necessary to be considered as time; and those who look a little further will find also the bulk of the thing moved necessary to be taken into the computation by anyone who will estimate or measure motion, so as to judge right of it. Nor, indeed, does motion any otherwise

conduce to the measuring of duration than as it constantly brings about the return of certain sensible *ideas*, in seeming equidistant periods. For if the motion of the sun were as unequal as of a ship driven by unsteady winds, sometimes very slow and at others irregularly very swift, or if being constantly equally swift, it yet was not circular and produced not the same appearances, it would not at all help us to measure time, any more than the seeming unequal motion of a comet does.

23. *Minutes, hours, days, and years* are then *no* more *necessary to time* or duration than inches, feet, yards, and miles marked out in any matter are to extension. For though we in this part of the universe, by the constant use of them as of periods set out by the revolutions of the sun, or as known parts of such periods, have fixed the *ideas* of such lengths of duration in our minds, which we apply to all parts of time, whose lengths we would consider: yet there may be other parts of the universe, where they no more use these measures of ours than in *Japan* they do our inches, feet, or miles; but yet something analogous to them there must be. For without some regular periodical returns, we could not measure ourselves, or signify to others, the length of any duration, though at the same time the world were as full of motion as it is now, but no part of it disposed into regular and apparently equidistant revolutions. But the different measures that may be made use of for the account of time do not at all alter the notion of duration, which is the thing to be measured; no more than the different standards of a foot and a cubit alter the notion of extension to those who make use of those different measures.

24. The mind, having once got such a measure of time as the annual revolution of the sun, can apply that measure to duration wherein that measure itself did not exist and with which, in the reality of its being, it had nothing to do; for should one say that *Abraham* was born in the two thousand seven hundred and twelfth year of the *Julian* period, it is altogether as intelligible as reckoning from the beginning of the world, though there were so far back no motion of the sun, nor any other motion at all. For though the *Julian* period be supposed to begin several hundred years before there were really either days, nights, or years marked out by any revolutions of the sun, yet we reckon as right, and thereby measure durations as well, as if really at that time the sun had existed and kept the same ordinary motion it doth

now. The *idea of duration equal to an annual revolution of the sun* is as easily *applicable* in our thoughts *to duration where no sun nor motion was*, as the *idea* of a foot or yard taken from bodies here can be applied in our thoughts to distances beyond the confines of the world, where are no bodies at all.

25.   For supposing it were 5639 miles or millions of miles from this place to the remotest body of the universe (for being finite, it must be at a certain distance), as we suppose it to be 5639 years from this time to the first existence of any body in the beginning of the world, *we can*, in our thoughts, *apply this measure of a year to duration before the creation*, or beyond the duration of bodies or motion, as we can this measure of a mile to space beyond the utmost bodies; and by the one measure duration, where there was no motion, as well as by the other measure space in our thoughts, where there is no body.

26.   If it be objected to me here that, in this way of explaining of time, I have begged what I should not, viz. that the world is neither eternal nor infinite, I answer that to my present purpose it is not needful, in this place, to make use of arguments to evince the world to be finite both in duration and extension. But it being at least as conceivable as the contrary, I have certainly the liberty to suppose it, as well as anyone hath to suppose the contrary; and I doubt not but that *everyone* that will go about it, may easily *conceive* in his mind *the beginning of motion, though not of all duration*, and so may come to a stop and *non ultra* in his consideration of motion. So also, in his thoughts, he may set limits to body, and the extension belonging to it; but not to space, where no body is, the utmost bounds of space and duration being beyond the reach of thought, as well as the utmost bounds of number are beyond the largest comprehension of the mind; and all for the same reason, as we shall see in another place.

27.   By the same means, therefore, and from the same original that we come to have *the idea of* time, we have also that *idea* which we call *eternity*: viz. having got the *idea* of succession and duration by reflecting on the train of our own *ideas* caused in us either by the natural appearances of those *ideas* coming constantly of themselves into our waking thoughts, or else caused by external objects successively affecting our senses; and having from the revolutions of the sun got the *ideas* of certain lengths of duration, we can in our thoughts add such lengths of duration to

one another as often as we please, and apply them, so added, to durations past or to come; and this we can continue to do, without bounds or limits, and proceed *in infinitum,* and apply thus the length of the annual motion of the sun to duration, supposed before the sun's or any other motion had its being; which is no more difficult or absurd than to apply the notion I have of the moving of a shadow one hour to-day upon the sun-dial to the duration of something last night, v.g. the burning of a candle, which is now absolutely separate from all actual motion; and it is as impossible for the duration of that flame for an hour last night to co-exist with any motion that now is, or forever shall be, as for any part of duration, that was before the beginning of the world, to co-exist with the motion of the sun now. But yet this hinders not but that, having the *idea* of the length of the motion of the shadow on a dial between the marks of two hours, I can as distinctly measure in my thoughts the duration of that candle-light last night, as I can the duration of anything that does now exist; and it is no more than to think that, had the sun shone then on the dial, and moved after the same rate it doth now, the shadow on the dial would have passed from one hour-line to another, whilst that flame of the candle lasted.

28.   The notion of an hour, day, or year, being only the *idea* I have of the length of certain periodical regular motions, neither of which motions do ever all at once exist but only in the *ideas* I have of them in my memory derived from my senses or reflection, I can with the same ease and for the same reason apply it in my thoughts to duration antecedent to all manner of motion as well as to anything that is but a minute, or a day antecedent to the motion that at this very moment the sun is in. All things past are equally and perfectly at rest; and to this way of consideration of them are all one, whether they were before the beginning of the world, or but yesterday: *the measuring of* any *duration* by some motion *depending* not at all *on* the real co-existence of that thing to that motion, or any other periods of revolution, but the having *a clear idea of the length of some* periodical known motion or other intervals of *duration* in my mind, and *applying that to the duration of the thing I would* *measure.*

29.   Hence we see that some men imagine the duration of the world from its first existence to this present year 1689 to have been 5639 years, or equal to 5639 annual revolutions of the

sun, and others a great deal more; as the *Egyptians* of old, who
in the time of *Alexander* counted 23,000 years from the reign of
the sun; and the *Chinese* now, who account the world 3,269,000
years old or more; which longer duration of the world according
to their computation, though I should not believe to be true, yet
I can equally imagine it with them and as truly understand and
say one is longer than the other, as I understand that *Methu-
salem's* life was longer than *Enoch's*. And if the common reckoning of 5639 should be true (as it may be as well as any other
assigned), it hinders not at all my imagining what others mean
when they make the world 1000 years older, since everyone
may with the same facility imagine (I do not say believe) the
world to be 50,000 years old as 5639, and may as well conceive
the duration of 50,000 years as 5639. Whereby it appears that
to the measuring the duration of anything by time, it is not requisite that that thing should be co-existent to the motion we
measure by, or any other periodical revolution; but *it suffices* to
this purpose *that we have the idea of the length of any regular
periodical appearances,* which we can in our minds apply to
duration, with which the motion or appearance never co-existed.
30.   For as in the history of the creation delivered by *Moses,* I
can imagine that light existed three days before the sun was or
had any motion, barely by thinking that the duration of light
before the sun was created was so long as (if the sun had moved
then as it doth now) would have been equal to three of his
diurnal revolutions; so by the same way I can have an *idea* of the
chaos or Angels being created before there was either light or
any continued motion, a minute, an hour, a day, a year, or
1000 years. For, if I can but consider *duration* equal to one
minute before either the being or motion of any body, I can add
one minute more till I come to sixty; and by the same way of
adding minutes, hours, or years (i.e. such or such parts of the
sun's revolution or any other period whereof I have the *idea*)
proceed *in infinitum,* and suppose a duration exceeding as many
such periods as I can reckon, let me add whilst I will, which I
think is the notion we have of *eternity*; of whose infinity we
have no other notion than we have of the infinity of number, to
which we can add forever without end.
31.   And thus I think it is plain that, *from* those two fountains
of all knowledge before mentioned, viz. *reflection and sensation,
we get the ideas of duration,* and the measures of it.

For, *First,* by observing what passes in our minds, how our *ideas* there in train constantly some vanish and others begin to appear, we come by the *idea* of *succession.*

Secondly, by observing a distance in the parts of this succession, we get the *idea* of *duration.*

Thirdly, by sensation observing certain appearances, at certain regular and seeming equidistant periods, we get the *ideas* of certain lengths or *measures of duration,* as minutes, hours, days, years, etc.

Fourthly, by being able to repeat those measures of time, or *ideas* of stated length of duration, in our minds as often as we will, we can come to *imagine duration, where nothing does really endure or exist*; and thus we imagine to-morrow, next year, or seven years hence.

Fifthly, by being able to repeat any such *idea* of any length of time, as of a minute, a year, or an age, as often as we will in our own thoughts, and add them one to another, without ever coming to the end of such addition any nearer than we can to the end of number, to which we can always add, we come by the *idea* of *eternity* as the future eternal duration of our souls, as well as the eternity of that infinite Being which must necessarily have always existed.

Sixthly, by considering any part of infinite duration as set out by periodical measures, we come by the *idea* of what we call *time* in general.

Chapter XV

OF DURATION AND EXPANSION, CONSIDERED TOGETHER

1. THOUGH we have in the precedent chapters dwelt pretty long on the considerations of space and duration, yet, they being *ideas* of general concernment that have something very abstruse and peculiar in their nature, the comparing them one with another may perhaps be of use for their illustration; and we may have the more clear and distinct conception of them by taking a view of them together. Distance or space, in its simple abstract conception, to avoid confusion, I call *expansion,* to distinguish it from *extension,* which by some is used to express this distance

only as it is in the solid parts of matter, and so includes, or at least intimates, the *idea* of body: whereas the *idea* of pure distance includes no such thing. I prefer also the word *expansion* to *space*, because *space* is often applied to distance of fleeting successive parts, which never exist together, as well as to those which are permanent. In both these (viz. *expansion* and *duration*) the mind has this common *idea* of continued lengths, capable of greater or less quantities: for a man has as clear an *idea* of the difference of the length of an hour and a day, as of an inch and a foot.

2. The *mind*, having got the *idea* of the length of any part of *expansion*, let it be a span or a pace or what length you will, *can*, as has been said, repeat that *idea* and so, adding it to the former, *enlarge its idea of length* and make it equal to two spans or two paces, and so, as often as it will, till it equals the distance of any parts of the earth one from another, and increase thus till it amounts to the distance of the sun or remotest star. By such a progression as this, setting out from the place where it is or any other place, it can proceed and pass beyond all those lengths and find nothing to stop its going on, either in or without body. It is true, we can easily in our thoughts come to the end of solid extension: the extremity and bounds of all body we have no difficulty to arrive at; but when the mind is there, it finds nothing to hinder its progress into this endless expansion: of that it can neither find nor conceive any end. Nor let anyone say that beyond the bounds of body there is nothing at all, unless he will confine GOD within the limits of matter. *Solomon*, whose understanding was filled and enlarged with wisdom, seems to have other thoughts, when he says, *Heaven, and the heaven of heavens, cannot contain thee*; and he, I think, very much magnifies to himself the capacity of his own understanding who persuades himself that he can extend his thoughts further than GOD exists, or imagine any expansion where He is not.

3. Just so is it in duration. *The mind, having got the idea of any length of duration, can double, multiply, and enlarge it,* not only beyond its own, but beyond the existence of all corporeal beings, and all the measures of time, taken from the great bodies of the world and their motions. But yet everyone easily admits that, though we make duration boundless, as certainly it is, we cannot yet extend it beyond all being. GOD, everyone easily allows, fills eternity; and it is hard to find a reason why

anyone should doubt that he likewise fills immensity. His infinite being is certainly as boundless one way as another; and methinks it ascribes a little too much to matter to say, where there is no body there is nothing.

4. Hence I think we may learn the reason *why everyone* familiarly and without the least hesitation speaks of and supposes eternity, and sticks not to *ascribe infinity to duration*; *but* it is *with more doubting* and reserve that many *admit* or suppose *the infinity of space*. The reason whereof seems to me to be this: that duration and extension being used as names of affections belonging to other beings, we easily conceive in GOD infinite duration, and we cannot avoid doing so; but, not attributing to him extension, but only to matter, which is finite, we are apter to doubt of the existence of expansion without matter, of which alone we commonly suppose it an attribute. And, therefore, when men pursue their thoughts of space, they are apt to stop at the confines of body: as if space were there at an end too, and reached no further. Or if their *ideas*, upon consideration, carry them further, yet they term what is beyond the limits of the universe, imaginary space: as if it were nothing, because there is no body existing in it. Whereas duration, antecedent to all body and to the motions which it is measured by, they never term imaginary: because it is never supposed void of some other real existence. And if the names of things may at all direct our thoughts towards the originals of men's *ideas* (as I am apt to think they may very much), one may have occasion to think, by the name *duration*, that the continuation of existence, with a kind of resistance to any destructive force, and the continuation of solidity (which is apt to be confounded with and, if we will look into the minute anatomical parts of matter, is little different from, hardness) were thought to have some analogy and gave occasion to words so near of kin as *durare* and *durum esse*. And that *durare* is applied to the *idea* of hardness, as well as that of existence, we see in *Horace*, Epod. xvi, *ferro duravit saecula*. But, be that as it will, this is certain, that whoever pursues his own thoughts will find them sometimes launch out beyond the extent of body, into the infinity of space or expansion, the *idea* whereof is distinct and separate from body and all other things; which may (to those who please) be a subject of further meditation.

5. *Time* in general is to *duration* as *place* to *expansion*. They

* G 332

are so much of those boundless oceans of eternity and immensity as is set out and distinguished from the rest, as it were by landmarks; and so are made use of to denote the position of finite real beings, in respect one to another, in those uniform infinite oceans of duration and space. These, rightly considered, are nothing but *ideas* of determinate distances from certain known points, fixed in distinguishable sensible things, and supposed to keep the same distance one from another. From such points fixed in sensible beings we reckon, and from them we measure our portions of those infinite quantities; which, so considered, are that which we call *time* and *place*. For duration and space being in themselves uniform and boundless, the order and position of things, without such known settled points, would be lost in them, and all things would lie jumbled in an incurable confusion.

6.   *Time* and *place* taken thus, for determinate distinguishable portions of those infinite abysses of space and duration, set out or supposed to be distinguished from the rest by marks and known boundaries, have each of them a two-fold acceptation.

First, Time in general is commonly taken for so much of infinite duration as is measured out by and co-existent with the existence and motions of the great bodies of the universe, as far as we know anything of them; and in this sense time begins and ends with the frame of this sensible world, as in these phrases before-mentioned, *before all time*, or *when time shall be no more*. *Place* likewise is taken sometimes for that portion of infinite space which is possessed by and comprehended within the material world, and is thereby distinguished from the rest of expansion, though this may be more properly called *extension* than place. Within these two are confined and, by the observable parts of them, are measured and determined the particular time or duration and the particular extension and place of all corporeal beings.

7.   *Secondly,* Sometimes the word *time* is used *in a larger sense*, and is applied to parts of that infinite duration, not that were really distinguished and measured out by this real existence and periodical motions of bodies that were appointed from the beginning to be for signs and for seasons and for days and years, and are accordingly our measures of time, but such other portions too of that infinite uniform duration, which we upon any occasion do suppose equal to certain lengths of measured

time, and so consider them as bounded and determined. For, if we should suppose the creation, or fall of the angels, was at the beginning of the *Julian* period, we should speak properly enough, and should be understood if we said it is a longer time, since the creation of angels than the creation of the world, by 764 years: whereby we would mark out so much of that undistinguished duration as we suppose equal to, and would have admitted, 764 annual revolutions of the sun, moving at the rate it now does. And thus likewise we sometimes speak of place, distance, or bulk, in the great *inane*, beyond the confines of the world, when we consider so much of that space as is equal to or capable to receive a body of any assigned dimensions, as a cubic foot, or do suppose a point in it at such a certain distance from any part of the universe.

8. *Where* and *when* are questions belonging to all finite existences, and are by us always reckoned from some known parts of this sensible world, and from some certain epochs marked out to us by the motions observable in it. Without some such fixed parts or periods, the order of things would be lost to our finite understandings, in the boundless invariable oceans of duration and expansion, which comprehend in them all finite beings and in their full extent belong only to the deity. And therefore we are not to wonder that we comprehend them not and do so often find our thoughts at a loss when we would consider them, either abstractly in themselves or as any way attributed to the first incomprehensible being. But when applied to any particular finite beings, the extension of any body is so much of that infinite space as the bulk of that body takes up. And place is the position of any body when considered at a certain distance from some other. As the *idea* of the particular *duration* of anything is an *idea* of that portion of infinite *duration* which passes during the existence of that thing: so the time *when* the thing existed is the *idea* of that space of duration which passed between some known and fixed period of duration and the being of that thing. One shows the distance of the extremities of the bulk or existence of the same thing, as that it is a foot square, or lasted two years; the other shows the distance of it in place or existence from other fixed points of space or duration, as that it was in the middle of *Lincoln's-Inn*-Fields, or the first degree of *Taurus*, and in the year of our Lord 1671, or the 1000th year of the *Julian* period: all which distances we

measure by preconceived *ideas* of certain lengths of space and duration, as inches, feet, miles, and degrees, and in the other minutes, days, and years, etc.

9.   There is one thing more wherein *space* and *duration* have a great conformity, and that is, though they are justly reckoned amongst our *simple ideas*, yet none of the distinct *ideas* we have of either is without all manner of *composition*[1]: it is the very nature of both of them to consist of parts; but their parts, being all of the same kind and without the mixture of any other *idea*, hinder them not from having a place amongst simple *ideas*.

[1] It has been objected to Mr. *Locke* that, if space consists of parts, as it is confessed in this place, he should not have reckoned it in the number of simple *ideas*: because it seems to be inconsistent with what he says elsewhere, that a simple *idea* is *uncompounded and contains in it nothing but one uniform appearance, or conception of the mind, and is not distinguishable into different* ideas, p. 90. It is further objected that Mr. *Locke* has not given in the Second Chapter of the Second Book, where he begins to speak of *simple ideas*, an exact definition of what he understands by the word *simple ideas*. To these difficulties, Mr. *Locke* answers thus: To begin with the last, he declares that he has not treated his subject in an order perfectly scholastic, having not had much familiarity with those sort of books during the writing of his, and not remembering at all the method in which they are written; and therefore his readers ought not to expect definitions regularly placed at the beginning of each new subject. Mr. *Locke* contents himself to employ the principal terms that he uses so that from his use of them the reader may easily comprehend what he means by them. But with respect to the term *simple idea*, he has had the good luck to define that in the place cited in the objection, and therefore there is no reason to supply that defect. The question then is to know whether the *idea* or *extension* agrees with this definition. Which will effectually agree to it if it be understood in the sense which Mr. *Locke* had principally in his view; for that composition which he designed to exclude in that definition was a composition of different *ideas* in the mind, and not a composition of the same kind in a thing whose essence consists in having parts of the same kind, where you can never come to a part entirely exempted from this composition. So that, if the *idea* of *extension* consists in having *partes extra partes* (as the Schools speak) it is always, in the sense of Mr. *Locke*, a *simple idea*: because the *idea* of having *partes extra partes* cannot be resolved into two other *ideas*. For the remainder of the objection made to Mr. *Locke* with respect to the nature of extension, Mr. *Locke* was aware of it, as may be seen in Section 9, Ch. XV of the Second Book, where he says that the least portion of space or extension whereof we have a clear and distinct *idea* may perhaps be the fittest to be considered by us as a *simple idea* of that kind, out of which our complex modes of space and extension are made up. So that, according to Mr. *Locke*, it may very fitly be called a *simple idea*, since it is the least *idea* of space that the mind can form to itself and that cannot be divided by the mind into any less whereof it has in itself any determined perception. From whence it follows that it is to the mind one *simple idea*; and that is sufficient to take away this objection, for it is not the design of Mr. *Locke*, in this place, to discourse of anything but concerning the *ideas* of the mind. But if this is not sufficient to clear the difficulty, Mr. *Locke* has nothing more to add but that, if the *idea* of extension is so peculiar that it cannot exactly agree with the definition that he has given of those *simple ideas* so that it differs in some manner from all others of that kind, he thinks it is better to leave it there exposed to this difficulty than to make a new division in his favour. It is enough for Mr. *Locke* that his meaning can be understood. It is very common to observe intelligible discourses spoiled by too much subtilty in nice divisions. We ought to put things together as well as we can, *doctrina causa*; but, after all, several things will not be bundled up together under our terms and ways of speaking.

Could the mind, as in number, come to so small a part of extension or duration as excluded divisibility, *that* would be, as it
were, the indivisible unit or *idea*, by repetition of which, it
would make its more enlarged *ideas* of extension and duration.
But, since the mind is not able to frame an *idea* of any space
without parts, instead thereof it makes use of the common
measures which, by familiar use in each country, have imprinted
themselves on the memory (as inches and feet, cubits and para-
sangs; and so seconds, minutes, hours, days, and years in
duration): the mind makes use, I say, of such *ideas* as these as
simple ones, and these are the component parts of larger ideas,
which the mind upon occasion makes by the addition of such
known lengths which it is acquainted with. On the other side,
the ordinary smallest measure we have of either is looked on as
an unit in number, when the mind by division would reduce
them into less fractions, though on both sides, both in addition
and division, either of space or duration, when the *idea* under
consideration becomes very big or very small, its precise bulk
becomes very obscure and confused; and it is the number of its
repeated additions or divisions that alone remains clear and
distinct; as will easily appear to anyone who will let his thoughts
loose in the vast expansion of space, or divisibility of matter.
Every part of duration is duration too, and every part of extension is extension, both of them capable of addition or division
in infinitum. But the least portions of either of them, whereof
we have clear and distinct *ideas*, may perhaps be fittest to be
considered by us as the *simple ideas* of that kind out of which our
complex modes of space, extension, and duration are made up,
and into which they can again be distinctly resolved. Such a
small part in duration may be called a *moment*, and is the time of
one *idea* in our minds in the train of their ordinary succession
there. The other, wanting a proper name, I know not whether I
may be allowed to call *a sensible point*, meaning thereby the
least particle of matter or space we can discern, which is ordinarily about a minute, and to the sharpest eyes seldom less than
thirty seconds of a circle, whereof the eye is the centre.

10. Expansion and duration have this further agreement: that,
though they are both considered by us as having parts, yet *their
parts* are *not separable* one from another, no, not even in thought:
though the parts of bodies from whence we take our measure
of the one, and the parts of motion, or rather the succession

of *ideas* in our minds, from whence we take the measure of the other, may be interrupted and separated; as the one is often by rest, and the other is by sleep, which we call rest too.

11.   But yet there is this manifest difference between them: that the *ideas* of length, which we have of *expansion, are turned every way*, and so make figure, and breadth, and thickness; but *duration is but as it were the length of one straight line*, extended *in infinitum*, not capable of multiplicity, variation, or figure; but is one common measure of all existence whatsoever, wherein all things, whilst they exist, equally partake. For this present moment is common to all things that are now in being, and equally comprehends that part of their existence as much as if they were all but one single being; and we may truly say, they all exist in the same moment of time. Whether angels and spirits have any analogy to this, in respect of expansion, is beyond my comprehension; and perhaps for us, who have understandings and comprehensions suited to our own preservation and the ends of our own being, but not to the reality and extent of all other beings, it is near as hard to conceive any existence or to have an *idea* of any real being, with a perfect negation of all manner of expansion, as it is to have the *idea* of any real existence with a perfect negation of all manner of duration; and therefore, what spirits have to do with space, or how they communicate in it, we know not. All that we know is that bodies do each singly possess its proper portion of it, according to the extent of solid parts, and thereby exclude all other bodies from having any share in that particular portion of space, whilst it remains there.

12.   *Duration*, and time which is a part of it, *is the idea* we have *of perishing distance, of which no two parts exist together*, but follow each other in succession, as *expansion is the* idea *of lasting distance, all whose parts exist together* and are not capable of succession. And therefore, though we cannot conceive any duration without succession, nor can put it together in our thoughts that any being does now exist tomorrow or possess at once more than the present moment of duration, yet we can conceive the eternal duration of the Almighty far different from that of man, or any other finite being. Because man comprehends not in his knowledge or power all past and future things: his thoughts are but of yesterday, and he knows not what to-morrow will bring forth. What is once past he can never recall;

and what is yet to come he cannot make present. What I say of
man, I say of all finite beings; who, though they may far exceed
man in knowledge and power, yet are no more than the meanest
creature in comparison with God himself. Finite of any magnitude holds not any proportion to infinite. God's infinite duration being accompanied with infinite knowledge and infinite
power, he sees all things, past and to come; and they are no more
distant from his knowledge, no further removed from his sight,
than the present: they all lie under the same view, and there is
nothing which he cannot make exist each moment he pleases.
For, the existence of all things depending upon his good pleasure, all things exist every moment that he thinks fit to have
them exist. To conclude: expansion and duration do mutually
embrace and comprehend each other, every part of space being
in every part of duration, and every part of duration in every
part of expansion. Such a combination of two distinct *ideas* is,
I suppose, scarce to be found in all that great variety we do or
can conceive, and may afford matter to further speculation.

Chapter XVI

OF NUMBER

1. AMONGST all the *ideas* we have, as there is none suggested to
the mind by more ways, so there is none more simple, than that
of unity, or one: it has no shadow of variety or composition in
it; every object our senses are employed about, every *idea* in our
understandings, every thought of our minds, brings this *idea*
along with it. And therefore it is the most intimate to our
thoughts, as well as it is, in its agreement to all other things, the
most universal *idea* we have. For number applies itself to men,
angels, actions, thoughts: everything that either doth exist, or
can be imagined.
2. By repeating this *idea* in our minds, and adding the repetitions together, we come by the *complex* ideas *of the modes of it*.
Thus, by adding one to one, we have the complex *idea* of a
couple; by putting twelve units together, we have the complex
idea of a dozen; and of a score, or a million, or any other number.

3. *The simple modes* of *number are of all other the most distinct*: every the least variation, which is an unit, making each combination as clearly different from that which approacheth nearest to it, as the most remote; two being as distinct from one, as two hundred; and the *idea* of two as distinct from the *idea* of three, as the magnitude of the whole earth is from that of a mite. This is not so in other simple modes, in which it is not so easy, nor perhaps possible, for us to distinguish betwixt two approaching *ideas*, which yet are really different. For who will undertake to find a difference between the white of this paper and that of the next degree to it; or can form distinct *ideas* of every the least excess in extension?

4. The clearness and *distinctness of each mode of number* from all others, even those that approach nearest, makes me apt to think that demonstrations in numbers, if they are not more evident and exact than in extension, yet they are more general in their use, and more determinate in their application. Because the *ideas* of numbers are more precise and distinguishable than in extension, where every equality and excess are not so easy to be observed or measured; because our thoughts cannot in space arrive at any determined smallness beyond which it cannot go, as an unit; and therefore the quantity or proportion of any the least excess cannot be discovered; which is clear otherwise in number where, as has been said, 91 is as distinguishable from 90 as from 9000, though 91 be the next immediate excess to 90. But it is not so in extension, where whatsoever is more than just a foot or an inch is not distinguishable from the standard of a foot or an inch; and in lines which appear of an equal length, one may be longer than the other by innumerable parts; nor can any-one assign an angle which shall be the next biggest to a right one.

5. By the repeating, as has been said, of the *idea* of an unit, and joining it to another unit, we make thereof one collective *idea*, marked by the name *two*. And whosoever can do this and pro-ceed on, still adding one more to the last collective *idea* which he had of any number and gave a name to it, may count or have *ideas* for several collections of units, distinguished one from another, as far as he hath a series of names for following num-bers, and a memory to retain that series, with their several names: all *numeration* being but still the adding of one unit more and giving to the whole together, as comprehended in one *idea*, a new or distinct name or sign, whereby to know it from

those before and after and distinguish it from every smaller or greater multitude of unities. So that he that can add one to one, and so to two, and so go on with his tale, taking still with him the distinct names belonging to every progression, and so again, by subtracting an unit from each collection, retreat and lessen them, is capable of all the *ideas* of numbers, within the compass of his language, or for which he hath names, though not perhaps, of more. For the several simple modes of numbers being in our minds but so many combinations of units, which have no variety nor are capable of any other difference but more or less, names or marks for each distinct combination seem more necessary than in any other sort of *ideas*. For without such names or marks, we can hardly well make use of numbers in reckoning, especially where the combination is made up of any great multitude of units; which put together, without a name or mark to distinguish that precise collection, will hardly be kept from being a heap in confusion.

6. This I think to be the reason why some *Americans* I have spoken with (who were otherwise of quick and rational parts enough) could not, as we do, by any means count to 1000; nor had any distinct *idea* of that number, though they could reckon very well to 20. Because their language, being scanty and accommodated only to the few necessaries of a needy, simple life, unacquainted either with trade or mathematics, had no words in it to stand for 1000; so that when they were discoursed with of those greater numbers, they would show the hairs of their head, to express a great multitude, which they could not number; which inability, I suppose, proceeded from their want of names. The *Tououpinambos* had no names for numbers above 5; any number beyond that, they made out by showing their fingers, and the fingers of others who were present[1]. And I doubt not but we ourselves might distinctly number in words a great deal further than we usually do, would we find out but some fit denominations to signify them by; whereas in the way we take now to name them by millions of millions of millions, etc., it is hard to go beyond eighteen, or at most four and twenty decimal progressions, without confusion. But to show how much *distinct names conduce to our well reckoning* or having useful *ideas* of numbers, let us set all these following figures in one continued line, as the marks of one number: v.g.

[1] Léry, *op. cit.*, ch. 20, p. 307.

Nonillions	*Octillions*	*Septillions*	*Sextillions*	*Quintillions*
857324	162486	345896	437916	423147

Quadrillions	*Trillions*	*Billions*	*Millions*	*Units*
248106	235421	261734	368149	623137

The ordinary way of naming this number in *English* will be the often repeating of millions, of millions, of millions, of millions, of millions, of millions, of millions, of millions (which is the denomination of the second six figures). In which way, it will be very hard to have any distinguishing notions of this number. But whether, by giving every six figures a new and orderly denomination, these and perhaps a great many more figures in progression might not easily be counted distinctly and *ideas* of them both got more easily to ourselves and more plainly signified to others, I leave it to be considered. This I mention only to show how necessary distinct names are to numbering, without pretending to introduce new ones of my invention.

7. Thus children, either for want of names to mark the several progressions of numbers or, not having yet the faculty to collect scattered *ideas* into complex ones and range them in a regular order and so retain them in their memories, as is necessary to reckoning, do not begin to number very early, nor proceed in it very far or steadily, till a good while after they are well furnished with good store of other *ideas*; and one may often observe them discourse and reason pretty well and have very clear conceptions of several other things, before they can tell twenty. And some, through the default of their memories, who cannot retain the several combinations of numbers, with their names annexed in their distinct orders, and the dependence of so long a train of numeral progressions and their relation one to another, are not able all their lifetime to reckon or regularly go over any moderate series of numbers. For he that will count 20, or have any *idea* of that number, must know that 19 went before, with the distinct name or sign of every one of them, as they stand marked in their order; for wherever this fails, a gap is made, the chain breaks, and the progress in numbering can go no further. So that *to reckon right, it is required*: (1) that the mind distinguish carefully two *ideas*, which are different one from another only by the addition or subtraction of one unit; (2) that it retain in memory the names or marks of the several combinations, from an unit to

that number, and that not confusedly and at random, but in that exact order that the numbers follow one another; in either of which, if it trips, the whole business of numbering will be disturbed, and there will remain only the confused *idea* of multitude, but the *ideas* necessary to distinct numeration will not be attained to.

8.   This further is observable in *number*, that it is that which the mind makes use of in *measuring all things* that by us are measurable, which principally are *expansion and duration*; and our *idea* of infinity, even when applied to those, seems to be nothing but the infinity of number. For what else are our *ideas* of eternity and immensity but the repeated additions of certain *ideas* of imagined parts of duration and expansion with the infinity of number, in which we can come to no end of addition? For such an inexhaustible stock, number, of all other our *ideas*, most clearly furnishes us with, as is obvious to everyone.   For let a man collect into one sum as great a number as he pleases, this multitude, how great soever, lessens not one jot the power of adding to it or brings him any nearer the end of the inexhaustible stock of number, where still there remains as much to be added as if none were taken out.   And this endless *addition* or *addibility* (if anyone like the word better) of numbers, so apparent to the mind, is that, I think, which gives us the clearest and most distinct *idea* of infinity; of which more in the following chapter.

CHAPTER XVII

OF INFINITY

1.   HE that would know what kind of *idea* it is to which we give the name of *infinity* cannot do it better than by considering to what infinity is by the mind more immediately attributed, and then how the mind comes to frame it.

Finite and *infinite* seem to me to be looked upon by the mind as the *modes of quantity*, and to be attributed primarily in their first designation only to those things which have parts, and are capable of increase or diminution by the addition or subtraction of any the least part; and such are the *ideas* of space, duration, and number, which we have considered in the foregoing chapters. It is true that we cannot but be assured that the great GOD, of whom and from whom are all things, is incomprehensibly infinite; but yet, when we apply to that first and supreme Being our idea of infinite, in our weak and narrow thoughts, we do it primarily in respect of his duration and ubiquity, and, I think, more figuratively to his power, wisdom, and goodness, and other attributes, which are properly inexhaustible and incomprehensible, etc. For, when we call them infinite, we have no other *idea* of this infinity but what carries with it some reflection on and intimation of that number or extent of the acts or objects of God's power, wisdom, and goodness which can never be supposed so great or so many which these attributes will not always surmount and exceed—let us multiply them in our thoughts as far as we can—with all the infinity of endless number. I do not pretend to say how these attributes are in GOD, who is infinitely beyond the reach of our narrow capacities; they do, without doubt, contain in them all possible perfection: but this, I say, is our way of conceiving them and these our *ideas* of their infinity.

2.   Finite then, and infinite being by the mind looked on as modifications of expansion and duration, the next thing to be considered is: *how the mind comes by them.* As for the *idea of finite*, there is no great difficulty. The obvious portions of extension that affect our senses carry with them into the mind the *idea* of finite; and the ordinary periods of succession, whereby we measure time and duration, as hours, days, and years, are bounded lengths. The difficulty is how we come by those boundless *ideas* of *eternity* and *immensity*, since the objects which we converse with come so much short of any approach or proportion to that largeness.

3.   Everyone that has any *idea* of any stated lengths of space, as a foot, finds that he can repeat that *idea*; and joining it to the former, make the *idea* of two feet; and by the addition of a third, three feet; and so on, without ever coming to an end of his additions, whether of the same *idea* of a foot, or, if he pleases, of doubling it, or any other *idea* he has of any length, as a mile, or diameter of the earth, or of the *orbis magnus*: for whichsoever of these he takes, and how often soever he doubles or any otherwise multiplies it, he finds that, after he has continued his doubling in his thoughts and enlarged his *idea* as much as he

pleases, he has no more reason to stop, nor is one jot nearer the end of such addition than he was at first setting out: the power of enlarging his *idea* of space by further additions remaining still the same, he hence takes *the idea of infinite space*.

4. This, I think, is the way whereby the mind gets the *idea of infinite space*. It is a quite different consideration to examine whether the mind has the *idea* of such a *boundless space actually existing*, since our *ideas* are not always proofs of the existence of things; but yet, since this comes here in our way, I suppose I may say that we are apt to think that space in itself is actually boundless, to which imagination the *idea* of space or expansion of itself naturally leads us. For, it being considered by us either as the extension of body, or as existing by itself, without any solid matter taking it up (for of such a void space we have not only the *idea*, but I have proved, as I think, from the motion of body, its necessary existence), it is impossible the mind should be ever able to find or suppose any end of it, or be stopped anywhere in its progress in this space, how far soever it extends its thoughts. Any bounds made with body, even adamantine walls, are so far from putting a stop to the mind in its further progress in space and extension that it rather facilitates and enlarges it. For so far as that body reaches, so far no one can doubt of extension; and when we are come to the utmost extremity of body, what is there that can there put a stop and satisfy the mind that it is at the end of space, when it perceives it is not; nay, when it is satisfied that body itself can move into it? For if it be necessary for the motion of body that there should be an empty space, though never so little, here amongst bodies; and it be possible for body to move in or through that empty space; nay, it is impossible for any particle of matter to move but into an empty space: the same possibility of a body's moving into a void space, beyond the utmost bounds of body as well as into a void space interspersed amongst bodies, will always remain clear and evident, the *idea* of empty pure space, whether within or beyond the confines of all bodies, being exactly the same, differing not in nature though in bulk, and there being nothing to hinder body from moving into it. So that wherever the mind places itself by any thought, either amongst or remote from all bodies, it can, in this uniform *idea* of space, nowhere find any bounds, any end, and so must necessarily conclude it, by the very nature and *idea* of each part of it, to be actually infinite.

5.   As, by the power we find in ourselves of repeating, as often
as we will, any *idea* of space, we get the *idea* of immensity: so, by
being able to repeat the *idea* of any length of duration we have
in our minds, with all the endless addition of number, we come
by the *idea* of *eternity*. For we find in ourselves we can no
more come to an end of such repeated *ideas* than we can come to
the end of number; which everyone perceives he cannot.   But
here again it is another question, quite different from our having
an *idea* of eternity, to know whether there were *any real being*,
whose duration has been *eternal*. And as to this, I say, he that
considers something now existing, must necessarily come to
something eternal. But having spoken of this in another place, I
shall say here no more of it, but proceed on to some other
considerations of our *idea* of infinity.

6.   If it be so, that our *idea* of infinity be got from the power
we observe in ourselves of repeating, without end, our own
ideas, it may be demanded: *Why we do not attribute infinity to
other* ideas, *as well as those of space and duration*, since they may
be as easily, and as often, repeated in our minds as the other;
and yet nobody ever thinks of infinite sweetness, or infinite
whiteness, though he can repeat the idea of sweet or white as
frequently as those of a yard or a day. To which I answer: All
the *ideas* that are considered as having parts, and are capable of
increase by the addition of any equal or less parts, afford us, by
their repetition, the *idea* of infinity; because, with this endless
repetition, there is continued an enlargement of which there can
be no end. But in other *ideas* it is not so. For to the largest *idea*
of extension or duration that I at present have, the addition of
any the least part makes an increase; but to the perfectest *idea* I
have of the whitest whiteness, if I add another of a less or equal
whiteness (and of a whiter than I have, I cannot add the *idea*),
it makes no increase, and enlarges not my *idea* at all; and therefore the different *ideas* of whiteness, etc., are called degrees.
For those *ideas* that consist of parts are capable of being augmented by every addition of the least part; but if you take the
idea of white, which one parcel of snow yielded yesterday to
your sight, and another *idea* of white from another parcel of
snow you see today, and put them together in your mind, they
embody, as it were, and run into one, and the *idea* of whiteness
is not at all increased; and if we add a less degree of whiteness to
a greater, we are so far from increasing, that we diminish it.

Those *ideas* that consist not of parts, cannot be augmented to what proportion men please, or be stretched beyond what they have received by their senses; but space, duration, and number, being capable of increase by repetition, leave in the mind an *idea* of an endless room for more; nor can we conceive anywhere a stop to a further addition or progression; and so those *ideas* alone lead our minds towards the thought of infinity.

7.   Though our *idea* of infinity arise from the contemplation of quantity and the endless increase the mind is able to make in quantity, by the repeated additions of what portions thereof it pleases, yet I guess we cause great confusion in our thoughts, when we join infinity to any supposed *idea* of quantity the mind can be thought to have, and so discourse or reason about an infinite quantity, viz. an infinite space or an infinite duration. For, *our idea of infinity* being, as I think, *an endless growing idea*, but the *idea* of any quantity the mind has being at that time terminated in that *idea* (for be it as great as it will, it can be no greater than it is), to join infinity to it is to adjust a standing measure to a growing bulk; and therefore I think it is not an insignificant subtilty, if I say that we are carefully to distinguish between the *idea* of the infinity of space and the *idea* of a space infinite. The first is nothing but a supposed endless progression of the mind over what repeated *ideas* of space it pleases; but to have actually in the mind the *idea* of a space infinite is to suppose the mind already passed over and actually to have a view of all those repeated *ideas* of space which an endless repetition can never totally represent to it; which carries in it a plain contradiction.

8.   This, perhaps, will be a little plainer, if we consider it in numbers. The infinity of numbers to the end of whose addition everyone perceives there is no approach, easily appears to anyone that reflects on it. But, how clear soever this *idea* of the infinity of number be, there is nothing yet more evident than the absurdity of the actual *idea* of an infinite number. Whatsoever positive *ideas* we have in our minds of any space, duration, or number, let them be never so great, they are still finite; but when we suppose an inexhaustible remainder, from which we remove all bounds, and wherein we allow the mind an endless progression of thought, without ever completing the *idea*, there we have our *idea* of infinity; which though it seems to be pretty clear when we consider nothing else in it but the negation of an

end, yet when we would frame in our minds the *idea* of an infinite space or duration, that *idea* is very obscure and confused because it is made up of two parts, very different if not inconsistent. For let a man frame in his mind an *idea* of any space or number as great as he will, it is plain the mind rests and terminates in that *idea* which is contrary to the *idea* of *infinity*, which *consists in a supposed endless progression*. And therefore, I think it is that we are so easily confounded when we come to argue and reason about infinite space or duration, etc. Because the parts of such an *idea* not being perceived to be, as they are, inconsistent, the one side or other always perplexes, whatever consequences we draw from the other: as an *idea* of motion not passing on would perplex anyone who should argue from such an *idea*, which is not better than an *idea* of motion at rest; and such another seems to me to be the *idea* of a space or (which is the same thing) a number infinite, i.e. of a space or number which the mind actually has and so views and terminates in, and of a space or number which in a constant and endless enlarging and progression it can in thought never attain to. For how large soever an *idea* of space I have in my mind, it is no larger than it is that instant that I have it, though I be capable the next instant to double it; and so on *in infinitum*. For that alone is infinite which has no bounds; and that the *idea* of infinity, in which our thoughts can find none.

9. But of all other *ideas*, it is *number*, as I have said, which I think *furnishes us with the clearest and most distinct* idea *of infinity* we are capable of. For, even in space and duration, when the mind pursues the *idea* of infinity, it there makes use of the *ideas* and repetitions of numbers, as of millions of millions of miles, or years, which are so many distinct *ideas*, kept best by number from running into a confused heap, wherein the mind loses itself; and when it has added together as many millions, etc., as it pleases, of known lengths of space or duration, the clearest *idea* it can get of infinity is the confused incomprehensible remainder of endless addable numbers, which affords no prospect of stop or boundary.

10. It will, perhaps, give us a little further light into the *idea* we have *of infinity*, and discover to us that it *is nothing but the infinity of number applied to determinate parts*, of which we have in our minds the distinct *ideas*, if we consider that number is not generally thought by us infinite, whereas duration and extension

are apt to be so; which arises from hence, that in number we are at one end, as it were: for there being in number nothing less than an unit, we there stop and are at an end; but in addition, or increase of number, we can set no bounds; and so it is like a line, whereof one end terminating with us, the other is extended still forwards, beyond all that we can conceive. But in space and duration it is otherwise. For in duration we consider it as if this line of number were extended both ways, to an unconceivable, undeterminate, and infinite length; which is evident to anyone that will but reflect on what consideration he hath of eternity; which, I suppose, will find to be nothing else but the turning this infinity of number both ways, *à parte ante*, and *à parte post*, as they speak. For when we would consider eternity *à parte ante*, what do we but, beginning from ourselves and the present time we are in, repeat in our minds the *ideas* of years or ages or any other assignable portion of duration past, with a prospect of proceeding in such addition with all the infinity of number; and when we would consider eternity *à parte post*, we just after the same rate begin from ourselves and reckon by multiplied periods yet to come, still extending that line of number as before; and these two, being put together, are that infinite duration we call *eternity*: which, as we turn our view either way, forwards or backwards, appears infinite, because we still turn that way the infinite end of number, i.e. the power still of adding more.

11. The same happens also in space, wherein, conceiving ourselves to be, as it were, in the centre, we do on all sides pursue those indeterminable lines of number; and reckoning any way from ourselves, a yard, mile, diameter of the earth, or *orbis magnus*, by the infinity of number, we add others to them, as often as we will. And having no more reason to set bounds to those repeated *ideas* than we have to set bounds to number, we have that indeterminable *idea of immensity*.

12. And since in any bulk of matter our thoughts can never arrive at the utmost *divisibility*, therefore there is an apparent infinity to us also in that which has the infinity also of number, but with this difference: that, in the former considerations of the infinity of space and duration, we only use addition of numbers; whereas this is like the division of an unit into its fractions, wherein the mind also can proceed *in infinitum*, as well as in the former additions, it being indeed but the addition still of new numbers; though in the addition of the one, we can have no

more the positive *idea* of a space infinitely great, than, in the division of the other, we can have the *idea* of a body infinitely little: our *idea* of infinity being, as I may say, a growing or fugitive *idea*, still in a boundless progression, that can stop nowhere.

13.   Though it be hard I think to find anyone so absurd as to say he has the positive *idea* of an actual infinite number, the infinity whereof lies only in a power still of adding any combination of units to any former number, and that as long and as much as one will; the like also being in the infinity of space and duration, which power leaves always to the mind room for endless additions: yet there be those who imagine they have *positive* ideas *of infinite* duration and space.   It would, I think, be enough to destroy any such positive *idea* of infinite, to ask him that has it whether he could add to it or no; which would easily show the mistake of such a positive *idea*.   We can, I think, have no positive *idea* of any space or duration which is not made up of and commensurate to repeated numbers of feet or yards, or days and years, which are the common measures whereof we have the *ideas* in our minds and whereby we judge of the greatness of these sort of quantities.   And therefore, since an *idea* of infinite space or duration must needs be made up of infinite parts, it can have no other infinity than that of number, capable still of further addition, but not an actual positive *idea* of a number infinite.   For I think it is evident that the addition of finite things together (as are all lengths whereof we have the positive *ideas*) can never otherwise produce the *idea* of infinite than as number does; which, consisting of additions of finite units one to another, suggests the *idea* of infinite, only by a power we find we have of still increasing the sum, and adding more of the same kind, without coming one jot nearer the end of such progression.

14.   They who would prove their *idea of infinite to be positive*, seem to me to do it by a pleasant argument, taken from the negation of an end; which being negative, the negation of it is positive.   He that considers that the end is in body, but the extremity or superficies of that body, will not perhaps be forward to grant that the end is a bare negative; and he that perceives the end of his pen is black or white, will be apt to think that the end is something more than a pure negation.   Nor is it, when applied to duration, the bare negation of existence, but more

properly the last moment of it. But if they will have the end to be nothing but the bare negation of existence, I am sure they cannot deny but that the beginning is the first instant of being and is not by anybody conceived to be a bare negation; and therefore by their own argument, the *idea* of eternal *à parte ante* or of a duration without a beginning, is but a negative *idea*.

15. The *idea* of infinite has, I confess, something of positive in all those things we apply to it. When we would think of infinite space or duration, we at first step usually make some very large *idea*, as perhaps of millions of ages, or miles, which possibly we double and multiply several times. All that we thus amass together in our thoughts is positive, and the assemblage of a great number of positive *ideas* of space or duration. But what still remains beyond this we have no more a positive distinct notion of than a mariner has of the depth of the sea where, having let down a large portion of his sounding-line, he reaches no bottom, whereby he knows the depth to be so many fathoms and more; but how much that more is, he hath no distinct notion at all; and could he always supply new line and find the plummet always sink without ever stopping, he would be something in the posture of the mind reaching after a complete and positive *idea* of infinity. In which case, let this line be 10 or 10,000 fathoms long, it equally discovers what is beyond it, and gives only this confused and comparative *idea*: that this is not all, but one may yet go further. So much as the mind comprehends of any space, it has a positive *idea* of; but in endeavouring to make it infinite, it being always enlarging, always advancing, the *idea* is still imperfect and incomplete. So much space as the mind takes a view of in its contemplation of greatness is a clear picture and positive in the understanding; but infinite is still greater. 1. Then *the* idea *of so much is positive* and clear. 2. *The* idea *of greater is also clear, but it* is but a *comparative* idea. 3. *The* idea *of so much greater, as cannot be comprehended*, and this is *plain negative*, not positive. For he has no positive clear *idea* of the largeness of any extension (which is that sought for in the *idea* of infinite) that has not a comprehensive *idea* of the dimensions of it; and such, nobody, I think, pretends to in what is infinite. For to say a man has a positive clear *idea* of any quantity, without knowing how great it is, is as reasonable as to say he has the positive clear *idea* of the number of the sands on the seashore who knows not how many

they be, but only that they are more than twenty. For just such a perfect and positive *idea* has he of an infinite space or duration, who says it is larger than the extent or duration of 10, 100, 1000, or any other number of miles, or years, whereof he has or can have a positive *idea*; which is all the *idea*, I think, we have of infinite. So that what lies beyond our positive *idea* towards infinity, lies in obscurity, and has the indeterminate confusion of a negative *idea*, wherein I know I neither do nor can comprehend all I would, it being too large for a finite and narrow capacity. And that cannot but be very far from a positive complete *idea*, wherein the greatest part of what I would comprehend is left out, under the indeterminate intimation of being still greater. For to say that, having in any quantity measured so much or gone so far, you are not yet at the end, is only to say that that quantity is greater. So that the negation of an end in any quantity is, in other words, only to say that it is bigger; and a total negation of an end is but the carrying this bigger still with you in all the progressions your thoughts shall make in quantity, and adding this *idea* of still greater to all the *ideas* you have or can be supposed to have of quantity. Now, whether such an *idea* as that be positive I leave anyone to consider.

16. I ask those who say they have a *positive* idea *of eternity* whether their *idea* of duration includes in it succession or not. If it does not, they ought to show the difference of their notion of duration, when applied to an eternal being, and to a finite: since, perhaps, there may be others, as well as I, who will own to them their weakness of understanding in this point, and acknowledge that the notion they have of duration forces them to conceive that whatever has duration is of a longer continuance today than it was yesterday. If, to avoid succession in eternal existence, they recur to the *punctum stans* of the Schools, I suppose they will thereby very little mend the matter, or help us to a more clear and positive *idea* of infinite duration: there being nothing more inconceivable to me than duration without succession. Besides, that *punctum stans*, if it signify anything, being not *quantum*, finite or infinite cannot belong to it. But, if our weak apprehensions cannot separate succession from any duration whatsoever, our *idea* of eternity can be nothing but of infinite succession of moments of duration wherein anything does exist; and whether anyone has, or can have, a

positive *idea* of an actual infinite number, I leave him to consider till his infinite number be so great that he himself can add no more to it; and as long as he can increase it, I doubt he himself will think the *idea* he hath of it a little too scanty for positive infinity.

17. I think it unavoidable for every considering, rational creature, that will but examine his own or any other existence, to have the notion of an eternal, wise being, who had no beginning; and such an *idea* of infinite duration I am sure I have. But this *negation of a beginning*, being but the negation of a positive thing, *scarce gives* me *a positive* idea *of infinity*; which whenever I endeavour to extend my thoughts to, I confess myself at a loss and find I cannot attain any clear comprehension of it.

18. He that thinks he has a positive *idea* of infinite space, will, when he considers it, find that he can *no* more have a *positive idea* of the greatest, than he has *of the least space*. For in this latter, which seems the easier of the two and more within our comprehension, we are capable only of a comparative *idea* of smallness, which will always be less than any one whereof we have the positive *idea*. All our positive *ideas* of any quantity, whether great or little, have always bounds, though our comparative *idea*, whereby we can always add to the one and take from the other, hath no bounds. For that which remains, either great or little, not being comprehended in that positive *idea* which we have, lies in obscurity; and we have no other *idea* of it, but of the power of enlarging the one and diminishing the other, without ceasing. A pestle and mortar will as soon bring any particle of matter to indivisibility, as the acutest thought of a mathematician; and a surveyor may as soon with his chain measure out infinite *space*, as a philosopher by the quickest flight of mind reach it, or by thinking comprehend it; which is to have a positive *idea* of it. He that thinks on a cube of an inch diameter, has a clear and positive *idea* of it in his mind, and so can frame one of $\frac{1}{2}$, $\frac{1}{4}$, $\frac{1}{8}$, and so on, till he has the *idea* in his thoughts of something very little; but yet reaches not the *idea* of that incomprehensible littleness which division can produce. What remains of smallness is as far from his thoughts as when he first began; and therefore he never comes at all to have a clear and positive *idea* of that smallness which is consequent to infinite divisibility.

19.   Everyone that looks towards infinity does, as I have said, at first glance make some very large *idea* of that which he applies it to, let it be space or duration; and possibly he wearies his thoughts by multiplying in his mind that first large *idea*; but yet by that he comes no nearer to the having a *positive clear idea* of what remains to make up a positive infinite than the country-fellow had of the water which was yet to come and pass the channel of the river where he stood:

> *Rusticus expectat dum transeat amnis, at ille*
> *Labitur, et labetur in omne volubilis aevum.*

20.   There are some I have met with that put so much differ-ence between infinite duration and infinite space, that they per-suade themselves that they have *a positive* idea *of eternity, but* that they *have not,* nor can have, any *idea of infinite space.* The reason of which mistake I suppose to be this: that finding, by a due contemplation of causes and effects, that it is necessary to admit some eternal being, and so to consider the real existence of that being as taking up and commensurate to their *idea* of eternity; but, on the other side, not finding it necessary but, on the contrary, apparently absurd that body should be infinite, they forwardly conclude they can have no *idea* of infinite space, because they can have no *idea* of infinite matter. Which consequence, I conceive, is very ill collected, because the exist-ence of matter is no ways necessary to the existence of space, no more than the existence of motion, or the sun, is necessary to duration, though duration used to be measured by it; and I doubt not but a man may have the idea of 10,000 miles square, without any body so big, as well as the idea of 10,000 years, without any body so old. It seems as easy to me to have the *idea* of space empty of body, as to think of the capacity of a bushel without corn, or the hollow of a nutshell without a kernel in it: it being no more necessary that there should be existing a solid body, infinitely extended, because we have an *idea* of the infinity of space, than it is necessary that the world should be eternal, because we have an *idea* of infinite duration; and why should we think our *idea* of infinite space requires the real existence of matter to support it, when we find that we have as clear an *idea* of infinite duration to come as we have of infinite duration past? Though, I suppose, nobody thinks it conceivable that anything does or has existed in that future

duration. Nor is it possible to join our *idea* of future duration with present or past existence, any more than it is possible to make the *ideas* of yesterday, today, and tomorrow to be the same, or bring ages past and future together and make them contemporary. But if these men are of the mind that they have clearer *ideas* of infinite duration than of infinite space, because it is past doubt that GOD has existed from all eternity, but there is no real matter co-extended with infinite space: yet those philosophers who are of opinion that infinite space is possessed by GOD's infinite omnipresence, as well as infinite duration by his eternal existence, must be allowed to have as clear an *idea* of infinite space as of infinite duration, though neither of them, I think, has any *positive* idea *of infinity* in either case. For whatsoever positive *ideas* a man has in his mind of any quantity, he can repeat it and add it to the former, as easy as he can add together the *ideas* of two days or two paces which are positive *ideas* of lengths he has in his mind, and so on as long as he pleases; whereby, if a man had a positive *idea* of infinite, either duration or space, he could add two infinites together: nay, make one infinite infinitely bigger than another, absurdities too gross to be confuted.

21. But yet if, after all this, there be men who persuade themselves that they have clear positive comprehensive *ideas* of infinity, it is fit they enjoy their privilege; and I should be very glad (with some others that I know, who acknowledge they have none such) to be better informed by their communication. For I have been hitherto apt to think that the great and *inextricable difficulties* which perpetually involve all discourses *concerning infinity*, whether of space, duration, or divisibility, have been the certain *marks of a defect in our* ideas *of infinity* and the disproportion the nature thereof has to the comprehension of our narrow capacities. For, whilst men talk and dispute of infinite space or duration, as if they had as complete and positive *ideas* of them as they have of the names they use for them, or as they have of a yard, or an hour, or any other determinate quantity, it is no wonder if the incomprehensible nature of the thing they discourse of, or reason about, leads them into perplexities and contradictions, and their minds be overlaid by an object too large and mighty to be surveyed and managed by them.

22. If I have dwelt pretty long on the considerations of duration, space, and number, and what arises from the contemplation

of them, infinity, it is possibly no more than the matter requires, there being few simple *ideas* whose modes give more exercise to the thoughts of men than these do. I pretend not to treat of them in their full latitude: it suffices to my design to show how the mind receives them, such as they are, from *sensation* and *reflection*; and how even the *idea* we have of *infinity*, how remote soever it may seem to be from any object of sense or operation of our mind, has, nevertheless, as all our other *ideas*, its original there. Some mathematicians perhaps, of advanced speculations, may have other ways to introduce into their minds *ideas* of infinity; but this hinders not but that they themselves, as well as all other men, got the first *ideas* which they had of infinity from sensation and reflection, in the method we have here set down.

Chapter XVIII

OF OTHER SIMPLE MODES

1. THOUGH I have in the foregoing chapters shown how, from simple *ideas* taken in by sensation, the mind comes to extend itself even to infinity (which, however it may of all others seem most remote from any sensible perception, yet at last hath nothing in it but what is made out of simple *ideas*: received into the mind by the senses, and afterwards there put together, by the faculty the mind has to repeat its own *ideas*) though, I say, these might be instances enough of simple modes of the simple *ideas* of sensation, and suffice to show how the mind comes by them, yet I shall, for method's sake, though briefly, give an account of some few more, and then proceed to more complex *ideas*.

2. To *slide, roll, tumble, walk, creep, run, dance, leap, skip,* and abundance of others that might be named, are words which are no sooner heard but everyone who understands *English* has presently in his mind distinct *ideas*, which are all but the different modifications of motion. *Modes of motion* answer those of extension; *swift* and *slow* are two different *ideas* of motion, the measures whereof are made of the distances of time and space put together; so they are complex *ideas*, comprehending time and space with motion.

3. The like variety have we in sounds. Every articulate word is a different *modification of sound*; by which we see that from the sense of hearing by such modifications the mind may be furnished with distinct *ideas* to almost an infinite number. Sounds also, besides the distinct cries of birds and beasts, are modified by diversity of notes of different length put together, which make that complex *idea* called a *tune*, which a musician may have in his mind when he hears or makes no sound at all, by reflecting on the *ideas* of those sounds so put together silently in his own fancy.

4. Those of colours are also very various: some we take notice of as the different degrees or, as they are termed, *shades of the same colour*. But since we very seldom make assemblages of colours, either for use or delight, but figure is taken in also, and has its part in it, as in painting, weaving, needleworks, etc., those which are taken notice of do most commonly belong to mixed modes, as being made up of *ideas* of divers kinds, viz. figure and colour, such as *beauty, rainbow,* etc.

5. All *compounded tastes and smells* are also modes, made up of these simple *ideas* of those senses. But they, being such as generally we have no names for, are less taken notice of and cannot be set down in writing, and therefore must be left without enumeration to the thoughts and experience of my reader.

6. In general it may be observed that those *simple modes which are considered but as different degrees of the same simple* idea, though they are in themselves many of them very distinct *ideas,* yet *have ordinarily no distinct names,* nor are much taken notice of, as distinct *ideas,* where the difference is but very small between them. Whether men have neglected these modes and given no names to them, as wanting measures nicely to distinguish them, or because, when they were so distinguished, that knowledge would not be of general or necessary use, I leave it to the thoughts of others: it is sufficient to my purpose to show that all our simple *ideas* come to our minds only by sensation and reflection, and that when the mind has them, it can variously repeat and compound them, and so make new complex *ideas.* But, though white, red, or sweet, etc., have not been modified or made into complex *ideas* by several combinations, so as to be named and thereby ranked into species, yet some others of the simple *ideas,* viz. those of unity, duration, motion, etc., above instanced in, as also power and thinking, have been thus

modified to a great variety of complex *ideas*, with names
belonging to them.

7.   *The reason whereof*, I suppose, has been this: that the great
concernment of men being with men one amongst another, the
knowledge of men, and their actions, and the signifying of them
to one another was most necessary; and therefore they made
ideas of actions very nicely modified, and gave those complex
ideas names, that they might the more easily record and discourse of those things they were daily conversant in, without
long ambages and circumlocutions, and that the things they
were continually to give and receive information about might be
the easier and quicker understood. That this is so and that men,
in framing different complex *ideas* and giving them names, have
been much governed by the end of speech in general (which is a
very short and expedite way of conveying their thoughts one to
another) is evident in the names which in several arts have been
found out and applied to several complex *ideas* of modified
actions belonging to their several trades for dispatch sake, in
their direction or discourses about them. Which *ideas* are not
generally framed in the minds of men not conversant about these
operations. And thence the words that stand for them, by the
greatest part of men of the same language, are not understood.
V.g., *colshire, drilling, filtration, cohobation* are words standing
for certain complex *ideas* which, being seldom in the minds of
any but those few whose particular employments do at every
turn suggest them to their thoughts, those names of them are
not generally understood but by smiths and chemists; who,
having framed the complex *ideas* which these words stand for,
and having given names to them or received them from others
upon hearing of these names in communication, readily conceive those *ideas* in their minds, as by *cohobation*: all the simple
ideas of distilling and the pouring the liquor, distilled from anything back upon the remaining matter and distilling it again.
Thus we see that there are great varieties of simple *ideas*, as of
tastes and smells, which have no names; and of modes many
more; which either not having been generally enough observed,
or else not being of any great use to be taken notice of in the
affairs and converse of men, they have not had names given to
them, and so pass not for species. This we shall have occasion
hereafter to consider more at large, when we come to speak of
words.

CHAPTER XIX

OF THE MODES OF THINKING

1. WHEN the mind turns its view inwards upon itself, and contemplates its own actions, *thinking* is the first that occurs. In it the mind observes a great variety of modifications, and from thence receives distinct *ideas*. Thus the perception which actually accompanies and is annexed to any impression on the body made by an external object, being distinct from all other modifications of *thinking*, furnishes the mind with a distinct *idea*, which we call *sensation*; which is, as it were, the actual entrance of any *idea* into the understanding by the senses. The same *idea*, when it again recurs without the operation of the like object on the external sensory, is *remembrance*; if it be sought after by the mind, and with pain and endeavour found, and brought again in view, it is *recollection*; if it be held there long under attentive consideration, it is *contemplation*; when *ideas* float in our mind, without any reflection or regard of the understanding, it is that which the *French* call *rêverie* (our language has scarce a name for it); when the *ideas* that offer themselves (for as I have observed in another place, whilst we are awake there will always be a train of *ideas* succeeding one another in our minds) are taken notice of and, as it were, registered in the memory, it is *attention*; when the mind with great earnestness and of choice fixes its view on any *idea*, considers it on all sides and will not be called off by the ordinary solicitation of other *ideas*, it is that we call *intention* or *study*; sleep, without dreaming, is rest from all these. And *dreaming* itself is the having of *ideas* (whilst the outward senses are stopped, so that they receive not outward objects with their usual quickness) in the mind not suggested by any external objects or known occasion, nor under any choice or conduct of the understanding at all; and whether that which we call *ecstasy* be not dreaming with the eyes open, I leave to be examined.

2. These are some few instances of those various *modes of thinking* which the mind may observe in itself and so have as distinct *ideas* of as it hath of *white* and *red*, a *square* or a *circle*.

I do not pretend to enumerate them all, nor to treat at large of this set of *ideas* which are got from *reflection*; that would be to make a volume. It suffices to my present purpose to have shown here, by some few examples, of what sort these *ideas* are and how the mind comes by them, especially since I shall have occasion hereafter to treat more at large of *reasoning*, *judging*, *volition*, and *knowledge*, which are some of the most considerable operations of the mind and *modes of thinking*.

3. But perhaps it may not be an unpardonable digression nor wholly impertinent to our present design, if we reflect here upon *the different state of the mind in thinking*, which those instances of attention, *rêverie*, and dreaming, etc., before mentioned, naturally enough suggest. That there are *ideas*, some or other, always present in the mind of a waking man, everyone's experience convinces him, though the mind employs itself about them with several degrees of attention. Sometimes the mind fixes itself with so much earnestness on the contemplation of some objects that it turns their *ideas* on all sides, remarks their relations and circumstances, and views every part so nicely and with such intention that it shuts out all other thoughts and takes no notice of the ordinary impressions made then on the senses, which at another season would produce very sensible perceptions; at other times, it barely observes the train of ideas that succeed in the understanding, without directing and pursuing any of them; and at other times it lets them pass almost quite unregarded, as faint shadows that make no impression.

4. This difference of *intention* and *remission* of the mind in thinking, with a great variety of degrees between earnest study and very near minding nothing at all, everyone, I think, has experimented in himself. Trace it a little further, and you find the mind in sleep retired as it were from the senses, and out of the reach of those motions made on the organs of sense, which at other times produce very vivid and sensible *ideas*. I need not, for this, instance in those who sleep out whole stormy nights without hearing the thunder or seeing the lightning or feeling the shaking of the house, which are sensible enough to those who are waking. But in this retirement of the mind from the senses it often retains a yet more loose and incoherent manner of *thinking* which we call *dreaming*; and last of all, sound sleep closes the scene quite and puts an end to all appearances. This, I think, almost everyone has experience of in himself and his

own observation without difficulty leads him thus far. That which I would further conclude from hence is that, since the mind can sensibly put on, at several times, several degrees of *thinking* and be sometimes even in a waking man so remiss as to have thoughts dim and obscure to that degree that they are very little removed from none at all; and at last in the dark retirements of sound sleep, loses the sight perfectly of all *ideas* whatsoever: since, I say, this is evidently so in matter of fact and constant experience, I ask whether it be not probable that *thinking is the action and not the essence of the soul*? since the operations of agents will easily admit of intention and remission; but the essences of things are not conceived capable of any such variation. But this by the by.

Chapter XX

OF MODES OF PLEASURE AND PAIN

1. AMONGST the simple *ideas* which we receive both from *sensation* and *reflection*, *pain* and *pleasure* are two very consider-able ones. For as in the body there is sensation barely in itself, or accompanied with *pain* or *pleasure*, so the thought or per-ception of the mind is simply so, or else accompanied also with *pleasure* or *pain*, delight or trouble, call it how you please. These, like other simple *ideas*, cannot be described, nor their names defined; the way of knowing them is, as of the simple *ideas* of the senses, only by experience. For, to define them by the presence of good or evil is no otherwise to make them known to us than by making us reflect on what we feel in our-selves, upon the several and various operations of good and evil upon our minds, as they are differently applied to or considered by us.

2. Things then are good or evil only in reference to pleasure or pain. That we call *good* which *is apt to cause or increase pleasure, or diminish pain in us, or else to procure or preserve us the posses-sion of any other good or absence of any evil*. And, on the contrary, we name that *evil* which *is apt to produce or increase any pain, or diminish any pleasure in us, or else to procure us any evil, or deprive us of any good*. By pleasure and pain, I must be

understood to mean of body or mind, as they are commonly distinguished, though in truth they be only different constitutions of the mind, sometimes occasioned by disorder in the body, sometimes by thoughts of the mind.

3.   *Pleasure* and *pain* and that which causes them, good and evil, are the hinges on which our *passions* turn.   And if we reflect on ourselves and observe how these, under various considerations, operate in us, what modifications or tempers of mind, what internal sensations (if I may so call them) they produce in us, we may thence form to ourselves the *ideas* of our *passions*.

4.   Thus anyone reflecting upon the thought he has of the delight which any present or absent thing is apt to produce in him has the *idea* we call *love*.   For when a man declares in autumn when he is eating them, or in spring when there are none, that he *loves* grapes, it is no more but that the taste of grapes delights him; let an alteration of health or constitution destroy the delight of their taste, and he then can be said to *love* grapes no longer.

5.   On the contrary, the thought of the pain which anything present or absent is apt to produce in us is what we call *hatred*. Were it my business here to inquire any further than into the bare *ideas* of our passions as they depend on different modifications of pleasure and pain, I should remark that our *love* and *hatred* of inanimate insensible beings is commonly founded on that pleasure and pain which we receive from their use and application any way to our senses, though with their destruction. But *hatred* or *love*, to beings capable of happiness or misery, is often the uneasiness or delight which we find in ourselves arising from a consideration of their very being or happiness. Thus the being and welfare of a man's children or friends producing constant delight in him, he is said constantly to *love* them.   But it suffices to note that our *ideas* of love and *hatred* are but the dispositions of the mind in respect of pleasure and pain in general, however caused in us.

6.   The uneasiness a man finds in himself upon the absence of anything whose present enjoyment carries the *idea* of delight with it is that we call *desire*; which is greater or less, as that uneasiness is more or less vehement.   Where, by the by, it may perhaps be of some use to remark that the chief, if not only, spur to human industry and action is uneasiness.   For whatever

good is proposed, if its absence carries no displeasure nor pain with it, if a man be easy and content without it, there is no desire of it nor endeavour after it; there is no more but a bare *velleity*, the term used to signify the lowest degree of desire and that which is next to none at all, when there is so little uneasiness in the absence of anything that it carries a man no further than some faint wishes for it, without any more effectual or vigorous use of the means to attain it. *Desire* also is stopped or abated by the opinion of the impossibility or unattainableness of the good proposed, as far as the uneasiness is cured or allayed by that consideration. This might carry our thoughts further, were it seasonable in this place.

7. *Joy* is a delight of the mind, from the consideration of the present or assured approaching possession of a good; and we are then possessed of any good when we have it so in our power that we can use it when we please. Thus a man almost starved has *joy* at the arrival of relief, even before he has the pleasure of using it. And a father in whom the very well-being of his children causes delight is always, as long as his children are in such a state, in the possession of that good; for he needs but to reflect on it to have that pleasure.

8. *Sorrow* is uneasiness in the mind upon the thought of a good lost, which might have been enjoyed longer; or the sense of a present evil.

9. *Hope* is that pleasure in the mind which everyone finds in himself upon the thought of a profitable future enjoyment of a thing which is apt to delight him.

10. *Fear* is an uneasiness of the mind upon the thought of future evil likely to befall us.

11. *Despair* is the thought of the unattainableness of any good, which works differently in men's minds, sometimes producing uneasiness or pain, sometimes rest and indolency.

12. *Anger* is uneasiness or discomposure of the mind upon the receipt of any injury, with a present purpose of revenge.

13. *Envy* is an uneasiness of mind, caused by the consideration of a good we desire obtained by one we think should not have had it before us.

14. These two last, *envy* and *anger*, not being caused by pain and pleasure simply in themselves, but having in them some mixed considerations of ourselves and others, are not therefore to be found in all men, because those other parts, of valuing

their merits, or intending revenge, is wanting in them; but all the rest, terminating purely in pain and pleasure, are, I think, to be found in all men. For we *love, desire, rejoice,* and *hope* only in respect of pleasure; we *hate, fear,* and *grieve* only in respect of pain ultimately; in fine, all these passions are moved by things only as they appear to be the causes of pleasure and pain, or to have pleasure or pain some way or other annexed to them. Thus we extend our hatred usually to the subject (at least, if a sensible or voluntary agent) which has produced pain in us, because the fear it leaves is a constant pain; but we do not so constantly love what has done us good, because pleasure operates not so strongly on us as pain, and because we are not so ready to have hope it will do so again. But this by the by.

15. By *pleasure and pain*, delight and uneasiness, I must all along be understood (as I have above intimated) to mean not only bodily pain and pleasure, but whatsoever *delight* or *uneasiness* is felt by us, whether arising from any grateful or unacceptable sensation or reflection.

16. It is further to be considered that, in reference to the passions, the removal or *lessening of a pain is* considered and operates as a *pleasure*: and the loss or diminishing of a pleasure, as a pain.

17. The passions too have most of them, in most persons, operations on the body, and cause various changes in it; which, not being always sensible, do not make a necessary part of the *idea* of each passion. For *shame*, which is an uneasiness of the mind upon the thought of having done something which is indecent or will lessen the valued esteem which others have for us, has not always blushing accompanying it.

18. I would not be mistaken here, as if I meant this as a discourse of the *passions*; they are *many more than those* I have here named; and those I have taken notice of would each of them require a much larger and more accurate discourse. I have only mentioned these here as so many instances of modes of pleasure and pain resulting in our minds from various considerations of good and evil. I might, perhaps, have instanced in other modes of pleasure and pain more simple than these, as the pain of *hunger* and *thirst*, and the pleasure of eating and drinking to remove them; the pain of tender eyes, and the pleasure of music; pain from captious uninstructive wrangling, and the pleasure of rational conversation with a friend, or of well-directed

study in the search and discovery of truth. But the passions being of much more concernment to us, I rather made choice to instance in them and show how the *ideas* we have of them are derived from sensation and reflection.

CHAPTER XXI

OF POWER

1. THE mind—being every day informed by the senses of the alteration of those simple *ideas* it observes in things without; and taking notice how one comes to an end, and ceases to be, and another begins to exist which was not before; reflecting also on what passes within itself, and observing a constant change of its *ideas*, sometimes by the impression of outward objects on the senses, and sometimes by the determination of its own choice; and concluding from what it has so constantly observed to have been, that the like changes will for the future be made in the same things, by like agents, and by the like ways—considers in one thing the possibility of having any of its simple *ideas* changed, and in another the possibility of making that change; and so comes by that *idea* which we call *power*. Thus we say fire has a *power* to melt gold, i.e. to destroy the consistency of its insensible parts, and consequently its hardness, and make it fluid; and gold has a *power* to be melted; that the sun has a *power* to blanch wax, and wax a *power* to be blanched by the sun, whereby the yellowness is destroyed, and whiteness made to exist in its room. In which, and the like cases, the *power* we consider is in reference to the change of perceivable *ideas*. For we cannot observe any alteration to be made in, or operation upon anything, but by the observable change of its sensible *ideas*, nor conceive any alteration to be made but by conceiving a change of some of its *ideas*.

2. *Power* thus considered is two-fold, viz. as able to make, or able to receive, any change; the one may be called *active*, and the other *passive power*. Whether matter be not wholly destitute of *active power*, as its author GOD is truly above all *passive power*, and whether the intermediate state of created spirits be not that alone which is capable of both *active* and *passive* power,

may be worth consideration. I shall not now enter into that inquiry, my present business being not to search into the original of power but how we come by the *idea* of it. But since *active powers* make so great a part of our complex *ideas* of natural substances (as we shall see hereafter) and I mention them as such according to common apprehension, yet they being not, perhaps, so truly *active powers* as our hasty thoughts are apt to represent them, I judge it not amiss, by this intimation, to direct our minds to the consideration of GOD and spirits for the clearest *idea* of *active power*.

3. I confess *power includes in it some kind of relation* (a relation to action or change), as indeed which of our *ideas*, of what kind soever, when attentively considered, does not? For our *ideas* of extension, duration, and number, do they not all contain in them a secret relation of the parts? Figure and motion have something relative in them much more visibly; and sensible qualities, as colours and smells, etc., what are they but the *powers* of different bodies in relation to our perception, etc.? And, if considered in the things themselves, do they not depend on the bulk, figure, texture, and motion of the parts? All which include some kind of relation in them. Our *idea* therefore of *power*, I think, may well have a place amongst other simple *ideas* and be considered as one of them, being one of those that make a principal ingredient in our complex *ideas* of substances, as we shall hereafter have occasion to observe.

4. We are abundantly furnished with the *idea* of *passive power* by almost all sorts of sensible things. In most of them we cannot avoid observing their sensible qualities, nay, their very substances, to be in a continual flux; and therefore with reason we look on them as liable still to the same change. Nor have we of *active power* (which is the more proper signification of the word *power*) fewer instances. Since whatever change is observed, the mind must collect a power somewhere able to make that change, as well as a possibility in the thing itself to receive it. But yet, if we will consider it attentively, bodies, by our senses, do not afford us so clear and distinct an *idea* of *active power*, as we have from reflection on the operations of our minds. For all *power* relating to action, and there being but two sorts of action whereof we have an *idea*, viz. thinking and motion, let us consider whence we have the clearest *ideas* of the *powers* which produce these actions. (1) Of thinking, body affords us no *idea*

at all; it is only from reflection that we have that. (2) Neither have we from body any *idea* of the beginning of motion. A body at rest affords us no *idea* of any *active power* to move; and when it is set in motion itself, that motion is rather a passion than an action in it. For, when the ball obeys the stroke of a billiard-stick, it is not any action of the ball, but bare passion; also when by impulse it sets another ball in motion that lay in its way, it only communicates the motion it had received from another, and loses in itself so much as the other received: which gives us but a very obscure *idea* of an *active power* of moving in body, whilst we observe it only to transfer, but not produce, any motion. For it is but a very obscure *idea* of *power* which reaches not the production of the action but the continuation of the passion. For so is motion in a body impelled by another, the continuation of the alteration made in it from rest to motion being little more an action than the continuation of the alteration of its figure by the same blow is an action. The *idea* of the beginning of motion we have only from reflection on what passes in ourselves, where we find by experience that barely by willing it, barely by a thought of the mind, we can move the parts of our bodies which were before at rest. So that it seems to me we have from the observation of the operation of bodies by our senses but a very imperfect obscure *idea* of *active power*, since they afford us not any *idea* in themselves of the *power* to begin any action, either motion or thought. But if, from the impulse bodies are observed to make one upon another, anyone thinks he has a clear *idea* of *power*, it serves as well to my purpose, *sensation* being one of those ways whereby the mind comes by its *ideas*; only I thought it worthwhile to consider here by the way whether the mind doth not receive its *idea* of *active power* clearer from reflection on its own operations than it doth from any external sensation.

5. This, at least, I think evident: that we find in ourselves a *power* to begin or forbear, continue or end several actions of our minds and motions of our bodies, barely by a thought or preference of the mind ordering or, as it were commanding, the doing or not doing such or such a particular action. This *power* which the mind has thus to order the consideration of any *idea*, or the forbearing to consider it, or to prefer the motion of any part of the body to its rest, and *vice versa*, in any particular instance, is that which we call the *will*. The actual exercise of

that power, by directing any particular action, or its forbearance, is that which we call *volition* or *willing*. The forbearance of that action, consequent to such order or command of the mind, is called *voluntary*. And whatsoever action is performed without such a thought of the mind is called *involuntary*. The power of perception is that which we call the *understanding*. Perception, which we make the act of the understanding, is of three sorts: (1) The perception of *ideas* in our minds. (2) The perception of the signification of signs. (3) The perception of the connexion or repugnancy, agreement or disagreement, that there is between any of our *ideas*. All these are attributed to the *understanding* or perceptive power, though it be the two latter only that use allows us to say we understand.

6.   These powers of the mind, viz. of *perceiving* and of *preferring*, are usually called by another name; and the ordinary way of speaking is that the *understanding* and *will* are two *faculties* of the mind: a word proper enough, if it be used, as all words should be, so as not to breed any confusion in men's thoughts, by being supposed (as I suspect it has been) to stand for some real beings in the soul that performed those actions of understanding and volition. For when we say the *will* is the commanding and superior faculty of the soul; that it is or is not free; that it determines the inferior faculties; that it follows the dictates of the *understanding*, etc.; though these and the like expressions, by those that carefully attend to their own *ideas* and conduct their thoughts more by the evidence of things than the sound of words, may be understood in a clear and distinct sense: yet I suspect, I say, that this way of speaking of *faculties* has misled many into a confused notion of so many distinct agents in us, which had their several provinces and authorities and did command, obey, and perform several actions, as so many distinct beings; which has been no small occasion of wrangling, obscurity, and uncertainty in questions relating to them.

7.   Everyone, I think, finds in himself a *power* to begin or forbear, continue or put an end to several actions in himself. From the consideration of the extent of this power of the mind over the actions of the man, which everyone finds in himself, arise the *ideas* of *liberty* and *necessity*.

8.   All the actions that we have any *idea* of, reducing themselves, as has been said, to these two, viz. thinking and motion: so

far as a man has power to think or not to think, to move or not to move, according to the preference or direction of his own mind, so far is a man *free*. Wherever any performance or forbearance are not equally in a man's power, wherever doing or not doing will not equally follow upon the preference of his mind directing it, there he is not *free*, though perhaps the action may be voluntary. So that the *idea* of *liberty* is the *idea* of a power in any agent to do or forbear any particular action, according to the determination or thought of the mind, whereby either of them is preferred to the other; where either of them is not in the power of the agent to be produced by him according to his *volition*, there he is not at *liberty*: that agent is under *necessity*. So that *liberty* cannot be where there is no thought, no volition, no will; but there may be thought, there may be will, there may be volition, where there is no *liberty*. A little consideration of an obvious instance or two may make this clear.

9. A tennis ball, whether in motion by the stroke of a racket, or lying still at rest, is not by anyone taken to be a *free agent*. If we inquire into the reason, we shall find it is because we conceive not a tennis ball to think, and consequently not to have any volition, or preference of motion to rest, or *vice versa*; and therefore has not *liberty*, is not a free agent; but all its both motion and rest come under our *idea* of *necessary*, and are so called. Likewise, a man falling into the water (a bridge breaking under him) has not herein liberty, is not a free agent. For though he has volition, though he prefers his not falling to falling, yet the forbearance of that motion not being in his power, the stop or cessation of that motion follows not upon his volition; and therefore therein he is not *free*. So a man striking himself or his friend by a convulsive motion of his arm, which it is not in his power by volition or the direction of his mind to stop or forbear, nobody thinks he has in this *liberty*; everyone pities him as acting by necessity and constraint.

10. Again, suppose a man be carried whilst fast asleep into a room where is a person he longs to see and speak with, and be there locked fast in, beyond his power to get out; he awakes and is glad to find himself in so desirable company, which he stays willingly in, i.e. prefers his stay to going away. I ask, is not this stay voluntary? I think nobody will doubt it; and yet being locked fast in, it is evident he is not at liberty not to stay, he has not freedom to be gone. So that *liberty is not an* idea *belonging to*

volition, or preferring, but to the person having the power of doing or forbearing to do, according as the mind shall choose or direct. Our *idea* of liberty reaches as far as that power and no further. For wherever restraint comes to check that power, or compulsion takes away that indifferency of ability on either side to act or to forbear acting, there *liberty,* and our notion of it, presently ceases.

11. We have instances enough and often more than enough in our own bodies. A man's heart beats and the blood circulates, which it is not in his power by any thought or volition to stop; and therefore in respect of these motions, where rest depends not on his choice nor would follow the determination of his mind if it should prefer it, he is not a *free agent.* Convulsive motions agitate his legs so that, though he *wills* it never so much, he cannot by any power of his mind stop their motion (as in that odd disease called *chorea Sancti Viti*), but he is perpetually dancing; he is not at liberty in this action but under as much necessity of moving as a stone that falls or a tennis ball struck with a racket. On the other side, a palsy or the stocks hinder his legs from obeying the determination of his mind if it would thereby transfer his body to another place. In all these there is want of *freedom,* though the sitting still even of a paralytic, whilst he prefers it to a removal, is truly voluntary. *Voluntary* then *is not opposed to necessary, but to involuntary.* For a man may prefer what he can do to what he cannot do; the state he is in, to its absence or change, though necessity has made it in itself unalterable.

12. As it is in the motions of the body, so it is in the thoughts of our minds: where anyone is such that we have power to take it up, or lay it by, according to the preference of the mind, there we are *at liberty.* A waking man, being under the necessity of having some *ideas* constantly in his mind, is not at *liberty* to think or not to think, no more than he is at *liberty* whether his body shall touch any other or no; but whether he will remove his contemplation from one *idea* to another is many times in his choice, and then he is, in respect of his *ideas,* as much at *liberty* as he is in respect of bodies he rests on; he can at pleasure remove himself from one to another. But yet some *ideas* to the mind, like some motions to the body, are such as in certain circumstances it cannot avoid, nor obtain their absence by the utmost effort it can use. A man on the rack is not at *liberty* to

lay by the *idea* of pain, and divert himself with other contemplations; and sometimes a boisterous passion hurries our thoughts, as a hurricane does our bodies, without leaving us the liberty of thinking on other things, which we would rather choose. But as soon as the mind regains the power to stop or continue, begin or forbear any of these motions of the body without, or thoughts within, according as it thinks fit to prefer either to the other, we then consider the man as a *free agent* again.

13. Wherever thought is wholly wanting or the power to act or forbear according to the direction of thought, there *necessity* takes place. This, in an agent capable of volition when the beginning or continuation of any action is contrary to that preference of his mind, is called *compulsion*; when the hindering or stopping any action is contrary to his volition, it is called *restraint*. Agents that have no thought, no volition at all, are in everything *necessary* agents.

14. If this be so (as I imagine it is), I leave it to be considered whether it may not help to put an end to that long agitated and, I think, unreasonable because unintelligible, question, viz. *whether man's will be free or no*. For if I mistake not, it follows from what I have said that the question itself is altogether improper; and it is as insignificant to ask whether man's *will* be free, as to ask whether his sleep be swift, or his virtue square: *liberty* being as little applicable to the *will*, as swiftness of motion is to sleep, or squareness to virtue. Everyone would laugh at the absurdity of such a question as either of these, because it is obvious that the modifications of motion belong not to sleep, nor the difference of figure to virtue; and when anyone well considers it, I think he will as plainly perceive that *liberty*, which is but a power, belongs only to agents and cannot be an attribute or modification of the *will*, which is also but a power.

15. Such is the difficulty of explaining and giving clear notions of internal actions by sounds that I must here warn my reader that *ordering*, *directing*, *choosing*, *preferring*, etc., which I have made use of, will not distinctly enough express *volition*, unless he will reflect on what he himself does when he *wills*. For example, *preferring*, which seems perhaps best to express the act of *volition*, does it not precisely. For though a man would prefer flying to walking, yet who can say he ever *wills* it? *Volition*, it is plain, is an act of the mind knowingly exerting that dominion it takes itself to have over any part of the man, by employing it

in, or withholding it from, any particular action. And what is the *will* but the faculty to do this? And is that faculty anything more in effect than a power, the power of the mind to determine its thought to the producing, continuing, or stopping any action as far as it depends on us? For can it be denied that whatever agent has a power to think on its own actions, and to prefer their doing or omission either to other, has that faculty called *will*? *Will*, then, is nothing but such a power. *Liberty*, on the other side, is the power a man has to do or forbear doing any particular action according as its doing or forbearance has the actual preference in the mind; which is the same thing as to say according as he himself *wills* it.

16. It is plain then that the *will* is nothing but one power or ability, and *freedom* another power or ability, so that to ask whether the *will has freedom* is to ask whether one power has another power, one ability another ability: a question at first sight too grossly absurd to make a dispute, or need an answer. For who is it that sees not that *powers* belong only to *agents* and *are attributes only of substances, and not of powers* themselves? So that this way of putting the question (viz. whether the *will be free*) is in effect to ask whether the *will* be a substance, an agent, or at least to suppose it, since freedom can properly be attributed to nothing else. If freedom can with any propriety of speech be applied to power, it may be attributed to the power that is in a man to produce or forbear producing motion in parts of his body by choice or preference; which is that which denominates him free and is freedom itself. But if anyone should ask whether freedom were free, he would be suspected not to understand well what he said; and he would be thought to deserve *Midas's* ears, who, knowing that rich was a denomination from the possession of riches, should demand whether riches themselves were rich.

17. However, the *name faculty*, which men have given to this power called the *will*, and whereby they have been led into a way of talking of the *will* as acting, may, by an appropriation that disguises its true sense, serve a little to palliate the absurdity; yet the *will*, in truth, signifies nothing but a power or ability to prefer or choose; and when the *will*, under the name of a *faculty*, is considered, as it is, barely as an ability to do something, the absurdity in saying it is free or not free will easily discover itself. For if it be reasonable to suppose and talk of *faculties* as distinct

beings that can act (as we do, when we say the *will* orders, and the *will* is free), it is fit that we should make a speaking *faculty*, and a walking *faculty*, and a dancing *faculty*, by which those actions are produced, which are but several modes of motion, as well as we make the *will* and *understanding* to be *faculties* by which the actions of choosing and perceiving are produced, which are but several modes of thinking. And we may as properly say that it is the singing *faculty* sings, and the dancing *faculty* dances, as that the *will* chooses, or that the understanding conceives; or, as is usual, that the *will* directs the understanding, or the understanding obeys or obeys not the *will*: it being altogether as proper and intelligible to say that the power of speaking directs the power of singing, or the power of singing obeys or disobeys the power of speaking.

18. This way of talking, nevertheless, has prevailed and, as I guess, produced great confusion. For these being all different powers in the mind or in the man to do several actions, he exerts them as he thinks fit. But the power to do one action is not operated on by the power of doing another action. For the power of thinking operates not on the power of choosing, nor the power of choosing on the power of thinking, no more than the power of dancing operates on the power of singing, or the power of singing on the power of dancing, as anyone who reflects on it will easily perceive. And yet this is it which we say when we thus speak, that *the will operates on the understanding, or the understanding on the will*.

19. I grant that this or that actual thought may be the occasion of volition, or exercising the power a man has to choose, or the actual choice of the mind, the cause of actual thinking on this or that thing, as the actual singing of such a tune may be the occasion of dancing such a dance, and the actual dancing of such a dance the occasion of singing such a tune. But in all these it is not one *power* that operates on another, but it is the mind that operates and exerts these powers; it is the man that does the action, it is the agent that has power, or is able to do. For *powers* are relations, not agents; and *that which has the power or not the power to operate is that alone which is or is not free*, and not the power itself. For freedom, or not freedom, can belong to nothing but what has or has not a power to act.

20. The attributing to *faculties* that which belonged not to them has given occasion to this way of talking; but the introducing

into discourses concerning the mind, with the name of *faculties*, a notion of their operating has, I suppose, as little advanced our knowledge in that part of ourselves as the great use and mention of the like invention of *faculties* in the operations of the body has helped us in the knowledge of physic. Not that I deny there are *faculties*, both in the body and mind: they both of them have their *powers* of operating, else neither the one nor the other could operate. For nothing can operate that is not able to operate; and that is not able to operate that has no *power* to operate. Nor do I deny that those words and the like are to have their place in the common use of languages that have made them current. It looks like too much affectation wholly to lay them by; and philosophy itself, though it likes not a gaudy dress, yet when it appears in public must have so much complacency as to be clothed in the ordinary fashion and language of the country, so far as it can consist with truth and perspicuity. But the fault has been that faculties have been spoken of and represented as so many distinct agents. For it being asked, what it was that digested the meat in our stomachs, it was a ready and very satisfactory answer to say that it was the *digestive faculty*. What was it that made anything come out of the body? The *expulsive faculty*. What moved? The *motive faculty*. And so in the mind, the *intellectual faculty*, or the understanding, understood; and the *elective faculty*, or the will, willed or commanded; which is, in short, to say that the ability to digest digested, and the ability to move moved, and the ability to understand understood. For *faculty*, *ability*, and *power*, I think, are but different names of the same things; which ways of speaking, when put into more intelligible words, will, I think, amount to thus much: that digestion is performed by something that is able to digest, motion by something able to move, and understanding by something able to understand. And, in truth, it would be very strange if it should be otherwise, as strange as it would be for a man to be free without being able to be free.

21. To return, then, to the inquiry about liberty, I think *the question is not proper, whether the will be free, but whether a man be free*. Thus, I think,

(1) That so far as anyone can, by the direction or choice of his mind, preferring the existence of any action to the non-existence of that action, and *vice versa*, make it to exist or not exist, so far he is *free*. For if I can, by a thought directing the

motion of my finger, make it move when it was at rest, or *vice versa*, it is evident that in respect of that I am free; and if I can, by a like thought of my mind, preferring one to the other, produce either words or silence, I am at liberty to speak or hold my peace; and *as far as this power reaches, of acting or not acting, by the determination of his own thought preferring either, so far is a man free.* For how can we think anyone freer than to have the power to do what he will? And so far as anyone can, by preferring any action to its not being, or rest to any action, produce that action or rest, so far can he do what he will. For such a preferring of action to its absence is the willing of it; and we can scarce tell how to imagine any *being* freer than to be able to do what he *wills*. So that in respect of actions within the reach of such a power in him, a man seems as free as it is possible for freedom to make him.

22.   But the inquisitive mind of man, willing to shift off from himself as far as he can all thoughts of guilt, though it be by putting himself into a worse state than that of fatal necessity, is not content with this: freedom, unless it reaches further than this will not serve the turn; and it passes for a good plea that a man is not free at all, if he be not as free to will as he is to act what he wills. Concerning a man's liberty, there yet, therefore, is raised this further question, *whether a man be free to will*, which I think is what is meant when it is disputed whether the *will* be free. And as to that I imagine:

23.   (2) That *willing*, or *volition*, being an action, and freedom consisting in a power of acting or not acting, *a man in respect of willing or the act of volition, when any action in his power is once proposed to his thoughts, as presently to be done, cannot be free.* The reason whereof is very manifest: for, it being unavoidable that the action depending on his *will* should exist or not exist, and its existence or not-existence following perfectly the determination and preference of his will, he cannot avoid willing the existence or not-existence of that action; it is absolutely necessary that he *will* the one or the other, i.e., *prefer* the one to the other, since one of them must necessarily follow; and that which does follow, follows by the choice and determination of his mind, that is, by his *willing it*: for if he did not *will* it, it would not be. So that in respect of the act of *willing*, a man in such case is not free: liberty consisting in a power to act or not to act, which in regard of volition a man,

upon such a proposal, has not. For it is unavoidably necessary
to prefer the doing or forbearance of an action in a man's power,
which is once so proposed to his thoughts: a man must necesarily
will the one or the other of them, upon which preference or
volition the action or its forbearance certainly follows and is
truly voluntary; but the act of volition, or preferring one of the
two, being that which he cannot avoid, a man, in respect of that
act of *willing*, is under a necessity, and so cannot be free, unless
necessity and freedom can consist together and a man can be
free and bound at once.

24.   This then is evident, that in all proposals of present action
*a man is not at liberty to will or not to will because he cannot
forbear willing*: liberty consisting in a power to act or to forbear
acting, and in that only. For a man that sits still is said yet to be
at liberty, because he can walk if he *wills* it. But if a man sitting
still has not a power to remove himself, he is not at liberty; so
likewise a man falling down a precipice, though in motion, is not
at liberty, because he cannot stop that motion if he would. This
being so, it is plain that a man that is walking, to whom it is
proposed to give off walking, is not at liberty whether he *will*
determine himself to walk or give off walking, or no: he must
necessarily prefer one or the other of them: walking or not
walking; and so it is in regard of all other actions in our power
so proposed, which are the far greater number. For considering
the vast number of voluntary actions that succeed one another
every moment that we are awake, in the course of our lives, there
are but few of them that are thought on or proposed to the *will*,
until the time they are to be done. And in all such actions, as I
have shown, the mind, in respect of *willing*, has not a power to
act or not to act, wherein consists liberty; the mind in that case
has not a power to forbear *willing*: it cannot avoid some determination concerning them, let the consideration be as short, the
thought as quick, as it will: it either leaves the man in the state he
was before thinking or changes it, continues the action or puts
an end to it. Whereby it is manifest that it orders and directs
one, in preference to or with neglect of the other, and thereby
either the continuation or change becomes unavoidably
voluntary.

25.   Since then it is plain that in most cases a man is not at
liberty whether he will *will* or no, the next thing demanded is
whether a man be at liberty to will which of the two he pleases,

motion or rest. This question carries the absurdity of it so manifestly in itself that one might thereby sufficiently be convinced
that liberty concerns not the will. For to ask whether a man be at
liberty to will either motion or rest, speaking or silence, which
he pleases, is to ask whether a man can *will* what he *wills*, or be
pleased with what he is pleased with. A question which, I
think, needs no answer; and they who can make a question of
it must suppose one will to determine the acts of another, and
another to determine that and so on *in infinitum.*

26. To avoid these and the like absurdities, nothing can be of
greater use than to establish in our minds determined *ideas* of
the things under consideration. If the *ideas* of liberty and
volition were well fixed in our understandings and carried
along with us in our minds, as they ought, through all the
questions that are raised about them, I suppose a great part of
the difficulties that perplex men's thoughts and entangle their
understandings would be much easier resolved; and we should
perceive where the confused signification of terms, or where the
nature of the thing caused the obscurity.

27. *First* then, it is carefully to be remembered that *freedom
consists in the dependence of the existence or not-existence of any
action upon our volition of it, and not in the dependence of any
action or its contrary on our preference.* A man standing on a
cliff is at liberty to leap twenty yards downwards into the sea,
not because he has a power to do the contrary action, which is
to leap twenty yards upwards, for that he cannot do; but he is
therefore free because he has a power to leap or not to leap.
But if a greater force than his either holds him fast or tumbles
him down, he is no longer free in that case: because the doing
or forbearance of that particular action is no longer in his power.
He that is a close prisoner in a room twenty-foot-square, being
at the north side of his chamber, is at liberty to walk twenty feet
southward, because he can walk or not walk it; but is not, at the
same time, at liberty to do the contrary, i.e. to walk twenty feet
northward.

In this, then, consists freedom, viz. in our being able to act or
not to act according as we shall choose or *will.*

28. *Secondly*, we must remember that *volition* or *willing* is an
act of the mind directing its thought to the production of any
action, and thereby exerting its power to produce it. To avoid
multiplying of words, I would crave leave here, under the word

action, to comprehend the forbearance too of any action proposed: *sitting still*, or *holding one's peace*, when *walking* or *speaking* are proposed, though mere forbearances, requiring as much the determination of the *will* and being often as weighty in their consequences as the contrary actions, may, on that consideration, well enough pass for actions too. But this I say that I may not be mistaken if for brevity's sake I speak thus.

29.   *Thirdly*, the *will* being nothing but a power in the mind to direct the operative faculties of a man to motion or rest, as far as they depend on such direction: to the question, What is it determines the will? the true and proper answer is, the mind. For that which determines the general power of directing, to this or that particular direction, is nothing but the agent itself exercising the power it has that particular way. If this answer satisfies not, it is plain the meaning of the question, *What determines the will?* is this: What moves the mind, in every particular instance, to determine its general power of directing to this or that particular motion or rest? And to this I answer: The motive for continuing in the same state or action is only the present satisfaction in it; the motive to change is always some *uneasiness*: nothing setting us upon the change of state, or upon any new action, but some *uneasiness*. This is the great motive that works on the mind to put it upon action, which for shortness's sake we will call *determining of the will*, which I shall more at large explain.

30.   But in the way to it, it will be necessary to premise that, though I have above endeavoured to express the act of *volition*, by *choosing, preferring*, and the like terms, that signify *desire* as well as *volition*, for want of other words to mark that act of the mind whose proper name is *willing* or *volition*, yet it being a very simple act, whosoever desires to understand what it is will better find it by reflecting on his own mind and observing what it does when it *wills*, than by any variety of articulate sounds whatsoever. This caution of being careful not to be misled by expressions that do not enough keep up the difference between the *will* and several acts of the mind that are quite distinct from it I think the more necessary, because I find the will often confounded with several of the affections, especially *desire*, and one put for the other, and that by men who would not willingly be thought not to have had very distinct notions of things and not to have writ very clearly about them. This I imagine has been

no small occasion of obscurity and mistake in this matter and therefore is, as much as may be, to be avoided. For he that shall turn his thoughts inwards upon what passes in his mind when he *wills* shall see that the *will* or power of *volition* is conversant about nothing but that particular determination of the mind whereby, barely by a thought, the mind endeavours to give rise, continuation, or stop to any action which it takes to be in its power. This, well considered, plainly shows that the *will* is perfectly distinguished from *desire*; which, in the very same action, may have a quite contrary tendency from that which our *will* sets us upon. A man, whom I cannot deny, may oblige me to use persuasions to another, which, at the same time I am speaking, I may wish may not prevail on him. In this case, it is plain the *will* and *desire* run counter. I will the action that tends one way, whilst my desire tends another, and that the direct contrary. A man who, by a violent fit of the gout in his limbs, finds a doziness in his head or a want of appetite in his stomach removed, desires to be eased too of the pain of his feet or hands (for wherever there is pain there is a desire to be rid of it) though yet, whilst he apprehends that the removal of the pain may translate the noxious humour to a more vital part, his *will* is never determined to any one action that may serve to remove this pain. Whence it is evident that *desiring* and *willing* are two distinct acts of the mind, and consequently that the *will*, which is but the power of *volition*, is much more distinct from *desire*. 31. To return, then, to the inquiry, *What is it that determines the will in regard to our actions?* And that, upon second thoughts, I am apt to imagine is not, as is generally supposed, the greater good in view, but some (and for the most part the most pressing) *uneasiness* a man is at present under. This is that which successively determines the *will* and sets us upon those actions we perform. This *uneasiness* we may call, as it is, *desire*; which is an *uneasiness* of the mind for want of some absent good. All pain of the body, of what sort soever, and disquiet of the mind, is *uneasiness*; and with this is always joined desire, equal to the pain or *uneasiness* felt, and is scarce distinguishable from it. For *desire* being nothing but an *uneasiness* in the want of an absent good, in reference to any pain felt, ease is that absent good; and till that ease be attained, we may call it *desire*, nobody feeling pain that he wishes not to be eased of, with a desire equal to that pain, and inseparable from it. Besides this desire of ease from pain, there is another of absent positive good; and here also the desire and *uneasiness* are equal. As much as we desire any absent good, so much are we in pain for it. But here all absent good does not, according to the greatness it has, or is acknowledged to have, cause pain equal to that greatness, as all pain causes desire equal to itself: because the absence of good is not always a pain, as the presence of pain is. And therefore absent good may be looked on and considered without *desire*. But so much as there is anywhere of *desire*, so much there is of *uneasiness*.

32.   That *desire* is a state of *uneasiness* everyone who reflects on himself will quickly find. Who is there that has not felt in *desire* what the wise man says of hope (which is not much different from it), that it being *deferred makes the heart sick*, and that still proportionable to the greatness of the *desire* which sometimes raises the *uneasiness* to that pitch that it makes people cry out, *give me children*, give me the thing desired, *or I die*? Life itself, and all its enjoyments, is a burden cannot be borne under the lasting and unremoved pressure of such an *uneasiness*.

33.   Good and evil, present and absent, it is true, work upon the mind; but that which immediately determines the *will*, from time to time, to every voluntary action, is the *uneasiness* of *desire*, fixed on some absent good: either negative, as indolence to one in pain; or positive, as enjoyment of pleasure. That it is this *uneasiness* that determines the *will* to the successive voluntary actions, whereof the greatest part of our lives is made up, and by which we are conducted through different courses to different ends, I shall endeavour to show, both from experience and the reason of the thing.

34.   When a man is perfectly content with the state he is in, which is when he is perfectly without any *uneasiness*, what industry, what action, what *will* is there left but to continue in it? Of this every man's observation will satisfy him. And thus we see our all-wise Maker, suitable to our constitution and frame, and knowing what it is that determines the *will*, has put into man the *uneasiness* of hunger and thirst, and other natural desires, that return at their seasons, to move and determine their *wills* for the preservation of themselves, and the continuation of their species. For I think we may conclude that, if the bare contemplation of these good ends to which we are carried by

these several *uneasinesses* had been sufficient to determine the *will* and set us on work, we should have had none of these natural pains, and perhaps in this world little or no pain at all. *It is better to marry than to burn,* says St. *Paul,* where we may see what it is that chiefly drives men into the enjoyments of a conjugal life. A little burning felt pushes us more powerfully than greater pleasures in prospect draw or allure.

35. It seems so established and settled a maxim, by the general consent of all mankind, that good, the greater good, determines the will, that I do not at all wonder that when I first published my thoughts on this subject I took it for granted; and I imagine that, by a great many, I shall be thought more excusable for having then done so, than that now I have ventured to recede from so received an opinion. But yet, upon a stricter inquiry, I am forced to conclude that *good,* the *greater good,* though apprehended and acknowledged to be so, does not determine the *will,* until our desire, raised proportionably to it, makes us *uneasy* in the want of it. Convince a man never so much that plenty has its advantages over poverty, make him see and own that the handsome conveniences of life are better than nasty penury: yet, as long as he is content with the latter, and finds no *uneasiness* in it, he moves not; his *will* never is determined to any action that shall bring him out of it. Let a man be never so well persuaded of the advantages of virtue, that it is as necessary to a man who has any great aims in this world, or hopes in the next, as food to life: yet till he *hungers and thirsts after righteousness,* till he feels an *uneasiness* in the want of it, his *will* will not be determined to any action in pursuit of this confessed greater good; but any other *uneasinesses* he feels in himself shall take place, and carry his *will* to other actions. On the other side, let a drunkard see that his health decays, his estate wastes; discredit and diseases, and the want of all things, even of his beloved drink, attends him in the course he follows; yet the returns of *uneasiness* to miss his companions, the habitual thirst after his cups at the usual time, drives him to the tavern, though he has in his view the loss of health and plenty, and perhaps of the joys of another life, the least of which is no inconsiderable good, but such as he confesses is far greater than the tickling of his palate with a glass of wine, or the idle chat of a soaking club. It is not for want of viewing the greater good, for he sees and acknowledges it and, in the intervals of his drinking hours, will take

resolutions to pursue the greater good; but when the *uneasiness* to miss his accustomed delight returns, the greater acknowledged good loses its hold and the present *uneasiness* determines the *will* to the accustomed action; which thereby gets stronger footing to prevail against the next occasion, though he at the same time makes secret promises to himself that he will do so no more: this is the last time he will act against the attainment of those greater goods. And thus he is, from time to time, in the state of that unhappy complainer, *video meliora proboque, deteriora sequor*: which sentence allowed for true and made good by constant experience may this, and possibly no other way, be easily made intelligible.

36. If we inquire into the reason of what experience makes so evident in fact, and examine why it is *uneasiness* alone operates on the *will* and determines it in its choice, we shall find that, we being capable but of one determination of the *will* to one action at once, the present *uneasiness* that we are under does naturally determine the will in order to that happiness which we all aim at in all our actions. For as much as whilst we are under any *uneasiness*, we cannot apprehend ourselves happy, or in the way to it: pain and *uneasiness* being, by everyone, concluded and felt to be inconsistent with happiness, spoiling the relish even of those good things which we have, a little pain serving to mar all the pleasure we rejoiced in. And, therefore, that which of course determines the choice of our *will* to the next action will always be the removing of pain, as long as we have any left, as the first and necessary step towards happiness.

37. Another reason why it is *uneasiness* alone determines the will, may be this: because that alone is present, and it is against the nature of things that what is absent should operate where it is not. It may be said that absent good may, by contemplation, be brought home to the mind and made present. The *idea* of it indeed may be in the mind, and viewed as present there; but nothing will be in the mind as a present good, able to counterbalance the removal of any *uneasiness* which we are under, till it raises our desire; and the *uneasiness* of that has the prevalency in determining the *will*. Till then the *idea* in the mind of whatever is good is there only like other *ideas*, the object of bare unactive speculation, but operates not on the *will*, nor sets us on work: the reason whereof I shall show by and by. How many are to be found that have had lively representations set

before their minds of the unspeakable joys of heaven, which they acknowledge both possible and probable too, who yet would be content to take up with their happiness here? And so the prevailing *uneasinesses* of their desires, let loose after the enjoyments of this life, take their turns in the determining their *wills*, and all that while they take not one step, are not one jot moved towards the good things of another life, considered as never so great.

38. Were the *will* determined by the views of good as it appears in contemplation greater or less to the understanding, which is the state of all absent good, and that which, in the received opinion, the *will* is supposed to move to and to be moved by, I do not see how it could ever get loose from the infinite eternal joys of heaven, once proposed and considered as possible. For all absent good, by which alone, barely proposed and coming in view, the *will* is thought to be determined, and so to set us on action, being only possible, but not infallibly certain: it is unavoidable that the infinitely greater possible good should regularly and constantly determine the *will* in all the successive actions it directs; and then we should keep constantly and steadily in our course towards heaven, without ever standing still, or directing our actions to any other end: the eternal condition of a future state infinitely outweighing the expectation of riches, or honour, or any other worldly pleasure which we can propose to ourselves, though we should grant these the more probable to be attained; for nothing future is yet in possession, and so the expectation even of these may deceive us. If it were so that the greater good in view determines the *will*, so great a good, once proposed, could not but seize the *will* and hold it fast to the pursuit of this infinitely greatest good, without ever letting it go again; for the *will* having a power over, and directing the thoughts, as well as other actions, would, if it were so, hold the contemplation of the mind fixed to that good.

This would be the state of the mind and regular tendency of the *will* in all its determinations, were it determined by that which is considered and in view the greater good. But that it is not so is visible in experience, the infinitely greatest confessed good being often neglected to satisfy the successive *uneasiness* of our desires pursuing trifles. But, though the greatest allowed, even everlasting, unspeakable good, which has sometimes moved and affected the mind, does not steadfastly hold the *will*, yet we see any very great and prevailing *uneasiness*, having once laid hold on the *will*, lets it not go; by which we may be convinced what it is that determines the *will*. Thus any vehement pain of the body, the ungovernable passion of a man violently in love, or the impatient desire of revenge keeps the *will* steady and intent; and the *will*, thus determined, never lets the understanding lay by the object, but all the thoughts of the mind and powers of the body are uninterruptedly employed that way, by the determinations of the *will*, influenced by that topping *uneasiness*, as long as it lasts; whereby it seems to me evident that the *will*, or power of setting us upon one action in preference to all others, is determined in us by *uneasiness*; and whether this be not so, I desire everyone to observe in himself.

39.   I have hitherto chiefly instanced in the *uneasiness* of desire, as that which determines the *will*, because that is the chief and most sensible; and the *will* seldom orders any action, nor is there any voluntary action performed, without some *desire* accompanying it; which I think is the reason why the *will* and *desire* are so often confounded. But yet we are not to look upon the *uneasiness* which makes up, or at least accompanies, most of the other passions as wholly excluded in the case. *Aversion, fear, anger, envy, shame*, etc., have each their *uneasiness* too, and thereby influence the *will*. These passions are scarce any of them, in life and practice, simple and alone, and wholly unmixed with others, though usually, in discourse and contemplation, that carries the name which operates strongest and appears most in the present state of the mind. Nay, there is, I think scarce any of the passions to be found without *desire* joined with it. I am sure, wherever there is *uneasiness*, there is *desire*: for we constantly desire happiness; and whatever we feel of *uneasiness*, so much, it is certain, we want of happiness, even in our own opinion, let our state and condition otherwise be what it will. Besides, the present moment not being our eternity, whatever our enjoyment be, we look beyond the present, and desire goes with our foresight, and that still carries the *will* with it. So that even in *joy* itself, that which keeps up the action whereon the enjoyment depends is the desire to continue it and fear to lose it. And whenever a greater *uneasiness* than that takes place in the mind, the *will* presently is by that determined to some new action and the present delight neglected.

40.   But we being in this world beset with sundry *uneasinesses*,

distracted with different *desires*, the next inquiry naturally will be, which of them has the precedency in determining the *will* to the next action? And to that the answer is that, ordinarily, which is the most pressing of those that are judged capable of being then removed. For the *will*, being the power of directing our operative faculties to some action for some end, cannot at any time be moved towards what is judged at that time unattainable: that would be to suppose an intelligent being designedly to act for an end only to lose its labour; for so it is to act for what is judged not attainable, and therefore very great *uneasinesses* move not the *will* when they are judged not capable of a cure: they, in that case, put us not upon endeavours. But these set apart, the most important and urgent *uneasiness* we at that time feel is that which ordinarily determines the *will* successively in that train of voluntary actions which make up our lives. The greatest present *uneasiness* is the spur to action that is constantly felt and for the most part determines the *will* in its choice of the next action. For this we must carry along with us that the proper and only object of the *will* is some action of ours and nothing else. For we producing nothing by our *willing* it but some action in our power, it is there the *will* terminates and reaches no further.

41. If it be further asked, what it is moves *desire*? I answer: happiness, and that alone. *Happiness* and *misery* are the names of two extremes, the utmost bounds whereof we know not; it is what *eye hath not seen, ear hath not heard, nor hath it entered into the heart of man to conceive*. But of some degrees of both we have very lively impressions, made by several instances of delight and joy on the one side, and torment and sorrow on the other; which, for shortness's sake, I shall comprehend under the names of pleasure and pain, there being pleasure and pain of the mind as well as the body: *With Him is fullness of joy, and pleasure for evermore*; or, to speak truly, they are all of the mind, though some have their rise in the mind from thought, others in the body from certain modifications of motion.

42. *Happiness*, then, in its full extent, is the utmost pleasure we are capable of, and *misery* the utmost pain; and the lowest degree of what can be called *happiness* is so much ease from all pain, and so much present pleasure, as without which anyone cannot be content. Now, because pleasure and pain are produced in us by the operation of certain objects either on our

minds or our bodies and in different degrees, therefore, what has
an aptness to produce pleasure in us is that we call *good*, and
what is apt to produce pain in us we call *evil*, for no other reason
but for its aptness to produce pleasure and pain in us, wherein
consists our *happiness* and *misery*. Further, though what is apt
to produce any degree of pleasure be in itself *good*, and what is
apt to produce any degree of pain be *evil*, yet it often happens
that we do not call it so when it comes in competition with a
greater of its sort, because, when they come in competition, the
degrees also of pleasure and pain have justly a preference. So
that if we will rightly estimate what we call *good* and *evil*, we
shall find it lies much in comparison: for the cause of every less
degree of pain, as well as every greater degree of pleasure, has
the nature of *good*, and *vice versa*.

43.   Though this be that which is called *good* and *evil*, and all
good be the proper object of *desire* in general, yet all good, even
seen and confessed to be so, does not necessarily move every
particular man's *desire*, but only that part, or so much of it as is
considered and taken to make a necessary part of his happiness.
All other good, however great in reality or appearance, excites
not a man's *desires* who looks not on it to make a part of that
happiness wherewith he, in his present thoughts, can satisfy
himself.   *Happiness*, under this view, everyone constantly
pursues and *desires* what makes any part of it: other things
acknowledged to be good, he can look upon without *desire*, pass
by, and be content without.   There is nobody, I think, so
senseless as to deny that there is pleasure in knowledge, and for
the pleasures of sense they have too many followers to let it be
questioned whether men are taken with them or no.   Now let
one man place his satisfaction in sensual pleasures, another in
the delight of knowledge: though each of them cannot but
confess there is great pleasure in what the other pursues, yet,
neither of them making the other's delight a part of his happiness, their *desires* are not moved, but each is satisfied without
what the other enjoys; and so his will is not determined to the
pursuit of it.   But yet, as soon as the studious man's hunger and
thirst make him *uneasy*, he whose *will* was never determined to
any pursuit of good cheer, poignant sauces, delicious wine, by
the pleasant taste he has found in them is, by the *uneasiness* of
hunger and thirst, presently determined to eating and drinking,
though possibly with great indifferency, what wholesome food

comes in his way. And, on the other side, the epicure buckles to study, when shame or the desire to recommend himself to his mistress shall make him *uneasy* in the want of any sort of knowledge. Thus, how much soever men are in earnest and constant in pursuit of happiness, yet they may have a clear view of good, great and confessed good, without being concerned for it or moved by it, if they think they can make up their happiness without it. Though as to pain, that they are always concerned for; they can feel no *uneasiness* without being moved. And therefore being *uneasy* in the want of whatever is judged necessary to their happiness, as soon as any good appears to make a part of their portion of happiness, they begin to *desire* it.

44. This, I think anyone may observe in himself and others, that the *greater visible good* does not always raise men's *desires* in proportion to the greatness it appears and is acknowledged to have, though every little trouble moves us and sets us on work to get rid of it. The reason whereof is evident from the nature of our *happiness* and *misery* itself. All present pain, whatever it be, makes a part of our present *misery*: but all absent good does not at any time make a necessary part of our present *happiness*, nor the absence of it make a part of our *misery*. If it did, we should be constantly and infinitely miserable, there being infinite degrees of happiness which are not in our possession. All *uneasiness* therefore being removed, a moderate portion of good serves at present to content men; and some few degrees of pleasure, in a succession of ordinary enjoyments, make up a happiness wherein they can be satisfied. If this were not so, there could be no room for those indifferent and visibly trifling actions, to which our *wills* are so often determined, and wherein we voluntarily waste so much of our lives; which remissness could by no means consist with a constant determination of *will* or *desire* to the greatest apparent good. That this is so, I think few people need go far from home to be convinced. And indeed in this life there are not many whose happiness reaches so far as to afford them a constant train of moderate mean pleasures, without any mixture of *uneasiness*; and yet they could be content to stay here forever, though they cannot deny but that it is possible there may be a state of eternal durable joys after this life, far surpassing all the good that is to be found here. Nay, they cannot but see that it is more possible than the attainment and continuation of that pittance of honour, riches, or pleasure which.

they pursue, and for which they neglect that eternal state. But yet in full view of this difference, satisfied of the possibility of a perfect, secure, and lasting happiness in a future state, and under a clear conviction that it is not to be had here whilst they bound their happiness within some little enjoyment or aim of this life and exclude the joys of heaven from making any necessary part of it, their desires are not moved by this greater apparent good, nor their *wills* determined to any action or endeavour for its attainment.

45.   The ordinary necessities of our lives fill a great part of them with the *uneasiness* of *hunger, thirst, heat, cold, weariness,* with labour, and *sleepiness* in their constant returns, etc. To which, if, besides accidental harms, we add the fantastical *uneasiness* (as itch after *honour, power,* or *riches,* etc.) which acquired habits, by fashion, example, and education, have settled in us, and a thousand other irregular desires which custom has made natural to us, we shall find that a very little part of our life is so vacant from these *uneasinesses* as to leave us free to the attraction of remoter absent good. We are seldom at ease and free enough from the solicitation of our natural or adopted desires, but a constant succession of *uneasinesses,* out of that stock which natural wants or acquired habits have heaped up, take the *will* in their turns; and no sooner is one action dispatched, which by such a determination of the *will* we are set upon, but another uneasiness is ready to set us on work. For the removing of the pains we feel, and are at present pressed with, being the getting out of misery, and consequently the first thing to be done in order to happiness: absent good, though thought on, confessed, and appearing to be good, not making any part of this unhappiness in its absence, is jostled out to make way for the removal of those *uneasinesses* we feel, till due and repeated contemplation has brought it nearer to our mind, given some relish of it, and raised in us some desire: which then, beginning to make a part of our present *uneasiness,* stands upon fair terms with the rest to be satisfied, and so, according to its greatness and pressure, comes in its turn to determine the *will.*

46.   And thus, by a due consideration, and examining any good proposed, it is in our power to raise our desires in a due proportion to the value of that good, whereby in its turn and place it may come to work upon the *will* and be pursued. For good,

though appearing and allowed never so great, yet till it has raised desires in our minds and thereby made us *uneasy* in its want, it reaches not our *wills*; we are not within the sphere of its activity, our *wills* being under the determination only of those *uneasinesses* which are present to us, which (whilst we have any) are always soliciting and ready at hand to give the *will* its next determination: the balancing, when there is any in the mind, being only which desire shall be next satisfied, which *uneasiness* first removed. Whereby it comes to pass that as long as any *uneasiness*, any desire remains in our mind, there is no room for *good* barely as such to come at the *will*, or at all to determine it. Because, as has been said, the first step in our endeavours after happiness being to get wholly out of the confines of misery and to feel no part of it, the *will* can be at leisure for nothing else till every *uneasiness* we feel be perfectly removed: which, in the multitude of wants and desires we are beset with in this imperfect state, we are not like to be ever freed from in this world.

47.   There being in us a great many *uneasinesses* always soliciting and ready to determine the *will*, it is natural, as I have said, that the greatest and most pressing should determine the *will* to the next action; and so it does for the most part, but not always. For the mind, having in most cases, as is evident in experience, a power to *suspend* the execution and satisfaction of any of its desires, and so all, one after another, is at liberty to consider the objects of them, examine them on all sides, and weigh them with others. In this lies the liberty man has; and from the not using of it right comes all that variety of mistakes, errors, and faults which we run into in the conduct of our lives and our endeavours after happiness, whilst we precipitate the determination of our *wills* and engage too soon, before due *examination*. To prevent this, we have a power to *suspend* the prosecution of this or that desire, as everyone daily may experiment in himself. This seems to me the source of all liberty; in this seems to consist that which is (as I think improperly) called *free will*. For, during this *suspension* of any desire, before the *will* be determined to action, and the action (which follows that determination) done, we have opportunity to examine, view, and judge of the good or evil of what we are going to do; and when, upon due *examination*, we have judged, we have done our duty, all that we can or ought to do, in pursuit of our happiness; and it is not a fault, but a

perfection of our nature, to desire, will, and act according to the last result of a fair *examination*.

48.   This is so far from being a restraint or diminution of *freedom* that it is the very improvement and benefit of it: it is not an abridgment, it is the end and use of our *liberty*; and the further we are removed from such a determination, the nearer we are to misery and slavery. A perfect indifference in the mind, not determinable by its last judgment of the good or evil that is thought to attend its choice, would be so far from being an advantage and excellency of any intellectual nature, that it would be as great an imperfection as the want of indifference to act or not to act till determined by the *will* would be an imperfection on the other side. A man is at liberty to lift up his hand to his head, or let it rest quiet: he is perfectly indifferent in either; and it would be an imperfection in him if he wanted that power, if he were deprived of that indifference. But it would be as great an imperfection if he had the same indifference, whether he would prefer the lifting up his hand or its remaining in rest, when it would save his head or eyes from a blow he sees coming: it is as much *a perfection that desire or the power of preferring should be determined by good* as that the power of acting should be determined by the *will*, and the certainer such determination is the greater is the perfection. Nay, were we determined by anything but the last result of our own minds, judging of the good or evil of any action, we were not free, the very end of our freedom being that we might attain the good we choose. And therefore every man is put under a necessity, by his constitution as an intelligent being, to be determined in *willing* by his own thought and judgment what is best for him to do, else he would be under the determination of some other than himself, which is want of liberty. And to deny that a man's *will*, in every determination, follows his own judgment is to say that a man *wills* and acts for an end that he would not have at the time that he *wills* and acts for it. For if he prefers it in his present thoughts before any other, it is plain he then thinks better of it and would have it before any other, unless he can have and not have it, *will* and not *will* it at the same time: a contradiction too manifest to be admitted!

49.   If we look upon those *superior beings* above us who enjoy perfect happiness, we shall have reason to judge that they are more steadily *determined in their choice of good* than we; and yet

we have no reason to think they are less happy or less free than we are. And if it were fit for such poor finite creatures as we are to pronounce what infinite wisdom and goodness could do, I think we might say that God himself cannot choose what is not good: the freedom of the Almighty hinders not his being determined by what is best.

50. But to give a right view of this mistaken part of liberty let me ask: Would anyone be a changeling because he is less determined by wise considerations than a wise man? Is it worth the name of *freedom* to be at liberty to play the fool and draw shame and misery upon a man's self? If to break loose from the conduct of reason and to want that restraint of examination and judgment which keeps us from choosing or doing the worse be *liberty*, true liberty, madmen and fools are the only freemen; but yet, I think, nobody would choose to be mad for the sake of such *liberty* but he that is mad already. The constant desire of happiness, and the constraint it puts upon us to act for it, nobody, I think, accounts an abridgment of *liberty*, or at least an abridgment of *liberty* to be complained of. God Almighty himself is under the necessity of being happy; and the more any intelligent being is so, the nearer is its approach to infinite perfection and happiness. That, in this state of ignorance, we short-sighted creatures might not mistake true felicity, we are endowed with a power to suspend any particular desire, and keep it from determining the *will*, and engaging us in action. This is *standing still*, where we are not sufficiently assured of the way; examination is *consulting a guide*. The determination of the *will*, upon inquiry, is *following the direction of that guide;* and he that has a power to act or not to act according as such determination directs is a *free agent:* such determination abridges not that power wherein liberty consists. He that has his chains knocked off and the prison doors set open to him is perfectly at *liberty*, because he may either go or stay as he best likes, though his preference be determined to stay by the darkness of the night or illness of the weather or want of other lodging. He ceases not to be free, though the desire of some convenience to be had there absolutely determines his preference and makes him stay in his prison.

51. As therefore the highest perfection of intellectual nature lies in a careful and constant pursuit of true and solid happiness, so the care of ourselves, that we mistake not imaginary for **real**

happiness, is the necessary foundation of our *liberty*. The stronger ties we have to an unalterable pursuit of happiness in general, which is our greatest good and which, as such, our desires always follow, the more are we free from any necessary determination of our *will* to any particular action, and from a necessary compliance with our desire, set upon any particular, and then appearing preferable good, till we have duly examined whether it has a tendency to, or be inconsonant with, our real happiness; and therefore, till we are as much informed upon this inquiry as the weight of the matter and the nature of the case demands, we are, by the necessity of preferring and pursuing true happiness as our greatest good, obliged to suspend the satisfaction of our desire in particular cases.

52.   This is the hinge on which turns the *liberty* of intellectual beings, in their constant endeavours after and a steady prosecution of true felicity, that they can *suspend* this prosecution in particular cases, till they have looked before them and informed themselves whether that particular thing which is then proposed or desired lies in the way to their main end, and make a real part of that which is their greatest good; for the inclination and tendency of their nature to happiness is an obligation and motive to them to take care not to mistake or miss it, and so necessarily puts them upon caution, deliberation, and wariness in the direction of their particular actions, which are the means to obtain it.   Whatever necessity determines to the pursuit of real bliss, the same necessity, with the same force, establishes *suspense*, *deliberation*, and scrutiny of each successive desire, whether the satisfaction of it does not interfere with our true happiness and mislead us from it.   This, as seems to me, is the great privilege of finite intellectual beings; and I desire it may be well considered whether the great inlet and exercise of all the *liberty* men have, are capable of, or can be useful to them, and that whereon depends the turn of their actions, does not lie in this: that they can *suspend* their desires and stop them from determining their *wills* to any action, till they have duly and fairly *examined* the good and evil of it, as far forth as the weight of the thing requires.   This we are able to do; and when we have done it, we have done our duty, and all that is in our power, and indeed all that needs.   For, since the *will* supposes knowledge to guide its choice, all that we can do is to hold our *wills* undetermined, till we have *examined* the good and evil of what we

desire. What follows after that follows in a chain of consequences, linked one to another, all depending on the last determination of the judgment, which, whether it shall be upon a hasty and precipitate view, or upon a due and mature *examination*, is in our power: experience showing us that in most cases we are able to suspend the present satisfaction of any desire.

53. But if any extreme disturbance (as sometimes it happens) possesses our whole mind, as when the pain of the rack, an impetuous *uneasiness*, as of love, anger, or any other violent passion, running away with us, allows us not the liberty of thought, and we are not masters enough of our own minds to consider thoroughly and examine fairly, God, who knows our frailty, pities our weakness, and requires of us no more than we are able to do, and sees what was and what was not in our power, will judge as a kind and merciful father. But the forbearance of a too hasty compliance with our desires, the moderation and restraint of our passions, so that our understandings may be *free* to examine, and reason unbiased give its judgment, being that whereon a right direction of our conduct to true happiness depends: it is in this we should employ our chief care and endeavours. In this we should take pains to suit the relish of our minds to the true intrinsic good or ill that is in things, and not permit an allowed or supposed possible great and weighty good to slip out of our thoughts, without leaving any relish, any desire of itself there, till, by a due consideration of its true worth, we have formed appetites in our minds suitable to it and made ourselves uneasy in the want of it, or in the fear of losing it. And how much this is in everyone's power, by making resolutions to himself such as he may keep, is easy for everyone to try. Nor let anyone say he cannot govern his passions, nor hinder them from breaking out, and carrying him into action; for what he can do before a prince or a great man, he can do alone or in the presence of God, if he will.

54. From what has been said it is easy to give an account how it comes to pass that, though all men desire happiness, yet their *wills carry them so contrarily*, and consequently some of them to what is evil. And to this I say that the various and contrary choices that men make in the world do not argue that they do not all pursue good, but that the same thing is not good to every man alike. This variety of pursuits shows that everyone does not place his happiness in the same thing or choose the same way to

it. Were all the concerns of man terminated in this life, why one
followed study and knowledge and another hawking and hunting, why one chose luxury and debauchery, and another
sobriety and riches, would not be because everyone of these
did not aim at his own happiness, but because their *happiness*
was placed in different things. And therefore it was a right
answer of the physician to his patient that had sore eyes: if you
have more pleasure in the taste of wine than in the use of your
sight, wine is good for you; but if the pleasure of seeing be
greater to you than that of drinking, wine is naught.

55.   The mind has a different relish, as well as the palate; and
you will as fruitlessly endeavour to delight all men with riches
or glory (which yet some men place their happiness in) as you
would to satisfy all men's hunger with cheese or lobsters; which,
though very agreeable and delicious fare to some, are to others
extremely nauseous and offensive. And many people would
with reason prefer the griping of an hungry belly to those
dishes which are a feast to others. Hence it was, I think, that the
philosophers of old did in vain inquire whether *summum
bonum* consisted in riches, or bodily delights, or virtue, or contemplation; and they might have as reasonably disputed, whether
the best relish were to be found in apples, plums, or nuts, and
have divided themselves into sects upon it. For, as pleasant
tastes depend not on the things themselves but their agreeableness to this or that particular palate, wherein there is great
variety, so the greatest happiness consists in the having those
things which produce the greatest pleasure, and in the absence of
those which cause any disturbance, any pain. Now these, to
different men, are very different things. If therefore men in this
life only have hope, if in this life they can only enjoy, it is not
strange nor unreasonable that they should seek their happiness
by avoiding all things that disease them here and by pursuing all
that delight them; wherein it will be no wonder to find variety
and difference. For if there be no prospect beyond the grave,
the inference is certainly right, *let us eat and drink,* let us enjoy
what we delight in, *for tomorrow we shall die.* This, I think, may
serve to show us the reason why, though all men's desires tend
to happiness, yet they are not moved by the same object. Men
may choose different things, and yet all choose right: supposing
them only like a company of poor insects, whereof some are bees,
delighted with flowers and their sweetness; others beetles,

delighted with other kinds of viands, which, having enjoyed for a season, they should cease to be and exist no more for ever.

56.   These things duly weighed, will give us, as I think, a clear view into the state of human liberty. Liberty, it is plain, consists in a power to do, or not to do; to do, or forbear doing, as we *will*. This cannot be denied. But this seeming to comprehend only the actions of a man consecutive to volition, it is further inquired whether he be at liberty to *will* or no. And to this it has been answered that, in most cases, a man is not at liberty to forbear the act of volition: he must exert an act of his *will*, whereby the action proposed is made to exist or not to exist. But yet there is a case wherein a man is at liberty in respect of *willing*, and that is the choosing of a remote good as an end to be pursued. Here a man may suspend the act of his choice from being determined for or against the thing proposed, till he has examined whether it be really of a nature, in itself and consequences, to make him happy or no. For when he has once chosen it, and thereby it is become a part of his happiness, it raises desire, and that proportionably gives him uneasiness which determines his *will* and sets him at work in pursuit of his choice on all occasions that offer. And here we may see how it comes to pass that a man may justly incur punishment, though it be certain that in all the particular actions that he *wills*, he does and necessarily does will that which he then judges to be good. For though his *will* be always determined by that which is judged good by his understanding, yet it excuses him not: because, by a too hasty choice of his own making, he has imposed on himself wrong measures of good and evil, which, however false and fallacious, have the same influence on all his future conduct as if they were true and right. He has vitiated his own palate and must be answerable to himself for the sickness and death that follows from it. The eternal law and nature of things must not be altered to comply with his ill-ordered choice. If the neglect or abuse of the liberty he had to examine what would really and truly make for his happiness misleads him, the miscarriages that follow on it must be imputed to his own election. He had a power to suspend his determination; it was given him that he might examine and take care of his own happiness and look that he were not deceived. And he could never judge that it was better to be deceived than not, in a matter of so great and near concernment.

What has been said may also discover to us the reason why men in this world prefer different things and pursue happiness by contrary courses. But yet, since men are always constant and in earnest in matters of happiness and misery, the question still remains, *how men come often to prefer the worse to the better*, and to choose that, which, by their own confession, has made them miserable.

57. To account for the various and contrary ways men take, though all aim at being happy, we must consider whence the various *uneasinesses* that determine the will, in the preference of each voluntary action, have their rise:

(1) Some of them come from causes not in our power, such as are often the pains of the body from want, disease, or outward injuries, as the rack, etc.; which, when present and violent, operate for the most part forcibly on the *will*, and turn the courses of men's lives from virtue, piety, and religion, and what before they judged to lead to happiness: everyone not endeavouring or, through disuse, not being able, by the contemplation of remote and future good, to raise in himself desires of them strong enough to counterbalance the uneasiness he feels in those bodily torments, and to keep his *will* steady in the choice of those actions which lead to future happiness. A neighbour country has been of late a tragical theatre from which we might fetch instances, if there needed any and the world did not in all countries and ages furnish examples enough to confirm that received observation, *necessitas cogit ad turpia*, and therefore there is great reason for us to pray *lead us not into temptation*.

(2) Other *uneasinesses* arise from our desires of absent good; which desires always bear proportion to and depend on the judgment we make and the relish we have of any absent good, in both which we are apt to be variously misled, and that by our own fault.

58. In the first place, I shall consider the wrong judgments men make of future good and evil, whereby their desires are misled. For, as to present happiness and misery, when that alone comes into consideration, and the consequences are quite removed, *a man never chooses amiss*: he knows what best pleases him, and that he actually prefers. Things in their present enjoyment are what they seem: the apparent and real good are, in this case, always the same. For, the pain or pleasure being just so great and no greater than it is felt, the present good or evil is

really so much as it appears. And therefore were every action of ours concluded within itself and drew no consequences after it, we should undoubtedly never err in our choice of good: we should always infallibly prefer the best. Were the pains of honest industry and of starving with hunger and cold set together before us, nobody would be in doubt which to choose; were the satisfaction of a lust and the joys of heaven offered at once to anyone's present possession, he would not balance or err in the determination of his choice.

59. But since our voluntary actions carry not all the happiness and misery that depend on them along with them in their present performance but are the precedent causes of good and evil, which they draw after them and bring upon us, when they themselves are past and cease to be, our desires look beyond our present enjoyments and carry the mind out to absent *good*, according to the necessity which we think there is of it, to the making or increase of our happiness. It is our opinion of such a necessity that gives it its attraction; without that, we are not moved by absent *good*. For in this narrow scantling of capacity which we are accustomed to and sensible of here, wherein we enjoy but one pleasure at once, which, when all uneasiness is away, is, whilst it lasts, sufficient to make us think ourselves happy, it is not all remote and even apparent good that affects us. Because the indolence and enjoyment we have sufficing for our present happiness, we desire not to venture the change, since we judge that we are happy already, being content, and that is enough. For who is content is happy. But as soon as any new uneasiness comes in, this happiness is disturbed and we are set afresh on work in the pursuit of happiness.

60. Their aptness therefore to conclude that they can be happy without it is one great occasion that men often are not raised to the desire of the greatest absent *good*. For, whilst such thoughts possess them, the joys of a future state move them not: they have little concern or uneasiness about them; and the *will*, free from the determination of such desires, is left to the pursuit of nearer satisfactions, and to the removal of those uneasinesses which it then feels, in its want of and longings after them. Change but man's view of these things; let him see that virtue and religion are necessary to his happiness; let him look into the future state of bliss or misery, and see there God, the righteous judge, ready to *render to every man according to his deeds: to*

them who, by patient continuance in well-doing, seek for glory and honour and immortality, eternal life; but unto every soul that doth evil, indignation and wrath, tribulation and anguish; to him, I say, who hath a prospect of the different state of perfect happiness or misery that attends all men after this life, depending on their behaviour here, the measures of good and evil that govern his choice are mightily changed. For, since nothing of pleasure and pain in this life can bear any proportion to endless happiness or exquisite misery of an immortal soul hereafter, actions in his power will have their preference, not according to the transient pleasure or pain that accompanies or follows them here, but as they serve to secure that perfect durable happiness hereafter.

61. But to account more particularly for the misery that men often bring on themselves, notwithstanding that they do all in earnest pursue happiness, we must consider how *things* come to be *represented* to our desires *under deceitful appearances*: and that is *by the judgment* pronouncing wrongly concerning them. To see how far this reaches and what are the causes of wrong judgment, we must remember that things are judged good or bad in a double sense.

First, that which is properly good or bad is nothing but barely pleasure or pain.

Secondly, but because not only present pleasure and pain but that also which is apt by its efficacy or consequences to bring it upon us at a distance is a proper object of our desires and apt to move a creature that has foresight, therefore *things* also *that draw after them pleasure and pain are considered as good and evil.*

62. The *wrong judgment* that *misleads us* and makes the will often fasten on the worse side lies in misreporting upon the various comparisons of these. The *wrong judgment* I am here speaking of is not what one man may think of the determination of another, but what every man himself must confess to be wrong. For, since I lay it for a certain ground that every intelligent being really seeks happiness, which consists in the enjoyment of pleasure without any considerable mixture of uneasiness, it is impossible anyone should willingly put into his own draught any bitter ingredient or leave out anything in his power that would tend to his satisfaction and the completing of his happiness, but only by *wrong judgment*. I shall not here speak of

that mistake which is the consequence of invincible error, which
scarce deserves the name of *wrong judgment*, but of that *wrong
judgment* which every man himself must confess to be so.

63. I. Therefore, as to present pleasure and pain, the mind, as
has been said, never mistakes that which is really good or evil;
that which is the greater pleasure, or the greater pain, is really
just as it appears. But, though present pleasure and pain show
their difference and degrees so plainly as not to leave room to
mistake, yet, *when we compare present pleasure or pain with future*
(which is usually the case in the most important determinations
of the will), *we often make wrong judgments* of them, taking our
measures of them in different positions of distance. Objects
near our view are apt to be thought greater than those of a larger
size that are more remote; and so it is with pleasures and
pains: the present is apt to carry it, and those at a distance have
the disadvantages in the comparison. Thus most men, like
spendthrift heirs, are apt to judge a little in hand better than a
great deal to come, and so, for small matters in possession, part
with great ones in reversion. But that this is a *wrong judgment*
everyone must allow, let his pleasure consist in whatever it will,
since that which is future will certainly come to be present, and
then, having the same advantage of nearness, will show itself in
its full dimensions and discover his wilful mistake who judged
of it by unequal measures. Were the pleasure of drinking
accompanied, the very moment a man takes off his glass, with
that sick stomach and aching head which in some men are sure
to follow not many hours after, I think nobody, whatever
pleasure he had in his cups, would on these conditions ever let
wine touch his lips, which yet he daily swallows, and the evil
side comes to be chosen only by the fallacy of a little difference
in time. But if pleasure or pain can be so lessened only by a few
hours' removal, how much more will it be so by a further
distance, to a man that will not by a right judgment do what
time will, i.e. bring it home upon himself and consider it as
present and there take its true dimensions? This is the way we
usually impose on ourselves, in respect of bare pleasure and pain
or the true degrees of happiness or misery: the future loses its
just proportion, and what is present obtains the preference as the
greater. I mention not here the *wrong judgment*, whereby the
absent are not only lessened, but reduced to perfect nothing,
when men enjoy what they can in present and make sure of that,

concluding amiss that no evil will thence follow. For that lies
not in comparing the greatness of future good and evil, which is
that we are here speaking of, but in another sort of *wrong
judgment*, which is concerning good or evil as it is considered to
be the cause and procurement of pleasure or pain that will follow
from it.

64.   *The cause of our judging amiss*, when we compare our present pleasure or pain with future, seems to me to be *the weak and
narrow constitution of our minds*. We cannot well enjoy two
pleasures at once, much less any pleasure almost, whilst pain
possesses us. The present pleasure, if it be not very languid and
almost none at all, fills our narrow souls and so takes up the
whole mind that it scarce leaves any thought of things absent;
or if among our pleasures there are some which are not
strong enough to exclude the consideration of things at a
distance, yet we have so great an abhorrence of pain that
a little of it extinguishes all our pleasures: a little bitter
mingled in our cup leaves no relish of the sweet. Hence it
comes that, at any rate, we desire to be rid of the present evil,
which we are apt to think nothing absent can equal, because
under the present pain we find not ourselves capable of any the
least degree of happiness. Men's daily complaints are a loud
proof of this: the pain that anyone actually feels is still of all
other the worst, and it is with anguish they cry out, *Any rather
than this; nothing can be so intolerable as what I now suffer*.
And therefore our whole endeavours and thoughts are intent to
get rid of the present evil before all things, as the first necessary
condition to our happiness, let what will follow. Nothing, as we
passionately think, can exceed or almost equal the uneasiness
that sits so heavy upon us. And because the abstinence from
a present pleasure that offers itself is a pain, nay, oftentimes a
very great one, the desire being inflamed by a near and tempting
object, it is no wonder that that operates after the same manner
pain does, and lessens in our thoughts what is future, and so
forces us, as it were, blindfold into its embraces.

65.   Add to this that absent good or, which is the same thing,
future pleasure, especially if of a sort which we are unacquainted
with, seldom is able to counterbalance any uneasiness, either of
pain or desire, which is present. For its greatness being no more
than what shall be really tasted when enjoyed, men are apt
enough to lessen that, to make it give place to any present

desire, and conclude with themselves that, when it comes to trial, it may possibly not answer the report or opinion that generally passes of it, they having often found that not only what others have magnified but even what they themselves have enjoyed with great pleasure and delight at one time has proved insipid or nauseous at another, and therefore they see nothing in it for which they should forego a present enjoyment. But that this is a *false* way of *judging*, when applied to the happiness of another life, they must confess, unless they will say God cannot make those happy he designs to be so. For that being intended for a state of happiness, it must certainly be agreeable to everyone's wish and desire; could we suppose their relishes as different there as they are here, yet the manna in heaven will suit everyone's palate. Thus much of the *wrong judgment* we make of present and future pleasure and pain, when they are compared together, and so the absent considered as future.

66. II. *As to things good or bad in their consequences,* and by the aptness that is in them to procure us good or evil in the future, *we judge amiss several ways*:

(1) When we *judge* that so much evil does not really depend on them, as in truth there does.

(2) When we *judge* that, though the consequence be of that moment, yet it is not of that certainty but that it may otherwise fall out, or else by some means be avoided, as by industry, address, change, repentance, etc. That these are *wrong* ways of *judging* were easy to show in every particular, if I would examine them at large singly; but I shall only mention this in general, viz., that it is a very wrong and irrational way of proceeding to venture a greater good for a less, upon uncertain guesses and before a due examination be made proportionable to the weightiness of the matter and the concernment it is to us not to mistake. This, I think, everyone must confess, especially if he considers the usual *causes* of this *wrong judgment*, whereof these following are some.

67. I. *Ignorance:* He that judges without informing himself to the utmost that he is capable cannot acquit himself of *judging amiss.*

II. *Inadvertency:* When a man overlooks even that which he does know. This is an affected and present ignorance, which misleads our judgments as much as the other. Judging is, as it were, balancing an account and determining on which side the

odds lie. If therefore either side be huddled up in haste, and
several of the sums that should have gone into the reckoning be
overlooked and left out, this precipitancy causes as *wrong* a
judgment as if it were a perfect ignorance. That which most
commonly causes this is the prevalence of some present pleasure
or pain, heightened by our feeble passionate nature, most
strongly wrought on by what is present. To check this precipitancy, our understanding and reason was given us, if we will
make a right use of it, to search and see, and then judge thereupon. Without liberty the understanding would be to no
purpose; and without understanding, liberty (if it could be)
would signify nothing. If a man sees what would do him good
or harm, what would make him happy or miserable, without
being able to move himself one step towards or from it, what is
he the better for seeing? And he that is at liberty to ramble in
perfect darkness, what is his liberty better than if he were driven
up and down as a bubble by the force of the wind? The being
acted by a blind impulse from without or from within is little
odds. The first, therefore, and great use of liberty is to hinder
blind precipitancy; the principal exercise of freedom is to stand
still, open the eyes, look about and take a view of the consequence of what we are going to do, as much as the weight of the
matter requires. How much sloth and negligence, heat and
passion, the prevalence of fashion or acquired indispositions do
severally contribute on occasion to these *wrong judgments* I shall
not here further inquire. I shall only add one other false
judgment which I think necessary to mention, because perhaps
it is little taken notice of, though of great influence.

68. All men desire happiness, that's past doubt; but, as has
been already observed, when they are rid of pain, they are apt to
take up with any pleasure at hand or that custom has endeared
to them, to rest satisfied in that; and so, being happy till some
new desire, by making them uneasy, disturbs that happiness and
shows them that they are not so, they look no further; nor is the
will determined to any action in pursuit of any other known or
apparent good. For since we find that we cannot enjoy all sorts
of good, but one excludes another, we do not fix our desires on
every apparent greater good, unless it be judged to be necessary
to our happiness: if we think we can be happy without it, it
moves us not. This is another occasion to men of *judging wrong*,
when they take not that to be necessary to their happiness which

really is so. This mistake misleads us both in the choice of the good we aim at and very often in the means to it, when it is a remote good. But, which way ever it be, either by placing it where really it is not or by neglecting the means as not necessary to it, when a man misses his great end, happiness, he will acknowledge he judged not right. That which contributes to this mistake is the real or supposed unpleasantness of the actions which are the way to this end: it seeming so preposterous a thing to men, to make themselves unhappy in order to happiness, that they do not easily bring themselves to it.

69. The last inquiry, therefore, concerning this matter is whether it be in a man's power to change the pleasantness and unpleasantness that accompanies any sort of action; and, to that, it is plain in many cases he can. Men may and should correct their palates and give relish to what either has, or they suppose has, none. The relish of the mind is as various as that of the body, and like that too may be altered; and it is a mistake to think that men cannot change the displeasingness or indifference that is in actions into pleasure and desire, if they will do but what is in their power. A due consideration will do it in some cases; and practice, application, and custom in most. Bread or tobacco may be neglected where they are shown to be useful to health, because of an indifference or disrelish to them; reason and consideration at first recommends and begins their trial, and use finds or custom makes them pleasant. That this is so in virtue, too, is very certain. Actions are pleasing or displeasing, either in themselves, or considered as a means to a greater and more desirable end. The eating of a well-seasoned dish, suited to a man's palate, may move the mind by the delight itself that accompanies the eating, without reference to any other end; to which the consideration of the pleasure there is in health and strength (to which that meat is subservient) may add a new gusto, able to make us swallow an ill-relished potion. In the latter of these, any action is rendered more or less pleasing only by the contemplation of the end and the being more or less persuaded of its tendency to it or necessary connexion with it; but the pleasure of the action itself is best acquired or increased by use and practice. Trials often reconcile us to that which at a distance we looked on with aversion, and by repetitions wear us into a liking of what possibly, in the first essay, displeased us. Habits have powerful charms and put so strong attractions of

easiness and pleasure into what we accustom ourselves to, that
we cannot forbear to do, or at least be easy in the omission of,
actions which habitual practice has suited and thereby recommends to us. Though this be very visible and everyone's
experience shows him he can do, yet it is a part, in the conduct
of men towards their happiness, neglected to a degree that it
will be possibly entertained as a paradox, if it be said that men
can make things or actions more or less pleasing to themselves,
and thereby remedy that to which one may justly impute a
great deal of their wandering. Fashion and the common
opinion having settled wrong notions, and education and
custom ill habits, the just values of things are misplaced and the
palates of men corrupted. Pains should be taken to rectify
these; and contrary habits change our pleasures and give a relish
to that which is necessary or conducive to our happiness. This
everyone must confess he can do; and when happiness is lost and
misery overtakes him, he will confess he did amiss in neglecting
it and condemn himself for it; and I ask everyone whether he
has not often done so?

70.   I shall not now enlarge any further on the *wrong judgments*
and neglect of what is in their power, whereby men mislead
themselves. This would make a volume and is not my business.
But whatever false notions or shameful neglect of what is in
their power may put men out of their way to happiness and
distract them, as we see, into so different courses of life, this yet
is certain: that morality, established upon its true foundations,
cannot but determine the choice in anyone that will but consider; and he that will not be so far a rational creature as to
reflect seriously upon infinite happiness and misery must needs
condemn himself as not making that use of his understanding
he should. The rewards and punishments of another life, which
the Almighty has established as the enforcements of his law,
are of weight enough to determine the choice against whatever
pleasure or pain this life can show, when the eternal state is
considered but in its bare possibility, which nobody can make
any doubt of. He that will allow exquisite and endless happiness
to be but the possible consequence of a good life here, and the
contrary state, the possible reward of a bad one, must own
himself to judge very much amiss if he does not conclude that a
virtuous life, with the certain expectation of everlasting bliss
which may come, is to be preferred to a vicious one with the fear

of that dreadful state of misery which, it is very possible, may overtake the guilty, or at best the terrible uncertain hope of annihilation. This is evidently so, though the virtuous life here had nothing but pain, and the vicious, continual pleasure: which yet is, for the most part, quite otherwise, and wicked men have not much the odds to brag of, even in their present possession; nay, all things rightly considered have, I think, even the worst part here. But when infinite happiness is put in one scale against infinite misery in the other; if the worst that comes to the pious man, if he mistakes, be the best that the wicked can attain to; if he be in the right, who can without madness run the venture? Who in his wits would choose to come within a possibility of infinite misery, which if he miss, there is yet nothing to be got by that hazard? Whereas on the other side, the sober man ventures nothing against infinite happiness to be got, if his expectation comes to pass. If the good man be in the right, he is eternally happy; if he mistakes, he is not miserable, he feels nothing. On the other side, if the wicked be in the right, he is not happy; if he mistakes, he is infinitely miserable. Must it not be a most manifest wrong judgment that does not presently see to which side, in this case, the preference is to be given? I have forborne to mention anything of the certainty or probability of a future state, designing here to show the *wrong judgment* that anyone must allow he makes upon his own principles, laid how he pleases, who prefers the short pleasures of a vicious life upon any consideration, whilst he knows and cannot but be certain that a future life is at least possible.

71. To conclude this inquiry into human liberty, which as it stood before, I myself from the beginning fearing, and a very judicious friend of mine, since the publication, suspecting to have some mistake in it, though he could not particularly show it me, I was put upon a stricter review of this chapter. Wherein lighting upon a very easy and scarce observable slip I had made in putting one seemingly indifferent word for another, that discovery opened to me this present view which here, in the *Second* Edition, I submitted to the learned world and which in short is this: *liberty* is a power to act or not to act, according as the mind directs. A power to direct the operative faculties to motion or rest in particular instances is that which we call the *will*. That which in the train of our voluntary actions determines the *will* to any change of operation is some present uneasiness,

which is, or at least is always accompanied with, that of *desire*. Desire is always moved by evil to fly it, because a total freedom from pain always makes a necessary part of our happiness; but every *good*, nay, every *greater good* does not constantly move *desire*, because it may not make, or may not be taken to make, any necessary part of our happiness. For all that we desire is only to be happy. But, though this general *desire* of happiness operates constantly and invariably, yet the satisfaction of any particular *desire* can be suspended from determining the *will* to any subservient action, till we have maturely examined whether the particular apparent good which we then desire makes a part of our real happiness, or be consistent or inconsistent with it. The result of our judgment upon that examination is what ultimately determines the man, who could not be *free* if his *will* were determined by anything but his own *desire*, guided by his own *judgment*. I know that liberty by some is placed in an *indifference* of the man, antecedent to the determination of his *will*. I wish they, who lay so much stress on such an *antecedent indifference*, as they call it, had told us plainly whether this supposed *indifference* be antecedent to the thought and judgment of the understanding as well as to the decree of the *will*. For it is pretty hard to state it between them, i.e. immediately after the judgment of the understanding and before the determination of the *will*, because the determination of the *will* immediately follows the judgment of the understanding; and to place liberty in an *indifference* antecedent to the thought and judgment of the understanding seems to me to place liberty in a state of darkness, wherein we can neither see nor say anything of it; at least it places it in a subject incapable of it, no agent being allowed capable of liberty but in consequence of thought and judgment. I am not nice about phrases, and therefore consent to say with those that love to speak so, that liberty is placed in *indifference*; but it is in an *indifference* that remains after the judgment of the understanding, yea, even after the determination of the *will*; and that is an indifference not of the man (for after he has once judged which is best, viz. to do or forbear, he is no longer indifferent) but an *indifference* of the operative powers of the man, which remaining equally able to operate or to forbear operating after as before the decree of the *will*, are in a state which, if one pleases, may be called *indifference*; and as far as this *indifference* reaches, a man is free and no further: v.g. I have the ability to move my hand or to let it rest, that operative power is indifferent to move or not to move my hand: I am then in that respect perfectly free. My *will* determines that operative power to rest, I am yet free, because the *indifference* of that my operative power to act or not to act still remains; the power of moving my hand is not at all impaired by the determination of my *will* which at present orders rest. The *indifference* of that power to act or not to act is just as it was before, as will appear if the *will* puts it to the trial by ordering the contrary. But if during the rest of my hand, it be seized by a sudden palsy, the *indifference* of that operative power is gone and with it my liberty: I have no longer freedom in that respect but am under a necessity of letting my hand rest. On the other side, if my hand be put into motion by a convulsion, the *indifference* of that operative faculty is taken away by that motion and my liberty in that case is lost, for I am under a necessity of having my hand move. I have added this to show in what sort of *indifference* liberty seems to me to consist and not in any other, real or imaginary.

72.   True notions concerning the nature and extent of *liberty* are of so great importance that I hope I shall be pardoned this digression which my attempt to explain it has led me into. The *ideas* of *will, volition, liberty* and *necessity* in this chapter of power came naturally in my way. In the former edition of this treatise, I gave an account of my thoughts concerning them according to the light I then had. And now, as a lover of truth, and not a worshipper of my own doctrines, I own some change of my opinion, which I think I have discovered ground for. In what I first writ, I with an unbiased indifference followed truth whither I thought she led me. But neither being so vain as to fancy infallibility, nor so disingenuous as to dissemble my mistakes for fear of blemishing my reputation, I have, with the same sincere design for truth only, not been ashamed to publish what a severer inquiry has suggested. It is not impossible but that some may think my former notions right and some (as I have already found) these later, and some neither. I shall not at all wonder at this variety in men's opinions: impartial deductions of reason in controverted points being so very rare, and exact ones in abstract notions not so very easy, especially if of any length. And therefore, I should think myself not a little beholding to anyone who would upon these, or any other grounds, fairly clear this subject of *liberty* from any difficulties that may yet remain.

Before I close this chapter, it may perhaps be to our purpose, and help to give us clearer conceptions about *power*, if we make our thoughts take a little more exact survey of *action*. I have said above that we have *ideas* but of two sorts of *action*, viz. *motion* and *thinking*. These, in truth, though called and counted *actions*, yet, if nearly considered, will not be found to be always perfectly so. For, if I mistake not, there are instances of both kinds, which, upon due consideration, will be found rather *passions* than *actions*, and consequently so far the effects barely of passive powers in those subjects, which yet on their account are thought *agents*. For, in these instances, the substance that hath motion or thought receives the impression whereby it is put into that *action* purely from without, and so acts merely by the capacity it has to receive such an impression from some external agent; and such a *power* is not properly an *active power*, but a mere passive capacity in the subject. Sometimes the substance or agent puts itself into *action* by its own power, and this is properly *active power*. Whatsoever modification a substance has whereby it produces any effect, that is called *action*: v.g., a solid substance by motion operates on or alters the sensible *ideas* of another substance, and therefore this modification of motion we call action. But yet this motion in that solid substance is, when rightly considered, but a passion, if it received it only from some external agent. So that the *active power* of motion is in no substance which cannot begin motion in itself, or in another substance when at rest. So likewise, in *thinking*, a power to receive *ideas* or thoughts from the operation of any external substance is called a *power* of thinking, but this is but a *passive power*, or capacity. But to be able to bring into view *ideas* out of sight at one's own choice, and to compare which of them one thinks fit, this is an *active power*. This reflection may be of some use to preserve us from mistakes about *powers* and *actions*, which grammar and the common frame of languages may be apt to lead us into, since what is signified by *verbs* that grammarians call *active*, does not always signify *action*: v.g., this proposition, I see the moon or a star, or I feel the heat of the sun, though expressed by a *verb active*, does not signify any *action* in me whereby I operate on those substances, but the reception of the *ideas* of light, roundness, and heat, wherein I am not active, but barely passive, and cannot in that position of my eyes or body avoid receiving them. But when I turn my eyes another way, or remove my body out of the sun-beams, I am properly active; because of my own choice, by a power within myself, I put myself into that motion. Such an *action* is the product of *active power*.

73. And thus I have, in a short draught, given a view of our *original ideas* from whence all the rest are derived, and of which they are made up; which, if I would consider as a philosopher, and examine on what causes they depend, and of what they are made, I believe they all might be reduced to these very few primary and original ones, viz.:

> *Extension,*
> *Solidity,*
> *Mobility,* or the power of being moved,

which by our senses we receive from body;

> *Perceptivity,* or the power of perception, or thinking,
> *Motivity,* or the power of moving,

which by reflection we receive from our minds. I crave leave to make use of these two new words, to avoid the danger of being mistaken in the use of those which are equivocal. To which if we add

> *Existence,*
> *Duration,*
> *Number,*

which belong both to the one and the other, we have, perhaps, all the original *ideas* on which the rest depend. For by these, I imagine, might be explained the nature of colours, sounds, tastes, smells, and all other *ideas* we have, if we had but faculties acute enough to perceive the severally modified extensions and motions of these minute bodies, which produce those several sensations in us. But my present purpose being only to inquire into the knowledge the mind has of things by those *ideas* and appearances which *God* has fitted it to receive from them, and how the mind comes by that knowledge, rather than into their causes or manner of production, I shall not, contrary to the design of this essay, set myself to inquire philosophically into the peculiar constitution of bodies and the configuration of parts whereby they have the power to produce in us the *ideas* of their sensible qualities. I shall not enter any further into that disquisition, it sufficing to my purpose to observe that gold or saffron has a power to produce in us the *idea* of yellow, and snow or milk, the *idea* of white, which we can only have by our sight, without examining the texture of the parts of those bodies, or the particular figures or motion of the particles which rebound from them, to cause in us that particular sensation: though, when we go beyond the bare *ideas* in our minds, and would inquire into their causes, we cannot conceive anything else to be in any sensible object whereby it produces different *ideas* in us but the different bulk, figure, number, texture, and motion of its insensible parts.

CHAPTER XXII

OF MIXED MODES

1. HAVING treated of *simple modes* in the foregoing chapters and given several instances of some of the most considerable of them, to show what they are and how we come by them, we are now in the next place to consider those we call *mixed modes*; such are the complex *ideas* we mark by the names *obligation, drunkenness,* a *lie,* etc.; which consisting of several combinations of simple *ideas* of different kinds, I have called *mixed modes,* to distinguish them from the more simple modes, which consist only of simple *ideas* of the same kind. These mixed modes, being also such combinations of simple *ideas* as are not looked upon to be characteristical marks of any real beings that have a steady existence, but scattered and independent *ideas* put together by the mind, are thereby distinguished from the complex *ideas* of substances.

2. That the mind, in respect of its simple *ideas*, is wholly passive and receives them all from the existence and operations of things, such as sensation or reflection offers them, without being able to make any one *idea*, experience shows us. But if we attentively consider these *ideas* I call *mixed modes* we are now speaking of, we shall find their original quite different. *The mind* often *exercises an active power in making these* several *combinations*; for, it being once furnished with simple *ideas*, it can put them together in several compositions and so make

variety of complex *ideas* without examining whether they exist so together in nature. And hence I think it is that these *ideas* are called *notions*: as if they had their original, and constant existence more in the thoughts of men than in the reality of things; and to form such *ideas*, it sufficed that the mind put the parts of them together, and that they were consistent in the understanding, without considering whether they had any real being, though I do not deny but several of them might be taken from observation and the existence of several simple *ideas* so combined, as they are put together in the understanding. For the man who first framed the *idea* of *hypocrisy* might have either taken it at first from the observation of one who made show of good qualities which he had not, or else have framed that *idea* in his mind without having any such pattern to fashion it by. For it is evident that, in the beginning of languages and societies of men, several of those complex *ideas*, which were consequent to the constitutions established amongst them, must needs have been in the minds of men before they existed anywhere else, and that many names that stood for such complex *ideas* were in use, and so those *ideas* framed, before the combinations they stood for ever existed.

3. Indeed, now that languages are made and abound with words standing for such combinations, *an usual way of getting these complex* ideas *is by the explication of those terms that stand for them.* For, consisting of a company of simple *ideas* combined, they may, by words standing for those simple *ideas*, be represented to the mind of one who understands those words, though that complex combination of simple *ideas* were never offered to his mind by the real existence of things. Thus a man may come to have the *idea* of *sacrilege* or *murder*, by enumerating to him the simple *ideas* which these words stand for, without ever seeing either of them committed.

4. Every *mixed mode* consisting of many distinct simple *ideas*, it seems reasonable to inquire *whence it has its unity*, and how such a precise multitude comes to make but one *idea*, since that combination does not always exist together in nature. To which I answer it is plain it has its unity from an act of the mind combining those several simple *ideas* together, and considering them as one complex one, consisting of those parts; and the mark of this union, or that which is looked on generally to complete it, is one name given to that combination. For it is by their names

that men commonly regulate their account of their distinct species of mixed modes, seldom allowing or considering any number of simple *ideas* to make one complex one, but such collections as there be names for. Thus, though the killing of an old man be as fit in nature to be united into one complex *idea* as the killing a man's father, yet there being no name standing precisely for the one as there is the name of *parricide* to mark the other, it is not taken for a particular complex *idea* nor a distinct species of actions from that of killing a young man, or any other man.

5. If we should inquire a little further to see *what* it is that *occasions men to make several combinations of simple* ideas into distinct and, as it were, settled *modes*, and neglect others, which in the nature of things themselves have as much an aptness to be combined and make distinct *ideas*, we shall find the reason of it to be the end of language; which being to mark or communicate men's thoughts to one another with all the dispatch that may be, they usually make such collections of *ideas* into complex modes and affix names to them, as they have frequent use of in their way of living and conversation, leaving others, which they have but seldom an occasion to mention, loose and without names that tie them together: they rather choosing to enumerate (when they have need) such *ideas* as make them up by the particular names that stand for them, than to trouble their memories by multiplying of complex *ideas* with names to them, which they shall seldom or never have any occasion to make use of.

6. This shows us *how it comes to pass that there are in every language many particular words which cannot be rendered by any one single word of another*. For the several fashions, customs, and manners of one nation making several combinations of *ideas* familiar and necessary in one, which another people have had never any occasion to make, or perhaps so much as take notice of, names come of course to be annexed to them, to avoid long periphrases in things of daily conversation, and so they become so many distinct complex *ideas* in their minds. Thus ὀστρακισμός amongst the *Greeks* and *proscriptio* amongst the *Romans* were words which other languages had no names that exactly answered, because they stood for complex *ideas* which were not in the minds of the men of other nations. Where there was no such custom, there was no notion of any

such actions, no use of such combinations of *ideas* as were united and, as it were, tied together by those terms: and therefore in other countries there were no names for them.

7.   Hence also we may see the reason *why languages constantly change*, take up new and lay by old terms. Because change of customs and opinions bringing with it new combinations of *ideas*, which it is necessary frequently to think on and talk about, new names, to avoid long descriptions, are annexed to them; and so they become new species of complex modes. What a number of different *ideas* are by this means wrapped up in one short sound and how much of our time and breath is thereby saved, anyone will see who will but take the pains to enumerate all the *ideas* that either *reprieve* or *appeal* stand for, and instead of either of those names, use a periphrasis to make anyone understand their meaning.

8.   Though I shall have occasion to consider this more at large, when I come to treat of words and their use, yet I could not avoid to take thus much notice here of the names of *mixed modes* which, being fleeting and transient combinations of simple *ideas*, which have but a short existence anywhere but in the minds of men, and there too have no longer any existence than whilst they are thought on, *have not so much anywhere the appearance of a constant and lasting existence as in their names*; which are therefore, in these sort of *ideas*, very apt to be taken for the *ideas* themselves. For if we should inquire where the *idea* of a *triumph* or *apotheosis* exists, it is evident they could neither of them exist altogether anywhere in the things themselves, being actions that required time to their performance, and so could never all exist together; and as to the minds of men, where the *ideas* of these actions are supposed to be lodged, they have there too a very uncertain existence, and therefore we are apt to annex them to the names that excite them in us.

9.   There are therefore *three ways whereby we get the complex* ideas *of mixed modes*: (1) By experience and *observation* of things themselves: thus, by seeing two men wrestle or fence, we get the *idea* of wrestling or fencing. (2) By *invention*, or voluntary putting together of several simple *ideas* in our own minds: so he that first invented printing or etching, had an *idea* of it in his mind before it ever existed. (3) Which is the most usual way, by *explaining the names* of actions we never saw, or motions we cannot see; and by enumerating, and thereby, as it

were, setting before our imaginations all those *ideas* which go
to the making them up, and are the constituent parts of them.
For, having by *sensation* and *reflection* stored our minds with
simple *ideas*, and by use got the names that stand for them, we
can by those names represent to another any complex *idea* we
would have him conceive, so that it has in it no simple *ideas*
but what he knows and has with us the same name for. For all
our complex *ideas* are ultimately resolvable into simple *ideas*, of
which they are compounded and originally made up, though
perhaps their immediate ingredients, as I may so say, are also
complex *ideas*. Thus the *mixed mode* which the word *lie* stands
for is made of these simple *ideas*: (1) articulate sounds; (2) certain *ideas* in the mind of the speaker; (3) those words the signs of
those *ideas*; (4) those signs put together by affirmation or
negation, otherwise than the *ideas* they stand for, are in the mind
of the speaker. I think I need not go any further in the analysis
of that complex *idea* we call a *lie*, what I have said is enough to
show that it is made up of simple *ideas*; and it could not be but
an offensive tediousness to my reader to trouble him with a more
minute enumeration of every particular simple *idea* that goes to
this complex one; which, from what has been said, he cannot
but be able to make out to himself. The same may be done in
all our complex *ideas* whatsoever, which, however compounded
and decompounded, may at last be resolved into simple *ideas*,
which are all the materials of knowledge or thought we have or
can have. Nor shall we have reason to fear that the mind is
hereby stinted to too scanty a number of *ideas*, if we consider
what an inexhaustible stock of simple modes number and
figure alone afford us. How far then *mixed modes*, which admit
of the various combinations of different simple *ideas* and their
infinite modes, are from being few and scanty we may easily
imagine. So that before we have done we shall see that nobody
need be afraid he shall not have scope and compass enough for
his thoughts to range in, though they be, as I pretend, confined
only to simple *ideas* received from sensation or reflection and
their several combinations.

10. It is worth our observing *which of all our simple* ideas *have
been most modified and had most mixed modes made out of them
with names given to them*; and those have been these three:
thinking and motion (which are the two *ideas* which comprehend
in them all action) and power, from whence these actions are

conceived to flow. These simple *ideas*, I say, of thinking, motion, and power have been those which have been most modified, and out of whose modifications have been made most complex modes with names to them. For action being the great business of mankind, and the whole matter about which all laws are conversant, it is no wonder that the several modes of thinking and motion should be taken notice of, the *ideas* of them observed and laid up in the memory and have names assigned to them, without which laws could be but ill-made, or vice and disorder repressed. Nor could any communication be well had amongst men without such complex *ideas* with names to them; and therefore men have settled names, and supposed settled *ideas* in their minds, of modes of actions distinguished by their causes, means, objects, ends, instruments, time, place, and other circumstances; and also of their powers fitted for those actions, v.g., boldness is the power to speak or do what we intend, before others, without fear or disorder; and the *Greeks* call the confidence of speaking by a peculiar name, παρρησία, which power or ability in man of doing anything, when it has been acquired by frequent doing the same thing, is that *idea* we name *habit*; when it is forward and ready upon every occasion to break into action, we *call* it *disposition*. Thus *testiness* is a disposition or aptness to be angry.

To conclude, let us examine any *modes of action*, v.g. *consideration* and *assent*, which are actions of the mind; *running* and *speaking*, which are actions of the body; *revenge* and *murder*, which are actions of both together; and we shall find them but so many *collections of simple ideas*, which together make up the complex ones signified by those names.

11. *Power* being the source from whence all action proceeds, the substances wherein these powers are, when they exert this power into act, are called *causes*; and the substances which thereupon are produced, or the simple *ideas* which are introduced into any subject by the exerting of that power, are called *effects*. The *efficacy* whereby the new substance or *idea* is produced is called, in the subject exerting that power, *action*; but in the subject wherein any simple idea is changed or produced, it is called *passion*: which efficacy however various, and the effects almost infinite, yet we can, I think, conceive it, in intellectual agents, to be nothing else but modes of thinking and willing; in corporeal agents, nothing else but modifications of motion. I say, I think

we cannot conceive it to be any other but these two. For whatever sort of action, besides these, produces any effects, I confess myself to have no notion or *idea* of; and so it is quite remote from my thoughts, apprehensions, and knowledge, and as much in the dark to me as five other senses, or as the *ideas* of colours to a blind man; and therefore *many words which seem to express some action* signify nothing of the action or *modus operandi* at all, *but* barely *the effect*, with some circumstances of the subject wrought on, or cause operating: v.g. creation, annihilation, contain in them no *idea* of the action or manner whereby they are produced, but barely of the cause and the thing done. And when a countryman says the cold freezes water, though the word freezing seems to import some *action*, yet truly it signifies nothing but the effect, viz. that water that was before fluid is become hard and consistent, without containing any *idea* of the action whereby it is done.

12. I think I shall not need to remark here that, though power and action make the greatest part of mixed modes, marked by names and familiar in the minds and mouths of men, yet other simple *ideas* and their several combinations are *not* excluded; much less, I think, will it be *necessary* for me *to enumerate all the mixed modes* which have been settled, with names to them. That would be to make a dictionary of the greatest part of the words made use of in divinity, ethics, law, and politics, and several other sciences. All that is requisite to my present design is to show what sort of *ideas* those are which I call *mixed modes*, how the mind comes by them, and that they are compositions made up of simple *ideas* got from sensation and reflection; which, I suppose, I have done.

CHAPTER XXIII

OF OUR COMPLEX IDEAS OF SUBSTANCES

1. THE mind being, as I have declared, furnished with a great number of the simple *ideas* conveyed in by the *senses*, as they are found in exterior things, or by *reflection* on its own operations, takes notice also that a certain number of these simple *ideas* go constantly together; which, being presumed to belong to one

thing, and words being suited to common apprehensions and made use of for quick dispatch, are called, so united in one subject, by one name; which, by inadvertency, we are apt afterward to talk of and consider as one simple *idea*, which indeed is a complication of many *ideas* together: because, as I have said, not imagining how these simple *ideas* can subsist by themselves, we accustom ourselves to suppose some *substratum* wherein they do subsist, and from which they do result; which therefore we call *substance*.

2. So that if anyone will examine himself concerning his *notion of pure substance in general*, he will find he has no other *idea* of it at all, but only a supposition of he knows not what support of such qualities which are capable of producing simple *ideas* in us; which qualities are commonly called accidents. If anyone should be asked what is the subject wherein colour or weight inheres, he would have nothing to say but, the solid extended parts; and if he were demanded what is it that that solidity and extension adhere in, he would not be in a much better case than the *Indian* before-mentioned who, saying that the world was supported by a great elephant, was asked what the elephant rested on, to which his answer was, a great tortoise; but being again pressed to know what gave support to the broad-backed tortoise, replied, something, he knew not what. And thus here, as in all other cases where we use words without having clear and distinct *ideas*, we talk like children who, being questioned what such a thing is which they know not, readily give this satisfactory answer, that it is *something*; which in truth signifies no more, when so used, either by children or men, but that they know not what, and that the thing they pretend to know and talk of is what they have no distinct *idea* of at all, and so are perfectly ignorant of it and in the dark. The *idea* then we have, to which we give the general name substance, being nothing but the supposed, but unknown, support of those qualities we find existing, which we imagine cannot subsist *sine re substante*, without something to support them, we call that support *substantia*; which, according to the true import of the word, is, in plain *English, standing under* or *upholding*.

3. An obscure and relative *idea* of substance in general being thus made, we come to have the *ideas of particular sorts of substances* by collecting such combinations of simple *ideas* as are, by experience and observation of men's senses, taken notice of

to exist together, and are therefore supposed to flow from the particular internal constitution or unknown essence of that substance. Thus we come to have the *ideas* of a man, horse, gold, water, etc.; of which substances, whether anyone has any other clear *idea*, further than of certain simple *ideas* co-existent together, I appeal to everyone's own experience. It is the ordinary qualities observable in iron, or a diamond, put together that make the true complex *idea* of those substances, which a smith or a jeweller commonly knows better than a philosopher; who, whatever substantial forms he may talk of, has no other *idea* of those substances than what is framed by a collection of those simple *ideas* which are to be found in them: only we must take notice that our complex *ideas* of substances, besides all these simple *ideas* they are made up of, have always the confused *idea* of *something* to which they belong, and in which they subsist; and therefore when we speak of any sort of substance, we say it is a *thing* having such or such qualities: as body is a *thing* that is extended, figured, and capable of motion; a spirit, a *thing* capable of thinking; and so hardness, friability, and power to draw iron, we say, are qualities to be found in a loadstone. These and the like fashions of speaking intimate that the substance is supposed always *something* besides the extension, figure, solidity, motion, thinking or other observable *ideas*, though we know not what it is.

4. Hence, when we talk or think of any particular sort of corporeal substances, as *horse, stone,* etc., though the *idea* we have of either of them be but the complication or collection of those several simple *ideas* of sensible qualities, which we use to find united in the thing called *horse* or *stone*: yet, because we cannot conceive how they should subsist alone, nor one in another, we suppose them existing in and supported by some common subject; *which support we denote by the name substance*, though it be certain we have no clear or distinct *idea* of that *thing* we suppose a support.

5. The same thing happens concerning the operations of the mind, viz. thinking, reasoning, fearing, etc., which we concluding not to subsist of themselves, nor apprehending how they can belong to body or be produced by it, we are apt to think these the actions of some other *substance*, which we call *spirit*; whereby yet it is evident that, having no other *idea* or notion of matter but *something* wherein those many sensible qualities which affect

our senses do subsist, by supposing a substance wherein *thinking, knowing, doubting,* and a power of moving, etc., do subsist, *we have as clear a notion of the substance of spirit as we have of body*: the one being supposed to be (without knowing what it is) the *substratum* to those simple *ideas* we have from without; and the other supposed (with a like ignorance of what it is) to be the *substratum* to those operations which we experiment in ourselves within. It is plain then that the *idea* of corporeal *substance* in matter is as remote from our conceptions and apprehensions as that of spiritual *substance,* or *spirit;* and therefore, from our not having any notion of the *substance* of spirit, we can no more conclude its non-existence than we can, for the same reason, deny the existence of body: it being as rational to affirm there is no body, because we have no clear and distinct *idea* of the *substance* of matter, as to say there is no spirit, because we have no clear and distinct *idea* of the *substance* of a spirit.

6. Whatever therefore be the secret and abstract nature of *substance* in general, all *the* ideas *we have of particular distinct sorts of substances* are nothing but several combinations of simple *ideas,* co-existing in such, though unknown, cause of their union as makes the whole subsist of itself. It is by such combinations of simple *ideas* and nothing else that we represent particular sorts of *substances* to ourselves; such are the *ideas* we have of their several species in our minds; and such only do we, by their specific names, signify to others, v.g. *man, horse, sun, water, iron;* upon hearing which words, everyone who understands the language frames in his mind a combination of those several simple *ideas* which he has usually observed or fancied to exist together under that denomination, all which he supposes to rest in and be, as it were, adherent to that unknown common subject which inheres not in anything else. Though in the meantime it be manifest, and everyone upon inquiry into his own thoughts will find, that he has no other *idea* of any *substance,* v.g., let it be *gold, horse, iron, man, vitriol, bread,* but what he has barely of those sensible qualities which he supposes to inhere, with a supposition of such a *substratum* as gives, as it were, a support to those qualities or simple *ideas* which he has observed to exist united together. Thus, the *idea* of the *sun,* what is it but an aggregate of those several simple *ideas,* bright, hot, roundish, having a constant regular motion, at a certain distance from us, and perhaps some other: as he who thinks and discourses of the

sun has been more or less accurate in observing those sensible qualities, *ideas*, or properties, which are in that thing which he calls the *sun*.

7.   For he has the perfectest *idea* of any of the particular sorts of *substances*, who has gathered and put together most of those simple *ideas* which do exist in it; among which are to be reckoned its active powers and passive capacities, which, though not simple *ideas*, yet in this respect, for brevity's sake, may conveniently enough be reckoned amongst them.   Thus, the power of drawing iron is one of the *ideas* of the complex one of that substance we call a *loadstone*; and a power to be so drawn is a part of the complex one we call *iron*: which powers pass for inherent qualities in those subjects.   Because every *substance*, being as apt, by the powers we observe in it, to change some sensible qualities in other subjects as it is to produce in us those simple *ideas* which we receive immediately from it, does, by those new sensible qualities introduced into other subjects, discover to us those powers which do thereby mediately affect our senses, as regularly as its sensible qualities do it immediately: v.g. we immediately by our senses perceive in *fire* its heat and colour, which are, if rightly considered, nothing but powers in it to produce those *ideas* in us; we also by our senses perceive the colour and brittleness of *charcoal*, whereby we come by the knowledge of another power in fire, which it has to change the colour and consistency of wood.   By the former, fire immediately, by the latter, it mediately discovers to us these several powers; which therefore we look upon to be a part of the qualities of fire, and so make them a part of the complex *idea* of it.   For all those powers that we take cognizance of terminating only in the alteration of some sensible qualities in those subjects on which they operate, and so making them exhibit to us new sensible *ideas*, therefore it is that I have reckoned these powers amongst the simple *ideas* which make the complex ones of the sorts of *substances*, though these powers considered in themselves are truly complex *ideas*.   And in this looser sense, I crave leave to be understood when I name any of these *potentialities amongst the simple ideas*, which we recollect in our minds when we think *of particular substances*.   For the powers that are severally in them are necessary to be considered, if we will have true distinct notions of the several sorts of substances.

8.   Nor are we to wonder that *powers make a great part of our*

complex ideas *of substances,* since their secondary qualities are those which in most of them serve principally to distinguish substances one from another, and commonly make a considerable part of the complex *idea* of the several sorts of them. For, our senses failing us in the discovery of the bulk, texture, and figure of the minute parts of bodies, on which their real constitutions and differences depend, we are fain to make use of their secondary qualities as the characteristical notes and marks whereby to frame *ideas* of them in our minds and distinguish them one from another: all which secondary qualities, as has been shown, are nothing but bare powers. For the colour and taste of *opium* are, as well as its soporific or anodyne virtues, mere powers, depending on its primary qualities, whereby it is fitted to produce different operations on different parts of our bodies.

9. *The* ideas *that make our complex ones of corporeal substances* are of these three sorts. *First,* the *ideas* of the primary qualities of things, which are discovered by our senses, and are in them even when we perceive them not; such are the bulk, figure, number, situation, and motion of the parts of bodies, which are really in them, whether we take notice of them or no. *Secondly,* the sensible secondary qualities, which, depending on these, are nothing but the powers those substances have to produce several *ideas* in us by our senses; which *ideas* are not in the things themselves otherwise than as anything is in its cause. *Thirdly,* the aptness we consider in any substance to give or receive such alterations of primary qualities, as that the substance so altered should produce in us different *ideas* from what it did before: these are called active and passive powers; all which powers, as far as we have any notice or notion of them, terminate only in sensible simple *ideas.* For whatever alteration a *loadstone* has the power to make in the minute particles of iron, we should have no notion of any power it had at all to operate on iron, did not its sensible motion discover it; and I doubt not but there are a thousand changes that bodies we daily handle have a power to cause in one another, which we never suspect, because they never appear in sensible effects.

10. *Powers* therefore justly *make a great part of our complex* ideas *of substances.* He that will examine his complex *idea* of gold will find several of its *ideas* that make it up to be only powers, as the power of being melted, but of not spending itself in the fire, of being dissolved in *aqua regia*, are *ideas* as nceessary

to make up our complex *idea* of gold as its colour and weight; which, if duly considered, are also nothing but different powers. For, to speak truly, yellowness is not actually in gold, but is a power in gold to produce that *idea* in us by our eyes, when placed in a due light; and the heat, which we cannot leave out of our *idea* of the sun, is no more really in the sun, than the white colour it introduces into wax. These are both equally powers in the sun, operating, by the motion and figure of its insensible parts, so on a man as to make him have the *idea* of heat; and so on wax, as to make it capable to produce in a man the *idea* of white.

11.   Had we senses acute enough to discern the minute particles of bodies and the real constitution on which their sensible qualities depend, I doubt not but they would produce quite different *ideas* in us; and that which is now the yellow colour of gold would then disappear, and instead of it we should see an admirable texture of parts, of a certain size and figure. This microscopes plainly discover to us; for what to our naked eyes produces a certain colour is, by thus augmenting the acuteness of our senses, discovered to be quite a different thing; and the thus altering, as it were, the proportion of the bulk of the minute parts of a coloured object to our usual sight produces different *ideas* from what it did before. Thus sand, or pounded glass, which is opaque and white to the naked eye, is pellucid in a microscope; and a hair seen this way loses its former colour and is in a great measure pellucid, with a mixture of some bright sparkling colours, such as appear from the refraction of diamonds and other pellucid bodies. Blood to the naked eye appears all red, but by a good microscope, wherein its lesser parts appear, shows only some few globules of red, swimming in a pellucid liquor; and how these red globules would appear, if glasses could be found that yet could magnify them a thousand or ten thousand times more, is uncertain.

12.   The infinite wise Contriver of us and all things about us hath fitted our senses, faculties, and organs to the conveniences of life, and the business we have to do here. We are able, by our senses, to know and distinguish things, and to examine them so far as to apply them to our uses, and several ways to accommodate the exigencies of this life. We have insight enough into their admirable contrivances and wonderful effects to admire and magnify the wisdom, power, and goodness of

their Author. Such a knowledge as this, which is suited to our present condition, we want not faculties to attain. But it appears not that God intended we should have a perfect, clear, and adequate knowledge of them: that perhaps is not in the comprehension of any finite being. We are furnished with faculties (dull and weak as they are) to discover enough in the creatures to lead us to the knowledge of the Creator and the knowledge of our duty, and we are fitted well enough with abilities to provide for the conveniences of living: these are our business in this world. But were our senses altered and made much quicker and acuter, the appearance and outward scheme of things would have quite another face to us and, I am apt to think, would be inconsistent with our being, or at least well-being in this part of the universe which we inhabit. He that considers how little our constitution is able to bear a remove into parts of this air, not much higher than that we commonly breathe in, will have reason to be satisfied that in this globe of earth allotted for our mansion, the all-wise Architect has suited our organs, and the bodies that are to affect them, one to another. If our sense of hearing were but a thousand times quicker than it is, how would a perpetual noise distract us. And we should in the quietest retirement be less able to sleep or meditate than in the middle of a sea-fight. Nay, if that most instructive of our senses, seeing, were in any man 1000 or 100,000 times more acute than it is now by the best microscope, things, several millions of times less than the smallest object of his sight now would then be visible to his naked eyes, and so he would come nearer the discovery of the texture and motion of the minute parts of corporeal things, and in many of them probably get *ideas* of their internal constitutions; but then he would be in a quite different world from other people: nothing would appear the same to him and others, the visible *ideas* of everything would be different. So that I doubt whether he and the rest of men could discourse concerning the objects of sight, or have any communication about colours, their appearances being so wholly different. And perhaps such a quickness and tenderness of sight could not endure bright sunshine or so much as open daylight, nor take in but a very small part of any object at once, and that too only at a very near distance. And if by the help of such microscopical eyes (if I may so call them), a man could penetrate further than ordinary into the secret composition and radical texture of bodies, he would not make any great advantage by the change, if such an acute sight would not serve to conduct him to the market and exchange, if he could not see things he was to avoid at a convenient distance, nor distinguish things he had to do with, by those sensible qualities others do. He that was sharp-sighted enough to see the configuration of the minute particles of the spring of a clock, and observe upon what peculiar structure and impulse its elastic motion depends, would no doubt discover something very admirable; but if eyes so framed could not view at once the hand and the characters of the hour-plate, and thereby at a distance see what o'clock it was, their owner could not be much benefited by that acuteness, which, whilst it discovered the secret contrivance of the parts of the machine, made him lose its use.

13.   And here give me leave to propose an extravagant conjecture of mine, viz. that, since we have some reason (if there be any credit to be given to the report of things that our philosophy cannot account for) to imagine that spirits can assume to themselves bodies of different bulk, figure, and conformation of parts, whether one great advantage some of them have over us may not lie in this: that they can so frame and shape to themselves organs of sensation or perception as to suit them to their present design and the circumstances of the object they would consider. For how much would that man exceed all others in knowledge who had but the faculty so to alter the structure of his eyes, that one sense, as to make it capable of all the several degrees of vision which the assistance of glasses (casually at first lighted on) has taught us to conceive? What wonders would he discover who could so fit his eye to all sorts of objects as to see, when he pleased, the figure and motion of the minute particles in the blood and other juices of animals as distinctly as he does, at other times, the shape and motion of the animals themselves. But to us, in our present state, unalterable organs so contrived as to discover the figure and motion of the minute parts of bodies whereon depend those sensible qualities we now observe in them would, perhaps, be of no advantage. God has, no doubt, made us so as is best for us in our present condition. He hath fitted us for the neighbourhood of the bodies that surround us and we have to do with; and though we cannot, by the faculties we have, attain to a perfect knowledge of things, yet they will serve us well enough for those ends above-mentioned,

which are our great concernment. I beg my reader's pardon for laying before him so wild a fancy concerning the ways of perception in beings above us; but how extravagant soever it be, I doubt whether we can imagine anything about the knowledge of angels but after this manner, some way or other, in proportion to what we find and observe in ourselves. And though we cannot but allow that the infinite power and wisdom of God may frame creatures with a thousand other faculties and ways of perceiving things without them than what we have, yet our thoughts can go no further than our own, so impossible it is for us to enlarge our very guesses beyond the *ideas* received from our own sensation and reflection. The supposition, at least, that angels do sometimes assume bodies need not startle us, since some of the most ancient and most learned fathers of the Church seemed to believe that they had bodies; and this is certain, that their state and way of existence is unknown to us.

14. But to return to the matter in hand, the *ideas* we have of substances and the ways we come by them: I say *our specific* ideas *of substances* are nothing else but *a collection of a certain number of simple* ideas, *considered as united in one thing*. These *ideas* of substances, though they are commonly called simple apprehensions, and the names of them simple terms, yet in effect are complex and compounded. Thus the *idea* which an *Englishman* signifies by the name *swan* is white colour, long neck, red beak, black legs, and whole feet, and all these of a certain size, with a power of swimming in the water, and making a certain kind of noise, and perhaps, to a man who has long observed this kind of birds, some other properties: which all terminate in sensible simple *ideas*, all united in one common subject.

15. Besides the complex *ideas* we have of material sensible substances, of which I have last spoken, by the simple *ideas* we have taken from those operations of our own minds which we experiment daily in ourselves, as thinking, understanding, willing, knowing and power of beginning motion, etc., coexisting in some substance, we are able to frame *the complex* idea *of an immaterial spirit*. And thus, by putting together the *ideas* of thinking, perceiving, liberty, and power of moving themselves and other things, we have as clear a perception and notion of immaterial substances as we have of material. For putting together the *ideas* of thinking and willing, or the power of moving or quieting corporeal motion, joined to substance, of which

we have no distinct *idea*, we have the *idea* of an immaterial spirit; and by putting together the *ideas* of coherent solid parts, and a power of being moved, joined with substance, of which likewise we have no positive *idea*, we have the *idea* of matter. The one is as clear and distinct an *idea* as the other: the *idea* of thinking, and moving a body, being as clear and distinct *ideas* as the *ideas* of extension, solidity, and being moved. For our *idea* of substance is equally obscure, or none at all, in both: it is but a supposed I know not what, to support those *ideas* we call accidents. It is for want of reflection that we are apt to think that our senses show us nothing but material things. Every act of sensation, when duly considered, gives us an equal view of both parts of nature, the corporeal and spiritual. For whilst I know, by seeing or hearing, etc., that there is some corporeal being without me, the object of that sensation, I do more certainly know that there is some spiritual being within me that sees and hears. This, I must be convinced, cannot be the action of bare insensible matter; nor ever could be, without an immaterial thinking being.

16.   By the complex *idea* of extended, figured, coloured, and all other sensible qualities, which is all that we know of it, we are as far from the *idea* of the substance of body, as if we knew nothing at all; *nor* after all the acquaintance and familiarity which we imagine we *have* with matter, and the many qualities *men* assure themselves they perceive and know in bodies, will it perhaps upon examination be found that they have any *more or clearer primary* ideas *belonging to body than they have belonging to immaterial spirit*.

17.   *The primary* ideas *we have peculiar to body*, as contra-distinguished to spirit, *are the cohesion of solid*, and consequently separable, *parts, and a power of communicating motion by impulse*. These, I think, are the original *ideas* proper and peculiar to body; for figure is but the consequence of finite extension.

18.   *The* ideas *we have* belonging and *peculiar to spirit are thinking and will*, or a power of putting body into motion by thought, and, which is consequent to it, liberty. For, as body cannot but communicate its motion by impulse to another body, which it meets with at rest, so the mind can put bodies into motion, or forbear to do so, as it pleases. The *ideas* of existence, duration, and mobility are common to them both.

19.   There is no reason why it should be thought strange that I

make *mobility belong to spirit*; for, having no other *idea* of motion but change of distance with other beings that are considered as at rest, and finding that spirits as well as bodies cannot operate but where they are, and that spirits do operate at several times in several places, I cannot but attribute change of place to all finite spirits; (for of the infinite spirit I speak not here). For my soul, being a real being as well as my body, is certainly as capable of changing distance with any other body or being, as body itself, and so is capable of motion. And if a mathematician can consider a certain distance, or a change of that distance between two points, one may certainly conceive a distance and a change of distance between two spirits, and so conceive their motion, their approach or removal, one from another.

20. Everyone finds in himself that his soul can think, will, and operate on his body in the place where that is, but cannot operate on a body, or in a place, an hundred miles distant from it. Nobody can imagine that his soul can think or move a body at *Oxford* whilst he is at *London*, and cannot but know that, being united to his body, it constantly changes place all the whole journey between *Oxford* and *London*, as the coach or horse does that carries him, and I think may be said to be truly all that while in motion; or, if that will not be allowed to afford us a clear *idea* enough of its motion, its being separated from the body in death I think will; for to consider it as going out of the body, or leaving it and yet to have no *idea* of its motion, seems to me impossible.

21. If it be said by anyone that it cannot change place because it hath none, for spirits are not in *loco* but *ubi*, I suppose that way of talking will not now be of much weight to many in an age that is not much disposed to admire or suffer themselves to be deceived by such unintelligible ways of speaking. But if anyone thinks there is any sense in that distinction, and that it is applicable to our present purpose, I desire him to put it into intelligible *English*, and then from thence draw a reason to show that immaterial spirits are not capable of motion. Indeed motion cannot be attributed to GOD, not because he is an immaterial, but because he is an infinite spirit.

22. Let us *compare* then our complex *idea* of an immaterial spirit with our complex *idea* of body and see whether there be any more obscurity in one than in the other, and in which most.

Our *idea* of body, as I think, is an extended solid substance, capable of communicating motion by impulse; and our *idea* of our soul, as an immaterial spirit, is of a substance that thinks, and has a power of exciting motion in body, by will or thought. These, I think, are *our complex* ideas *of soul and body, as contra-distinguished*; and now let us examine which has most obscurity in it and difficulty to be apprehended. I know that people whose thoughts are immersed in matter and have so subjected their minds to their senses that they seldom reflect on anything beyond them, are apt to say they cannot comprehend a thinking thing, which perhaps is true; but I affirm, when they consider it well, they can no more comprehend an extended thing.

23. If anyone say he knows not what it is thinks in him, he means he knows not what the substance is of that thinking thing; no more, say I, knows he what the substance is of that solid thing. Further, if he says he knows not how he thinks, I answer: neither knows he how he is extended, how the solid parts of body are united or cohere together to make extension. For though the pressure of the particles of air may account for the *cohesion of several parts of matter* that are grosser than the particles of air, and have pores less than the corpuscles of air, yet the weight or pressure of the air will not explain, nor can be a cause of, the coherence of the particles of air themselves. And if the pressure of the aether, or any subtiler matter than the air, may unite and hold fast together the parts of a particle of air, as well as other bodies, yet it cannot make bonds for itself and hold together the parts that make up every the least corpuscle of that *materia subtilis*. So that that hypothesis, how ingeniously soever explained, by showing that the parts of sensible bodies are held together by the pressure of other external insensible bodies, reaches not the parts of the aether itself; and by how much the more evident it proves that the parts of other bodies are held together by the external pressure of the aether, and can have no other conceivable cause of their cohesion and union, by so much the more it leaves us in the dark concerning the cohesion of the parts of the corpuscles of the aether itself; which we can neither conceive without parts, they being bodies and divisible, nor yet how their parts cohere, they wanting that cause of cohesion which is given of the cohesion of the parts of all other bodies.

24. But in truth, *the pressure of any ambient fluid*, how great soever, *can be no* intelligible *cause of the cohesion of the solid parts*

of matter. For though such a pressure may hinder the avulsion of two polished superficies one from another in a line perpendicular to them, as in the experiment of two polished marbles, yet it can never in the least hinder the separation by a motion in a line parallel to those surfaces. Because the ambient fluid, having a full liberty to succeed in each point of space deserted by a lateral motion, resists such a motion of bodies so joined, no more than it would resist the motion of that body, were it on all sides environed by that fluid and touched no other body; and therefore, if there were no other cause of cohesion, all parts of bodies must be easily separable by such a lateral sliding motion. For if the pressure of the aether be the adequate cause of cohesion, wherever that cause operates not, there can be no cohesion. And since it cannot operate against such a lateral separation (as has been shown), therefore in every imaginary plane intersecting any mass of matter, there could be no more cohesion than of two polished surfaces, which will always, notwithstanding any imaginable pressure of a fluid, easily slide one from another. So that, perhaps, how clear an *idea* soever we think we have of the extension of body, which is nothing but the cohesion of solid parts, he that shall well consider it in his mind may have reason to conclude that it is *as easy* for him *to have a clear* idea *how the soul thinks as how body is extended.* For, since body is no further nor otherwise extended than by the union and cohesion of its solid parts, we shall very ill comprehend the *extension* of body, without understanding wherein consists the union and cohesion of its parts; which seems to me as incomprehensible as the manner of thinking, and how it is performed.

25. I allow it is usual for most people to wonder how anyone should find a difficulty in what they think they every day observe. Do we not see, will they be ready to say, the parts of bodies stick firmly together? Is there anything more common? And what doubt can there be made of it? And the like I say concerning *thinking* and *voluntary motion*: do we not every moment experiment it in ourselves, and therefore can it be doubted? The matter of fact is clear, I confess; but when we would a little nearer look into it and consider how it is done, there I think we are at a loss, both in the one and the other, and can as little understand how the parts of body cohere as how we ourselves perceive or move. I would have anyone intelligibly explain to me how the parts of gold or brass (that but now in

* K 332

fusion were as loose from one another as the particles of water or the sands of an hour-glass) come in a few moments to be so united and adhere so strongly one to another that the utmost force of men's arms cannot separate them; a considering man will, I suppose, be here at a loss to satisfy his own or another man's understanding.

26.   The little bodies that compose that fluid we call *water* are so extremely small that I have never heard of anyone who by a microscope (and yet I have heard of some that have magnified to 10,000; nay, to much above 100,000 times) pretended to perceive their distinct bulk, figure, or motion; and the particles of *water* are also so perfectly loose one from another that the least force sensibly separates them.   Nay, if we consider their perpetual motion, we must allow them to have no cohesion one with another; and yet let but a sharp cold come and they unite, they consolidate, these little atoms cohere and are not, without great force, separable.   He that could find the bonds that tie these heaps of loose little bodies together so firmly, he that could make known the cement that makes them stick so fast one to another, would discover a great and yet unknown secret; and yet when that was done, would he be far enough from making the extension of body (which is the cohesion of its solid parts) intelligible, till he could show wherein consisted the union or consolidation of the parts of those bonds or of that cement or of the least particle of matter that exists?   Whereby it appears that this primary and supposed obvious quality of body will be found, when examined, to be as incomprehensible as anything belonging to our minds, and *a solid extended substance as hard to be conceived as a thinking immaterial one*, whatever difficulties some would raise against it.

27.   For to extend our thoughts a little further, that pressure which is brought to explain the cohesion of bodies is as unintelligible as the cohesion itself.   For if matter be considered, as no doubt it is, finite, let anyone send his contemplation to the extremities of the universe and there see what conceivable hoops, what bond he can imagine to hold this mass of matter in so close a pressure together, from whence steel has its firmness, and the parts of a diamond their hardness and indissolubility.   If matter be finite, it must have its extremes, and there must be something to hinder it from scattering asunder.   If, to avoid this difficulty, anyone will throw himself into the supposition and abyss of

infinite matter, let him consider what light he thereby brings to the *cohesion* of body, and whether he be ever the nearer making it intelligible, by resolving it into a supposition the most absurd and most incomprehensible of all other: so far is our extension of body (which is nothing but the cohesion of solid parts) from being clearer or more distinct, when we would inquire into the nature, cause, or manner of it, than the *idea* of thinking.

28. Another *idea* we have of body is the power of *communication of motion by impulse*; and of our souls, the power of *exciting of motion by thought*. These *ideas*, the one of body, the other of our minds, every day's experience clearly furnishes us with; but if here again we inquire how this is done, we *are equally in the dark*. For in the communication of motion by impulse, wherein as much motion is lost to one body as is got to the other, which is the ordinariest case, we can have no other conception but of the passing of motion out of one body into another; which, I think, is as obscure and inconceivable as how our minds move or stop our bodies by thought, which we every moment find they do. The increase of motion by impulse, which is observed or believed sometimes to happen, is yet harder to be understood. We have by daily experience clear evidence of motion produced both by impulse and by thought, but the manner how hardly comes without our comprehension: we are equally at a loss in both. So that however we consider motion and its communication either from body or spirit, *the* idea *which belongs to spirit is at least as clear as that that belongs to body*. And if we consider the active power of moving or, as I may call it, *motivity*, it is much clearer in spirit than body, since two bodies, placed by one another at rest, will never afford us the *idea* of a power in the one to move the other, but by a borrowed motion; whereas the mind every day affords us *ideas* of an active power of moving of bodies; and therefore it is worth our consideration whether active power be not the proper attribute of spirits, and passive power of matter. Hence may be conjectured that created spirits are not totally separate from matter, because they are both active and passive. Pure spirit, viz. God, is only active; pure matter is only passive; those beings that are both active and passive we may judge to partake of both. But, be that as it will, I think, we have as many and as clear *ideas* belonging to spirit as we have belonging to body, the substance of each being equally unknown to us, and the *idea* of thinking in spirit as clear as of

extension in body; and the communication of motion by
thought which we attribute to spirit is as evident as that by
impulse, which we ascribe to body. Constant experience makes
us sensible of both of these, though our narrow understandings
can comprehend neither. For when the mind would look beyond
those original *ideas* we have from sensation or reflection and
penetrate into their causes and manner of production, we find
still it discovers nothing but its own short-sightedness.

29. To conclude. Sensation convinces us that there are solid,
extended substances, and reflection, that there are thinking ones;
experience assures us of the existence of such beings, and that the
one hath a power to move body by impulse, the other by thought:
this we cannot doubt of. Experience, I say, every moment furnishes us with the clear *ideas* both of the one and the other. But
beyond these *ideas*, as received from their proper sources, our
faculties will not reach. If we would inquire further into their
nature, causes, and manner, we perceive not the nature of
extension clearer than we do of thinking. If we would explain
them any further, one is as easy as the other; and there is no
more difficulty to conceive how a substance we know not should,
by thought, set body into motion, than how a substance we know
not should, by impulse, set body into motion. So that we are
no more able to discover wherein the *ideas* belonging to body
consist than those belonging to spirit. From whence it seems
probable to me that the simple *ideas* we receive from sensation
and reflection are the boundaries of our thoughts; beyond which
the mind, whatever efforts it would make, is not able to advance
one jot; nor can it make any discoveries, when it would pry into
the nature and hidden causes of those *ideas*.

30. So that, in short, *the idea* we have *of spirit, compared with
the* idea we have *of body*, stands thus: the substance of spirits is
unknown to us, and so is the substance of body equally unknown
to us. Two primary qualities or properties of body, viz. solid
coherent parts and impulse, we have distinct clear *ideas* of; so
likewise we know and have distinct clear *ideas* of two primary
qualities or properties of spirit, viz. thinking, and a power of
action, i.e. a power of beginning or stopping several thoughts
or motions. We have also the *ideas* of several qualities inherent
in bodies, and have the clear distinct *ideas* of them; which
qualities are but the various modifications of the extension of
cohering solid parts, and their motion. We have likewise the

ideas of the several modes of thinking, viz. believing, doubting, intending, fearing, hoping, all which are but the several modes of thinking. We have also the *ideas* of willing, and moving the body consequent to it, and with the body itself too; for, as has been shown, spirit is capable of motion.

31. Lastly, if this notion of immaterial spirit may have, perhaps, some difficulties in it not easily to be explained, we have therefore no more reason to deny or doubt the existence of such spirits than we have to deny or doubt the existence of body, because the notion of body is cumbered with some difficulties very hard, and perhaps impossible, to be explained or understood by us. For I would fain have instanced anything in our notion of spirit more perplexed or nearer a contradiction than the very notion of body includes in it, the divisibility *in infinitum* of any finite extension involving us, whether we grant or deny it, in consequences impossible to be explicated or made in our apprehensions consistent: consequences that carry greater difficulty and more apparent absurdity than anything can follow from the notion of an immaterial knowing substance.

32. Which we are not at all to wonder at, since we, having but some few superficial *ideas* of things, discovered to us only by the senses from without or by the mind reflecting on what it experiments in itself within, have no knowledge beyond that, much less of the internal constitution and true nature of things, being destitute of faculties to attain it. And therefore experimenting and discovering in ourselves knowledge and the power of voluntary motion, as certainly as we experiment or discover in things without us the cohesion and separation of solid parts, which is the extension and motion of bodies, *we have as much reason to be satisfied with our notion of immaterial spirit as with our notion of body, and the existence of the one as well as the other*. For it being no more a contradiction that thinking should exist separate and independent from solidity than it is a contradiction that solidity should exist separate and independent from thinking, they being both but simple *ideas* independent one from another; and having as clear and distinct *ideas* in us of thinking as of solidity, I know not why we may not as well allow a thinking thing without solidity, i.e. *immaterial*, to exist, as a solid thing without thinking, i.e. *matter*, to exist, especially since it is no harder to conceive how thinking should exist

without matter than how matters should think. For whensoever we would proceed beyond these simple *ideas* we have from sensation and reflection and dive further into the nature of things, we fall presently into darkness and obscurity, perplexedness and difficulties, and can discover nothing further but our own blindness and ignorance. But which ever of these complex *ideas* be clearest, that of body or immaterial spirit, this is evident, that the simple *ideas* that make them up are no other than what we have received from sensation or reflection; and so is it of all our other *ideas* of substances, even of God himself.

33.   For if we examine the *idea* we have of the incomprehensible supreme Being, we shall find that we come by it the same way, and that the complex *ideas* we have both of God and separate spirits are made of the simple *ideas* we receive from *reflection*: v.g., having, from what we experiment in ourselves, got the *ideas* of existence and duration, of knowledge and power, of pleasure and happiness, and of several other qualities and powers which it is better to have than to be without; when we would frame an *idea* the most suitable we can to the supreme Being, we enlarge every one of these with our *idea* of infinity, and so, putting them together, make our complex *idea of God*. For that the mind has such a power of enlarging some of its *ideas*, received from sensation and reflection, has been already shown.

34.   If I find that I know some few things and some of them or all perhaps imperfectly, I can frame an *idea* of knowing twice as many; which I can double again as often as I can add to number and thus enlarge my *idea* of knowledge by extending its comprehension to all things existing or possible. The same also I can do of knowing them more perfectly: i.e., all their qualities, powers, causes, consequences and relations, etc., till all be perfectly known that is in them or can any way relate to them, and thus frame the *idea* of infinite or boundless knowledge. The same may also be done of power till we come to that we call infinite, and also of the duration of existence without beginning or end, and so frame the *idea* of an eternal being. The degrees or extent wherein we ascribe existence, power, wisdom and all other perfection (which we can have any *ideas* of) to that sovereign being which we call God being all boundless and infinite, we frame the best *idea* of him our minds are capable of; all which is done, I say, by enlarging those simple *ideas* we have taken from the operations of our own minds by reflection or by

our senses from exterior things to that vastness to which infinity can extend them.

35. For it is infinity which, joined to our *ideas* of existence, power, knowledge, etc., makes that complex *idea* whereby we represent to ourselves, the best we can, the supreme Being. For, though in his own essence (which certainly we do not know, not knowing the real essence of a pebble, or a fly, or of our own selves) God be simple and uncompounded, yet I think I may say we have no other *idea* of him but a complex one of existence, knowledge, power, happiness, etc., infinite and eternal; which are all distinct *ideas*, and some of them, being relative, are again compounded of others; all which, being as has been shown originally got from *sensation* and *reflection*, go to make up the *idea* or notion we have of God.

36. This further is to be observed, that there is no *idea* we attribute to God, bating infinity, which is not also a part of our complex *idea* of other spirits. Because, being capable of no other simple *ideas*, belonging to anything but body, but those which by reflection we receive from the operation of our own minds, we can attribute to spirits no other but what we receive from thence; and all the difference we can put between them in our contemplation of spirits is only in the several extents and degrees of their knowledge, power, duration, happiness, etc. For that in our *ideas*, as well *of spirits* as of other things, we are *restrained to those we receive from sensation and reflection* is evident from hence: that in our *ideas* of spirits, how much soever advanced in perfection beyond those of bodies, even to that of infinite, we cannot yet have any *idea* of the manner wherein they discover their thoughts one to another, though we must necessarily conclude that separate spirits, which are beings that have perfecter knowledge and greater happiness than we, must needs have also a perfecter way of communicating their thoughts than we have who are fain to make use of corporeal signs and particular sounds; which are therefore of most general use as being the best and quickest we are capable of. But of immediate communication, having no experiment in ourselves and consequently no notion of it at all, we have no *idea* how spirits which use not words can, with quickness, or much less, how spirits that have no bodies can be masters of their own thoughts and communicate or conceal them at pleasure, though we cannot but necessarily suppose they have such a power.

37.   And thus we have seen *what kind of* ideas *we have of sub-stances of all kinds*, wherein they consist, and how we come by them. From whence, I think, it is very evident:

First, That all our *ideas* of the several sorts of substances are nothing but collections of simple *ideas*, with a supposition of something to which they belong, and in which they subsist, though of this supposed something we have no clear distinct *idea* at all.

Secondly, That all the simple *ideas* that, thus united in one common *substratum*, make up our complex *ideas* of several sorts of the substances are no other but such as we have received from *sensation* or *reflection*. So that even in those which we think we are most intimately acquainted with, and come nearest the comprehension of our most enlarged conceptions, we cannot reach beyond those simple *ideas*. And even in those which seem most remote from all we have to do with and do infinitely surpass anything we can perceive in ourselves by *reflection* or discover by *sensation* in other things, we can attain to nothing but those simple *ideas* which we originally received from *sensa-tion* or *reflection*, as is evident in the complex *ideas* we have of angels and particularly of God himself.

Thirdly, That most of the simple *ideas* that make up our complex *ideas* of substances, when truly considered, are only powers, however we are apt to take them for positive qualities: v.g. the greatest part of the *ideas* that make our complex *idea* of *gold* are yellowness, great weight, ductility, fusibility, and solubility in *aqua regia*, etc., all united together in an unknown *substratum*; all which *ideas* are nothing else but so many relations to other substances, and are not really in the gold, considered barely in itself, though they depend on those real and primary qualities of its internal constitution, whereby it has a fitness differ-ently to operate and be operated on by several other substances.

Chapter XXIV

OF COLLECTIVE IDEAS OF SUBSTANCES

1.   BESIDES these complex *ideas* of several single substances, as of man, horse, gold, violet, apple, etc., the mind hath also

complex collective ideas of substances; which I so call, because
such *ideas* are made up of many particular substances considered
together, as united into one *idea,* and which so joined are looked
on as one: v.g., the *idea* of such a collection of men as make an
army, though consisting of a great number of distinct substances,
is as much one *idea* as the *idea* of a man; and the great collective
idea of all bodies whatsoever signified by the name world is as
much one *idea* as the *idea* of any the least particle of matter in
it, it sufficing to the unity of any *idea* that it be considered as one
representation or picture, though made up of never so many
particulars.
2. These collective *ideas* of substances the mind makes by its
power of composition and uniting severally either simple or
complex *ideas* into one, as it does by the same faculty make the
complex *ideas* of particular substances, consisting of an aggregate of diverse simple *ideas,* united in one substance. And as
the mind, by putting together the repeated *ideas* of unity, makes
the collective mode or complex *idea* of any number, as a score,
or a gross, etc., so, by putting together several particular substances, it makes collective *ideas* of substances, as a troop, an
army, a swarm, a city, a fleet; each of which everyone finds that
he represents to his own mind by one *idea,* in one view, and so
under that notion considers those several things as perfectly one,
as one ship, or one atom. Nor is it harder to conceive how an
army of ten thousand men should make one *idea* than how a
man should make one *idea*: it being as easy to the mind to unite
into one the *idea* of a great number of men and consider it as
one, as it is to unite into one particular all the distinct *ideas* that
make up the composition of a man and consider them all together
as one.
3. Amongst such kind of collective *ideas* are to be counted
most part of artificial things, at least such of them as are made
up of distinct substances; and, in truth, if we consider all these
collective *ideas* aright, as *army, constellation, universe,* as they
are united into so many single *ideas,* they are but the artificial
draughts of the mind, bringing things very remote and independent on one another into one view, the better to contemplate
and discourse of them, united into one conception and signified
by one name. For these are no things so remote nor so contrary which the mind cannot, by this art of composition, bring
into one *idea*; as is visible in that signified by the name *universe.*

CHAPTER XXV

OF RELATION

1. BESIDES the *ideas*, whether simple or complex, that the mind has of things as they are in themselves, there are others it gets from their comparison one with another. The understanding, in the consideration of anything, is not confined to that precise object: it can carry any *idea*, as it were, beyond itself or, at least, look beyond it to see how it stands in conformity to any other. When the mind so considers one thing that it does, as it were, bring it to and set it by another and carry its view from one to the other, this is, as the words import, *relation* and *respect*; and the denominations given to positive things, intimating that respect, and serving as marks to lead the thoughts beyond the subject itself denominated to something distinct from it, are what we call *relatives*; and the things so brought together, *related*. Thus, when the mind considers *Caius* as such a positive being, it takes nothing into that *idea* but what really exists in *Caius*: v.g. when I consider him as a man, I have nothing in my mind but the complex *idea* of the species, man. So likewise, when I say *Caius* is a white man, I have nothing but the bare consideration of man who hath that white colour. But when I give *Caius* the name *husband*, I intimate some other person; and when I give him the name *whiter*, I intimate some other thing; in both cases my thought is led to something beyond *Caius*, and there are two things brought into consideration. And since any *idea*, whether simple or complex, may be the occasion why the mind thus brings two things together and, as it were, takes a view of them at once, though still considered as distinct, therefore any of our *ideas* may be the foundation of relation. As in the above-mentioned instance, the contract and ceremony of marriage with *Sempronia* is the occasion of the denomination or relation of husband, and the colour white the occasion why he is said whiter than freestone.

2. These and the like *relations expressed by relative terms that have others answering them with a reciprocal intimation*, as father and son, bigger and less, cause and effect, *are very obvious* to

everyone, and everybody at first sight perceives the relation. For father and son, husband and wife, and such other correlative terms seem so nearly to belong one to another and, through custom, do so readily chime and answer one another in people's memories, that upon the naming of either of them the thoughts are presently carried beyond the things so named; and nobody overlooks or doubts of a relation where it is so plainly intimated. But where languages have failed to give correlative names, there the relation is not always so easily taken notice of. *Concubine* is, no doubt, a relative name as well as wife; but in languages where this and the like words have not a correlative term, there people are not so apt to take them to be so, as wanting that evident mark of relation which is between correlatives, which seem to explain one another and not to be able to exist but together. Hence it is that many of those names, which duly considered do include evident relations, have been called external denominations. But all names that are more than empty sounds must signify some *idea* which is either in the thing to which the name is applied, and then it is positive and is looked on as united to and existing in the thing to which the denomination is given, or else it arises from the respect the mind finds in it to something distinct from it, with which it considers it, and then it includes a relation.

3. Another sort of *relative terms* there is, which are not looked on to be either relative or so much as external denominations; *which* yet, under the form and appearance of signifying something absolute in the subject, do conceal a tacit, though less observable, relation. Such are the *seemingly positive* terms of *old, great, imperfect*, etc., whereof I shall have occasion to speak more at large in the following chapters.

4. This further may be observed, that the *ideas* of relation may be the same in men who have far different *ideas* of the things that are related, or that are thus compared: v.g. those who have far different *ideas* of a *man* may yet agree in the notion of a *father*, which is a notion superinduced to the substance, or man, and refers only to an act of that thing called man whereby he contributed to the generation of one of his own kind, let man be what it will.

5. The *nature* therefore *of relation* consists in the referring or comparing two things one to another, from which comparison one or both comes to be denominated. And if either of those

things be removed or cease to be, the relation ceases, and the denomination consequent to it, though the other receive in itself no alteration at all: v.g. *Caius*, whom I consider today as a father, ceases to be so tomorrow only by the death of his son, without any alteration made in himself. Nay, barely by the mind's changing the object to which it compares anything, the same thing is capable of having contrary denominations at the same time: v.g. *Caius*, compared to several persons, may truly be said to be older and younger, stronger and weaker, etc.

6.   Whatsoever doth or can exist or be considered as one thing is positive; and so not only simple *ideas* and substances, but modes also, are positive beings, though the parts of which they consist are very often relative one to another; but the whole together considered as one thing, and producing in us the complex *idea* of one thing, which *idea* is in our minds as one picture, though an aggregate of divers parts and under one name, it is a positive or absolute thing, or *idea*. Thus a triangle, though the parts thereof compared one to another be *relative*, yet the *idea* of the whole is a positive absolute *idea*. The same may be said of a family, a tune, etc.; for there can be no relation but betwixt two things considered as two things. There must always be in relation two *ideas* or things, either in themselves really separate, or considered as distinct, and then a ground or occasion for their comparison.

7.   Concerning relation in general, these things may be considered:

First, That there is *no one thing*, whether simple *idea*, substance, mode, or relation, or name of either of them, *which is not capable of almost an infinite number of* considerations in reference to other things; and therefore this makes no small part of men's thoughts and words. V.g., one single man may at once be concerned in and sustain all these following *relations*, and many more, viz. father, brother, son, grandfather, grandson, father-in-law, son-in-law, husband, friend, enemy, subject, general, judge, patron, client, professor, *European*, *Englishman*, islander, servant, master, possessor, captain, superior, inferior, bigger, less, older, younger, contemporary, like, unlike, etc., to an almost infinite number: he being capable of as many relations as there can be occasions of comparing him to other things, in any manner of agreement, disagreement, or respect whatsoever. For, as I said, *relation* is a way of comparing or considering two things together and giving one or both of them some appellation from that comparison, and sometimes giving even the relation itself a name.

8.   *Secondly*, This further may be considered concerning *relation*: that, though it be not contained in the real existence of things, but something extraneous and superinduced, yet the *ideas* which relative words stand for are often clearer and more distinct than of those substances to which they do belong. The notion we have of a father or brother is a great deal clearer and more distinct than that we have of a man; or, if you will, *paternity* is a thing whereof it is easier to have a clear *idea* than of *humanity*. And I can much easier conceive what a friend is than what GOD, because the knowledge of one action or one simple *idea* is oftentimes sufficient to give me the notion of a relation; but to the knowing of any substantial being, an accurate collection of sundry *ideas* is necessary. A man, if he compares two things together, can hardly be supposed not to know what it is wherein he compares them, so that, when he compares any things together, he cannot but have a very clear *idea* of that relation. The *ideas*, then, of *relations are capable* at least *of being more perfect and distinct in our minds than those of substances*. Because it is commonly hard to know all the simple *ideas* which are really in any substance, but for the most part easy enough to know the simple *ideas* that make up any relation I think on, or have a name for: v.g. comparing two men in reference to one common parent, it is very easy to frame the *ideas* of brothers, without having yet the perfect *idea* of a man. For significant relative words, as well as others, standing only for *ideas*, and those being all either simple or made up of simple ones, it suffices, for the knowing the precise *idea* the relative term stands for, to have a clear conception of that which is the foundation of the relation; which may be done without having a perfect and clear *idea* of the thing it is attributed to. Thus having the notion that one laid the egg out of which the other was hatched, I have a clear *idea* of the relation of *dam* and *chick*, between the two cassowaries in St. *James'* Park, though perhaps I have but a very obscure and imperfect *idea* of those birds themselves.

9.   *Thirdly*, Though there be a great number of considerations wherein things may be compared one with another, and so a multitude of *relations*, yet they *all terminate in* and are concerned about those *simple ideas*, either of sensation or reflection;

which I think to be the whole materials of all our knowledge. To clear this, I shall show it in the most considerable relations that we have any notion of, and in some that seem to be the most remote from *sense* or *reflection*; which yet will appear to have their *ideas* from thence and leave it past doubt that the notions we have of them are but certain simple *ideas*, and so originally derived from sense or reflection.

10.   *Fourthly*, That *relation* being the considering of one thing with another which is extrinsical to it, it is evident that all words that necessarily lead the mind to any other *ideas* than are supposed really to exist in that thing to which the word is applied are *relative words:* v.g. a *man, black, merry, thoughtful, thirsty, angry, extended*; these and the like are all absolute, because they neither signify nor intimate anything but what does or is supposed really to exist in the man thus denominated; but *father, brother, king, husband, blacker, merrier*, etc., are words which, together with the thing they denominate, imply also something else separate and exterior to the existence of that thing.

11.   Having laid down these premises concerning *relation* in general, I shall now proceed to show in some instances how all the *ideas* we have of *relation* are made up, as the others are, only of simple *ideas*, and that they all, how refined or remote from sense soever they seem, terminate at last in simple *ideas*. I shall begin with the most comprehensive relation wherein all things that do or can exist are concerned, and that is the relation of *cause* and *effect*. The *idea* whereof, how derived from the two fountains of all our knowledge, *sensation* and *reflection*, I shall in the next place consider.

CHAPTER XXVI

OF CAUSE AND EFFECT, AND OTHER RELATIONS

1.   IN the notice that our senses take of the constant vicissitude of things, we cannot but observe that several particular, both qualities and substances, begin to exist, and that they receive this their existence from the due application and operation of some other being. From this observation we get our *ideas* of *cause* and *effect*. That which produces any simple or complex

idea we denote by the general name, *cause*, and that which is produced, *effect*. Thus, finding that, in that substance which we call wax, fluidity, which is a simple *idea* that was not in it before, is constantly produced by the application of a certain degree of heat, we call the simple *idea* of heat, in relation to fluidity in wax, the cause of it, and fluidity the effect. So also, finding that the substance, wood, which is a certain collection of simple *ideas* so called, by the application of fire is turned into another substance, called ashes, i.e. another complex *idea*, consisting of a collection of simple *ideas*, quite different from that complex *idea* which we call wood, we consider fire, in relation to ashes, as cause, and the ashes, as effect. So that whatever is considered by us to conduce or operate to the producing any particular simple *idea*, or collection of simple *ideas* whether substance or mode, which did not before exist, hath thereby in our minds the relation of a cause, and so is denominated by us.

2. Having thus, from what our senses are able to discover in the operations of bodies on one another, got the notion of *cause* and *effect*, viz. that a *cause* is that which makes any other thing, either simple *idea*, substance, or mode, begin to be, and an *effect* is that which had its beginning from some other thing: the mind finds no great difficulty to distinguish the several originals of things into two sorts:

First, When the thing is wholly made new, so that no part thereof did ever exist before, as when a new particle of matter doth begin to exist *in rerum natura*, which had before no being; and this we call *creation*.

Secondly, When a thing is made up of particles which did all of them before exist, but that very thing, so constituted of pre-existing particles which, considered all together, make up such a collection of simple *ideas*, had not any *existence* before, as this man, this egg, rose, or cherry, etc. And this, when referred to a substance, produced in the ordinary course of nature by an internal principle, but set on work by and received from some external agent or cause, and working by insensible ways which we perceive not, we call *generation*. When the cause is extrinsical, and the effect produced by a sensible separation or *juxta-position* of discernible parts, we call it *making*; and such are all artificial things. When any simple *idea* is produced which was not in that subject before, we call it *alteration*. Thus a man is generated, a picture made; and either of them altered, when any new sensible quality or simple *idea* is produced in either of them, which was not there before; and the things thus made to exist, which were not there before, are *effects*; and those things which operated to the existence, *causes*. In which and all other cases, we may observe that the notion of *cause* and *effect* has its rise from *ideas* received by sensation or reflection, and that this relation, how comprehensive soever, terminates at last in them. For to have the *idea* of *cause* and *effect*, it suffices to consider any simple *idea* or substance as beginning to exist by the operation of some other, without knowing the manner of that operation.

3.   *Time* and *place* are also the foundations of very large relations, and all finite beings at least are concerned in them. But having already shown in another place how we get these *ideas*, it may suffice here to intimate that most of the denominations of things, received from time, are only relations. Thus when anyone says that Queen *Elizabeth* lived sixty-nine and reigned forty-five years, these words import only the relation of that duration to some other and mean no more but this, that the duration of her existence was equal to sixty-nine, and the duration of her government to forty-five annual revolutions of the sun; and so are all words answering *how long*. Again, *William* the Conqueror invaded *England* about the year 1070, which means this: that taking the duration from our Saviour's time till now for one entire great length of time, it shows at what distance this invasion was from the two extremes. And so do all words of time answering to the question *when*, which show only the distance of any point of time from the period of a longer duration, from which we measure and to which we thereby consider it as related.

4.   There are yet, besides those, other words of time, that ordinarily are thought to stand for positive *ideas*, which yet will, when considered, be found to be relative, such as are *young*, *old*, etc., which include and intimate the relation anything has to a certain length of duration whereof we have the *idea* in our minds. Thus having settled in our thoughts the *idea* of the ordinary duration of a man to be seventy years, when we say a man is *young*, we mean that his age is yet but a small part of that which usually men attain to; and when we denominate him *old*, we mean that his duration is run out almost to the end of that which men do not usually exceed. And so it is but comparing the particular age or duration of this or that man to the

idea of that duration which we have in our minds as ordinarily belonging to that sort of animals; which is plain in the application of these names to other things, for a man is called young at twenty years and very young at seven years old; but yet a horse we call old at twenty, and a dog at seven years, because in each of these we compare their age to different *ideas* of duration, which are settled in our minds as belonging to these several sorts of animals, in the ordinary course of nature. But the sun and stars, though they have outlasted several generations of men, we call not old, because we do not know what period GOD hath set to that sort of beings: this term belonging properly to those things which we can observe in the ordinary course of things, by a natural decay, to come to an end in a certain period of time; and so have in our minds, as it were, a standard to which we can compare the several parts of their duration; and by the relation they bear thereunto, call them young or old; which we cannot therefore do to a ruby or a diamond, things whose usual periods we know not.

5. The *relation* also that things have to one another in their *places* and distances is very obvious to observe: as above, below, a mile distant from *Charing-Cross*, in *England*, and in *London*. But as in duration, so in *extension* and bulk, there are some *ideas* that are relative, which we signify by names that are thought positive, as *great and little are* truly *relations*. For here also having, by observation, settled in our minds the *ideas* of the bigness of several species of things from those we have been most accustomed to, we make them, as it were, the standards whereby to denominate the bulk of others. Thus we call a great apple such a one as is bigger than the ordinary sort of those we have been used to; and a little horse, such a one as comes not up to the size of that *idea* which we have in our minds to belong ordinarily to horses; and that will be a great horse to a *Welshman* which is but a little one to a *Fleming*: they two having, from the different breed of their countries, taken several sized *ideas* to which they compare and in relation to which they denominate their great and their little.

6. So likewise *weak and strong are* but *relative denominations* of power, compared to some *ideas* we have at that time of greater or less power. Thus when we say a weak man, we mean one that has not so much strength or power to move as usually men have, or usually those of his size have; which is a comparing

his strength to the *idea* we have of the usual strength of men, or men of such a size. The like when we say the creatures are all weak things: weak, there, is but a relative term, signifying the disproportion there is in the power of GOD and the creatures. And so abundance of words in ordinary speech stand only for relations (and, perhaps, the greatest part) which at first sight, seem to have no such signification: v.g., the ship has necessary stores. *Necessary* and *stores* are both relative words, one having a relation to the accomplishing the voyage intended, and the other to future use. All which relations, how they are confined to and terminate in *ideas* derived from *sensation* or *reflection,* is too obvious to need any explication.

Chapter XXVII

OF IDENTITY AND DIVERSITY

1. ANOTHER occasion the mind often takes of comparing is the very being of things, when, considering anything as existing at any determined time and place, we compare it with itself existing at another time, and thereon form the *ideas* of *identity* and *diversity.* When we see anything to be in any place in any instant of time, we are sure (be it what it will) that it is that very thing, and not another which at that same time exists in another place, how like and undistinguishable soever it may be in all other respects; and in this consists *identity,* when the *ideas* it is attributed to vary not at all from what they were that moment wherein we consider their former existence, and to which we compare the present. For we never finding nor conceiving it possible that two things of the same kind should exist in the same place at the same time, we rightly conclude that whatever exists anywhere at any time, excludes all of the same kind, and is there itself alone. When therefore we demand whether anything be the same or no, it refers always to something that existed such a time in such a place, which it was certain, at that instant, was the same with itself, and no other; from whence it follows that one thing cannot have two beginnings of existence, nor two things one beginning: it being impossible for two things of the same

kind to be or exist in the same instant in the very same place, or one and the same thing in different places. That, therefore, that had one beginning is the same thing; and that which had a different beginning in time and place from that is not the same, but diverse. That which has made the difficulty about this relation has been the little care and attention used in having precise notions of the things to which it is attributed.

2.   We have the *ideas* but of three sorts of substances: (1) God. (2) Finite intelligences. (3) *Bodies*. First, God is without beginning, eternal, unalterable, and everywhere, and therefore concerning his identity there can be no doubt. Secondly, Finite spirits having had each its determinate time and place of beginning to exist, the relation to that time and place will always determine to each of them its identity, as long as it exists.

Thirdly, The same will hold of every particle of matter to which, no addition or subtraction of matter being made, it is the same. For, though these three sorts of substances, as we term them, do not exclude one another out of the same place, yet we cannot conceive but that they must necessarily each of them exclude any of the same kind out of the same place; or else the notions and names of identity and diversity would be in vain, and there could be no such distinction of substances, or anything else one from another. For example: could two bodies be in the same place at the same time, then those two parcels of matter must be one and the same, take them great or little; nay, all bodies must be one and the same. For by the same reason that two particles of matter may be in one place, all bodies may be in one place: which, when it can be supposed, takes away the distinction of identity and diversity of one and more, and renders it ridiculous. But it being a contradiction that two or more should be one, identity and diversity are relations and ways of comparing well-founded and of use to the understanding. All other things being but modes or relations ultimately terminated in substances, the identity and diversity of each particular existence of them too will be by the same way determined; only as to things whose existence is in succession, such as are the actions of finite beings, v.g. *motion* and *thought*, both which consist in a continued train of succession, concerning their diversity there can be no question: because each perishing the moment it begins, they cannot exist in different times or in different places, as permanent beings can at different times exist in distant places; and therefore no motion or thought, considered as at different times, can be the same, each part thereof having a different beginning of existence.

3. From what has been said, it is easy to discover what is so much inquired after, the *principium individuationis*; and that, it is plain, is existence itself, which determines a being of any sort to a particular time and place, incommunicable to two beings of the same kind. This, though it seems easier to conceive in simple substances or modes, yet, when reflected on, is not more difficult in compounded ones, if care be taken to what it is applied: v.g. let us suppose an atom, i.e. a continued body under one immutable superficies, existing in a determined time and place; it is evident, that, considered in any instant of its existence, it is in that instant the same with itself. For, being at that instant what it is, and nothing else, it is the same, and so must continue as long as its existence is continued; for so long it will be the same, and no other. In like manner, if two or more atoms be joined together into the same mass, every one of those atoms will be the same, by the foregoing rule; and whilst they exist united together, the mass, consisting of the same atoms, must be the same mass, or the same body, let the parts be never so differently jumbled; but if one of these atoms be taken away, or one new one added, it is no longer the same mass or the same body. In the state of living creatures, their identity depends not on a mass of the same particles but on something else. For in them the variation of great parcels of matter alters not the identity: an oak growing from a plant to a great tree, and then lopped, is still the same oak; and a colt grown up to a horse, sometimes fat, sometimes lean, is all the while the same horse, though in both these cases there may be a manifest change of the parts, so that truly they are not either of them the same masses of matter, though they be truly one of them the same oak, and the other the same horse. The reason whereof is that, in these two cases of a mass of matter and a living body, *identity* is not applied to the same thing.

4. We must therefore consider wherein an oak differs from a mass of matter; and that seems to me to be in this: that the one is only the cohesion of particles of matter any how united; the other such a disposition of them as constitutes the parts of an oak, and such an organization of those parts as is fit to receive and distribute nourishment, so as to continue and frame the

wood, bark, and leaves, etc., of an oak, in which consists the vegetable life. That being then one plant which has such an organization of parts in one coherent body, partaking of one common life, it continues to be the same plant as long as it partakes of the same life, though that life be communicated to new particles of matter vitally united to the living plant, in a like continued organization, conformable to that sort of plants. For this organization, being at any one instant in any one collection of *matter*, is in that particular concrete distinguished from all other and is that individual life; which existing constantly from that moment both forwards and backwards, in the same continuity of insensibly suceeding parts united to the living body of the plant, it has that identity which makes the same plant and all the parts of it parts of the same plant during all the time that they exist united in that continued organization, which is fit to convey that common life to all the parts so united.

5. The case is not so much different in *brutes* but that anyone may hence see what makes an animal and continues it the same. Something we have like this in machines and may serve to illustrate it. For example, what is a watch? It is plain it is nothing but a fit organization or construction of parts to a certain end, which, when a sufficient force is added to it, it is capable to attain. If we would suppose this machine one continued body, all whose organized parts were repaired, increased, or diminished by a constant addition or separation of insensible parts, with one common life, we should have something very much like the body of an animal, with this difference: that in an animal the fitness of the organization and the motion wherein life consists begin together, the motion coming from within; but in machines, the force, coming sensibly from without, is often away when the organ is in order and well-fitted to receive it.

6. This also shows wherein the identity of the same *man* consists: viz. in nothing but a participation of the same continued life, by constantly fleeting particles of matter, in succession vitally united to the same organized body. He that shall place the *identity* of man in anything else but, like that of other animals, in one fitly organized body, taken in any one instant and from thence continued under one organization of life in several successively fleeting particles of matter united to it, will find it hard to make an *embryo*, one of years, mad, and sober, the same man, by any supposition that will not make it possible for

Seth, Ismael, Socrates, Pilate, St. Austin, and *Caesar Borgia* to be the same man. For if the *identity* of soul alone makes the same man, and there be nothing in the nature of matter why the same individual spirit may not be united to different bodies, it will be possible that those men living in distant ages, and of different tempers, may have been the same man: which way of speaking must be, from a very strange use of the word *man,* applied to an *idea* out of which body and shape are excluded. And that way of speaking would agree yet worse with the notions of those philosophers who allow of transmigration and are of opinion that the souls of men may, for their miscarriages, be detruded into the bodies of beasts, as fit habitations, with organs suited to the satisfaction of their brutal inclinations. But yet I think, nobody, could he be sure that the soul of *Heliogabalus* were in one of his hogs, would yet say that hog were a *man* or *Heliogabalus.*

7. It is not therefore unity of substance that comprehends all sorts of *identity* or will determine it in every case; but to conceive and judge of it aright, we must consider what *idea* the word it is applied to stands for: it being one thing to be the same *substance,* another the same *man,* and a third the same *person,* if *person, man,* and *substance* are three names standing for three different *ideas;* for such as is the *idea* belonging to that name, such must be the *identity;* which, if it had been a little more carefully attended to, would possibly have prevented a great deal of that confusion which often occurs about this matter, with no small seeming difficulties, especially concerning *personal identity,* which therefore we shall in the next place a little consider.

8. An animal is a living organized body; and consequently the same animal, as we have observed, is the same continued life communicated to different particles of matter as they happen successively to be united to that organized living body. And whatever is talked of other definitions, ingenuous observation puts it past doubt that the *idea* in our minds of which the sound *man* in our mouths is the sign, is nothing else but of an animal of such a certain form: since I think I may be confident that whoever should see a creature of his own shape and make, though it had no more reason all its life than a *cat* or a *parrot,* would call him still a *man;* or whoever should hear a *cat* or a *parrot* discourse, reason, and philosophize would call or think it

nothing but a *cat* or a *parrot* and say the one was a dull irrational *man*, and the other a very intelligent rational *parrot*. A relation we have in an author of great note is sufficient to countenance the supposition of a rational *parrot*. His words[1] are:

'I had a mind to know from his (Prince *Maurice's*) own mouth the account of a common but much credited story, that I had heard so often from many others, of an old *parrot* he had in *Brazil* during his government there, that spoke and asked and answered common questions like a reasonable creature, so that those of his train there generally concluded it to be witchery or possession; and one of his chaplains, who lived long afterwards in *Holland*, would never from that time endure a *parrot* but said they all had a devil in them. I had heard many particulars of this story and assevered by people hard to be discredited, which made me ask Prince *Maurice* what there was of it. He said, with his usual plainness and dryness in talk, there was something true but a great deal false of what had been reported. I desired to know of him what there was of the first? He told me short and coldly that he had heard of such an old *parrot* when he came to *Brazil*; and though he believed nothing of it and it was a good way off, yet he had so much curiosity as to send for it; that it was a very great and a very old one; and when it came first into the room where the Prince was, with a great many *Dutchmen* about him, it said presently: *What a company of white men are here?* They asked it what he thought that man was, pointing at the Prince. It answered, *some general or other*. When they brought it close to him, he asked it: *D'où venez-vous?* It answered: *De Marinnan.* The Prince: *À qui êtes-vous?* The parrot: *À un Portugais.* Prince: *Que fais-tu là?* Parrot: *Je garde les poules.* The Prince laughed and said: *Vous gardez les poules?* The parrot answered: *Oui, moi, & je sais bien faire,* and made the chuck four or five times that people use to make to chickens when they call them. I set down the words of this worthy dialogue in *French*, just as Prince *Maurice* said them to me. I asked him in what language the *parrot* spoke and he said in *Brazilian.* I asked whether he understood *Brazilian*; he said no, but he had taken care to have two interpreters by him, the one a *Dutchman* that spoke *Brazilian*, and the other a *Brazilian* that spoke *Dutch*; that he asked them separately and privately,

[1] Temple, Sir Wm. *Memoirs of what past in Christendom, begun* 1672 *to . . .* 1679. 1692. pp. 57-60.

and both of them agreed in telling him just the same thing that the *parrot* said. I could not but tell this odd story because it is so much out of the way, and from the first hand, and what may pass for a good one; for I dare say this Prince at least believed himself in all he told me, having ever passed for a very honest and pious man. I leave it to naturalists to reason, and to other men to believe as they please upon it; however, it is not perhaps amiss to relieve or enliven a busy scene sometimes with such digressions, whether to the purpose or no.'

I have taken care that the reader should have the story at large in the author's own words, because he seems to me not to have thought it incredible; for it cannot be imagined that so able a man as he, who had sufficiency enough to warrant all the testimonies he gives of himself, should take so much pains, in a place where it had nothing to do, to pin so close not only on a man whom he mentions as his friend, but on a prince, in whom he acknowledges very great honesty and piety, a story which, if he himself thought incredible, he could not but also think ridiculous. The Prince, it is plain, who vouches this story, and our author who relates it from him, both of them call this talker a *parrot*; and I ask anyone else who thinks such a story fit to be told, whether, if this *parrot* and all of its kind had always talked, as we have a prince's word for it, as this one did, whether, I say, they would not have passed for a race of *rational animals*; but yet whether for all that they would have been allowed to be men and not *parrots*? For I presume it is not the *idea* of a thinking or rational being alone that makes the *idea* of a *man* in most people's sense, but of a body so and so shaped, joined to it; and if that be the *idea* of a *man*, the same successive body not shifted all at once must, as well as the same immaterial spirit, go to the making of the same *man*.

9.   This being premised, to find wherein *personal identity* consists, we must consider what *person* stands for; which, I think, is a thinking intelligent being that has reason and reflection and can consider itself as itself, the same thinking thing in different times and places; which it does only by that consciousness which is inseparable from thinking and, as it seems to me, essential to it: it being impossible for anyone to perceive without perceiving that he does perceive. When we see, hear, smell, taste, feel, meditate, or will anything, we know that we do so. Thus it is always as to our present sensations and perceptions, and by this

everyone is to himself that which he calls *self*: it not being considered in this case whether the same *self* be continued in the
same or divers substances. For since consciousness always
accompanies thinking, and it is that that makes everyone to be
what he calls *self*, and thereby distinguishes himself from all
other thinking things: in this alone consists *personal identity*,
i.e. the sameness of a rational being. And as far as this consciousness can be extended backwards to any past action or
thought, so far reaches the identity of that *person*: it is the same
self now it was then, and it is by the same *self* with this present
one that now reflects on it, that that action was done.

10. But it is further inquired whether it be the same identical
substance? This, few would think they had reason to doubt of,
if these perceptions, with their consciousness, always remained
present in the mind whereby the same thinking thing would be
always consciously present and, as would be thought, evidently
the same to itself. But that which seems to make the difficulty
is this: that this consciousness being interrupted always by
forgetfulness, there being no moment of our lives wherein we
have the whole train of all our past actions before our eyes in one
view, but even the best memories losing the sight of one part
whilst they are viewing another; and we sometimes, and that the
greatest part of our lives, not reflecting on our past selves, being
intent on our present thoughts, and in sound sleep having no
thoughts at all, or at least none with that consciousness which
remarks our waking thoughts; I say, in all these cases, our consciousness being interrupted, and we losing the sight of our past
selves, doubts are raised whether we are the same thinking thing,
i.e. the same substance, or no. Which, however reasonable or
unreasonable, concerns not *personal identity* at all: the question
being what makes the same *person*, and not whether it be the
same identical substance, which always thinks in the same person; which, in this case, matters not at all: different substances,
by the same consciousness (where they do partake in it) being
united into one person, as well as different bodies by the same
life are united into one animal, whose *identity* is preserved in
that change of substances by the unity of one continued life.
For, it being the same consciousness that makes a man be himself to himself, *personal identity* depends on that only, whether
it be annexed only to one individual substance, or can be
continued in a succession of several substances. For as far as

any intelligent being can repeat the *idea* of any past action with the same consciousness it had of it at first, and with the same consciousness it has of any present action, so far it is the same *personal self*. For it is by the consciousness it has of its present thoughts and actions that it is *self* to *itself* now, and so will be the same *self* as far as the same consciousness can extend to actions past or to come, and would be by distance of time or change of substance no more two *persons* than a man be two men by wearing other clothes today than he did yesterday, with a long or short sleep between: the same consciousness uniting those distant actions into the same *person*, whatever substances contributed to their production.

11.   That this is so, we have some kind of evidence in our very bodies, all whose particles, whilst vitally united to this same thinking conscious self so that we feel when they are touched and are affected by and conscious of good or harm that happens to them, are a part of our *selves*, i.e. of our thinking conscious *self*. Thus, the limbs of his body are to everyone a part of *himself*; he sympathizes and is concerned for them. Cut off a hand, and thereby separate it from that consciousness he had of its heat, cold, and other affections, and it is then no longer a part of that which is *himself*, any more than the remotest part of matter. Thus, we see the *substance* whereof *personal self* consisted at one time may be varied at another, without the change of personal *identity*: there being no question about the same person, though the limbs, which but now were a part of it, be cut off.

12.   But the question is whether, if the same substance, which thinks, be changed, it can be the same person, or, remaining the same, it can be different persons.

And to this I answer, first, this can be no question at all to those who place thought in a purely material animal constitution, void of an immaterial substance. For, whether their supposition be true or no, it is plain they conceive personal identity preserved in something else than identity of substance, as animal identity is preserved in identity of life and not of substance. And therefore those who place thinking in an immaterial substance only, before they can come to deal with these men, must show why personal identity cannot be preserved in the change of immaterial substances, or variety of particular immaterial substances, as well as animal identity is preserved in the change of material substances, or variety of particular bodies: unless they will say, it is one immaterial spirit that makes the same life in brutes, as it is one immaterial spirit that makes the same person in men; which the *Cartesians* at least will not admit, for fear of making brutes thinking things too.

13. But next, as to the first part of the question, whether, if the same thinking substance (supposing immaterial substances only to think) be changed, it can be the same person, I answer: That cannot be resolved but by those who know what kind of substances they are that do think, and whether the consciousness of past actions can be transferred from one thinking substance to another. I grant, were the same consciousness the same individual action, it could not; but, it being but a present representation of a past action, why it may not be possible that that may be represented to the mind to have been which really never was, will remain to be shown. And therefore how far the consciousness of past actions is annexed to any individual agent, so that another cannot possibly have it, will be hard for us to determine, till we know what kind of action it is that cannot be done without a reflex act of perception accompanying it, and how performed by thinking substances, who cannot think without being conscious of it. But that which we call the *same consciousness* not being the same individual act, why one intellectual substance may not have represented to it, as done by itself, what it never did, and was perhaps done by some other agent: why, I say, such a representation may not possibly be without reality of matter of fact, as well as several representations in dreams are, which yet whilst dreaming we take for true, will be difficult to conclude from the nature of things. And that it never is so will by us, till we have clearer views of the nature of thinking substances, be best resolved into the goodness of God, who, as far as the happiness or misery of any of his sensible creatures is concerned in it, will not, by a fatal error of theirs, transfer from one to another that consciousness which draws reward or punishment with it. How far this may be an argument against those who would place thinking in a system of fleeting animal spirits, I leave to be considered. But yet, to return to the question before us, it must be allowed that, if the same consciousness (which, as has been shown, is quite a different thing from the same numerical figure or motion in body) can be transferred from one thinking substance to another, it will be possible that

two thinking substances may make but one person. For the same consciousness being preserved, whether in the same or different substances, the personal identity is preserved.

14. As to the second part of the question, whether, the same immaterial substance remaining, there may be two distinct persons, which question seems to me to be built on this: whether the same immaterial being, being conscious of the actions of its past duration, may be wholly stripped of all the consciousness of its past existence and lose it beyond the power of ever retrieving again and so, as it were beginning a new account from a new period, have a consciousness that cannot reach beyond this new state. All those who hold pre-existence are evidently of this mind, since they allow the soul to have no remaining consciousness of what it did in that pre-existent state, either wholly separate from body, or informing any other body; and if they should not, it is plain experience would be against them. So that, personal identity reaching no further than consciousness reaches, a pre-existent spirit, not having continued so many ages in a state of silence, must needs make different persons. Suppose a *Christian Platonist* or *Pythagorean* should, upon God's having ended all his works of creation the seventh day, think his soul hath existed ever since, and should imagine it has revolved in several human bodies, as I once met with one who was persuaded his had been the soul of *Socrates* (how reasonably I will not dispute; this I know, that in the post he filled, which was no inconsiderable one, he passed for a very rational man, and the press has shown that he wanted not parts or learning); would anyone say that he, being not conscious of any of *Socrates's* actions or thoughts, could be the same person with *Socrates*? Let anyone reflect upon himself and conclude that he has in himself an immaterial spirit, which is that which thinks in him and in the constant change of his body keeps him the same and is that which he calls himself; let him also suppose it to be the same soul that was in *Nestor* or *Thersites* at the siege of *Troy* (for souls being, as far as we know anything of them, in their nature indifferent to any parcel of matter, the supposition has no apparent absurdity in it), which it may have been, as well as it is now the soul of any other man; but he now having no consciouness of any of the actions either of *Nestor* or *Thersites*, does or can he conceive himself the same person with either of them? Can he be concerned in either of their actions, attribute

them to himself, or think them his own, more than the actions of any other men that ever existed? So that, this consciousness not reaching to any of the actions of either of those men, he is no more one *self* with either of them than if the soul or immaterial spirit that now informs him had been created and began to exist, when it began to inform his present body, though it were never so true that the same spirit that informed *Nestor's* or *Thersites's* body were numerically the same that now informs his. For this would no more make him the same person with *Nestor* than if some of the particles of matter that were once a part of *Nestor* were now a part of this man: the same immaterial substance, without the same consciousness, no more making the same person by being united to any body than the same particle of matter, without consciousness, united to any body, makes the same person. But let him once find himself conscious of any of the actions of *Nestor*, he then finds himself the same person with *Nestor*.

15. And thus may we be able, without any difficulty, to conceive the same person at the resurrection, though in a body not exactly in make or parts the same which he had here, the same consciousness going along with the soul that inhabits it. But yet the soul alone, in the change of bodies, would scarce, to anyone but to him that makes the soul the *man*, be enough to make the same *man*. For should the soul of a prince, carrying with it the consciousness of the prince's past life, enter and inform the body of a cobbler as soon as deserted by his own soul, everyone sees he would be the same person with the prince, accountable only for the prince's actions; but who would say it was the same man? The body too goes to the making the man and would, I guess, to everybody, determine the man in this case, wherein the soul, with all its princely thoughts about it, would not make another man: but he would be the same cobbler to everyone besides himself. I know that in the ordinary way of speaking, the same person and the same man stand for one and the same thing. And indeed, everyone will always have a liberty to speak as he pleases and to apply what articulate sounds to what *ideas* he thinks fit, and change them as often as he pleases. But yet when we will inquire what makes the same *spirit, man,* or *person,* we must fix the *ideas* of *spirit, man,* or *person* in our minds; and having resolved with ourselves what we mean by them, it will not be hard to determine in either of them or the like when it is the *same* and when not.

16.   But though the same immaterial substance or soul does not alone, wherever it be, and in whatsoever state, make the same man: yet, it is plain, consciousness, as far as ever it can be extended, should it be to ages past, unites existences and actions very remote in time into the same person, as well as it does the existence and actions of the immediately preceding moment, so that whatever has the consciousness of present and past actions is the same person to whom they both belong. Had I the same consciousness that I saw the ark and *Noah's* flood as that I saw an overflowing of the *Thames* last winter, or as that I write now, I could no more doubt that I that write this now, that saw the *Thames* overflowed last winter, and that viewed the flood at the general deluge, was the same *self*, place that *self* in what substance you please, than I that write this am the same *myself* now whilst I write (whether I consist of all the same substance, material or immaterial, or no) that I was yesterday. For as to this point of being the same *self*, it matters not whether this present *self* be made up of the same or other substances, I being as much concerned and as justly accountable for any action that was done a thousand years since, appropriated to me now by this self-consciousness, as I am for what I did the last moment.

17.   *Self* is that conscious thinking thing (whatever substance made up of, whether spiritual or material, simple or compounded, it matters not) which is sensible or conscious of pleasure and pain, capable of happiness or misery, and so is concerned for *itself*, as far as that consciousness extends. Thus everyone finds that, whilst comprehended under that consciousness, the little finger is as much as part of *itself* as what is most so. Upon separation of this little finger, should this consciousness go along with the little finger and leave the rest of the body, it is evident the little finger would be the *person*, the *same person*; and self then would have nothing to do with the rest of the body. As in this case it is the consciousness that goes along with the substance, when one part is separate from another, which makes the same *person* and constitutes this inseparable *self*: so it is in reference to substance remote in time. That with which the *consciousness* of this present thinking thing can join itself makes the same *person* and is one *self* with it, and with nothing else, and so attributes to *itself* and owns all the actions of that thing as its own, as far as that consciousness reaches, and no further; as everyone who reflects will perceive.

18.   In this *personal identity* is founded all the right and justice of reward and punishment: happiness and misery being that for which everyone is concerned for *himself*, not mattering what becomes of any substance not joined to or affected with that consciousness. For, as it is evident in the instance I gave but now, if the consciousness went along with the little finger when it was cut off, that would be the same *self* which was concerned for the whole body yesterday, as making part of *itself*, whose actions then it cannot but admit as its own now. Though, if the same body should still live and immediately from the separation of the little finger have its own peculiar consciousness, whereof the little finger knew nothing, it would not at all be concerned for it as a part of *itself*, or could own any of its actions, or have any of them imputed to him.

19.   This may show us wherein *personal identity* consists: not in the identity of substance but, as I have said, in the identity of *consciousness*, wherein, if *Socrates* and the present mayor of *Queenborough* agree, they are the same person; if the same *Socrates* waking and sleeping do not partake of the same *consciousness*, *Socrates* waking and sleeping is not the same person. And to punish *Socrates* waking for what sleeping *Socrates* thought, and waking *Socrates* was never conscious of, would be no more of right than to punish one twin for what his brother-twin did, whereof he knew nothing, because their outsides were so like that they could not be distinguished; for such twins have been seen.

20.   But yet possibly it will still be objected, suppose I wholly lose the memory of some parts of my life beyond a possibility of retrieving them, so that perhaps I shall never be conscious of them again: yet am I not the same person that did those actions, had those thoughts that I once was conscious of, though I have now forgot them? To which I answer that we must here take notice what the word *I* is applied to, which, in this case, is the man only. And the same man being presumed to be the same person, *I* is easily here supposed to stand also for the same person. But if it be possible for the same man to have distinct incommunicable consciousness at different times, it is past doubt the same man would at different times make different persons; which, we see, is the sense of mankind in the solemnest declaration of their opinions, human laws not punishing the *mad man* for the *sober man*'s actions, nor the *sober man* for what the

mad man did, thereby making them two persons: which is some-what explained by our way of speaking in *English* when we say such an one *is not himself*, or is *beside himself*; in which phrases it is insinuated, as if those who now, or at least first used them, thought that *self* was changed, the *self*-same person was no longer in that man.

21. But yet it is hard to conceive that *Socrates*, the same individual man, should be two persons. To help us a little in this, we must consider what is meant by *Socrates* or the same individual *man*.

First, it must be either the same individual, immaterial, thinking substance; in short, the same numerical soul, and nothing else.

Secondly, or the same animal, without any regard to an immaterial soul.

Thirdly, or the same immaterial spirit united to the same animal.

Now, take which of these suppositions you please, it is im-possible to make personal identity to consist in anything but consciousness, or reach any further than that does.

For, by the first of them, it must be allowed possible that a man born of different women, and in distant times, may be the same man. A way of speaking which, whoever admits, must allow it possible for the same man to be two distinct persons, as any two that have lived in different ages without the knowledge of one another's thoughts.

By the second and third, *Socrates*, in this life and after it, cannot be the same man any way but by the same conscious-ness; and so, making *human identity* to consist in the same thing wherein we place *personal identity*, there will be no difficulty to allow the same man to be the same person. But then they who place *human identity* in consciousness only, and not in some-thing else, must consider how they will make the infant *Socrates* the same man with *Socrates* after the resurrection. But whatso-ever to some men makes a *man*, and consequently the same individual man, wherein perhaps few are agreed, personal identity can by us be placed in nothing but consciousness (which is that alone which makes what we call *self*), without involving us in great absurdities.

22. But is not a man drunk and sober the same person, why else is he punished for the fact he commits when drunk, though

he be never afterwards conscious of it? Just as much the same person as a man that walks and does other things in his sleep is the same person and is answerable for any mischief he shall do in it. Human laws punish both, with a justice suitable to their way of knowledge; because, in these cases, they cannot distinguish certainly what is real, what counterfeit; and so the ignorance in drunkenness or sleep is not admitted as a plea. For, though punishment be annexed to personality, and personality to consciousness, and the drunkard perhaps be not conscious of what he did, yet human judicatures justly punish him, because the fact is proved against him, but want of consciousness cannot be proved for him. But in the Great Day, wherein the secrets of all hearts shall be laid open, it may be reasonable to think no one shall be made to answer for what he knows nothing of, but shall receive his doom, his conscience accusing or excusing him.

23. Nothing but consciousness can unite remote existences into the same person: the identity of substance will not do it; for whatever substance there is however framed, without consciousness there is no person; and a carcass may be a person, as well as any sort of substance be so, without consciousness.

Could we suppose two distinct incommunicable consciousnesses acting the same body, the one constantly by day, the other by night; and, on the other side, the same consciousness, acting by intervals, two distinct bodies: I ask, in the first case whether the *day-* and the *night-man* would not be two as distinct persons as *Socrates* and *Plato*? And whether, in the second case, there would not be one person in two distinct bodies, as much as one man is the same in two distinct clothings? Nor is it at all material to say that this same and this distinct *consciousness*, in the cases above mentioned, is owing to the same and distinct immaterial substances, bringing it with them to those bodies; which, whether true or no, alters not the case, since it is evident the *personal identity* would equally be determined by the consciousness, whether that consciousness were annexed to some individual immaterial substance or no. For, granting that the thinking substance in man must be necessarily supposed immaterial, it is evident that immaterial thinking thing may sometimes part with its past consciousness and be restored to it again, as appears in the forgetfulness men often have of their past actions; and the mind many times recovers the memory of a past consciousness, which it had lost for twenty years together. Make these intervals of memory and forgetfulness to take their turns regularly by day and night, and you have two persons with the same immaterial spirit, as much as in the former instance two persons with the same body. So that *self* is not determined by identity or diversity of substance, which it cannot be sure of, but only by identity of consciousness.

24. Indeed it may conceive the substance whereof it is now made up to have existed formerly, united in the same conscious being; but consciousness removed, that substance is no more *itself* or makes no more a part of it than any other substance, as is evident in the instance we have already given of a limb cut off, of whose heat or cold or other affections having no longer any consciousness, it is no more of a man's self than any other matter of the universe. In like manner it will be in reference to any immaterial substance which is void of that consciousness whereby I am my *self* to *myself*. If there be any part of its existence which I cannot upon recollection join with that present consciousness whereby I am now my *self*, it is in that part of its existence no more my *self* than any other immaterial being. For whatsoever any substance has thought or done, which I cannot recollect and by my consciousness make my own thought and action, it will no more belong to me, whether a part of me thought or did it, than if it had been thought or done by any other immaterial being anywhere existing.

25. I agree the more probable opinion is that this consciousness is annexed to and the affection of one individual immaterial substance.

But let men, according to their divers hypotheses, resolve of that as they please. This every intelligent being, sensible of happiness or misery, must grant: that there is something that is *himself* that he is concerned for and would have happy; that this *self* has existed in a continued duration more than one instant, and therefore it is possible may exist, as it has done, months and years to come, without any certain bounds to be set to its duration; and may be the same *self* by the same consciousness, continued on for the future. And thus, by this consciousness, he finds himself to be the *same self* which did such or such an action some years since, by which he comes to be happy or miserable now. In all which account of *self*, the same numerical substance is not considered as making the same *self*, but the same continued consciousness, in which several substances may have been united and again separated from it, which, whilst they continued in a vital union with that wherein this consciousness then resided, made a part of that same *self*. Thus any part of our bodies, vitally united to that which is conscious in us, makes a part of our *selves*; but upon separation from the vital union, by which that consciousness is communicated, that which a moment since was part of our *selves* is now no more so than a part of another man's *self* is a part of me; and it is not impossible but in a little time may become a real part of another person. And so we have the same numerical substance become a part of two different persons, and the same person preserved under the change of various substances. Could we suppose any spirit wholly stripped of all its memory or consciousness of past actions, as we find our minds always are of a great part of ours, and sometimes of them all, the union or separation of such a spiritual substance would make no variation of personal identity, any more than that of any particle of matter does. Any substance vitally united to the present thinking being is a part of that very *same self* which now is; anything united to it by a consciousness of former actions makes also a part of the *same self* which is the same both then and now.

26. *Person*, as I take it, is the name for this *self*. Wherever a man finds what he calls *himself*, there, I think, another may say is the *same person*. It is a forensic term, appropriating actions and their merit, and so belongs only to intelligent agents, capable of a law, and happiness and misery. This personality extends *itself* beyond present existence to what is past, only by consciousness; whereby it becomes concerned and accountable, owns and imputes to *itself* past actions, just upon the same ground and for the same reason that it does the present. All which is founded in a concern for happiness, the unavoidable concomitant of consciousness: that which is conscious of pleasure and pain desiring that that self that is conscious should be happy. And therefore whatever past actions it cannot reconcile or appropriate to that present *self* by consciousness, it can be no more concerned in than if they had never been done; and to receive pleasure or pain, i.e. reward or punishment, on the account of any such action, is all one as to be made happy or miserable in its first being, without any demerit at all. For supposing a man punished now for what he had done in another life, whereof he could be made to have no consciousness at all, what difference is

there between that punishment and being created miserable? And therefore conformable to this, the Apostle tells us, that at the Great Day, when everyone shall *receive according to his doings, the secrets of all hearts shall be laid open.* The sentence shall be justified by the consciousness all persons shall have that they *themselves,* in what bodies soever they appear, or what substances soever that consciousness adheres to, are the *same* that committed those actions and deserve that punishment for them.

27.   I am apt enough to think I have, in treating of this subject, made some suppositions that will look strange to some readers, and possibly they are so in themselves. But yet I think they are such as are pardonable in this ignorance we are in of the nature of that thinking thing that is in us and which we look on as our *selves.* Did we know what it was or how it was tied to a certain system of fleeting animal spirits, or whether it could or could not perform its operations of thinking and memory out of a body organized as ours is, and whether it has pleased God that no one such spirit shall ever be united to any but one such body, upon the right constitution of whose organs its memory should depend, we might see the absurdity of some of those suppositions I have made. But taking, as we ordinarily now do (in the dark concerning these matters), the soul of a man for an immaterial substance, independent from matter and indifferent alike to it all, there can from the nature of things be no absurdity at all to suppose that the same soul may at different times be united to different bodies and with them make up, for that time, one man: as well as we suppose a part of a sheep's body yesterday should be a part of a man's body tomorrow and in that union make a vital part of *Meliboeus* himself, as well as it did of his ram.

28.   To conclude: whatever substance begins to exist, it must during its existence necessarily be the same; whatever compositions of substances begin to exist during the union of those substances, the concrete must be the same; whatsoever mode begins to exist, during its existence it is the same; and so if the composition be of distinct substances and different modes, the same rule holds. Whereby it will appear that the difficulty or obscurity that has been about this matter rather rises from the names ill-used than from any obscurity in things themselves. For whatever makes the specific *idea* to which the name is

applied, if that *idea* be steadily kept to, the distinction of any-thing into the same and divers will easily be conceived, and there can arise no doubt about it.

29.   For supposing a rational spirit be the *idea* of a *man*, it is easy to know what is the *same man*, viz. the *same spirit*, whether separate or in a body, will be the *same man*.   Supposing a rational spirit vitally united to a body of a certain conformation of parts to make a *man*: whilst that rational spirit, with that vital conformation of parts, though continued in a fleeting successive body, remains, it will be the *same man*.   But if to anyone the *idea* of a *man* be but the vital union of parts in a certain shape: as long as that vital union and shape remains in a concrete, no otherwise the same but by a continued succession of fleeting particles, it will be the same *man*.   For whatever be the composi-tion whereof the complex *idea* is made, whenever existence makes it one particular thing under any denomination, the same existence continued preserves it the same individual under the same denomination.

Chapter XXVIII

OF OTHER RELATIONS

1.   Besides the before-mentioned occasions of time, place, and causality of comparing or referring things one to another, there are, as I have said, infinite others, some whereof I shall mention.

First, The first I shall name is some one simple *idea* which, being capable of parts or degrees, affords an occasion of com-paring the subjects wherein it is to one another, in respect of that simple *idea*, v.g. *whiter, sweeter, bigger, equal, more*, etc. These relations, depending on the equality and excess of the same simple *idea* in several subjects may be called, if one will, *proportional*; and that these are only conversant about those simple *ideas* received from sensation or reflection is so evident that nothing need be said to evince it.

2.   *Secondly*, Another occasion of comparing things together, or considering one thing so as to include in that consideration some other thing, is the circumstances of their origin or beginning; which, being not afterwards to be altered, make the relations

depending thereon as lasting as the subjects to which they
belong, v.g. *father* and *son, brothers, cousin-germans*, etc., which
have their relations by one community of blood, wherein they
partake in several degrees; *countrymen*, i.e. those who were born
in the same country or tract of ground; and these I call *natural
relations*, wherein we may observe that mankind have fitted
their notions and words to the use of common life and not to the
truth and extent of things. For it is certain that in reality the
relation is the same betwixt the begetter and the begotten in the
several races of other animals as well as men; but yet it is seldom
said this bull is the grandfather of such a calf, or that two
pigeons are cousin-germans. It is very convenient that by
distinct names these relations should be observed and marked
out in mankind, there being occasion, both in laws and other
communications one with another, to mention and take notice
of men under these relations; from whence also arise the
obligations of several duties amongst men; whereas in brutes,
men having very little or no cause to mind these relations, they
have not thought fit to give them distinct and peculiar names.
This, by the way, may give us some light into the different state
and growth of languages; which, being suited only to the convenience of communication, are proportioned to the notions men
have, and the commerce of thoughts familiar amongst them, and
not to the reality or extent of things, nor to the various respects
might be found among them, nor the different abstract considerations might be framed about them. Where they had no
philosophical notions, there they had no terms to express them;
and it is no wonder men should have framed no names for those
things they found no occasion to discourse of. From whence it
is easy to imagine why, as in some countries, they may not have
so much as the name for a horse, and in others, where they are
more careful of the pedigrees of their horses than of their own,
that there they may have not only names for particular horses
but also of their several relations of kindred one to another.

3. *Thirdly*, Sometimes the foundation of considering things,
with reference to one another, is some act whereby anyone
comes by a moral right, power, or obligation to do something.
Thus, a *general* is one that hath power to command an army;
and an army under a general is a collection of armed men obliged
to obey one man. A *citizen*, or a *burgher*, is one who has a right
to certain privileges in this or that place. All this sort depending

upon men's wills or agreement in society, I call *instituted* or *voluntary*, and may be distinguished from the natural in that they are most, if not all of them, some way or other alterable and separable from the persons to whom they have sometimes belonged, though neither of the substances so related be destroyed. Now, though these are all reciprocal, as well as the rest, and contain in them a reference of two things one to the other, yet, because one of the two things often wants a relative name importing that reference, men usually take no notice of it and the relation is commonly overlooked: v.g. a *patron* and *client* are easily allowed to be relations, but a *constable* or *dictator* are not so readily at first hearing considered as such, because there is no peculiar name for those who are under the command of a dictator or constable, expressing a relation to either of them, though it be certain that either of them hath a certain power over some others, and so is so far related to them as well as a patron is to his client or general to his army.

4. *Fourthly,* There is another sort of relation which is the conformity or disagreement men's voluntary actions have to a rule to which they are referred, and by which they are judged of; which, I think, may be called *moral relation,* as being that which denominates our moral actions, and deserves well to be examined, there being no part of knowledge wherein we should be more careful to get determined *ideas* and avoid, as much as may be, obscurity and confusion. Human actions, when with their various ends, objects, manners, and circumstances they are framed into distinct complex *ideas,* are, as has been shown, so many *mixed modes,* a great part whereof have names annexed to them. Thus, supposing gratitude to be a readiness to acknowledge and return kindness received, polygamy to be the having more wives than one at once: when we frame these notions thus in our minds, we have there so many determined *ideas* of mixed modes. But this is not all that concerns our actions; it is not enough to have determined *ideas* of them and to know what names belong to such and such combinations of *ideas.* We have a further and greater concernment, and that is to know whether such actions so made up are morally good or bad.

5. Good and evil, as hath been shown (Bk. II, chap. xx, § 2, and chap. xxi, § 42), are nothing but pleasure or pain, or that which occasions or procures pleasure or pain to us. *Morally good and evil,* then, is only the conformity or disagreement of our

voluntary actions to some law, whereby good or evil is drawn on us from the will and power of the law-maker; which good and evil, pleasure or pain, attending our observance or breach of the law by the decree of the law-maker, is that we call *reward* and *punishment*.

6.   Of these *moral rules* or laws to which men generally refer, and by which they judge of the rectitude or pravity of their actions, there seem to me to be *three sorts* with their three different enforcements or rewards and punishments. For since it would be utterly in vain to suppose a rule set to the free actions of man without annexing to it some enforcement of good and evil to determine his will, we must, wherever we suppose a law, suppose also some reward or punishment annexed to that law. It would be in vain for one intelligent being to set a rule to the actions of another if he had it not in his power to reward the compliance with and punish deviation from his rule by some good and evil that is not the natural product and consequence of the action itself. For that, being a natural convenience or inconvenience, would operate of itself without a law. This, if I mistake not, is the true nature of all *law*, properly so called.

7.   The laws that men generally refer their actions to, to judge of their rectitude or obliquity, seem to me to be these three: (1) The *divine* law. (2) The *civil* law. (3) The law of *opinion* or *reputation*, if I may so call it. By the relation they bear to the first of these, men judge whether their actions are sins or duties; by the second, whether they be criminal or innocent; and by the third, whether they be virtues or vices.

8.   *First*, The *divine* law, whereby I mean that law which God has set to the actions of men, whether promulgated to them by the light of nature or the voice of revelation. That God has given a rule whereby men should govern themselves, I think there is nobody so brutish as to deny. He has a right to do it, we are his creatures; he has goodness and wisdom to direct our actions to that which is best; and he has power to enforce it by rewards and punishments of infinite weight and duration in another life; for nobody can take us out of his hands. This is the only true touchstone of *moral rectitude*; and by comparing them to this law, it is that men judge of the most considerable *moral good* or *evil* of their actions: that is, whether, as *duties or sins*, they are like to procure them happiness or misery from the hands of the ALMIGHTY.

9. *Secondly,* The *civil* law, the rule set by the commonwealth to the actions of those who belong to it, is another rule to which men refer their actions, to judge whether they be *criminal* or no. This law nobody overlooks, the rewards and punishments that enforce it being ready at hand and suitable to the power that makes it; which is the force of the commonwealth, engaged to protect the lives, liberties, and possessions of those who live according to its laws, and has power to take away life, liberty, or goods from him who disobeys; which is the punishment of offences committed against this law.

10. *Thirdly,* The *law of opinion or reputation.* Virtue and vice are names pretended and supposed everywhere to stand for actions in their own nature right and wrong; and as far as they really are so applied, they so far are coincident with the *divine law* above mentioned. But yet, whatever is pretended, this is visible: that these names, *virtue* and *vice,* in the particular instances of their application, through the several nations and societies of men in the world, are constantly attributed only to such actions as in each country and society are in reputation or discredit. Nor is it to be thought strange that men everywhere should give the name of *virtue* to those actions which amongst them are judged praiseworthy, and call that *vice* which they account blamable: since otherwise they would condemn themselves, if they should think anything *right* to which they allowed not commendation, anything *wrong* which they let pass without blame. Thus the measure of what is everywhere called and esteemed *virtue* and *vice* is this approbation or dislike, praise or blame, which by a secret and tacit consent establishes itself in the several societies, tribes, and clubs of men in the world, whereby several actions come to find credit or disgrace amongst them according to the judgment, maxims, or fashions of that place. For though men, uniting into politic societies, have resigned up to the public the disposing of all their force, so that they cannot employ it against any fellow-citizen any further than the law of the country directs, yet they retain still the power of thinking well or ill, approving or disapproving of the actions of those whom they live amongst and converse with; and by this approbation and dislike they establish amongst themselves what they will call *virtue* and *vice.*

11. That this is the common *measure of virtue and vice* will appear to anyone who considers that, though that passes for

vice in one country which is counted a *virtue*, or at least not *vice*, in another, yet everywhere *virtue* and praise, *vice* and blame, go together. *Virtue* is everywhere that which is thought praise-worthy; and nothing else but that which has the allowance of public esteem is called *virtue*.[1] *Virtue* and praise are so united

[1] Our author, in his Preface to the 2nd Edition, taking notice how apt men have been to mistake him, added what here follows: Of this the ingenious author of the *Discourse concerning the Nature of Man* has given me a late instance, to mention no other. For the civility of his expressions and the candour that belongs to his order forbid me to think that he would have closed his Preface with an insinuation, as if in what I had said, Book II, Chapter xxviii, concerning the third rule which men refer their actions to, I went about to make *virtue vice*, and *vice virtue*, unless he had mis-taken my meaning; which he could not have done if he had but given himself the trouble to consider what the argument was I was then upon, and what was the chief design of that chapter, plainly enough set down in the fourth section and those following. For I was there not laying down moral rules, but showing the original and nature of moral *ideas*, and enumerating the rules men make use of in moral relations, whether those rules were true or false; and pursuant thereunto, I tell what has everywhere that denomination, which in the language of that place answers to *virtue* and *vice* in ours, which *alters not the nature of things*, though men generally do judge of and denominate their actions according to the esteem and fashion of the place or sect they are of.

If he had been at the pains to reflect on what I had said, B. I, c. iii, section 18, and in this present chapter, sections 13, 14, 15, and 20, he would have known what I think of the eternal and unalterable nature of right and wrong and what I call *virtue* and *vice*; and if he had observed that, in the place he quotes, I only report as matter of fact what others call *virtue* and *vice*, he would not have found it liable to any great exception. For I think I am not much out in saying that one of the rules made use of in the world for a ground or measure of a moral relation is that esteem and reputation which several sorts of actions find variously in the several societies of men, according to which they are there called *virtues* or *vices*; and whatever authority the learned Mr. *Lowde* places in his *old English dictionary*, I dare say it nowhere tells him (if I should appeal to it) that the same action is not in credit called and counted a *virtue* in one place which, being in disrepute, passes for and under the name of *vice* in another. The taking notice that men bestow the names of *virtue* and *vice* according to this rule of reputation is all I have done, or can be laid to my charge to have done, towards the making *vice virtue* and *virtue vice*. But the good man does well, and as becomes his calling, to be watchful in such points and to take the alarm, even at expressions which, standing alone by themselves, might sound ill and be suspected.

It is to this zeal, allowable in his function, that I forgive his citing as he does these words of mine in section 11 of this chapter (*The exhortations of inspired teachers have not feared to appeal to common repute, whatsoever things lovely, whatsoever things are of good report, if there be any virtue, if there be any praise*, etc., *Phil.* iv, 8) without taking notice of those immediately preceding, which introduce them and run thus: *Whereby in the corruption of manners, the true boundaries of the law of nature, which ought to be the rule of virtue and vice, were pretty well preserved. So that even the exhortations of inspired teachers*, etc. By which words and the rest of that section, it is plain that I brought that passage of St. *Paul* not to prove that the general measure of what men call *virtue* and *vice* throughout the world was the reputation and fashion of each particular society within itself, but to show that, though it were so, yet, for reasons I there give, men, in that way of denominating their actions, did not for the most part much vary from the law of nature, which is that standing and unalterable rule by which they ought to judge of the moral rectitude and pravity of their actions and accordingly denominate them *virtues* or *vices*. Had Mr. *Lowde* considered this, he would have found it little to his purpose to have quoted that passage in a sense I used it not and would, I imagine, have spared the explication he

that they are called often by the same name. *Sunt sua praemia laudi*, says *Virgil*; and so *Cicero*, *nihil habet natura praestantius, quam honestatem, quam laudem, quam dignitatem, quam decus,* which he tells you are all names for the same thing, *Tuscul. Quaest.*, lib. ii, 20. This is the language of the heathen philosophers who well understood wherein their notions of *virtue* and *vice* consisted. And though, perhaps, by the different temper, education, fashion, maxims, or interest of different sorts of men, it fell out that what was thought praiseworthy in one place escaped not censure in another, and so in different societies, *virtues* and *vices* were changed: yet as to the main, they for the most part kept the same everywhere. For since nothing can be more natural than to encourage with esteem and reputation that wherein everyone finds his advantage, and to blame and

---

subjoins to it as not very necessary. But I hope this Second Edition will give him satisfaction in the point, and that this matter is now so expressed as to show him there was no cause of scruple.

Though I am forced to differ from him in those apprehensions he has expressed in the latter end of his Preface concerning what I had said about *virtue* and *vice*, yet we are better agreed than he thinks in what he says in his third chapter, p. 78, concerning *natural inscription* and *innate notions*. I shall not deny him the privilege he claims, p. 52, to state the question as he pleases, especially when he states it so as to leave nothing in it contrary to what I have said: for, according to him, *innate notions being conditional things, depending upon the concurrence of several other circumstances in order to the soul's exerting them*, all that he says for *innate, imprinted, impressed notions* (for of *innate ideas* he says nothing at all) amounts at last only to this: that there are certain propositions which, though the soul from the beginning or when a man is born does not know, yet by *assistance from the outward senses and the help of some previous cultivation* it may afterwards come certainly to know the truth of; which is no more than what I have affirmed in my First Book. For I suppose by the *soul's* exerting them he means its beginning to know them, or else the *soul's exerting of notions* will be to me a very unintelligible expression; and I think at best is a very unfit one in this case, it misleading men's thoughts by an insinuation, as if these notions were in the mind before the *soul exerts them,* i.e. before they are known; whereas truly, before they are known, there is nothing of them in the mind but a capacity to know them, when the *concurrence of those circumstances*, which this ingenious author thinks necessary, *in order to the soul's exerting them*, brings them into our knowledge.

Page 52, I find him express it thus: *These natural notions are not so imprinted upon the soul as that they naturally and necessarily exert themselves (even in children and idiots) without any assistance from the outward senses or without the help of some previous cultivation.* Here he says: *they exert themselves,* as, p. 78, that the *soul exerts them.* When he has explained to himself or others what he means by the *soul's exerting innate notions* or *their exerting themselves,* and what that *previous cultivation* and *circumstances, in order* to their being *exerted,* are, he will, I suppose, find there is so little of controversy between him and me in the point, bating that he calls that *exerting of notions* which I in a more vulgar style call *knowing,* that I have reason to think he brought in my name upon this occasion only out of the pleasure he has to speak civilly of me, which I must gratefully acknowledge he has done everywhere he mentions me, not without conferring on me, as some others have done, a title I have no right to.

discountenance the contrary, it is no wonder that esteem and discredit, virtue and vice, should in a great measure everywhere correspond with the unchangeable rule of right and wrong, which the law of God hath established: there being nothing that so directly and visibly secures and advances the general good of mankind in this world as obedience to the laws he has set them, and nothing that breeds such mischiefs and confusion as the neglect of them. And therefore men, without renouncing all sense and reason and their own interest, which they are so constantly true to, could not generally mistake in placing their commendation and blame on that side that really deserved it not. Nay, even those men whose practice was otherwise failed not to give their approbation right, few being depraved to that degree as not to condemn at least in others the faults they themselves were guilty of: whereby even in the corruption of manners, the true boundaries of the law of nature, which ought to be the rule of virtue and vice, were pretty well preserved. So that even the exhortations of inspired teachers have not feared to appeal to common repute. *Whatsoever is lovely, whatsoever is of good report, if there be any virtue, if there be any praise,* etc. (Phil. iv, 8.)

12. If anyone shall imagine that I have forgot my own notion of a law, when I make *the law* whereby men judge *of virtue and vice* to be nothing else but the consent of private men, who have not authority enough to make a law, especially wanting that which is so necessary and essential to a law, a power to enforce it: I think I may say that he who imagines commendation and disgrace not to be strong motives on men to accommodate themselves to the opinions and rules of those with whom they converse seems little skilled in the nature or history of mankind, the greatest part whereof he shall find to govern themselves chiefly, if not solely, by this law of fashion; and so they do that which keeps them in reputation with their company, little regard the laws of God or the magistrate. The penalties that attend the breach of God's laws some, nay, perhaps most men seldom seriously reflect on; and amongst those that do, many, whilst they break the law, entertain thoughts of future reconciliation and making their peace for such breaches. And as to the punishments due from the laws of the commonwealth, they frequently flatter themselves with the hopes of impunity. But no man escapes the punishment of their censure and dislike who

offends against the fashion and opinion of the company he keeps and would recommend himself to. Nor is there one of ten thousand who is stiff and insensible enough to bear up under the constant dislike and condemnation of his own club. He must be of a strange and unusual constitution who can content himself to live in constant disgrace and disrepute with his own particular society. Solitude many men have sought and been reconciled to; but nobody that has the least thought or sense of a man about him can live in society under the constant dislike and ill opinion of his familiars and those he converses with. This is a burden too heavy for human sufferance, and he must be made up of irreconcilable contradictions who can take pleasure in company and yet be insensible of contempt and disgrace from his companions.

13.   These three then: *first*, the law of God; *secondly*, the law of politic societies; *thirdly*, the law of fashion or private censure, are those to which men variously compare their actions; and it is by their conformity to one of these laws that they take their measures when they would judge of their moral rectitude and denominate their actions good or bad.

14.   Whether the rule to which, as to a touchstone, we bring our voluntary actions to examine them by, and try their goodness, and accordingly to name them, which is, as it were, the mark of the value we set upon them: whether, I say, we take that rule from the fashion of the country or the will of a law-maker, the mind is easily able to observe the relation any action hath to it, and to judge whether the action agrees or disagrees with the rule, and so hath a notion of *moral goodness or evil*, which is either conformity or not conformity of any action to that rule, and therefore is often called moral rectitude. This rule being nothing but a collection of several simple *ideas*, the conformity thereto is but so ordering the action that the simple *ideas* belonging to it may correspond to those which the law requires. And thus we see how moral beings and notions are founded on and terminated in these simple *ideas* we have received from sensation or reflection. For example, let us consider the complex *idea* we signify by the word murder; and when we have taken it asunder and examined all the particulars, we shall find them to amount to a collection of simple *ideas* derived from reflection or sensation. Viz. *First*, from reflection on the operations of our own minds, we have the *ideas* of willing, considering, purposing

beforehand, malice, or wishing ill to another; and also of life, or perception, and self-motion. *Secondly*, from sensation we have the collection of those simple sensible *ideas* which are to be found in a man and of some action whereby we put an end to perception and motion in the man: all which simple *ideas* are comprehended in the word murder. This collection of simple *ideas* being found by me to agree or disagree with the esteem of the country I have been bred in, and to be held by most men there worthy praise or blame, I call the action virtuous or vicious; if I have the will of a supreme invisible law-maker for my rule, then, as I supposed the action commanded or forbidden by God, I call it good or evil, sin or duty; and if I compare it to the civil law, the rule made by the legislative of the country, I call it lawful or unlawful, a crime or no crime. So that whence-soever we take the rule of moral actions or by what standard soever we frame in our minds the *ideas* of virtues or vices, they consist only and are made up of collections of simple *ideas* which we originally received from sense or reflection, and their rectitude or obliquity consists in the agreement or disagreement with those patterns prescribed by some law.

15.   To conceive rightly of *moral actions*, we must take notice of them under this two-fold consideration. *First*, as they are in themselves, each made up of such a collection of simple *ideas*. Thus *drunkenness* or *lying* signify such or such a collection of simple *ideas*, which I call mixed modes; and in this sense they are as much *positive absolute ideas*, as the drinking of a horse, or speaking of a parrot. *Secondly*, our actions are considered as good, bad, *or* indifferent; and in this respect they are *relative*, it being their conformity to, or disagreement with, some rule that makes them to be regular or irregular, good or bad; and so, as far as they are compared with a rule, and thereupon denominated, they come under relation. Thus the challenging and fighting with a man, as it is a certain positive mode or particular sort of action, by particular *ideas* distinguished from all others, is called *duelling*: which, when considered in relation to the law of God, will deserve the name of sin; to the law of fashion, in some countries, valour and virtue; and to the municipal laws of some governments, a capital crime. In this case, when the positive mode has one name, and another name as it stands in relation to the law, the distinction may as easily be observed as

it is in substances, where one name, v.g. *man*, is used to signify the thing, another, v.g. *father*, to signify the relation.

16. But because very frequently the positive *idea* of the action and its moral relation are comprehended together under one name, and the same word made use of to express both the mode or action and its moral rectitude or obliquity, therefore the relation itself is less taken notice of; and there is often no *distinction* made *between the positive idea* of the action *and the reference it has to a rule*. By which confusion of these two distinct considerations under one term, those who yield too easily to the impressions of sounds and are forward to take names for things are often misled in their judgment of actions. Thus the taking from another what is his, without his knowledge or allowance, is properly called *stealing*; but that name being commonly understood to signify also the moral pravity of the action and to denote its contrariety to the law, men are apt to condemn whatever they hear called stealing as an ill action, disagreeing with the rule of right. And yet the private taking away his sword from a madman to prevent his doing mischief, though it be properly denominated *stealing*, as the name of such a *mixed mode*: yet when compared to the law of God and considered in its relation to that supreme rule, it is no sin or transgression, though the name *stealing* ordinarily carries such an intimation with it.

17. And thus much for the relation of human actions to a law, which therefore I call *moral relations*.

It would make a volume to go over all sorts of *relations*; it is not therefore to be expected that I should here mention them all. It suffices to our present purpose to show by these what the *ideas* are we have *of* this comprehensive consideration called *relation*; which is so *various* and the occasions of it so *many* (as many as there can be of comparing things one to another) that it is not very easy to reduce it to rules or under just heads. Those I have mentioned, I think, are some of the most considerable and such as may serve to let us see from whence we get our *ideas* of relations and wherein they are founded. But before I quit this argument, from what has been said, give me leave to observe:

18. *First*, That it is evident that *all relation terminates in* and is ultimately founded on those *simple ideas* we have *got from*

sensation or reflection, so that all we have in our thoughts ourselves (if we think of anything or have any meaning) or would
signify to others, when we use words standing for relations, is
nothing but some simple *ideas*, or collections of simple *ideas*,
compared one with another. This is so manifest in that sort
called *proportional* that nothing can be more. For when a man
says honey is sweeter than wax, it is plain that his thoughts in
this relation terminate in this simple *idea*, sweetness; which is
equally true of all the rest: though, where they are compounded
or decompounded, the simple *ideas* they are made up of are
perhaps seldom taken notice of: v.g. when the word father is
mentioned: *first*, there is meant that particular species or collective *idea* signified by the word man; *secondly*, those sensible
simple *ideas* signified by the word generation; and *thirdly*, the
effects of it and all the simple *ideas* signified by the word child.
So the word friend, being taken for a man who loves and is
ready to do good to another, has all those following *ideas* to the
making of it up. *First*, all the simple *ideas* comprehended in the
word man or intelligent being. *Secondly*, the *idea* of love.
Thirdly, the *idea* of readiness or disposition. *Fourthly*, the *idea*
of action, which is any kind of thought or motion. *Fifthly*, the
idea of good, which signifies anything that may advance his
happiness; and terminates at last, if examined, in particular
simple *ideas* of which the word *good* in general signifies any one,
but if removed from all simple *ideas* quite, it signifies nothing at
all. And thus also all moral words terminate at last, though
perhaps more remotely, in a collection of simple *ideas*: the
immediate signification of relative words being very often other
supposed known relations, which, if traced one to another, still
end in simple *ideas*.

19.   *Secondly*, That in relations we have for the most part, if
not always, *as clear a notion of the relation as we have of those
simple* ideas *wherein it is founded*: agreement or disagreement,
whereon relation depends, being things whereof we have commonly as clear *ideas* as of any other whatsoever: it being but the
distinguishing simple *ideas* or their degrees one from another
without which we could have no distinct knowledge at all.
For, if I have a clear *idea* of sweetness, light, or extension, I have,
too, of equal or more or less of each of these; if I know what it is
for one man to be born of a woman, viz. *Sempronia*, I know what
it is for another man to be born of the same woman, *Sempronia*,

and so have as clear a notion of brothers as of births, and perhaps clearer. For if I believed that *Sempronia* digged *Titus* out of the parsley-bed (as they used to tell children) and thereby became his mother, and that afterwards in the same manner she digged *Caius* out of the parsley-bed, I had as clear a notion of the relation of brothers between them, as if I had all the skill of a midwife: the notion that the same woman contributed, as mother, equally to their births (though I were ignorant or mistaken in the manner of it) being that on which I grounded the relation, and that they agreed in that circumstance of birth, let it be what it will. The comparing them then in their descent from the same person, without knowing the particular circumstances of that descent, is enough to found my notion of their having or not having the relation of brothers. But though the *ideas* of particular *relations* are capable of being as clear and distinct in the minds of those who will duly consider them as those of mixed modes, and more determinate than those of substances: yet, the names belonging to *relation* are often of as doubtful and uncertain signification as those of substances or mixed modes, and much more than those of simple *ideas*. Because relative words being the marks of this comparison, which is made only by men's thoughts and is an *idea* only in men's minds, men frequently apply them to different comparisons of things according to their own imaginations; which do not always correspond with those of others using the same names.

20. *Thirdly,* That in these I call *moral relations*, I have a true notion of relation by comparing the action with the rule, whether the rule be true or false. For if I measure anything by a yard, I know whether the thing I measure be longer or shorter than that supposed yard, though, perhaps, the yard I measure by be not exactly the standard: which, indeed, is another inquiry. For though the rule be erroneous and I mistaken in it, yet the agreement or disagreement observable in that which I compare with it makes me perceive the relation. Though measuring by a wrong rule, I shall thereby be brought to judge amiss of its moral rectitude, because I have tried it by that which is not the true rule; but I am not mistaken in the relation which that action bears to that rule I compare it to, which is agreement or disagreement.

Chapter XXIX

OF CLEAR AND OBSCURE, DISTINCT AND CONFUSED IDEAS

1. HAVING shown the original of our *ideas* and taken a view of
their several sorts; considered the difference between the simple
and the complex, and observed how the complex ones are
divided into those of modes, substances, and relations: all which,
I think, is necessary to be done by anyone who would acquaint
himself thoroughly with the progress of the mind in its apprehension and knowledge of things: it will, perhaps, be thought
I have dwelt long enough upon the examination of *ideas*. I
must, nevertheless, crave leave to offer some few other considerations concerning them. The first is that some are *clear* and
others *obscure*, some *distinct* and others *confused*.

2. The perception of the mind being most aptly explained by
words relating to the sight, we shall best understand what is
meant by *clear* and *obscure* in our *ideas* by reflecting on what we
call *clear* and *obscure* in the objects of sight. Light being that
which discovers to us visible objects, we give the name of *obscure*
to that which is not placed in a light sufficient to discover
minutely to us the figure and colours which are observable in it,
and which, in a better light, would be discernible. In like
manner, our *simple ideas* are *clear*, when they are such as the
objects themselves from whence they were taken did or might,
in a well-ordered sensation or perception, present them. Whilst
the memory retains them thus and can produce them to the
mind whenever it has occasion to consider them, they are *clear
ideas*. So far as they either want anything of the original exactness, or have lost any of their first freshness and are, as it were,
faded or tarnished by time, so far are they *obscure*. *Complex
ideas*, as they are made up of simple ones, so they are *clear*, when
the *ideas* that go to their composition are clear; and the number
and order of those simple *ideas* that are the ingredients of any
complex one is determinate and certain.

3. The *cause* of *obscurity*, in simple *ideas*, seems to be either
dull organs, or very slight and transient impressions made by
the objects, or else a weakness in the memory, not able to retain

them as received. For to return again to visible objects, to help us to apprehend this matter: if the organs or faculties of perception, like wax over-hardened with cold, will not receive the impression of the seal from the usual impulse wont to imprint it; or, like wax of a temper too soft, will not hold it well, when well imprinted; or else supposing the wax of a temper fit, but the seal not applied with a sufficient force to make a clear impression: in any of these cases, the print left by the seal will be *obscure*. This, I suppose, needs no application to make it plainer.

4. As a *clear idea* is that whereof the mind has such a full and evident perception as it does receive from an outward object operating duly on a well-disposed organ, so a *distinct idea* is that wherein the mind perceives a difference from all other; and a *confused idea* is such an one as is not sufficiently distinguishable from another, from which it ought to be different.

5. If no *idea* be *confused* but such as is not sufficiently distinguishable from another, from which it should be different, it will be hard, may anyone say, to find anywhere a *confused idea*. For let any *idea* be as it will, it can be no other but such as the mind perceives it to be; and that very perception sufficiently distinguishes it from all other *ideas* which cannot be other, i.e. different, without being perceived to be so. No *idea* therefore can be indistinguishable from another from which it ought to be different, unless you would have it different from itself: for from all other it is evidently different.

6. To remove this difficulty, and to help us to conceive aright what it is that makes the *confusion ideas* are at any time chargeable with, we must consider that things ranked under distinct names are supposed different enough to be distinguished, that so each sort, by its peculiar name, may be marked and discoursed of apart upon any occasion. And there is nothing more evident than that the greatest part of different names are supposed to stand for different things. Now every *idea* a man has being visibly what it is and distinct from all other *ideas* but itself, that which makes it *confused* is, when it is such, that it may as well be called by another name as that which it is expressed by: the difference which keeps the things (to be ranked under those two different names) distinct, and makes some of them belong rather to the one and some of them to the other of those names, being left out, and so the distinction which

was intended to be kept up by those different names is quite lost.

7.   The *defaults which* usually *occasion* this *confusion,* I think, are chiefly these following:

First, When any complex *idea* (for it is complex *ideas* that are most liable to confusion) is made up of *too small a number of simple ideas,* and such only as are common to other things, whereby the differences that make it deserve a different name are left out. Thus, he that has an *idea* made up of barely the simple ones of a beast with spots has but a confused *idea* of a leopard, it not being thereby sufficiently distinguished from a lynx and several other sorts of beasts that are spotted. So that such an *idea,* though it hath the peculiar name leopard, is not distinguishable from those designed by the names lynx or panther, and may as well come under the name lynx as leopard. How much the custom of defining words by general terms contributes to make the *ideas* we would express by them confused and undetermined, I leave others to consider. This is evident, that confused *ideas* are such as render the use of words uncertain and take away the benefit of distinct names. When the *ideas* for which we use different terms have not a difference answerable to their distinct names and so cannot be distinguished by them, there it is that they are truly confused.

8.   *Secondly,* Another default which makes our *ideas* confused is when, though the particulars that make up any *idea* are in number enough, yet they are so *jumbled together* that it is not easily discernible whether it more belongs to the name that is given it than to any other. There is nothing more proper to make us conceive this confusion than a sort of pictures usually shown as surprising pieces of art, wherein the colours, as they are laid by the pencil on the table itself, mark out very odd and unusual figures and have no discernible order in their position. This draught thus made up of parts wherein no symmetry nor order appears is, in itself, no more a confused thing than the picture of a cloudy sky wherein, though there be as little order of colours or figures to be found, yet nobody thinks it a confused picture. What is it then that makes it be thought confused, since the want of symmetry does not? As it is plain it does not; for another draught made, barely in imitation of this, could not be called confused. I answer, that which makes it be thought confused is the applying it to some name to which it does no more discernibly belong than to some other. V.g.: When it is

said to be the picture of a man, or *Caesar*, then anyone with reason counts it confused; because it is not discernible in that state to belong more to the name man or *Caesar* than to the name baboon or *Pompey*, which are supposed to stand for different *ideas* from those signified by man or *Caesar*. But when a cylindrical mirror, placed right, hath reduced those irregular lines on the table into their due order and proportion, then the confusion ceases and the eye presently sees that it is a man or *Caesar*, i.e. that it belongs to those names and that it is sufficiently distinguishable from a baboon or *Pompey*, i.e. from the *ideas* signified by those names. Just thus it is with our *ideas* which are, as it were, the pictures of things. No one of these mental draughts, however the parts are put together, can be called confused (for they are plainly discernible as they are) till it be ranked under some ordinary name, to which it cannot be discerned to belong any more than it does to some other name of an allowed different signification.

9.   *Thirdly*, A third defect that frequently gives the name of confused to our *ideas* is when any one of them is *uncertain and undetermined*. Thus we may observe men who, not forbearing to use the ordinary words of their language till they have learned their precise signification, change the *idea* they make this or that term stand for almost as often as they use it. He that does this out of uncertainty of what he should leave out or put into his *idea* of *church* or *idolatry* every time he thinks of either, and holds not steady to any one precise combination of *ideas* that makes it up, is said to have a confused *idea* of idolatry or the church: though this be still for the same reason that the former, viz. because a mutable *idea* (if we will allow it to be one *idea*) cannot belong to one name rather than another, and so loses the distinction that distinct names are designed for.

10.   By what has been said, we may observe how much *names*, as supposed steady signs of things, and by their difference to stand for and keep things distinct that in themselves are different, are the *occasion of denominating* ideas *distinct or confused*, by a secret and unobserved reference the mind makes of its *ideas* to such names. This, perhaps, will be fuller understood after what I say of words in the Third Book has been read and considered. But without taking notice of such a reference of *ideas* to distinct names, as the signs of distinct things, it will be hard to say what a *confused idea* is. And therefore when a man

designs by any name a sort of things or any one particular thing, distinct from all others, the complex *idea* he annexes to that name is the more distinct, the more particular the *ideas* are, and the greater and more determinate the number and order of them is whereof it is made up. For the more it has of these, the more has it still of the perceivable differences whereby it is kept separate and distinct from all *ideas* belonging to other names, even those that approach nearest to it, and thereby all confusion with them is avoided.

11.   *Confusion*, making it a difficulty to separate two things that should be separated, *concerns always two ideas*, and those most which most approach one another. Whenever, therefore, we suspect any *idea* to be *confused*, we must examine what other it is in danger to be confounded with, or which it cannot easily be separated from; and that will always be found an *idea* belonging to another name, and so should be a different thing, from which yet it is not sufficiently distinct: being either the same with it, or making a part of it, or at least as properly called by that name as the other it is ranked under, and so keeps not that difference from that other *idea* which the different names import.

12.   This, I think, is the *confusion* proper to *ideas*; which still carries with it a secret reference to names. At least, if there be any other confusion of *ideas*, this is that which most of all disorders men's thoughts and discourses: *ideas* as ranked under names being those that for the most part men reason of within themselves and always those which they commune about with others. And therefore where there are supposed two different *ideas* marked by two different names, which are not as distinguishable as the sounds that stand for them, there never fails to be *confusion*; and where any *ideas* are distinct as the *ideas* of those two sounds they are marked by, there can be between them no confusion. The way to prevent it is to collect and unite into our complex *idea* as precisely as is possible all those ingredients whereby it is differenced from others, and to them so united in a determinate number and order apply steadily the same name. But this neither accommodating men's ease or vanity or serving any design but that of naked truth, which is not always the thing aimed at, such exactness is rather to be wished than hoped for. And since the loose application of names to undetermined, variable, and almost no *ideas* serves both to cover our own ignorance as well as to perplex and confound others, which goes

for learning and superiority in knowledge, it is no wonder that most men should use it themselves, whilst they complain of it in others. Though, I think, no small part of the *confusion* to be found in the notions of men might by care and ingenuity be avoided, yet I am far from concluding it everywhere wilful. Some *ideas* are so complex and made up of so many parts that the memory does not easily retain the very same precise combination of simple *ideas* under one name; much less are we able constantly to divine for what precise complex *idea* such a name stands in another man's use of it. From the first of these follows *confusion* in a man's own reasonings and opinions within himself; from the latter, frequent *confusion* in discoursing and arguing with others. But having more at large treated of words, their defects and abuses in the following book, I shall here say no more of it.

13.   Our *complex ideas*, being made up of collections, and so variety of simple ones, *may* accordingly *be very clear and distinct in one part, and very obscure and confused in another*. In a man who speaks of a *chiliahedron*, or a body of a thousand sides, the *idea* of the figure may be very confused, though that of the number be very distinct: so that he being able to discourse and demonstrate concerning that part of his complex *idea* which depends upon the number of a thousand, he is apt to think he has a distinct *idea* of a *chiliahedron*, though it be plain he has no precise *idea* of its figure so as to distinguish it, by that, from one that has but 999 sides; the not observing whereof causes no small error in men's thoughts and confusion in their discourses.

14.   He that thinks he has a distinct *idea* of the figure of a *chiliahedron*, let him for trial's sake take another parcel of the same uniform matter, viz. gold or wax, of an equal bulk, and make it into a figure of 999 sides. He will, I doubt not, be able to distinguish these two *ideas* one from another by the number of sides, and reason and argue distinctly about them, whilst he keeps his thoughts and reasoning to that part only of these *ideas* which is contained in their numbers: as that the sides of the one could be divided into two equal numbers; and of the other, not, etc. But when he goes about to distinguish them by their figure, he will there be presently at a loss and not be able, I think, to frame in his mind two *ideas*, one of them distinct from the other, by the bare figure of these two pieces of gold, as he could if the same parcels of gold were made one into a cube, the

other a figure of five sides. In which incomplete *ideas* we are very apt to impose on ourselves and wrangle with others, especially where they have particular and familiar names. For being satisfied in that part of the *idea* which we have clear, and the name which is familiar to us being applied to the whole containing that part also which is imperfect and obscure, we are apt to use it for that confused part and draw deductions from it in the obscure part of its signification, as confidently as we do from the other.

15. Having frequently in our mouths the name *eternity*, we are apt to think we have a positive comprehensive *idea* of it, which is as much as to say that there is no part of that duration which is not clearly contained in our *idea*. It is true that he that thinks so may have a clear *idea* of duration; he may also have a clear *idea* of a very great length of duration; he may also have a clear *idea* of the comparison of that great one with still a greater; but it not being possible for him to include in his *idea* of any duration, let it be as great as it will, the whole extent together of a duration where he supposes no end, that part of his *idea* which is still beyond the bounds of that large duration he represents to his own thoughts is very obscure and undetermined. And hence it is that in disputes and reasonings concerning eternity, or any other *infinite*, we are apt to blunder and involve ourselves in manifest absurdities.

16. In matter, we have no clear *ideas* of the smallness of parts much beyond the smallest that occur to any of our senses; and therefore, when we talk of the divisibility of matter *in infinitum*, though we have clear *ideas* of division and divisibility and have also clear *ideas* of parts made out of a whole by division, yet we have but very obscure and confused *ideas* of corpuscles or minute bodies so to be divided, when, by former divisions, they are reduced to a smallness much exceeding the perception of any of our senses; and so all that we have clear and distinct *ideas* of is of what division in general or abstractly is, and the relation of *totum* and *pars*; but of the bulk of the body to be thus infinitely divided after certain progressions, I think we have no clear nor distinct *idea* at all. For I ask anyone whether, taking the smallest atom of dust he ever saw, he has any distinct *idea* (bating still the number which concerns not extension) betwixt the 100,000th and the 1,000,000th part of it. Or if he thinks he can refine his *ideas* to that degree without losing sight of

them, let him add ten cyphers to each of those numbers. Such a degree of smallness is not unreasonable to be supposed, since a division carried on so far brings it no nearer the end of infinite division than the first division into two halves does. I must confess, for my part I have no clear distinct *ideas* of the different bulk or extension of those bodies, having but a very obscure one of either of them. So that, I think, when we talk of division of bodies *in infinitum*, our *idea* of their distinct bulks, which is the subject and foundation of division, comes, after a little progression, to be confounded and almost lost in obscurity. For that *idea* which is to represent only bigness must be very obscure and confused, which we cannot distinguish from one ten times as big but only by number: so that we have clear, distinct *ideas* we may say of ten and one, but no distinct *idea* of two such extensions. It is plain from hence that, when we talk of infinite divisibility of body or extension, our distinct and clear *ideas* are only of numbers: but the clear, distinct *ideas* of extension, after some progress of division, are quite lost; and of such minute parts we have no distinct *ideas* at all; but it returns, as all our *ideas* of infinite do, at last to that of number always to be added, but thereby never amounts to any distinct *idea* of actual, infinite parts. We have, it is true, a clear *idea* of division as often as we will think of it; but thereby we have no more a clear *idea* of infinite parts in matter than we have a clear *idea* of an infinite number by being able still to add new numbers to any assigned number we have: endless divisibility giving us no more a clear and distinct *idea* of actually infinite parts than endless addibility (if I may so speak) gives us a clear and distinct *idea* of an actually infinite number, they both being only in a power still of increasing the number, be it already as great as it will. So that of what remains to be added (wherein consists the infinity) we have but an obscure, imperfect, and confused *idea*, from or about which we can argue or reason with no certainty or clearness, no more than we can in arithmetic about a number of which we have no such distinct *idea*, as we have of 4 or 100, but only this relative obscure one: that compared to any other, it is still bigger; and we have no more a clear, positive *idea* of it, when we say or conceive it is bigger or more than 400,000,000 than if we should say, it is bigger than 40 or 4: 400,000,000 having no nearer a proportion to the end of addition or number than 4. For he that adds only 4 to 4, and so proceeds, shall as

soon come to the end of all addition as he that adds 400,000,000
to 400,000,000. And so likewise in eternity, he that has an *idea*
of but four years has as much a positive complete *idea* of eternity
as he that has one of 400,000,000 of years: for what remains of
eternity beyond either of these two numbers of years is as clear
to the one as the other, i.e. neither of them has any clear,
positive *idea* of it at all. For he that adds only 4 years to 4, and
so on, shall as soon reach eternity as he that adds 400,000,000 of
years and so on, or, if he please, doubles the increase as often as
he will: the remaining abyss being still as far beyond the end of
all these progressions as it is from the length of a day or an
hour. For nothing finite bears any proportion to infinite; and
therefore our *ideas*, which are all finite, cannot bear any. Thus
it is also in our *idea* of *extension*, when we increase it by addition,
as well as when we diminish it by division, and would enlarge
our thoughts to infinite space. After a few doublings of those
ideas of extension, which are the largest we are accustomed to
have, we lose the clear distinct *idea* of that space; it becomes a
confusedly great one with a surplus of still greater, about which,
when we would argue or reason, we shall always find ourselves
at a loss: confused *ideas* in our arguings, and deductions from
that part of them which is confused, always leading us into
confusion.

Chapter XXX

OF REAL AND FANTASTICAL IDEAS

1. BESIDES what we have already mentioned concerning *ideas*,
other considerations belong to them in reference to things from
whence they are taken, or which they may be supposed to
represent; and thus, I think, they may come under a threefold
distinction, and are:

First, either real or fantastical;

Secondly, adequate or inadequate;

Thirdly, true or false.

First, By *real ideas*, I mean such as have a foundation in
nature, such as have a conformity with the real being and
existence of things, or with their archetypes. *Fantastical or*

chimerical I call such as have no foundation in nature, nor have any conformity with that reality of being to which they are tacitly referred, as to their archetypes. If we examine the several sorts of *ideas* before-mentioned, we shall find that:

2. *First,* Our *simple* ideas *are all real*, all agree to the reality of things, not that they are all of them the images or representations of what does exist; the contrary whereof, in all but the primary qualities of bodies, hath been already shown. But, though whiteness and coldness are no more in snow than pain is, yet those *ideas* of whiteness and coldness, pain, etc., being in us the effects of powers in things without us, ordained by our Maker to produce in us such sensations, they are real *ideas* in us whereby we distinguish the qualities that are really in things themselves. For these several appearances being designed to be the marks whereby we are to know and distinguish things which we have to do with, our *ideas* do as well serve us to that purpose and are as real distinguishing characters, whether they be only constant effects or else exact resemblances of something in the things themselves: the reality lying in that steady correspondence they have with the distinct constitutions of real beings. But whether they answer to those constitutions, as to causes or patterns, it matters not: it suffices that they are constantly produced by them. And thus our simple *ideas* are all real and true, because they answer and agree to those powers of things which produce them in our minds, that being all that is requisite to make them real and not fictions at pleasure. For in simple *ideas* (as has been shown) the mind is wholly confined to the operation of things upon it, and can make to itself no simple *idea* more than what it has received.

3. Though the mind be wholly passive in respect of its simple *ideas,* yet, I think, we may say it is not so in respect of its complex *ideas;* for those being combinations of simple *ideas* put together and united under one general name, it is plain that the mind of man uses some kind of liberty in forming those complex *ideas:* how else comes it to pass that one man's *idea* of gold or justice is different from another's but because he has put in or left out of his, some simple *idea* which the other has not? The question then is which of these are real and which barely imaginary combinations? What collections agree to the reality of things and what not? And to this I say that:

4. *Secondly, Mixed modes and relations* having no other *reality*

but what they have in the minds of men, there is nothing more
required to this kind of *ideas* to make them *real*, but that they be
so framed that there be a possibility of existing conformable to
them. These *ideas*, being themselves archetypes, cannot differ
from their archetypes and so *cannot be chimerical*, unless anyone
will jumble together in them inconsistent *ideas*. Indeed, as any
of them have the names of a known language assigned to them,
by which he that has them in his mind would signify them to
others, so bare possibility of existing is not enough: they must
have a conformity to the ordinary signification of the name that
is given them, that they may not be thought fantastical, as if a
man would give the name of justice to that *idea* which common
use calls liberality. But this fantasticalness relates more to
propriety of speech than reality of *ideas*; for a man to be undisturbed in danger, sedately to consider what is fittest to be
done, and to execute it steadily is a mixed mode or a complex
idea of an action which may exist. But to be undisturbed in
danger, without using one's reason or industry, is what is also
possible to be, and so is as real an *idea* as the other. Though the
first of these, having the name *courage* given to it, may in respect
of that name be a right or wrong *idea*; but the other, whilst it
has not a common received name of any known language assigned
to it, is not capable of any deformity, being made with no
reference to anything but itself.

5.   *Thirdly*, Our *complex* ideas *of substances*, being made all of
them in reference to things existing without us, and intended
to be representations of substances as they really are, are no
further *real* than as they are such combinations of simple *ideas*
as are really united and co-exist in things without us. On the
contrary, those are *fantastical* which are made up of such collections of simple *ideas* as were really never united, never were
found together in any substance: v.g. a rational creature, consisting of a horse's head, joined to a body of human shape, or
such as the *centaurs* are described; or a body yellow, very
malleable, fusible, and fixed, but lighter than common water;
or an uniform, unorganized body, consisting, as to sense, all of
similar parts, with perception and voluntary motion joined to it.
Whether such substances as these can possibly exist or no, it is
probable we do not know; but, be that as it will, these *ideas* of
substances being made conformable to no pattern existing that
we know, and consisting of such collections of *ideas* as no

substance ever showed us united together, they ought to pass with us for barely imaginary; but much more are those complex *ideas* so, which contain in them any inconsistency or contradiction of their parts.

CHAPTER XXXI

OF ADEQUATE AND INADEQUATE IDEAS

1. OF our real *ideas*, some are adequate, and some are inadequate. Those I call *adequate* which perfectly represent those archetypes which the mind supposes them taken from, which it intends them to stand for, and to which it refers them. *Inadequate ideas* are such which are but a partial or incomplete representation of those archetypes to which they are referred. Upon which account it is plain,

2. *First*, That *all our simple* ideas *are adequate*. Because, being nothing but the effects of certain powers in things, fitted and ordained by GOD to produce such sensations in us, they cannot but be correspondent and adequate to those powers; and we are sure they agree to the reality of things. For, if sugar produce n us the *ideas* which we call whiteness and sweetness, we are sure there is a power in sugar to produce those *ideas* in our minds, or else they could not have been produced by it. And so each sensation answering the power that operates on any of our senses, the *idea* so produced is a real *idea* (and not a fiction of the mind, which has no power to produce any simple *idea*) and cannot but be adequate, since it ought only to answer that power; and so all simple *ideas* are adequate. It is true, the things producing in us these simple *ideas* are but few of them denominated by us as if they were only the causes of them, but as if those *ideas* were real beings in them. For though fire be called painful to the touch, whereby is signified the power of producing in us the *idea* of pain, yet it is denominated also light and hot, as if light and heat were really something in the fire, more than a power to excite these *ideas* in us, and therefore are called *qualities* in or of the fire. But these being nothing, in truth, but powers to excite such *ideas* in us, I must in that sense be understood when I speak of secondary *qualities* as being in

things, or of their *ideas* as being in the objects that excite them in us. Such ways of speaking, though accommodated to the vulgar notions without which one cannot be well understood, yet truly signify nothing but those powers which are in things to excite certain sensations or *ideas* in us: since, were there no fit organs to receive the impressions fire makes on the sight and touch, nor a mind joined to those organs to receive the *ideas* of light and heat by those impressions from the fire or the sun, there would yet be no more light or heat in the world than there would be pain if there were no sensible creature to feel it, though the sun should continue just as it is now, and Mount *Aetna* flame higher than ever it did. Solidity and extension and the termination of it, figure, with motion and rest, whereof we have the *ideas*, would be really in the world as they are whether there were any sensible being to perceive them or no, and therefore those we have reason to look on as the real modifications of matter, and such as are the exciting causes of all our various sensations from bodies. But this being an inquiry not belonging to this place, I shall enter no further into it, but proceed to show what complex *ideas* are *adequate* and what not.

3.   *Secondly,* Our *complex* ideas *of modes*, being voluntary collections of simple *ideas*, which the mind puts together without reference to any real archetypes or standing patterns existing anywhere, *are* and cannot but be *adequate ideas*. Because they, not being intended for copies of things really existing, but for archetypes made by the mind to rank and denominate things by, cannot want anything: they having each of them that combination of *ideas* and thereby that perfection which the mind intended they should, so that the mind acquiesces in them and can find nothing wanting. Thus, by having the *idea* of a figure with three sides meeting at three angles, I have a complete *idea* wherein I require nothing else to make it perfect. That the mind is satisfied with the perfection of this its *idea* is plain, in that it does not conceive that any understanding hath, or can have, a more complete or perfect *idea* of that thing it signifies by the word *triangle*, supposing it to exist, than itself has in that complex *idea* of three sides and three angles, in which is contained all that is or can be essential to it or necessary to complete it, wherever or however it exists. But in our *ideas* of *substances* it is otherwise. For there, desiring to copy things as they really do exist, and to represent to ourselves that constitution on which

all their properties depend, we perceive our *ideas* attain not that perfection we intend: we find they still want something we should be glad were in them, and so are all *inadequate*, But *mixed modes* and *relations*, being archetypes without patterns, and so having nothing to represent but themselves, cannot but be adequate, everything being so to itself. He that at first put together the *idea* of danger perceived, absence of disorder from fear, sedate consideration of what was justly to be done, and executing that without disturbance or being deterred by the danger of it, had certainly in his mind that complex *idea* made up of that combination; and intending it to be nothing else but what it is, nor to have in it any other simple *ideas* but what it hath, it could not also but be an *adequate idea*; and laying this up in his memory, with the name *courage* annexed to it to signify it to others, and denominate from thence any action he should observe to agree with it, had thereby a standard to measure and denominate actions by, as they agreed to it. This *idea*, thus made and laid up for a pattern, must necessarily be *adequate*, being referred to nothing else but itself, nor made by any other original but the good-liking and will of him that first made this combination.

4. Indeed another, coming after and in conversation learning from him the word *courage*, may make an *idea*, to which he gives that name *courage*, different from what the first author applied it to and has in his mind when he uses it. And in this case, if he designs that his *idea* in thinking should be conformable to the other's *idea*, as the name he uses in speaking is conformable in sound to his from whom he learned it, his *idea* may be very wrong and *inadequate*. Because in this case, making the other man's *idea* the pattern of his *idea* in thinking, as the other man's word or sound is the pattern of his in speaking, his *idea* is so far defective and *inadequate* as it is distant from the archetype and pattern he refers it to and intends to express and signify by the name he uses for it, which name he would have to be a sign of the other man's *idea* (to which, in its proper use, it is primarily annexed) and of his own, as agreeing to it: to which, if his own does not exactly correspond, it is faulty and inadequate.

5. Therefore these *complex* ideas *of modes*, when they are referred by the mind and intended to correspond to the *ideas* in the mind of some other intelligent being, expressed by the names we apply to them, they *may be* very deficient, wrong, and

inadequate, because they agree not to that which the mind designs to be their archetype and pattern: in which respect only any *idea* of *modes* can be wrong, imperfect, or *inadequate*. And on this account our *ideas* of *mixed modes* are the most liable to be faulty of any other; but this refers more to proper speaking than knowing right.

6.   *Thirdly*, What *ideas we have of substances*, I have above shown. Now, those *ideas* have in the mind a double reference: (1) Sometimes they are referred to a supposed real essence of each species of things. (2) Sometimes they are only designed to be pictures and representations in the mind of things that do exist, by *ideas* of those qualities that are discoverable in them. In both which ways these copies of those originals and archetypes *are* imperfect and *inadequate*.

First, It is usual for men to make the names of substances stand for things as supposed to have certain real essences, whereby they are of this or that species; and names standing for nothing but the *ideas* that are in men's minds, they must consequently refer their *ideas* to such real essences, as to their archetypes. That men (especially such as have been bred up in the learning taught in this part of the world) do suppose certain specific essences of substances, which each individual in its several kinds is made conformable to and partakes of, is so far from needing proof that it will be thought strange if anyone should do otherwise. And thus they ordinarily apply the specific names they rank particular substances under to things as distinguished by such specific real essences. Who is there almost, who would not take it amiss if it should be doubted whether he called himself man with any other meaning than as having the real essence of a man? And yet if you demand what those real essences are, it is plain men are ignorant and know them not. From whence it follows that the *ideas* they have in their minds, being referred to real essences, as to archetypes which are unknown, must be so far from being *adequate* that they cannot be supposed to be any representation of them at all. The complex *ideas* we have of substances are, as it has been shown, certain collections of simple *ideas* that have been observed or supposed constantly to exist together. But such a complex *idea* cannot be the real essence of any substance; for then the properties we discover in that body would depend on that complex *idea* and be deducible from it, and their necessary connexion with it be known: as all properties of a triangle depend on and, as far as they are discoverable, are deducible from the complex *idea* of three lines including a space. But it is plain that in our complex *ideas* of substances are not contained such *ideas*, on which all the other qualities that are to be found in them do depend. The common *idea* men have of *iron* is a body of a certain colour, weight, and hardness; and a property that they look on as belonging to it is malleableness. But yet this property has no necessary connexion with that complex *idea*, or any part of it; and there is no more reason to think that malleableness depends on that colour, weight, and hardness than that that colour or that weight depends on its malleableness. And yet, though we know nothing of these real essences, there is nothing more ordinary than that men should attribute the sorts of things to such essences. The particular parcel of matter which makes the ring I have on my finger is forwardly by most men supposed to have a real essence whereby it is *gold*, and from whence those qualities flow which I find in it, viz. its peculiar colour, weight, hardness, fusibility, fixedness, and change of colour upon a slight touch of mercury, etc. This essence, from which all these properties flow, when I inquire into it and search after it, I plainly perceive I cannot discover: the furthest I can go is only to presume that, it being nothing but body, its real essence or internal constitution, on which these qualities depend, can be nothing but the figure, size, and connexion of its solid parts; of neither of which I having any distinct perception at all, I can have no *idea* of its essence, which is the cause that it has that particular shining yellowness, a greater weight than anything I know of the same bulk, and a fitness to have its colour changed by the touch of quicksilver. If anyone will say that the real essence and internal constitution on which these properties depend is not the figure, size, and arrangement or connexion of its solid parts, but something else called its particular *form*, I am further from having any *idea* of its real essence than I was before; for I have an *idea* of figure, size, and situation of solid parts in general, though I have none of the particular figure, size, or putting together of parts whereby the qualities above-mentioned are produced; which qualities I find in that particular parcel of matter that is on my finger, and not in another parcel of matter with which I cut the pen I write with. But when I am told that something besides the figure, size, and posture of the solid parts of that body is its essence, something called *substantial form*, of that I confess I have no *idea* at all, but only of the sound *form*; which is far enough from an *idea* of its real essence or constitution. The like ignorance as I have of the real essence of this particular substance, I have also of the real essence of all other natural ones: of which essences, I confess, I have no distinct *ideas* at all; and I am apt to suppose others, when they examine their own knowledge, will find in themselves, in this one point, the same sort of ignorance.

7. Now then, when men apply to this particular parcel of matter on my finger a general name already in use and denominate it *gold*, do they not ordinarily or are they not understood to give it that name as belonging to a particular species of bodies, having a real internal essence, by having of which essence this particular substance comes to be of that species and to be called by that name? If it be so, as it is plain it is, the name by which things are marked as having that essence must be referred primarily to that essence; and consequently the *idea* to which that name is given must be referred also to that essence and be intended to represent it. Which essence, since they who so use the names know not, their ideas *of substances* must be *all inadequate* in that respect, as not containing in them that real essence which the mind intends they should.

8. *Secondly*, Those who, neglecting that useless supposition of unknown real essences, whereby they are distinguished, endeavour to copy the substances that exist in the world by putting together the *ideas* of those sensible qualities which are found co-existing in them, though they come much nearer a likeness of them than those who imagine they know not what real specific essences, yet they arrive not at perfectly adequate *ideas* of those substances they would thus copy into their minds; nor do those copies exactly and fully contain all that is to be found in their archetypes. Because those qualities and powers of substances, whereof we make their complex *ideas*, are so many and various that no man's complex *idea* contains them all. That our abstract *ideas* of substances do not contain in them all the simple *ideas* that are united in the things themselves is evident in that men do rarely put into their complex *idea* of any substance all the simple *ideas* they do know to exist in it. Because, endeavouring to make the signification of their specific names as clear and as little cumbersome as they can, they make their specific *ideas* of

the sorts of substances, for the most part, of a few of those simple *ideas* which are to be found in them; but these having no original precedency or right to be put in and make the specific *idea* more than others that are left out, it is plain that, both these ways, *our* ideas *of substances* are deficient and *inadequate*. The simple *ideas* whereof we make our complex ones of substances are all of them (bating only the figure and bulk of some sorts) powers; which being relations to other substances, we can never be sure that we know all the powers that are in any one body till we have tried what changes it is fitted to give to or receive from other substances in their several ways of application; which being impossible to be tried upon any one body, much less upon all, it is impossible we should have adequate *ideas* of any substance made up of a collection of all its properties.

9. Whosoever first lighted on a parcel of that sort of substance we denote by the word *gold* could not rationally take the bulk and figure he observed in that lump to depend on its real essence or internal constitution. Therefore those never went into his *idea* of that species of body; but its peculiar colour, perhaps, and weight were the first he abstracted from it to make the complex *idea* of that species. Which both are but powers, the one to affect our eyes after such a manner and to produce in us that *idea* we call yellow, and the other to force upwards any other body of equal bulk, they being put into a pair of equal scales one against another. Another, perhaps, added to these the *ideas* of fusibility and fixedness, two other passive powers, in relation to the operation of fire upon it; another, its ductility and solubility in *aqua regia*, two other powers relating to the operation of other bodies in changing its outward figure or separation of it into insensible parts. These, or part of these, put together, usually make the complex *idea* in men's minds of that sort of body we call *gold*.

10. But no one who hath considered the properties of bodies in general, or this sort in particular, can doubt that this, called *gold*, has infinite other properties not contained in that complex *idea*. Some, who have examined this species more accurately, could, I believe, enumerate ten times as many properties in *gold*, all of them as inseparable from its internal constitution as its colour or weight; and it is probable, if anyone knew all the properties that are by divers men known of this metal, there would an hundred times as many *ideas* go to the complex *idea* of

gold as any one man yet has in his, and yet, perhaps, that not be
the thousandth part of what is to be discovered in it: the changes
that that one body is apt to receive and make in other bodies,
upon a due application, exceeding far not only what we know
but what we are apt to imagine. Which will not appear so much
a paradox to anyone who will but consider how far men are yet
from knowing all the properties of that one, no very compound
figure, a *triangle*, though it be no small number that are already
by mathematicians discovered of it.

11.   So that *all our complex* ideas *of substances are* imperfect
and *inadequate*.   Which would be so also in mathematical
figures, if we were to have our complex *ideas* of them only by
collecting their properties in reference to other figures. How
uncertain and imperfect would our *ideas* be of an *ellipsis*, if we
had no other *idea* of it but some few of its properties? Whereas,
having in our plain *idea* the whole essence of that figure, we
from thence discover those properties, and demonstratively see
how they flow and are inseparable from it.

12.   Thus the mind has three sorts of abstract *ideas* or nominal
essences:

First, Simple ideas, which *are* ἔκτυπα or *copies*, but yet certainly *adequate*.   Because, being intended to express nothing
but the power in things to produce in the mind such a sensation,
that sensation, when it is produced, cannot but be the effect of
that power.   So the paper I write on having the power in the
light (I speak according to the common notion of light) to
produce in me the sensation which I call white, it cannot but
be the effect of such a power in something without the mind,
since the mind has not the power to produce any such *idea* in
itself; and being meant for nothing else but the effect of such a
power, that simple *idea* is real and *adequate*; the sensation of
white in my mind, being the effect of that power which is in the
paper to produce it, is perfectly *adequate* to that power, or else
that power would produce a different *idea*.

13.   *Secondly*, The *complex* ideas *of substances are ectypes,
copies* too, but not perfect ones, not *adequate*; which is very
evident to the mind, in that it plainly perceives that, whatever
collection of simple *ideas* it makes of any substance that exists,
it cannot be sure that it exactly answers all that are in that substance; since, not having tried all the operations of all other
substances upon it and found all the alterations it would

receive from or cause in other substances, it cannot have an exact *adequate* collection of all its active and passive capacities; and so *not* have an *adequate* complex *idea* of the powers of any substance existing and its relations, which is that sort of complex *idea* of substances we have. And, after all, if we could have and actually had in our complex *idea* an exact collection of all the secondary qualities or powers of any substance, we should not yet thereby have an *idea* of the essence of that thing. For, since the powers or qualities that are observable by us are not the real essence of that substance but depend on it and flow from it, any collection whatsoever of these qualities cannot be the real essence of that thing. Whereby it is plain that our *ideas* of substances are not *adequate*, are not what the mind intends them to be. Besides, a man has no *idea* of substance in general, nor knows what substance is in itself.

14. *Thirdly, Complex* ideas *of modes and relations are* originals and *archetypes*, are not copies, nor made after the pattern of any real existence to which the mind intends them to be conformable and exactly to answer. These being such collections of simple *ideas* that the mind itself puts together, and such collections that each of them contains in it precisely all that the mind intends that it should, they are archetypes and essences of modes that may exist, and so are designed only for and belong only to such modes as, when they do exist, have an exact conformity with those complex *ideas*. The *ideas*, therefore, of modes and relations cannot but be *adequate*.

CHAPTER XXXII

OF TRUE AND FALSE IDEAS

1. THOUGH truth and falsehood belong, in propriety of speech, only to propositions, yet *ideas* are oftentimes termed *true or false* (as what words are there that are not used with great latitude and with some deviation from their strict and proper significations?): though I think that, when *ideas* themselves are termed true or false, there is still some secret or tacit proposition which is the foundation of that denomination, as we shall see if we

examine the particular occasions wherein they come to be called true or false. In all which we shall find some kind of affirmation or negation, which is the reason of that denomination. For our *ideas*, being nothing but bare appearances or perceptions in our minds, cannot properly and simply in themselves be said to be *true* or *false*, no more than a single name of anything can be said to be *true* or *false*.

2.   Indeed both *ideas* and words *may* be said to be *true*, *in a metaphysical sense* of the word truth, as all other things that any way exist are said to be true, i.e. really to be such as they exist: though in things called *true* even in that sense, there is perhaps a secret reference to our *ideas*, looked upon as the standards of that truth; which amounts to a mental proposition, though it be usually not taken notice of.

3.   But it is not in that metaphysical sense of truth which we inquire here, when we examine whether our *ideas* are capable of being *true* or *false*, but in the more ordinary acceptation of those words; and so I say that the *ideas* in our minds, being only so many perceptions or appearances there, none of them are *false*: the *idea* of a centaur having no more falsehood in it when it appears in our minds than the name centaur has falsehood in it when it is pronounced by our mouths or written on paper. For truth or falsehood lying always in some affirmation or negation, mental or verbal, our *ideas* are *not capable*, any of them, *of being false*, till the mind passes some judgment on them, that is, affirms or denies something of them.

4.   Whenever the mind refers any of its *ideas* to anything extraneous to them, they are then *capable to be called true or false*. Because the mind, in such a reference, makes a tacit supposition of their conformity to that thing; which supposition as it happens to be *true* or *false*, so the *ideas* themselves come to be denominated. The most usual cases wherein this happens are these following:

5.   *First*, When the mind supposes any *idea* it has *conformable to* that in *other men's* minds, called by the same common name: v.g. when the mind intends or judges its *ideas* of *justice, temperance, religion* to be the same with what other men give those names to.

    Secondly, When the mind supposes any *idea* it has in itself to be *conformable to some real existence*. Thus the two *ideas* of a man and a centaur, supposed to be the *ideas* of real substances, are the one *true* and the other *false*: the one having a conformity to what has really existed, the other not.

Thirdly, When the mind *refers* any of its *ideas to* that *real* constitution and *essence* of anything whereon all its properties depend; and thus the greatest part, if not all our *ideas* of substances are *false*.

6. These suppositions the mind is very apt tacitly to make concerning its own *ideas*. But yet, if we will examine it, we shall find it is chiefly, if not only, concerning its abstract complex *ideas*. For the natural tendency of the mind being towards knowledge, and finding that, if it should proceed by and dwell upon only particular things, its progress would be very slow and its work endless: therefore to shorten its way to knowledge and make each perception the more comprehensive, the first thing it does as the foundation of the easier enlarging its knowledge, either by contemplation of the things themselves that it would know or conference with others about them, is to bind them into bundles and rank them so into sorts, that what knowledge it gets of any of them it may thereby with assurance extend to all of that sort, and so advance by larger steps in that which is its great business, knowledge. This, as I have elsewhere shown, is the reason why we collect things under comprehensive *ideas*, with names annexed to them, into *genera* and *species*, i.e. into kinds and sorts.

7. If therefore we will warily attend to the motions of the mind and observe what course it usually takes in its way to knowledge, we shall, I think, find that, the mind having got any *idea* which it thinks it may have use of either in contemplation or discourse, the first thing it does is to abstract it, and then get a name to it, and so lay it up in its storehouse, the memory, as containing the essence of a sort of things of which that name is always to be the mark. Hence it is that we may often observe that, when anyone sees a new thing of a kind that he knows not, he presently asks what it is, meaning by that inquiry nothing but the name, as if the name carried with it the knowledge of the species or the essence of it, whereof it is indeed used as the mark and is generally supposed annexed to it.

8. But, this abstract *idea* being something in the mind between the thing that exists and the name that is given to it, it is in our *ideas* that both the rightness of our knowledge and the propriety or intelligibleness of our speaking consists. And hence it is

that men are so forward to suppose that the abstract *ideas* they
have in their minds are such as agree to the things existing without them to which they are referred, and are the same also to
which the names they give them do by the use and propriety of
that language belong. For without this *double conformity of* their
ideas, they find they should both think amiss of things in themselves, and talk of them unintelligibly to others.

9. *First,* then, I say that, *when the truth of our* ideas *is judged
of by the conformity they have to the* ideas *which other men have
and commonly signify by the same name, they may be any of
them false.* But yet *simple* ideas are *least* of all *liable to be so
mistaken,* because a man, by his senses and every day's observation, may easily satisfy himself what the simple *ideas* are which
their several names that are in common use stand for: they being
but few in number and such as, if he doubts or mistakes in, he
may easily rectify by the objects they are to be found in. Therefore it is seldom that anyone mistakes in his names of simple
ideas, or applies the name *red* to the *idea* of green, or the name
sweet to the *idea* bitter; much less are men apt to confound the
names of *ideas* belonging to different senses and call a colour by
the name of a taste, etc., whereby it is evident that the simple
ideas they call by any name are commonly the same that others
have and mean when they use the same names.

10. *Complex* ideas *are much more liable to be false in this
respect; and the complex* ideas *of mixed modes, much more than
those of substances;* because in substances (especially those
which the common and unborrowed names of any language are
applied to) some remarkable sensible qualities, serving ordinarily to distinguish one sort from another, easily preserve those
who take any care in the use of their words from applying them
to sorts of substances to which they do not at all belong. But in
mixed modes we are much more uncertain: it being not so easy
to determine of several actions whether they are to be called
justice or *cruelty, liberality* or *prodigality.* And so in referring
our *ideas* to those of other men, called by the same names, ours
may be *false;* and the *idea* in our minds which we express by the
word *justice* may perhaps be that which ought to have another
name.

11. But whether or no our *ideas* of mixed modes are more
liable than any sort to be different from those of other men
which are marked by the same names, this at least is certain:

that *this sort of falsehood is much more familiarly attributed to our ideas of mixed modes than to any other*. When a man is thought to have a false *idea* of *justice*, or *gratitude*, or *glory*, it is for no other reason but that his agrees not with the *ideas* which each of those names are the signs of in other men.

12. *The reason whereof* seems to me to be this: that the abstract *ideas* of mixed modes being men's voluntary combinations of such a precise collection of simple *ideas*, and so the essence of each species being made by men alone, whereof we have no other sensible standard existing anywhere but the name itself, or the definition of that name: we have nothing else to refer these our *ideas* of mixed modes to, as a standard to which we would conform them, but the *ideas* of those who are thought to use those names in their most proper significations; and so, as our *ideas* conform or differ from them, they pass for true or false. And thus much concerning the *truth* and *falsehood* of our *ideas* in reference to their names.

13. *Secondly*, As to the *truth and falsehood of our* ideas *in reference* to the *real existence* of things: when that is made the standard of their truth, none of them can be termed false, but only our complex *ideas* of substances.

14. *First*, Our simple *ideas* being barely such perceptions as God has fitted us to receive and given power to external objects to produce in us by established laws and ways, suitable to his wisdom and goodness, though incomprehensible to us, their truth consists in nothing else but in such appearances as are produced in us and must be suitable to those powers he has placed in external objects, or else they could not be produced in us; and thus answering those powers, they are what they should be, *true ideas*. Nor do they become liable to any imputation of *falsehood*, if the mind (as in most men I believe it does) judges these *ideas* to be in the things themselves. For God in his wisdom having set them as marks of distinction in things whereby we may be able to discern one thing from another and so choose any of them for our uses, as we have occasion, it alters not the nature of our simple *idea* whether we think that the *idea* of blue be in the violet itself or in our mind only; and only the power of producing it, by the texture of its parts reflecting the particles of light after a certain manner, to be in the violet itself. For that texture in the object, by a regular and constant operation, producing the same *idea* of blue in us, it

serves us to distinguish, by our eyes, that from any other thing: whether that distinguishing mark, as it is really in the *violet*, be only a peculiar texture of parts or else that very colour, the *idea* whereof (which is in us) is the exact resemblance. And it is equally from that appearance to be denominated *blue*, whether it be that real colour or only a peculiar texture in it that causes in us that *idea*: since the name *blue* notes properly nothing but that mark of distinction that is in a *violet*, discernible only by our eyes, whatever it consists in, that being beyond our capacities distinctly to know and, perhaps, would be of less use to us if we had faculties to discern.

15.   Neither would it carry any imputation of *falsehood* to our simple *ideas if*, by the different structure of our organs, it were so ordered that *the same object should produce in several men's minds different* ideas at the same time: v.g. if the *idea* that a *violet* produced in one man's mind by his eyes were the same that a *marigold* produced in another man's, and *vice versa*. For, since this could never be known, because one man's mind could not pass into another man's body to perceive what appearances were produced by those organs, neither the *ideas* hereby, nor the names, would be at all confounded, or any *falsehood* be in either. For all things that had the texture of a *violet* producing constantly the *idea* which he called *blue*, and those which had the texture of a *marigold* producing constantly the *idea* which he as constantly called *yellow*, whatever those appearances were in his mind, he would be able as regularly to distinguish things for his use by those appearances, and understand and signify those distinctions marked by the names *blue* and *yellow*, as if the appearances or *ideas* in his mind, received from those two flowers, were exactly the same with the *ideas* in other men's minds. I am nevertheless very apt to think that the sensible *ideas* produced by any object in different men's minds are most commonly very near and undiscernibly alike. For which opinion, I think, there might be many reasons offered; but, that being besides my present business, I shall not trouble my reader with them, but only mind him that the contrary supposition, if it could be proved, is of little use either for the improvement of our knowledge or conveniency of life, and so we need not trouble ourselves to examine it.

16.   From what has been said concerning our simple *ideas*, I think it evident that our *simple* ideas can *none of them* be *false in*

respect of things existing without us. For the truth of these appearances or perceptions in our minds consisting, as has been said, only in their being answerable to the powers in external objects to produce by our senses such appearances in us, and each of them being in the mind such as it is suitable to the power that produced it, and which alone it represents, it cannot upon that account, or as referred to such a pattern, be *false*. *Blue* or *yellow*, *bitter* or *sweet*, can never be false *ideas*: these perceptions in the mind are just such as they are there, answering the powers appointed by God to produce them, and so are truly what they are and are intended to be. Indeed the names may be misapplied, but that in this respect makes no falsehood in the *ideas*, as if a man ignorant in the *English* tongue should call *purple scarlet*.

17. *Secondly, Neither can* our *complex* ideas *of modes, in reference to the essence of anything really existing, be false*; because whatever complex *idea* I have of any mode, it hath no reference to any pattern existing and made by nature; it is not supposed to contain in it any other *ideas* than what it hath, nor to represent anything but such a complication of *ideas* as it does. Thus, when I have the *idea* of such an action of a man who forbears to afford himself such meat, drink, and clothing, and other conveniencies of life as his riches and estate will be sufficient to supply and his station requires, I have no *false idea* but such an one as represents an action either as I find or imagine it, and so is capable of neither *truth* nor *falsehood*. But when I give the name *frugality* or *virtue* to this action, then it may be called a *false idea*, if thereby it be supposed to agree with that *idea* to which, in propriety of speech, the name of *frugality* doth belong, or to be conformable to that law which is the standard of virtue and vice.

18. *Thirdly,* Our complex *ideas of substances, being all referred to patterns in things themselves, may be false.* That they are all *false*, when looked upon as the representations of the unknown essences of things, is so evident that there needs nothing to be said of it. I shall therefore pass over that chimerical supposition and consider them as collections of simple *ideas* in the mind, taken from combinations of simple *ideas* existing together constantly in things, of which patterns they are the supposed copies; and in this reference of them to the existence of things, they *are false* ideas: (1) *when* they put together simple *ideas*,

which in the real existence of things have no union; as when, to the shape and size that exist together in a horse is joined in the same complex *idea* the power of barking like a dog: which three *ideas*, however put together into one in the mind, were never united in nature; and this therefore may be called a *false idea* of an horse. (2) *Ideas* of substances are in this respect also *false*, when, from any collection of simple *ideas* that do always exist together, there is separated, by a direct negation, any other simple *idea* which is constantly joined with them. Thus, if to extension, solidity, fusibility, the peculiar weightiness, and yellow colour of gold, anyone join in his thoughts the negation of a greater degree of fixedness than is in lead or copper, he may be said to have a false complex *idea*, as well as when he joins to those other simple ones the *idea* of perfect absolute fixedness. For either way, the complex *idea* of gold, being made up of such simple ones as have no union in nature, may be termed false. But if he leave out of this his complex *idea* that of fixedness quite, without either actually joining to or separating of it from the rest in his mind, it is, I think, to be looked on as an inadequate and imperfect *idea* rather than a *false* one, since, though it contains not all the simple *ideas* that are united in nature, yet it puts none together but what do really exist together.

19.   Though in compliance with the ordinary way of speaking, I have shown in what sense and upon what ground our *ideas* may be sometimes called *true* or *false*, yet if we will look a little nearer into the matter in all cases, where any *idea* is called *true* or *false*, it is from some judgment that the mind makes or is supposed to make that is *true* or *false*. For *truth or falsehood* being *never without some affirmation or negation*, express or tacit, it is not to be found but where signs are joined or separated, according to the agreement or disagreement of the things they stand for. The signs we chiefly use are either *ideas* or words, wherewith we make either mental or verbal propositions. *Truth* lies in so joining or separating these representatives as the things they stand for do in themselves agree or disagree; and *falsehood* in the contrary, as shall be more fully shown hereafter.

20.   Any *idea*, then, which we have in our minds, whether conformable or not to the existence of things, or to any *ideas* in the minds of other men, cannot properly for this alone be called *false*. For these representations, if they have nothing in them

but what is really existing in things without, cannot be thought *false*, being exact representations of something; nor yet if they have anything in them differing from the reality of things, can they properly be said to be false representations, or *ideas* of things they do not represent. But the mistake and *falsehood* is:

21. *First, When the mind* having any *idea*, it *judges* and concludes *it the same that is in other men's minds signified by the same name*, or that it is conformable to the ordinary received signification or definition of that word, when indeed it is not; which is the most usual mistake in mixed modes, though other *ideas* also are liable to it.

22. *Secondly*, When, it having a complex *idea* made up of such a collection of simple ones as nature never puts together, *it judges it to agree to a species of creatures really existing*: as when it joins the weight of tin to the colour, fusibility, and fixedness of gold.

23. *Thirdly*, When in its complex *idea* it has united a certain number of simple *ideas* that do really exist together in some sorts of creatures but has also left out others, as much inseparable, *it judges this to be a perfect complete* idea *of a sort of things which really it is not*: v.g. having joined the *ideas* of substance, yellow, malleable, most heavy and fusible, it takes that complex *idea* to be the complete *idea* of gold, when yet its peculiar fixedness and solubility in *aqua regia* are as inseparable from those other *ideas* or qualities of that body as they are one from another.

24. *Fourthly*, The mistake is yet greater, *when I judge that this complex* idea *contains in it the real essence of any body existing*, when at least it contains but some few of those properties which flow from its real essence and constitution. I say only some few of those properties; for those properties consisting mostly in the active and passive powers it has in reference to other things, all that are vulgarly known of any one body and of which the complex *idea* of that kind of things is usually made are but a very few, in comparison of what a man that has several ways tried and examined it knows of that one sort of things; and all that the most expert man knows are but few in comparison of what are really in that body and depend on its internal or essential constitution. The essence of a triangle lies in a very little compass, consists in a very few *ideas*: three lines, including a space, make up that essence; but the properties that flow from this essence are more than can be easily known or enumerated.

So I imagine it is in substances: their real essences lie in a little compass, though the properties flowing from that internal constitution are endless.

25.   To conclude, a man having no notion of anything without him but by the *idea* he has of it in his mind (which *idea* he has a power to call by what name he pleases), he may indeed make an *idea* neither answering the reality of things, nor agreeing to the *ideas* commonly signified by other people's words; but cannot make a wrong or *false idea* of a thing which is no otherwise known to him but by the *idea* he has of it: v.g. when I frame an *idea* of the legs, arms, and body of a man, and join to this a horse's head and neck, I do not make a *false idea* of anything, because it represents nothing without me. But when I call it a *man* or *Tartar*, and imagine it either to represent some real being without me, or to be the same *idea* that others call by the same name: in either of these cases I may err. And upon this account it is that it comes to be termed a *false idea*, though indeed the *falsehood* lies not in the *idea*, but in that tacit mental proposition wherein a conformity and resemblance is attributed to it which it has not. But yet, if, having framed such an *idea* in my mind, without thinking either that existence or the name *man* or *Tartar* belongs to it, I will call it *man* or *Tartar*, I may be justly thought fantastical in the naming, but not erroneous in my judgment, nor the *idea* any way *false*.

26.   Upon the whole matter, I think that our *ideas*, as they are considered by the mind either in reference to the proper signification of their names or in reference to the reality of things, *may* very fitly *be called right or wrong* ideas, according as they agree or disagree to those patterns to which they are referred. But if anyone had rather call them *true* or *false*, it is fit he use a liberty, which everyone has, to call things by those names he thinks best: though, in propriety of speech, *truth* or *falsehood* will, I think, scarce agree to them but as they, some way or other, virtually contain in them some mental proposition. The *ideas* that are in a man's mind, simply considered, cannot be wrong, unless complex ones, wherein inconsistent parts are jumbled together. All other *ideas* are in themselves right, and the knowledge about them right and true knowledge; but when we come to refer them to anything, as to their patterns and archetypes, then they are capable of being wrong as far as they disagree with such archetypes.

Chapter XXXIII

OF THE ASSOCIATION OF IDEAS

1. THERE is scarce anyone that does not observe something that seems odd to him, and is in itself really extravagant, in the opinions, reasonings, and actions of other men. The least flaw of this kind, if at all different from his own, everyone is quick-sighted enough to espy in another, and will by the authority of reason forwardly condemn, though he be guilty of much greater unreasonableness in his own tenets and conduct, which he never perceives and will very hardly, if at all, be convinced of.

2. This proceeds not wholly from self-love, though that has often a great hand in it. Men of fair minds, and not given up to the overweening of self-flattery, are frequently guilty of it; and in many cases one with amazement hears the arguings and is astonished at the obstinacy of a worthy man who yields not to the evidence of reason, though laid before him as clear as daylight.

3. This sort of unreasonableness is usually imputed to educa-tion and prejudice, and for the most part truly enough, though that reaches not the bottom of the disease nor shows distinctly enough whence it rises or wherein it lies. Education is often rightly assigned for the cause, and prejudice is a good general name for the thing itself; but yet, I think, he ought to look a little further, who would trace this sort of madness to the root it springs from and so explain it, as to show whence this flaw has its original in very sober and rational minds, and wherein it consists.

4. I shall be pardoned for calling it by so harsh a name as *madness*, when it is considered that opposition to reason deserves that name and is really madness; and there is scarce a man so free from it but that, if he should always on all occasions argue or do as in some cases he constantly does, would not be thought fitter for Bedlam than civil conversation. I do not here mean when he is under the power of an unruly passion, but in the steady calm course of his life. That which will yet more apolo-gize for this harsh name and ungrateful imputation on the

greatest part of mankind is that, inquiring a little by the by
into the nature of madness (bk. II, chap. xi, § 13), I found it to
spring from the very same root and to depend on the very same
cause we are here speaking of. This consideration of the thing
itself, at a time when I thought not the least on the subject which
I am now treating of, suggested it to me. And if this be a
weakness to which all men are so liable, if this be a taint which so
universally infects mankind, the greater care should be taken to
lay it open under its due name, thereby to excite the greater
care in its prevention and cure.

5. Some of our *ideas* have a natural correspondence and connexion one with another; it is the office and excellency of our
reason to trace these, and hold them together in that union and
correspondence which is founded in their peculiar beings. Besides this, there is another connexion of *ideas* wholly owing to
chance or custom: *ideas*, that in themselves are not at all of kin,
come to be so united in some men's minds that it is very hard
to separate them, they always keep in company, and the one no
sooner at any time comes into the understanding but its associate
appears with it; and if they are more than two which are thus
united, the whole gang, always inseparable, show themselves
together.

6. This strong combination of *ideas*, not allied by nature, the
mind makes in itself either voluntarily or by chance; and hence
it comes in different men to be very different, according to their
different inclinations, educations, interests, etc. Custom settles
habits of thinking in the understanding, as well as of determining in the will, and of motions in the body: all which seem
to be but trains of motion in the animal spirits, which, once set
a-going, continue in the same steps they have been used to;
which, by often treading, are worn into a smooth path, and the
motion in it becomes easy and, as it were, natural. As far as we
can comprehend thinking, thus *ideas* seem to be produced in
our minds; or, if they are not, this may serve to explain their
following one another in an habitual train, when once they are
put into that track, as well as it does to explain such motions of
the body. A musician used to any tune will find that, let it but
once begin in his head, the *ideas* of the several notes of it will
follow one another orderly in his understanding, without any
care or attention, as regularly as his fingers move orderly over
the keys of the organ to play out the tune he has begun, though

his unattentive thoughts be elsewhere a-wandering. Whether the natural cause of these *ideas*, as well as of that regular dancing of his fingers, be the motion of his animal spirits, I will not determine, how probable soever, by this instance, it appears to be so; but this may help us a little to conceive of intellectual habits and of the tying together of *ideas*.

7. That there are such associations of them made by custom in the minds of most men, I think nobody will question who has well considered himself or others; and to this, perhaps, might be justly attributed most of the sympathies and antipathies observable in men, which work as strongly and produce as regular effects as if they were natural; and are therefore called so, though they at first had no other original but the accidental connexion of two *ideas*, which either the strength of the first impression or future indulgence so united that they always afterwards kept company together in that man's mind, as if they were but one *idea*. I say most of the antipathies, I do not say all: for some of them are truly natural, depend upon our original constitution, and are born with us; but a great part of those which are counted natural would have been known to be from unheeded, though perhaps early, impressions or wanton fancies at first, which would have been acknowledged the original of them, if they had been warily observed. A grown person surfeiting with honey no sooner hears the name of it, but his fancy immediately carries sickness and qualms to his stomach, and he cannot bear the very *idea* of it; other *ideas* of dislike and sickness and vomiting presently accompany it, and he is disturbed, but he knows from whence to date this weakness and can tell how he got this indisposition: had this happened to him by an overdose of honey when a child, all the same effects would have followed, but the cause would have been mistaken, and the antipathy counted natural.

8. I mention this not out of any great necessity there is in this present argument to distinguish nicely between natural and acquired antipathies, but I take notice of it for another purpose, viz. that those who have children or the charge of their education would think it worth their while diligently to watch and carefully to prevent the undue connexion of *ideas* in the minds of young people. This is the time most susceptible of lasting impressions; and though those relating to the health of the body are by discreet people minded and fenced against, yet I am apt

to doubt that those which relate more peculiarly to the mind, and terminate in the understanding or passions, have been much less heeded than the thing deserves: nay, those relating purely to the understanding have, as I suspect, been by most men wholly overlooked.

9.   This wrong connexion in our minds of *ideas*, in themselves loose and independent one of another, has such an influence and is of so great force to set us awry in our actions as well moral as natural, passions, reasonings, and notions themselves, that perhaps there is not any one thing that deserves more to be looked after.

10.   The *ideas* of *goblins* and *sprites* have really no more to do with darkness than light: yet let but a foolish maid inculcate these often on the mind of a child and raise them there together, possibly he shall never be able to separate them again so long as he lives, but darkness shall ever afterwards bring with it those frightful *ideas*, and they shall be so joined that he can no more bear the one than the other.

11.   A man receives a sensible injury from another, thinks on the man and that action over and over, and by ruminating on them strongly, or much, in his mind, so cements those two *ideas* together that he makes them almost one; never thinks on the man, but the pain and displeasure he suffered comes into his mind with it, so that he scarce distinguishes them, but has as much an aversion for the one as the other. Thus hatreds are often begotten from slight and almost innocent occasions, and quarrels propagated and continued in the world.

12.   A man has suffered pain or sickness in any place, he saw his friend die in such a room: though these have in nature nothing to do one with another, yet when the *idea* of the place occurs to his mind, it brings (the impression being once made) that of the pain and displeasure with it, he confounds them in his mind, and can as little bear the one as the other.

13.   When this combination is settled and whilst it lasts, it is not in the power of reason to help us and relieve us from the effects of it. *Ideas* in our minds, when they are there, will operate according to their natures and circumstances; and here we see the cause why time cures certain affections, which reason, though in the right and allowed to be so, has not power over nor is able against them to prevail with those who are apt to hearken to it in other cases. The death of a child, that was

the daily delight of his mother's eyes and joy of her soul, rends from her heart the whole comfort of her life and gives her all the torment imaginable; use the consolations of reason in this case, and you were as good preach ease to one on the rack and hope to allay, by rational discourses, the pain of his joints tearing asunder. Till time has by disuse separated the sense of that enjoyment and its loss from the *idea* of the child returning to her memory, all representations, though never so reasonable, are in vain; and therefore some in whom the union between these *ideas* is never dissolved spend their lives in mourning and carry an incurable sorrow to their graves.

14. A friend of mine knew one perfectly cured of madness by a very harsh and offensive operation. The gentleman, who was thus recovered, with great sense of gratitude and acknowledgement owned the cure all his life after as the greatest obligation he could have received; but whatever gratitude and reason suggested to him, he could never bear the sight of the operator: that image brought back with it the *idea* of that agony which he suffered from his hands, which was too mighty and intolerable for him to endure.

15. Many children, imputing the pain they endured at school to their books they were corrected for, so join those *ideas* together that a book becomes their aversion; and they are never reconciled to the study and use of them all their lives after; and thus reading becomes a torment to them, which otherwise possibly they might have made the great pleasure of their lives. There are rooms convenient enough that some men cannot study in; and fashions of vessels which, though never so clean and commodious, they cannot drink out of, and that by reason of some accidental *ideas* which are annexed to them and make them offensive; and who is there that hath not observed some man to flag at the appearance or in the company of some certain person, not otherwise superior to him, but because having once on some occasion got the ascendant, the *idea* of authority and distance goes along with that of the person, and he that has been thus subjected is not able to separate them.

16. Instances of this kind are so plentiful everywhere that, if I add one more, it is only for the pleasant oddness of it. It is of a young gentleman, who having learnt to dance, and that to great perfection, there happened to stand an old trunk in the room where he learnt. The *idea* of this remarkable piece of

household stuff had so mixed itself with the turns and steps of
all his dances that, though in that chamber he could dance ex-
cellently well, yet it was only whilst that trunk was there; nor
could he perform well in any other place, unless that or some
such other trunk had its due position in the room. If this story
shall be suspected to be dressed up with some comical circumstances, a little beyond precise nature, I answer for myself that
I had it some years since from a very sober and worthy man,
upon his own knowledge, as I report it; and I dare say there are
very few inquisitive persons who read this, who have not met
with accounts, if not examples, of this nature that may parallel,
or at least justify this.

17.   Intellectual habits and defects, this way contracted, are not
less frequent and powerful, though less observed. Let the *ideas*
of being and matter be strongly joined, either by education or
much thought: whilst these are still combined in the mind, what
notions, what reasonings will there be about separate spirits?
Let custom from the very childhood have joined figure and
shape to the *idea* of God, and what absurdities will that mind be
liable to about the Deity?

Let the *idea* of infallibility be inseparably joined to any
person, and these two constantly together possess the mind; and
then one body in two places at once shall unexamined be
swallowed for a certain truth, by an implicit faith, whenever that
imagined infallible person dictates and demands assent without
inquiry.

18.   Some such wrong and unnatural combinations of *ideas*
will be found to establish the irreconcilable opposition between
different sects of philosophy and religion; for we cannot imagine
everyone of their followers to impose wilfully on himself and
knowingly refuse truth offered by plain reason.   Interest,
though it does a great deal in the case, yet cannot be thought to
work whole societies of men to so universal a perverseness as
that every one of them to a man should knowingly maintain
falsehood: some at least must be allowed to do what all pretend
to, i.e. to pursue truth sincerely; and therefore there must be
something that blinds their understandings and makes them not
see the falsehood of what they embrace for real truth. That
which thus captivates their reasons and leads men of sincerity
blindfold from common sense will, when examined, be found
to be what we are speaking of: some independent *ideas* of no

alliance to one another are, by education, custom, and the constant din of their party, so coupled in their minds that they always appear there together, and they can no more separate them in their thoughts than if they were but one *idea*, and they operate as if they were so. This gives sense to *jargon*, demonstration to absurdities, and consistency to nonsense, and is the foundation of the greatest, I had almost said of all, the errors in the world; or if it does not reach so far, it is at least the most dangerous one, since, so far as it obtains, it hinders men from seeing and examining. When two things, in themselves disjoined, appear to the sight constantly united, if the eye sees these things riveted which are loose, where will you begin to rectify the mistakes that follow in two *ideas* that they have been accustomed so to join in their minds as to substitute one for the other and, as I am apt to think, often without perceiving it themselves? This, whilst they are under the deceit of it, makes them incapable of conviction, and they applaud themselves as zealous champions for truth, when indeed they are contending for error; and the confusion of two different *ideas*, which a customary connexion of them in their minds hath to them made in effect but one, fills their heads with false views and their reasonings with false consequences.

19. Having thus given an account of the original, sorts, and extent of our *ideas*, with several other considerations about these (I know not whether I may say) instruments, or materials of our knowledge, the method I at first proposed to myself would now require that I should immediately proceed to show what use the understanding makes of them, and what knowledge we have by them. This was that which, in the first general view I had of this subject, was all that I thought I should have to do; but, upon a nearer approach, I find that there is so close a connexion between *ideas* and words, and our abstract *ideas* and general words have so constant a relation one to another, that it is impossible to speak clearly and distinctly of our knowledge, which all consists in propositions, without considering first the nature, use, and signification of language; which, therefore, must be the business of the next book.

EVERYMAN'S LIBRARY was founded in 1906, and the series stands without rival today as the world's most comprehensive low-priced collection of books of classic measure. It was conceived as a library covering the whole field of English literature, including translations of the ancient classics and outstanding foreign works; a series to make widely available those great books which appeal to every kind of reader, and which in essence form the basis of western culture. The aim and scope of the series was crystallized in the title Everyman's Library, justified by world sales totalling (by 1960) some forty-four millions.

There were, of course, already in being in 1906 other popular series of reprints, but none on the scale proposed for Everyman. One hundred and fifty-five volumes were published in three batches in the Library's first year; they comprised a balanced selection from many branches of literature and set the standard on which the Library has been built up. By the outbreak of the First World War the Library was moving towards its 750th volume; and, in spite of the interruptions of two world wars, the aim of the founder-publisher, a library of a thousand volumes, was achieved by the jubilee in 1956, with Aristotle's *Metaphysics*, translated by John Warrington.

In March 1953 a fresh development of the Library began: new volumes and all new issues of established volumes in Everyman's Library were now made in a larger size. The larger volumes have new title-pages, bindings and wrappers, and the text pages have generous margins. Four hundred and twenty-two volumes in this improved format had been issued by 1960. In that year new pictorial wrappers appeared and they have provided the volumes with a surprisingly contemporary 'look'.

Editorially the Library is under constant survey; volumes are examined and brought up to date, with new introductions, annotations and additional matter; often a completely new translation or a newly edited text is substituted when transferring an old volume to the new format. New editions of Pepys's *Diary*, Caesar's *War Commentaries*, *The Anglo-Saxon Chronicle* and Professor T. M. Raysor's reorganization of Coleridge's *Shakespearean Criticism* are examples of this type of revision.

The new larger volumes are in keeping with the original 'home-library' plan but are also in a suitable size for the shelves of all institutional libraries, more so since many important works in Everyman's Library are unobtainable in any other edition. This development entails no break in the continuity of the Library; and fresh titles and verified editions are being constantly added.

A Classified Annotated Catalogue of the library is available free, the annotations giving the year of birth and death of the author, the date of first publication of the work and in many instances descriptive notes on the contents of the last revised Everyman's Library edition. Also available (as a volume in the Library, No. 889) is A. J. Hoppe's *The Reader's Guide to Everyman's Library*, revised and reissued in 1961. It gives in one alphabetical sequence references and cross-references of a comprehensive kind, including all authors and all works, even works included in anthologies, and a factual annotation of each work. Running to more than 400 pages, and referring to 1,260 authors, it is virtually a guide to all books of classic standing in the English language.

EVERYMAN'S LIBRARY: A Selected List

BIOGRAPHY

Baxter, Richard (1615–91).
    THE AUTOBIOGRAPHY OF RICHARD BAXTER.   868

Boswell, James (1740–95). *See* Johnson.

Brontë, Charlotte (1816–55).
    LIFE, 1857. By *Mrs Gaskell*. Introduction by *May Sinclair*. (*See also* Fiction.) 318

Burns, Robert (1759–96).
    LIFE, 1828. By *J. G. Lockhart* (1794–1854). With Introduction by *Prof. James Kinsley*, M.A., PH.D.   (*See also* Poetry and Drama.) 156

Byron, Lord (1788–1824).
    LETTERS. Edited by *R. G. Howarth*, B.LITT., and with an Introduction by *André Maurois*.   (*See also* Poetry and Drama.) 931

Canton, William (1845–1926).
    A CHILD'S BOOK OF SAINTS, 1898.   (*See also* Essays.) 61

Cellini, Benvenuto (1500–71).
    THE LIFE OF BENVENUTO CELLINI, written by himself. Translated by *Anne Macdonell*. Introduction by *William Gaunt*.   51

Cowper, William (1731–1800).
    SELECTED LETTERS. Edited, with Introduction, by *W. Hadley*, M.A.   774
    (*See also* Poetry and Drama.)

Dickens, Charles (1812–70).
    LIFE, 1874. By *John Forster* (1812–76). Introduction by *G. K. Chesterton*. 2 vols. (*See also* Fiction.) 781–2

Evelyn, John (1620–1706).
    DIARY. Edited by *William Bray*, 1819. Intro. by *G. W. E. Russell*. 2 vols.   220–1

Fox, George (1624–91).
    JOURNAL, 1694. Revised by *Norman Penney*, with Account of Fox's last years. Introduction by *Rufus M. Jones*.   754

Franklin, Benjamin (1706–90).
    AUTOBIOGRAPHY, 1817. With Introduction and Account of Franklin's later life by *W. Macdonald*. Reset new edition (1949), with a newly compiled Index.   316

Goethe, Johann Wolfgang von (1749–1832).
    LIFE, 1855. By *G. H. Lewes* (1817–78). Introduction by *Havelock Ellis*. Index. (*See also* Poetry and Drama.) 269

Hudson, William Henry (1841–1922).
    FAR AWAY AND LONG AGO, 1918. Intro. by *John Galsworthy*.   956

Johnson, Samuel (1709–84).
    LIVES OF THE ENGLISH POETS, 1781. Introduction by *Mrs L. Archer-Hind*. 2 vols. (*See also* Essays, Fiction.) 770–1
    BOSWELL'S LIFE OF JOHNSON, 1791. A new edition (1949), with Introduction by *S. C. Roberts*, M.A., LL.D., and a 30-page Index by Alan Dent. 2 vols.   1–2

Keats, John (1795–1821).
    LIFE AND LETTERS, 1848. By *Lord Houghton* (1809–85). Introduction by *Robert Lynd*. Note on the letters by Lewis Gibbs.   (*See also* Poetry and Drama.) 801

Lamb, Charles (1775–1834).
    LETTERS. New edition (1945) arranged from the Complete Annotated Edition of the Letters. 2 vols.   (*See also* Essays and Belles-Lettres, Fiction.) 342–3

Napoleon Buonaparte (1769–1821).
    HISTORY OF NAPOLEON BUONAPARTE, 1829. By *J. G. Lockhart* (1794–1854).   3
    (*See also* Essays and Belles-Lettres.)

Nelson, Horatio, Viscount (1758–1805).
    LIFE, 1813. By *Robert Southey* (1774–1843).   (*See also* Essays.) 52

Outram, General Sir James (1803–63), 'the Bayard of India.'
    LIFE, 1903. Deals with important passages in the history of India in the nineteenth century. By *L. J. Trotter* (1827–1912).   396

Pepys, Samuel (1633–1703).
    DIARY. Newly edited (1953), with modernized spelling, by *John Warrington*, from the edition of Mynors Bright (1875–9). 3 vols.   53–5

Plutarch (46?–120).
    LIVES OF THE NOBLE GREEKS AND ROMANS. Dryden's edition, 1683–6. Revised, with Introduction, by *A. H. Clough* (1819–61). 3 vols.   407–9

Rousseau, Jean Jacques (1712–78).
    CONFESSIONS, 1782. 2 vols. Complete and unabridged English translation. New Introduction by *Prof. R. Niklaus*, B.A., PH.D., of Exeter University.   859–60
    (*See also* Essays, Theology and Philosophy.)

Scott, Sir Walter (1771–1832).
    LOCKHART'S LIFE OF SCOTT. An abridgement by *J. G. Lockhart* himself from the original 7 volumes. New Introduction by *W. M. Parker*, M.A.   39

CLASSICAL

ESSAYS AND BELLES-LETTRES

HISTORY

ORATORY

POETRY AND DRAMA

11

Palgrave, Francis Turner (1824–97). *See* 'Golden Treasury of English Songs and Lyrics, The.' 96

Persian Poems. Selected and edited by *Prof. A. J. Arberry*, M.A., LITT.D., F.B.A. 996

Poe, Edgar Allan (1809–49).
POEMS AND ESSAYS. Introduction by *Andrew Lang*. (*See also* Fiction.) 791

Poems of our Time. An Anthology edited by *Richard Church*, C.B.E., *M. M. Bozman* and *Edith Sitwell*, D.LITT., D.B.E. Nearly 400 poems by about 130 poets. 981

Pope, Alexander (1688–1744).
COLLECTED POEMS. Edited with Intro. (1956) by *Prof. Bonamy Dobrée*, O.B.E., M.A. 760

Restoration Plays. Introduction by *Edmund Gosse*. Includes Dryden's 'All for Love,' Wycherley's 'The Country Wife,' Congreve's 'The Way of the World,' Otway's 'Venice Preserved,' Farquhar's 'Beaux-Stratagem,' Vanbrugh's 'Provoked Wife,' Etherege's 'Man of Mode.' 604

Rossetti, Dante Gabriel (1828–82).
POEMS AND TRANSLATIONS. Introduction by *E. G. Gardner*. 627

Shakespeare, William (1564–1616).
A Complete Edition, based on Clark and Wright's Cambridge text, and edited by *Oliphant Smeaton*. With biographical Introduction, Chronological Tables and full Glossary. 3 vols.
Comedies, 153; Histories, Poems and Sonnets, 154; Tragedies, 155

Shelley, Percy Bysshe (1792–1822).
POETICAL WORKS. Introduction by *A. H. Koszul*. 2 vols. 257–8

Sheridan, Richard Brinsley (1751–1816).
COMPLETE PLAYS. Introduction and notes by *Lewis Gibbs*. 95

Silver Poets of the Sixteenth Century. Edited by *Gerald Bullett*. The works of Sir Thomas Wyatt (1503–42), Henry Howard, Earl of Surrey (1517?–47), Sir Philip Sidney (1554–86), Sir Walter Ralegh (1552–1618) and Sir John Davies (1569–1626.) 985

Spenser, Edmund (1552–99).
THE FAERIE QUEENE. Introduction by *Prof. J. W. Hales*, and Glossary. 2 vols. The reliable Morris text and glossary are used for this edition. 443–4
THE SHEPHERD'S CALENDAR, 1579; and OTHER POEMS. Introduction by *Philip Henderson*. 879

Stevenson, Robert Louis (1850–94).
POEMS. A CHILD'S GARDEN OF VERSES, 1885; UNDERWOODS, 1887; SONGS OF TRAVEL, 1896; and BALLADS, 1890, Introduction by *Ernest Rhys*. 768
(*See also* Essays, Fiction, Travel.)

Swinburne, Algernon Charles (1837–1909).
POEMS AND PROSE. A selection, edited with an Intro. by *Richard Church*. 961

Synge, J. M. (1871–1909).
PLAYS, POEMS AND PROSE. Introduction by *Michaél Mac Liammóir*. 968

Tchekhov, Anton (1860–1904).
PLAYS AND STORIES. 'The Cherry Orchard,' 'The Seagull,' 'The Wood Demon,' 'Tatyana Riepin' and 'On the Harmfulness of Tobacco' are included, as well as 13 of his best stories. The translation is by *S. S. Koteliansky*. Introduction by *David Magarshack*. 941

Tennyson, Alfred, Lord (1809–92).
POEMS. A comprehensive edition (1950), with an Introduction by *Mildred Bozman*. 2 vols. 44, 626

Twenty-four One-Act Plays. Enlarged edition, new Introduction by *John Hampden*. Contains plays by T. S. Eliot, Sean O'Casey, Laurence Housman, W. B. Yeats, James Bridie, Noel Coward, Lord Dunsany, Wolf Mankowitz and others. 947

Webster, John (1580?–1625?), and Ford, John (1586–1639).
SELECTED PLAYS. Introduction by *Prof. G. B. Harrison*, M.A., PH.D. In one volume: 'The White Devil,' 'The Duchess of Malfi,' 'The Broken Heart,' ''Tis Pity She's a Whore.' 899

Whitman, Walt (1819–92).
LEAVES OF GRASS, 1855–92. New edition (1947) by *Dr Emory Holloway*. 573

Wilde, Oscar (1854–1900).
PLAYS, PROSE WRITINGS, AND POEMS. Edited, with Introduction, by *Hesketh Pearson*. Including the two plays, 'The Importance of Being Earnest' and 'Lady Windermere's Fan'; his novel, 'The Picture of Dorian Gray'; the poem, 'The Ballad of Reading Gaol'; the essay, 'The Soul of Man,' etc. 858

Wordsworth, William (1770–1850).
POEMS. Edited, with Introductory study, notes, bibliography and full index, by *Philip Wayne*, M.A. 203, 311, 998

REFERENCE

Reader's Guide to Everyman's Library. Compiled by *A. J. Hoppé*. This volume is a new compilation and gives in one alphabetical sequence the names of all the authors, titles and subjects in Everyman's Library and its supplementary series, Everyman's Reference Library and the Children's Illustrated Classics. 889
Many volumes formerly included in Everyman's Library reference section are now included in Everyman's Reference Library and are bound in larger format.

ROMANCE

Aucassin and Nicolette, with other Medieval Romances. Translated, with Introduction, by *Eugene Mason.* 497

Boccaccio, Giovanni (1313-75).
DECAMERON, 1471. Translated by *J. M. Rigg*, 1903. Introduction by *Edward Hutton*, 2 vols. Unabridged. 845-6

Bunyan, John (1628-88).
PILGRIM'S PROGRESS, Parts I and II, 1678-84. Reset edition. Introduction by *Prof. G. B. Harrison*, M.A., PH.D. (*See also* Theology and Philosophy.) 204

Cervantes, Saavedra Miguel de (1547-1616).
DON QUIXOTE DE LA MANCHA. Translated by *P. A. Motteux*. Notes by *J. G. Lockhart*. Introduction and supplementary Notes by *L. B. Walton*, M.A., B.LITT. 2 vols. 385-6

Chrétien de Troyes (fl. 12th cent.).
ARTHURIAN ROMANCES ('Erec et Enide'; 'Cligés'; 'Yvain' and 'Lancelot'). Translated into prose, with Introduction, notes and bibliography, by *William Wistar Comfort*. 698

Kalevala, or The Land of Heroes. Translated from the Finnish by W. F. Kirby. 2 vols. 259-60

Mabinogion, The. Translated with Introduction by *Thomas Jones*, M.A., D.LITT., and *Gwyn Jones*, M.A. 97

Malory, Sir Thomas (fl. 1400 ?-70).
LE MORTE D'ARTHUR. Introduction by *Sir John Rhys.* 2 vols. 45-6

Marie de France (12th century), LAYS OF, AND OTHER FRENCH LEGENDS. Eight of Marie's 'Lais' and two of the anonymous French love stories of the same period translated with an Introduction by *Eugene Mason.* 557

Njal's Saga. THE STORY OF BURNT NJAL (written about 1280-90). Translated from the Icelandic by *Sir G. W. Dasent* (1861). Introduction (1957) and Index by *Prof. Edward Turville-Petre*, B.LITT., M.A. 558

Rabelais, François (1494 ?-1553).
THE HEROIC DEEDS OF GARGANTUA AND PANTAGRUEL, 1532-5. Introduction by *D. B. Wyndham Lewis.* 2 vols. A complete unabridged edition of Urquhart and Motteux's translation, 1653-94. 826-7

SCIENCE

Boyle, Robert (1627-91).
THE SCEPTICAL CHYMIST, 1661. Introduction by *M. M. Pattison Muir.* 559

Darwin, Charles (1809-82).
THE ORIGIN OF SPECIES, 1859. The sixth edition embodies Darwin's final additions and revisions. New Introduction (1956) by *W. R. Thompson*, F.R.S. 811
(*See also* Travel and Topography.)

Eddington, Arthur Stanley (1882-1944).
THE NATURE OF THE PHYSICAL WORLD, 1928. Introduction by *Sir Edmund Whittaker*, F.R.S., O.M. 922

Euclid (fl. c. 330-c. 275 B.C.).
THE ELEMENTS OF EUCLID. Edited by *Isaac Todhunter*, with Introduction by *Sir Thomas L. Heath*, K.C.B., F.R.S. 891

Faraday, Michael (1791-1867).
EXPERIMENTAL RESEARCHES IN ELECTRICITY, 1839-55. With Plates and Diagrams, and an appreciation by *Prof. John Tyndall.* 576

Harvey, William (1578-1657).
THE CIRCULATION OF THE BLOOD. Introduction by *Ernest Parkyn.* 262

Howard, John (1726 ?-90).
THE STATE OF THE PRISONS, 1777. Intro. and Notes by *Kenneth Ruck.* 835

Marx, Karl (1818-83).
CAPITAL, 1867. Translated by *Eden* and *Cedar Paul.* 2 vols. Introduction by *Prof. G. D. H. Cole.* 848-9

Mill, John Stuart (1806-73). *See* Wollstonecraft.

Owen, Robert (1771-1858).
A NEW VIEW OF SOCIETY, 1813; and OTHER WRITINGS. Introduction by *G. D. H. Cole.* 799

Pearson, Karl (1857-1936).
THE GRAMMAR OF SCIENCE, 1892. 939

Ricardo, David (1772-1823).
THE PRINCIPLES OF POLITICAL ECONOMY AND TAXATION, 1817. Introduction by *Prof. Michael P. Fogarty*, M.A. 590

Smith, Adam (1723-90).
THE WEALTH OF NATIONS, 1766. Intro. by *Prof. Edwin Seligman.* 2 vols. 412-13

White, Gilbert (1720-93).
A NATURAL HISTORY OF SELBORNE, 1789. New edition (1949). Introduction and Notes by *R. M. Lockley.* 48

Wollstonecraft, Mary (1759-97), THE RIGHTS OF WOMAN, 1792; and **Mill, John Stuart** (1806-73), THE SUBJECTION OF WOMEN, 1869. New Introduction by *Pamela Frankau.* 825

14

THEOLOGY AND PHILOSOPHY